Cultural Legal Studies

What can law's popular cultures do for law, as a constitutive and interrogative critical practice? This collection explores such a question through the lens of the 'cultural legal studies' movement, which proffers a new encounter with the 'cultural turn' in law and legal theory. Moving beyond the 'law ands' (literature, humanities, culture, film, visual and aesthetics) on which it is based, this book demonstrates how the techniques and practices of cultural legal studies can be used to metamorphose law and the legalities that underpin its popular imaginary. By drawing on three different modes of cultural legal studies – storytelling, technology and jurisprudence – the collection showcases the intersectional practices of cultural legal studies, and law in its popular cultural mode.

The contributors to the collection deploy differentiated modes of cultural legal studies practice, adopting diverse philosophical, disciplinary, methodological and theoretical approaches and subjects of examination. The collection draws on this mix of diversity and homogeneity to thread together its overarching theme: that we must take seriously an interrogation of law as culture and in its cultural form. That is, it does not ask how a text 'represents' law; but rather how the representational nature of both law and culture intersect so that the 'juridical' become visible in various cultural manifestations. In short, it asks: how law's popular cultures actively effect the metamorphosis of law.

Cassandra Sharp's research draws on a range of disciplinary methods to empirically explore individual responses to law. Her focus is the use of popular stories by individuals in challenging and constructing legal meaning and identity. She is a member of the Legal Intersections Research Centre (LIRC) at the University of Wollongong, Australia.

Marett Leiboff is a cultural legal studies and law and humanities scholar who is working on a monograph that explores theatrical jurisprudence. Her scholarship is grounded in her pre-law background in academic theatre studies. Marett is a member of the Legal Intersections Research Centre, University of Wollongong, Australia.

Cultural Legal Studies

Law's popular cultures and the metamorphosis of Law

Edited by
Cassandra Sharp and
Marett Leiboff

Routledge
Taylor & Francis Group
LONDON AND NEW YORK

First published 2016
by Routledge
4 Park Square, Milton Park, Abingdon, Oxon OX14 4RN
605 Third Avenue, New York, NY 10017

a GlassHouse Book

Routledge is an imprint of the Taylor & Francis Group, an informa business

First issued in paperback 2017

British Library Cataloguing in Publication Data
A catalogue record for this book is available from the British Library

Library of Congress Cataloging-in-Publication Data
Cultural legal studies: law's popular cultures and the metamorphosis of law/edited by Cassandra Sharp and Marett Leiboff.
pages cm
Includes bibliographical references and index.
ISBN 978-1-138-80106-6 (hardback) – ISBN 978-1-315-75515-1 (ebk)
1. Sociological jurisprudence. 2. Culture and law. 3. Law and literature. I. Sharp, Cassandra, editor. II. Leiboff, Marett, editor.
K376.C848 2015
340'.115 – dc23
2015008845

ISBN: 978-1-138-80106-6 (hbk)
ISBN: 978-0-8153-8220-1 (pbk)

Typeset in Baskerville and Gill Sans
by Florence Production Ltd, Stoodleigh, Devon, UK

Contents

Figures

Preface

This collection had its origins in the symposium '*Cultural Legal Studies Methodology – Wherefore Art Thou?*' held at the University of Wollongong (UOW), Australia, in September 2012. Organised by Cassandra Sharp and Marett Leiboff, it was the first formal outing of the *Law and Popular Cultures Theme* of the Legal Intersections Research Centre (LIRC), in the then Faculty of Law at UOW. The symposium had two important objectives at its core: first, to seek to identify and frame how we define 'cultural legal studies'; and second to illuminate the methodologies and practices that draw upon the practices of cultural legal studies in order to shape law and popular culture/humanities research.[1] As well as presentations on these topics by the participants, the symposium featured an open session around the question: 'What is Cultural Legal Studies?'

While it was apparent that work in this diverse field was connected by a desire to explore the meaning and representation of law within a variety of cultural contexts, and that its scholarship sought to illuminate a complex encounter between contemporary culture and law, it was still too amorphous, too ill-defined. There did exist something called *cultural legal studies* (and at one stage we had even thought of rebadging our LIRC research theme with the moniker), yet seemingly, there was nothing to ground it. What did seem apparent though, was that there might be something different about the Australian approach to the field, and in particular something unique perhaps about the methodologies deployed by Antipodean scholars. Even though there had been a wealth of opportunities in conferences and special issues of journals to mark the field, as well as the methodology, there had been nothing other than a title, a name, a badge through which to identify the use of *cultural legal studies* in the Australian context. And so . . . the symposium was conceived as a mechanism for directly addressing the *what* and *how* of *cultural legal studies*.

1 Of course, this is far from the first time that symposia or conference streams have been directed towards this field. See Chapter 1 which describes the developing academic attention to cultural legal studies over the last several decades.

Cultural Legal Studies: Law's Popular Cultures and the Metamorphosis of Law builds on the themes and connections that originated in this 2012 symposium, and includes contributions by the original participants (MacNeil, Turnbull, Leiboff, Sharp, Duncanson, Crawley, Peters) and additional contributors inspired by the outcomes of the symposium. It brings together leading scholars from Australia, Canada, the United Kingdom and the United States including Professor William MacNeil (Griffith), Professor Jessica Silbey (Suffolk) and Professor Sue Turnbull (Media Studies, Wollongong).

We wish to thank all the participants (speakers and attendees) in the original symposium for their preparation, insight, and willingness to engage in robust discussion that opened pathways into the field. In particular, we thank Judy Grbich, Ian Duncanson, Trish Luker, and Rick Mohr whose animation of the ideas helped lead to expanding the scope of what we wanted to achieve in this collection. We also wish to thank the contributors to the collection who have been incredibly patient through the publication process (we may even have set a record with six babies being born between the symposium and the collection coming to fruition!).

We also want to thank Nan Seuffert, LIRC director, for her support of both the symposium and the publication, and for the way she has supported and encouraged contextual research and scholarship within LIRC since her arrival, for her mentorship and inspired leadership and friendship. We thank Felicia Martin for her wonderful admin support, and Adam Friend and Kristen Orr who helped out with some editorial assistance. We also wish to acknowledge the support of our colleagues in the law school and in LIRC, who are collegial, engaging and fun to be around: Karina Murray, Margaret Bond, Patricia Mundy, Linda Steele, Kate Tubridy, Luis Gómez Romero, Gabriel Garcia and Elena Marchetti.

Both of us also want to acknowledge the influence of Penny Pether in our academic careers, and remember her in this collection. Although in Chapter 1, we discuss her scholarly influence in the field, we also wanted to recognise the impact of Penny on our academic lives. In particular, as a UOW first year law student in the early 1990s, Cassandra had the privilege of enrolling in a subject developed and taught by Penny called *Perspectives on Law – English Literature*. It was a subject devoted to exploring the ways in which law was not only represented, but also critiqued, challenged and distorted in literature; and it involved the study of work by James Boyd White, Peter Goodrich, Richard Weisberg and Terry Threadgold; with texts like *Merchant of Venice*, *the Paper Chase*, *Presumed Innocent* and *Billy Budd Sailor*. Having enrolled in Arts/Law (and expecting them to be quite different), it was a wonderful revelation that the two degrees were so intimately connected. This provoked in Cassandra what has now become a lifelong passion for law and humanities research, and she is grateful for the inspiration of Penny in that first year of law to pursue the relationship between law and the humanities.

Cassandra would also like to thank Rob for his enduring encouragement and for always being the voice of reason; Nathaniel for his continual interest in my 'pop culture' work and suggestions of topics to research; and to Caitlin for being my 'biggest fan'. She also thanks Elena Marchetti and Marett Leiboff for their support and advice, and the insight they provide which strengthens her work.

Marett would like to thank Shaun McVeigh, Peter Goodrich, Les Moran, Jeanne Gaakeer, Connal Parsley in particular for their contribution to this collection, and to everyone else who I probably should have acknowledged. You know who you are.

We would also both like to acknowledge the influence of the closely knit cultural legal studies crowd in Australia and associated networks through a range of institutions in particular the Law, Literature and Humanities Association of Australasia, and the Law and Society Association of Australia and New Zealand. At UTS, Katherine Biber, Honni van Rijswijk, Trish Luker, Olivia Barr and Penny Crofts; at Melbourne, Shaun McVeigh, Sundhya Pahuja, Ann Genovese, Peter Rush, Alison Young; at Griffith, Tim Peters, Karen Crawley and Bill MacNeil; and at ANU, Des Manderson and Joshua Neoh.

We want to thank Colin Perrin for his support and enthusiasm for this collection. Rebekah Jenkins and Laura Muir have been fantastic. We also want to thank each other!

Cassandra Sharp and Marett Leiboff
Wollongong
February 2015

Contributors

Book editors

Cassandra Sharp
Senior Lecturer
Law and Popular Cultures Research Theme, Legal Intersections Research Centre
School of Law, University of Wollongong
Dr Sharp's research draws on cultural studies, literary theory, criminology, and legal theory to interrogate public interaction with legal consciousness. Her primary research interest lies in the expression and transmission of law within the public imaginary through mediated popular fictions, and she deploys an interdisciplinary empirical methodology to explore the ways that the concept of justice is challenged and/or maintained through contemporary stories of law.

Marett Leiboff
Law and Popular Cultures Research Theme, Legal Intersections Research Centre
School of Law, University of Wollongong
Associate Professor Leiboff's work is concerned with interpretative extroversion as a mode of cultural legal studies. She has published around legal accounts of visual culture, *histoire* as a mode of reading embodied law, and has drawn on her background in academic theatre studies to develop a theatrical jurisprudence. The co-author of *Legal Theories: Contexts and Practices*, Marett co-edited a 2010 special issue of the journal Law Text Culture on 'Law's Theatrical Presence' and edited a 2012 special issue of the *Australian Feminist Law Journal* on 'Law and Humanities Futures'. She is Vice President of the Law Literature and Humanities Association of Australasia and Managing Editor and Board Member of *Law Text Culture.*

Book contributors

Katherine Biber
Faculty of Law
University of Technology, Sydney

Associate Professor Biber is a legal scholar, criminologist and historian. She researches crime and evidence, with a specific focus on photography, visual culture and adversarial litigation. With a background in community legal centres, Katherine studies the relationship between social disadvantage and transgression. Katherine is currently undertaking an ARC funded project *Open justice and open secrets: the cultural afterlife of criminal evidence*, investigating what happens to the evidence tendered in criminal proceedings after the conclusion of the trial, in order to develop an appropriate response to the cultural proliferation of material that was previously tightly regulated. Formally regarded as part of the court record, and subject to the rules of evidence during the trial, this material has aroused the interest of creative and commercial users who wish to access it, sometimes for purposes which might be transgressive, dangerous or insensitive. This project asks what is at stake in opening this criminal archive, and what might be at stake if we try to regulate it.

Karen Crawley
Lecturer
Griffith Law School

Dr Crawley is a graduate of the University of Sydney, with Honours in English Literature and in Law, and received her LLM and PhD from McGill University, where her postgraduate research was supported by the Canada Research Chair in Law and Discourse. Her dissertation, *Seeing Double: Ironic Encounters between Art and Law*, explored the potential of irony for understanding and critiquing law's authoritative representations. Karen's research draws on literary theory, visual culture, and critical theory. She has published on the history of censorship, the theatricality of the police, the prosecution of street artists, and the ethics of photography. She is Managing Editor of the *Australian Feminist Law Journal* and serves on the board of the *Law, Literature and the Humanities Association of Australasia*.

Kirsty Duncanson
Legal Studies
La Trobe University

While maintaining a central focus on the intersections of law, crime and the social world, Dr Duncanson's work is strongly interdisciplinary, drawing on theory and method from across the fields of socio-legal studies, criminology, political science, gender studies, visual culture and media studies. Her key areas of interest include the negotiation of sexual assault through the criminal justice system and the greater community, and strategies of prevention; and popular engagements with law and sovereignty as they take place in the production and consumption of visual culture.

Luis Gómez Romero
Lecturer
Law and Popular Cultures Research Theme, Legal Intersections Research Centre
School of Law
University of Wollongong
Dr Gómez Romero joined the School of Law at the University of Wollongong in June 2013. Prior to this, Luis developed a postdoctoral research project at the Institute for the Public Life of Arts and Ideas (IPLAI) at McGill University (Montreal, Canada). While at McGill, Luis co-edited with Ian Dahlman a special issue of *Law Text Culture* (volume 16, 2012) that addressed comics as a distinct source of legal theory and legal ideology. His main research interests are Human Rights; Political Theory; Cultural Studies; Utopianism; Law and Literature; Law and Popular Culture; Critical Legal Theory and Feminist Jurisprudence. A member of the advisory board of *Isonomía*, the leading Legal Theory and Jurisprudence journal in the Spanish-speaking world, he is the author of, among other things, *Fantasía, Distopía y Justicia: La Saga de Harry Potter como Instrumento para la Enseñanza de los Derechos Humanos* (*Fantasy, Dystopia and Justice: Harry Potter's saga as an Instrument for Teaching Human Rights*) Madrid: Ministerio de Sanidad, Política Sociale Igualdad/Instituto de la Juventud, 2011.

William MacNeil
Griffith Law School
Professor William MacNeil is a scholar of jurisprudence and cultural legal studies, having published widely in both fields. His first book, *Lex Populi: The Jurisprudence of Popular Culture*, was published by Stanford University Press in 2007. Bill's second book, *Novel Judgements: Legal Theory as Fiction* was published by Routledge (London) in 2011. At present, Bill is at work on a third book, entitled *Speculative Legalism: The Philosophy of Law in Science Fiction, Fantasy and Horror* and continues, as ever, to 'share the love' of legal theory. As well as slaying vampires, he was the Dean of Law and Head of School of the Griffith Law School from 2010–2014.

Timothy D Peters
Lecturer
Griffith Law School
Dr Peters is a lecturer at the Griffith Law School and a Managing Editor of the *Griffith Law Review*. His research focuses on the intersections of legal theory, theology and popular culture and he has published legal readings of a range of pop culture texts including Batman and *Star Wars*. He recently completed his PhD: 'Reading the Law Made Strange: A Theological Jurisprudence of Popular Culture'.

Peter Robson
School of Law
University of Strathclyde
Professor Robson's scholarship explores how popular culture affects the practice and perception of law that built on earlier work that grew out of his PhD. He has recently been examining the study of images of law in popular culture and expanding his concerns on the methodology of cultural studies, while the second edition of the acclaimed *Film and the Law* book appeared in October 2010. His current work focuses on television and examines the constraints on writers and producers of TV lawyer shows and has involved interviewing those involved in the production process. He co-edited with Jessica Silbey a collection of essays focusing on the methodology of cultural scholarship entitled *Law and Justice on the Small Screen*.

Jessica Silbey
Law School
Suffolk University
Professor Silbey's scholarship engages the cultural analysis of law, asking how popular cultural forms (of film and literature, for example) shape legal disputes and explanations. One of her interests is in the interdiscipline of law and film, exploring how film is used as a legal tool and how it becomes an object of legal analysis in light of its history as a cultural object and art form. How does automated surveillance film become testimony in a court of law? How do cultural perceptions about film affect its evaluation by jurors, advocates and judges? How might legal actors and lay citizens mobilise the audiovisual technology of our twenty-first century to further the promises of our justice system? She has written widely on the use of film in law (as a tool and a method of analysis) as well as the use of law in film (its popular representation as a manner by which legal consciousness is created and shaped). Her new project concerns popular conceptions of intellectual property and how those conceptions motivate and structure various statutory intellectual property regimes.

Sue Turnbull
Professor of Communication and Media Studies
University of Wollongong
Sue Turnbull is Professor of Communication and Media Studies at the University of Wollongong. Her research interests include media education, media audiences and television studies. She is the author of *The TV Crime Drama* (Edinburgh University Press, 2014) and has recently co-edited a book with Dr Kate Darian-Smith entitled *Remembering Television* (2012) which brings together television history and memory studies. She is a former President of the Australian and New Zealand Communication Association and currently editor of the academic journal *Media International Australia* and co-editor of *Participations*,

the online journal of audience and reception studies. Sue is a frequent media commentator on television and radio and is crime fiction reviewer for the *Sydney Morning Herald*.

Honni van Rijswijk
Senior Lecturer
Faculty of Law
University of Technology, Sydney
Dr Honni van Rijswijk is a graduate of Sydney Law School and received her PhD from the University of Washington, where she was a Fellow in the Society of Scholars at the Simpson Center for the Humanities. Her research is interdisciplinary, and she writes primarily at the intersections of law, literature and critical theory. She has published on feminist theories of harm, formulations of responsibility in law and literature, the role of history in the common law, and on questions of justice relating to the Stolen Generations.

Part I

Cultural legal studies

The urgency of method and story

Chapter 1

Cultural legal studies and law's popular cultures

Marett Leiboff and Cassandra Sharp

Naming

Something unfinished resides in the phrase *cultural legal studies*, a slipperiness conveyed by the overlapping parts of speech, the adjectives that could be nouns, the nouns that could be verbs. Structural incongruities like this can be invigorating, countenancing heterogeneous possibilities and postures, but this interpretative slipperiness is its bane as well as its blessing. Twenty or so years have elapsed since cultural legal studies emerged in its contemporary manifestations,[1] sometimes in a nominate form,[2] but mostly innominate. It sits alongside its confrères: the cultural studies of law;[3] law and cultural studies;[4]

1 In 1951, Jerome Hall proposed nothing less than a School of Cultural Legal Studies at the University of Indiana, to be formed around law, the humanities and the social sciences: Jerome Hall, 'Open Letter Proposing a School of Cultural Legal Studies' (1951) 4 *Journal of Legal Education* 181.

2 In 2001, MacNeil and Hutchings called the contributions to their special issue of the Griffith Law Review on *Law's Cultural Mediations* a 'millennial "snapshot" of cultural legal studies around the common law world'. William MacNeil and Peter Hutchings, 'Law's Cultural Mediations: An Introduction by Way of Introduction' (2001) 10 *Griffith Law Review* 1, 6.

3 Rosemary J Coombe, 'Critical Cultural Legal Studies' (1998) 10 *Yale Journal of Law & the Humanities* 463; Rosemary J Coombe and Jonathan Cohen, 'Law and Late Modern Culture: Reflections on Between Facts and Norms from the Perspective of Critical Cultural Legal Studies' (1998–1999) 76 *Denver University Law Review* 1029; Paul W Kahn, *The Cultural Study of Law: Reconstructing Legal Scholarship* (University of Chicago Press, 1999). Sara L Knox and Cristyn Davies, 'The Force of Meaning' Special issue *The Force of Meaning: Cultural Studies of Law* (2013) 27 *Cultural Studies* 1, 1–10, offer in this introductory article to a special issue of the journal, a darkly political cultural studies of law. The collection was also published as C Davies and S Knox (eds), *Cultural Studies of Law* (Routledge, 2014).

4 Ian Duncanson, 'Cultural Studies Encounters Legal Pluralism: Certain Objects of Order, Law and Culture' (1997) 12 *Canadian Journal of Law and Society* 115; Austin Sarat and Jonathan Simon 'Beyond Legal Realism: Cultural Analysis, Cultural Studies, and the Situation of Legal Scholarship' (2001) 13 *Yale Journal of Law & Humanities* 3; Austin Sarat and Jonathan Simon (eds), *Cultural Analysis, Cultural Studies, and the Law: Moving Beyond Legal Realism* (Duke University Press, 2003).

law and popular culture[5] (or popular cultures and law);[6] law as culture;[7] law in the domains of culture;[8] as cultural-legal studies;[9] and its myriad compatriot 'law-ands', ranging from law and literature, to law and film,[10] law and aesthetics,[11] to law and humanities.[12] Over that time, its grammatical lacunae, the overlaps in terminology, as well as its disparate techniques, methodologies and interests means that it can and has been coded, decoded and recoded to denote and connote many different things. Confusion exists because the term has been used differently by scholars who refer to different practices, methods, approaches and concerns, through references to particular literatures and not others, and to different parsings of the phrase.[13] So while some cultural legal studies scholars use methods drawn from anthropology, such as ethnographies, cultural legal studies is not a study of culture or cultures. Nor is cultural legal

5 Steve Redhead, *Unpopular Cultures: The Birth of Law and Popular Culture* (Manchester University Press, 1995); Richard K Sherwin, *When Law Goes Pop: The Vanishing Line Between Law and Popular Culture* (University of Chicago Press, 2000); Margaret Thornton (ed.), *Romancing the Tomes: Popular Culture, Law and Feminism* (Cavendish, 2002); Richard K Sherwin (ed.), *Popular Culture and Law* (Ashgate, 2008); Austin Sarat (ed.), *Imagining Legality: Where Law Meets Popular Culture* (University of Alabama Press, 2011); Michael Asimow, Kathryn Brown and David Ray Papke (eds), *Law and Popular Culture: International Perspectives* (Cambridge Scholars Press, 2014).

6 Christy Collis and Jason Bainbridge, 'Introduction – Popular Cultures and the *Law*' (2005) 19 *Continuum: Journal of Media and Cultural Studies* 159; Daniela Carpi, 'Focus: Law, Literature and (Popular) Culture' (2014) 8 *Pólemos: Journal of Law, Literature and Culture* 1, 1–7.

7 Naomi Mezey, 'Law as Culture' (2001) 13 *Yale Journal of Law & the Humanities* 35.

8 Austin Sarat and Thomas R Kearns (eds), *Law in the Domains of Culture* (University of Michigan Press, 1997).

9 Austin Sarat and Martha Merrill Umphrey, 'Temporal Horizons: On the Possibilities of Law and Fatherhood in *To Kill a Mockingbird*' (2013) 27 *Cultural Studies* 30, 30.

10 Leslie J Moran *et al.* (eds), *Law's Moving Image* (GlassHouse Press, 2004); Orit Kamir, *Framed: Women in Law and Film* (Duke University Press, 2006); Alison Young, *The Scene of Violence: Cinema, Crime, Affect* (Routledge, 2010); Steve Greenfield, Guy Osborn and Peter Robson, *Film and the Law* (Hart Publishing, 2nd edn, 2010); Peter Robson and Jessica Silbey (eds), *Law and Justice on the Small Screen* (Hart, 2012).

11 Costas Douzinas and Linda Nead (eds), *Law and the Image: The Authority of Art and the Aesthetics of Law* (The University of Chicago Press, 1999); Peter Rush and Andrew Kenyon (eds), *Aesthetics of Law and Culture: Texts, Images, Screens* (Emerald Group Publishing Ltd, 2004); Alison Young, *Judging The Image: Art, Value, Law* (Routledge, 2005); Katherine Biber, *Captive Images: Race, Crime, Photography* (Routledge-Cavendish, 2007); Richard Sherwin (ed.), 'Visualizing Law in the Digital Age' (2012–2013) 57 *New York Law School Review*; Anne Wagner and Richard K Sherwin (eds), *Law, Culture and Visual Studies* (Springer, 2014); Leif Dahlberg (ed.), *Visualising Law and Authority: Essays on Legal Aesthetics* (De Gruyter, 2012); Alison Young, S*treet Art, Public City: Law, Crime and the Urban Imagination* (Routledge, 2014); Katherine Biber and Trish Luker, 'Evidence and the Archive: Ethics, Aesthetics, and Emotion' (2014) 40 *Australian Feminist Law Journal* 1.

12 For example, Law Culture and the Humanities; Law and Humanities; Yale Journal of Law and the Humanities; Law and Humanities; Austin Sarat, Matthew Anderson and Cathrine O Frank, *Law and the Humanities: An Introduction* (Cambridge University Press, 2010).

13 Karen Crawley in Chapter 9 adopts a different definition of cultural studies of law.

studies 'cultural studies', though most cultural legal scholars draw on the techniques, approaches and methods drawn from cultural studies either explicitly or by association.[14] Others who work within cultural legal studies work with the humanities (language, semiotics, literature, biography, history, theatre, visual art), in addition to popular culture media, photography, television, film, video games, digital communication practices, and so on. Yet it is not a study of cultural forms and products, though some cultural legal scholars work with those fields and practices.

To cut to the chase, cultural legal studies is concerned with animating law's popular cultures – the multivalenced forms and practices ranging from the humanities to video games and beyond – as a means through which to transform or animate questions of law and justice. We do not mean to stop with this sentence, but over the next few pages, will tease with and tease out these concepts a bit more. But we do want to start by marking out a few lines in the sand, the allusion being altogether more apt than might seem (as opposed to law's brightlines, touchstones and sharp reliefs), because sand, as we know, is made up of grains that can be formed and unformed at will, or through a puff of wind, or the crashing of waves. We want to make a claim, that cultural legal studies and its qualifier, law's popular cultures, are concerned with something that is present, existing, and engaged vis-à-vis law. From Gilbert and Sullivan to *The Matrix*, from *Dial M for Murder* to Ovid, from Shakespeare to *The Bridge*, from the *Book of Common Prayer* to *The Hunger Games*, from page to stage, from screen to scream – law's popular cultures are the agents through which complex encounters between contemporary culture in all its forms,[15] and law are played out.

Through the agency of law's popular cultures, cultural legal studies is concerned with questions of law; interrogating legality, justice and the politics of law. Through these agents, cultural legal studies speaks to the politics of legal negation, offers new forms of law within and beyond formally constituted

14 See Crawley, Chapter 9, for an exhaustive exploration of *representation* as a jurisprudence and method of cultural legal studies, and for an overview of the scholarship in this facet of the field.

15 The use of the plural form denotes a broad range of cultural forms, practices and techniques. For example, the Popular Cultures Research Network at the University of Leeds comprehends popular cultures as the national and the transnational, boundaries and crossing boundaries, gender, the global, local and glocal, high, popular and mass cultures, identity, identities and ethnicities, performativity, place and space, cultural policy and the creative industries, education, youth, art and aesthetics, architecture and the city, and law: www.leeds.ac.uk/arts/info/40011/popular_cultures_research_network/1148/about. The Law and Popular Cultures theme of the Legal Intersections Research Centre, University of Wollongong accounts for popular cultures as language, semiotics, literature, biography, history, theatre, visual art, cultural studies, legal theory, as the site of a complex encounter between contemporary culture and law: http://lha.uow.edu.au/law/LIRC/themes/UOW165568.html

legal assemblages, and speaks to the politics and practices of law as representation and vice versa. It looks like a multiplex, with multiple sites and screens, generating, producing and creating complex encounters between different manifestations of the popular cultural and law as jurisprudence,[16] as a means through which to think about how to *do* law well.[17] In its diverse manifestations, cultural legal studies ranges from MacNeil's *Lex Populi* and *Legal Fictions* to Manderson's *Kangaroo Courts*, from Dorsett and McVeigh's *Jurisdiction* to Seuffert's postcolonial historiography, from Cassandra Sharp's ethnographic modes of justice and ethics, to Rick Mohr's modes of practice, from Young's critical cultural criminologies of visual culture, to Leiboff and Thomas' call to Monty Python as jurisprudence.[18] A tiny snapshot of a huge and diverse field, this work reveals cultural legal studies as a jurisprudence of materialities,[19] 'at once concrete and textual as it takes place in the daily lives of contemporary subjects'.[20] Cultural legal studies plays out through embodied action and movement – of law, its scholars and sites of engagement and encounter,[21] through law's popular cultures.

16 As an illustration of the oeuvre of one cultural legal scholar, see Desmond Manderson (ed.), *Courting Death: the Law of Mortality* (Pluto Press, 1999); *Songs Without Music: Aesthetic Dimensions of Law and Justice* (University of California Press, 2000); *Kangaroo Courts and the Rule of Law: The Legacy of Modernism* (Routledge, 2012); and 'Memory and Echo: Pop Cult, Hi Tech and the Irony of Tradition' (2013) 27 *Cultural Studies* 11.

17 Cf Rosemary J Coombe, 'Is there a Cultural Studies of Law?' in Toby Miller (ed.), *A Companion to Cultural Studies* (Basil Blackwell, 2001), 36.

18 William P MacNeil, *Lex Populi: The Jurisprudence of Popular Culture* (Stanford University Press, 2007); William P MacNeil, *Novel Judgements: Legal Theory as Fiction* (Routledge-Cavendish, 2011); Desmond Manderson (2012) above n 16; Shaunnagh Dorsett and Shaun McVeigh, *Jurisdiction* (Routledge, 2012); Nan Seuffert, *Jurisprudence of National Identity: Kaleidoscopes of Imperialism And Globalisation from Aotearoa New Zealand* (Ashgate, 2006); Cassandra Sharp, 'Let's See How Far We've Come: The Role of Empirical Methodology in Exploring Television Audiences' in Peter Robson and Jessica Silbey (eds), *Law and Justice on the Small Screen* (Hart Publishing, 2012) 111; Cassandra Sharp, 'Justice with a Vengeance – Retributive Desire in Popular Imagination' in Michael Asimow, Kathryn Brown and David Ray Papke (eds), *Law and Popular Culture: International Perspectives* (Cambridge Scholars Publishing, 2014) 153; Richard Mohr, 'Signature and Illusion: Lessons from the Baroque for "Truth" in Law and the Humanities' (2012) 36 *The Australian Feminist Law Journal* 45; Richard Mohr, 'Flesh and the Person' (2008) 29 *The Australian Feminist Law Journal* 31; Young, above n 10 and n 11; Marett Leiboff and Mark Thomas, *Legal Theories: Contexts and Practices* (Thomson Law Book Co, 2nd edn, 2014).

19 Andreas Philippopoulos-Mihalopoulos, *Spatial Justice: Body, Lawscape, Atmosphere* (Routledge, 2015).

20 Ibid, 483.

21 Olivia Barr, 'A Moving Theory: Remembering the Office of Scholar' (2010) 14 *Law Text Culture* 40; Marett Leiboff,'Law, Muteness and the Theatrical' (2010) 14 *Law Text Culture* 384; Marett Leiboff, 'Towards a Jurisprudence of the Embodied Mind – Sarah Lund, Forbrydelsen and the Mindful Body' in Hanne Petersen and Rubya Mehdi (eds), Special issue on 'Law and Art' Volume 2 (2015) 6 *NAVEIÑ REET: Nordic Journal of Law and Social Research.*

What this suggests is that *cultural legal studies* is concerned with the real,[22] which makes law's popular cultures its agent of exploration, of criticism, of practice. But what counts as the real, as Peter Goodrich has so elegantly put it, is 'aereall and spectral, mediated by the calculus and other signs through which we know it',[23] and so too the illusion,[24] or 'play—of interdisciplinary scholarship, the indiscipline and irreverence to the study of law's use of figurative and visual media'.[25] But cultural legal studies is also concerned with physical and literal encounters, so rather than speak of the psychoanalytic real (Real), or reality, we also turn to actuality, actualité, actualities, with all of the filmic resonance ('actuality film'), and its grounding in the conditions or circumstances or realities of existence.[26] From apologue to diegesis, the representational to the judgment and beyond, cultural legal studies mobilises a constitutive and interrogative critical practice for and about law, through law's popular cultures as the agent of encounter. As Collis and Bainbridge observed in 2005, 'popular culture is not simply a domain in which the law is represented; rather, it is a domain in which law is practised, negotiated, legitimized, and embodied',[27] while for MacNeil and Hutchings, cultural legal studies (through law's cultural mediations),[28] reveals to the legal unconscious and legal imaginary 'its abiding antagonisms like "What is the connection to, or conflict between law and morality?", "Law and power?" "Law and rights?" and especially "Law and justice?"'[29] Each of these positions speaks to the jurisprudential project of cultural legal studies, albeit at different ends of the spectrum – a jurisprudence of practice and existence on the one hand, and through the representational, foundational jurisprudential concepts on the other.

To designate cultural legal studies as a jurisprudence, or even to identify its features is all very well, but it still does not name what it is. Indeed, it seems more than a little careless for cultural legal studies to have been left hanging – as parts of speech, or as a mere negation against related fields, as allusory but operative concepts.[30] Naming and marking out a field of this kind has its hazards,

22 Jerry Leonard and Marie Asche (eds), *Legal Studies As Cultural Studies: A Reader in (post) Modern Critical Theory* (State University of New York Press, 1995) 3; cf Julie Stone Peters, 'Law, Literature and the Vanishing Real: On the Future of the Interdisciplinary Illusion' (2005) 120(2) *PMLA* 442.

23 Peter Goodrich, 'Screening Law' (2009) 21 *Law & Literature* 1, 20.

24 Ibid, 2. Goodrich reminds that illusion derives from the Latin *ludere*, to play.

25 Ibid, 21.

26 'actuality, n.' *OED Online* (Oxford University Press, December 2014) Accessed 15 December 2014.

27 Collis and Bainbridge, above n 6, 162.

28 MacNeil and Hutchings, above n 2, 1.

29 MacNeil and Hutchings, above n 2, 1–2.

30 In addition to MacNeil and Hutchings' use of the phrase, Leiboff used it without definition: Marett Leiboff, 'Of the Monstrous Regiment and the Family Jewels' (2005) 23 *Australian Feminist Law Journal* 33, 35.

not least the possibility of ossification, but the hazards work both ways. To name is to take responsibility for a field.[31] The slip to *illusion*, that there is name without field, is a small step away where names are left hanging, even if it is possible to decipher something of its genre. But naming cultural legal studies is not elusive. Parsing the individual words of the phrase does part of the job – the invocation to cultural studies and critical jurisprudence gives clues to its morphology, where the cultural turn met critical legal theory (and since then, the archival turn, the historical turn, the theatrical turn and so on), but without more, this is mere bricolage or syncretism. Cultural legal studies is not the same as its confrères and compatriots, or cultural studies or critical jurisprudences. It has done something different (from the outset, as we will come to), with *doing* being the operative word, as the surplus of parts of speech that reside in the phrase enact.

Cultural legal studies is not constituted by its words but the words *as they play on each other*. This is imperative in understanding its name. First, these words need to be understood as *complect*,[32] manifested through complex sticky embraces, connections and interweavings made up of those who encounter law, and the popular cultural formations through which law is encountered, shaped and conceived. Second, whether concerned with actualities or reality, or theory, cultural legal scholars *enfold* diverse fields and genres within law and back again. This *action* of enfolding is necessarily grounded within Philippopoulos-Mihalopoulos' lawscape, with its folds, its spatialisation, its embodiment and materiality,[33] and is productive of the complexities and dynamics of cultural legal studies.[34] Cultural legal studies is thus an active form of the dyadics of the 'law ands' – of literature, humanities, culture, film, visual and aesthetics. Its name denotes what it does, complecting and enfolding myriad fields, binding the aereall and spectral, with the grittiness of actualities (sand in its most minute form), with law.

Cultural legal studies had, in short, jumped over the disciplinary divide of the dyads, and had done so at least a decade before Julie Stone Peters spoke

31 Cf Matthew Stone, Illan rua Wall and Costas Douzinas (eds), *New Critical Legal Thinking: Law and the Political* (Birkbeck Law Press, 2012).

32 Formed from two Latin derivatives, it conjoins *complecti* to embrace, encircle with *plectĕre* to plait, twine. In its transitive form, complect as verb is obsolete, meaning to embrace. Its extant form is defined to mean to weave or connect together; to interweave. We are using the term in both obsolete and extant forms. As an adjective, complected means interwoven, complicated. It needs to be distinguished from the US adjective complected, meaning complexion. 'complect, v.'. *OED Online* (Oxford University Press, December 2014) Accessed 15 December 2014. 'complected, adj.2'. *OED Online* (Oxford University Press, December 2014) Accessed 15 December 2014.

33 Philippopoulos-Mihalopoulos, above n 19.

34 These questions are also present in related fields such as legal geography: Irus Braverman, Nicholas Blomley, David Delaney and Alexandre Keda, *The Expanding Spaces of Law: A Timely Legal Geography* (Stanford University Press, 2014).

of the end of the law and literature project in 2005,[35] where it was perhaps undergoing a 'transformation into something bigger and necessarily more amorphous'.[36] Cultural legal studies, then not yet named, had already moved down that path, in Australia at least, in the early 1990s. For MacNeil and Hutchings, it was the move to the cultural in the last decade of the twentieth century and the first decade of the twenty-first, that meant that cultural legal studies marked a change at a textual and interpretative level that was so fundamental that it 'entails a jurisprudential reorientation . . . and even of juristic vision'.[37] That is, they recognised that there was now an actual shift in the way law was done, marking a point where a metamorphosis that had begun a decade earlier, by the time they wrote in 2001, could now be called cultural legal studies. How cultural legal studies got to that point is the direction to which we now turn.

Antipodean cultural legal studies

Ann Genovese and Shaun McVeigh call the practice of writing jurisprudence through history, or as history, 'jurisography'.[38] In keeping with its own practices, cultural legal studies, too, is best understood through its jurisography, through its histories and trajectories, its people and places, its connections and relations, its actualities. What its jurisography reveals is that something happened in Australia at a crucial period in the early 1990s, a rapprochement between critical legal scholars, critical literature scholars, law and society and socio-legal scholars, law and literature and law and history scholars out of which cultural legal studies grew. Its links were formed through conditions that were uniquely Australian, especially the genius and energies of a small group of founding scholars and a group of unique institutions, journals and associations, with abiding commitments to justice and to the effects of law. Along with critical legal theories, broadly described, with work grounded in the cultural and aesthetic and a keen eye to the social impact of law, something happened in Australia that was *same, same, but different* from the practices and methods that took shape in the north.

In order to account for a jurisography of cultural legal studies, we need to name something else, or at least bring it from the shadows. There is an operative occult word, ever present but never named when we speak of cultural legal studies – that it is an *antipodean* cultural legal studies. We know the antipodean

35 Peters, above n 22, 451–452; see also Anna Schur, 'Flourishing or Perishing? Law and Literature Airbrushed' (2014) 26 *Law & Literature* 105.

36 Peters, above n 22, 451.

37 MacNeil and Hutchings, above n 2, 1.

38 Ann Genovese, 'Critical Decision, 1982: Remembering *Koowarta v Bjelke-Petersen*' (2014) 23 *Griffith Law Review* 1, 2.

will be immediately read as referring to the geographic south from where we write, and about which we write, but there is more to the concept of the antipodes than a determinist geography would suggest. The antipodes is not *antonymic* of a geographic north, though antipodean cultural legal studies is very much grounded in the south. As Matthew Goldie points out, the antipodes are not merely spatial, geographic or oppositional, but 'correspond with us and correspond to us . . . evanescent and disorienting'.[39] That which is antipodean is not just a place *opposite* but a different way of being, in Goldie's terms (drawing on Eve Sedgwick) to one side of, or beside.[40] That is, antipodean cultural legal studies grew to the side, or beside the law and literature, law and popular culture, and critical legal theories, that emerged in the UK and US,[41] creating new and different forms of complection and enfolding out of the foundational grammars and techniques of the north, and indeed, from the south as well. What seems to be critical, in all senses of the word, is that in Australia and New Zealand, the critical tradition took its shape not through *critical* legal movements but through law and society, law and history and law and literature associations, conferences,[42] and journals,[43] that mingled disciplines, individuals and techniques. That the *Australian Journal of Law and Society* was to devote a special issue in 1991 to 'Law and Literature', made up of pieces presented at the first Law and Literature conference held in Australia in 1990, sets the tone for the sticky encounters and complection – law and literature in a law and society journal – that characterise cultural legal studies.[44]

39 Matthew Boyd Goldie, 'Island Theory – The Antipodes' in Maeve McCusker and Anthony Soares (eds), *Islanded Identities: Constructions of Postcolonial Cultural Insularity* (Editions Rodopi, 2011) 1–40, 3.

40 Matthew Boyd Goldie, *The Idea of the Antipodes: Place People and Voices* (Routledge, 2010) 4–5; ibid, 12.

41 Costas Douzinas, 'A Short History of the British Critical Legal Conference or, the Responsibility of the Critic' (2014) 25 *Law and Critique* 187; the US Law and Humanities Institute was formed in 1978/1979 and eventually led to the formation of the journal *Cardozo Studies in Law and Literature* in 1989/1990, which became *Law and Literature* in 2000. The *Yale Journal of Law and the Humanities* was founded in 1988/1989. For a history of US law culture and humanities: see Sarat, Anderson and Frank, above n 12.

42 A long-established Law and Society Association going back to the early 1980s, later rebranded in 2005 as the Law and Society Association of Australia and New Zealand, and in 1990 the Law and Literature Association was established at its first conference at Sydney University, later re-established as the Law Literature and Humanities Association of Australia in 2009.

43 The socio-legal journal established at La Trobe in 1983, *Law in Context*, was followed by the Macquarie Law School's *Australian Journal of Law and Society*, first published in the early 1980s; the *Australian Feminist Law Journal*, published first in 1993; *Law Text Culture* in 1994; and the *Griffith Law Review* which moved towards a theory orientation in 1996.

44 The editors noted in their introduction that they did not include contributions that were not 'strictly' law and literature. They noted they had to leave out David Fraser's 'Sex, Lies and Videotape: Images of Lawyers in Popular Culture', which analysed the TV series *LA Law* from a critical legal studies perspective: see Penny Pether and Simon Petch, 'Literature and Law' (1991) 7 *Australian Journal of Law and Society* 1, 1.

We date antipodean cultural legal studies as at 1994, with the publication of the first issue of the journal *Law Text Culture* (then styled *Law/Text/Culture*) and its foundational role in producing and generating a singular form of legal theory and practice that is emblematically an *antipodean* cultural legal studies. 1994 will do, though it is not perfect. *Law Text Culture* created a different idiom that could move beyond the limitations of the dyads of law and literature. Its publication might mark the inception of cultural legal studies, but cultural legal studies did not form, Athena-like, out of the head of Zeus. Cultural legal studies did not limit itself to the assumptions and techniques that resided in these fields. Instead, a series of antecedents and points of departure, not least the energy and genius of a singular group of scholars, created the conditions for the emergence of cultural legal studies, and its use of multiple techniques and practices.

To obtain a sense of the conditions that led to its development, we wish to identify – briefly – four arcs that shaped antipodean cultural legal studies. They are temporally and spatially distinct and in no particular order. The first we wish to mention are the *Brit Crits*: Douzinas, Goodrich, and its younger members who moved to Australia in the early-mid 1990s – Shaun McVeigh to the new Griffith Law School, followed by Peter Rush (returning to Australia) and Alison Young to Melbourne – first at the Law Department at the University of Lancaster in the late 1980s, then Birkbeck in the early 1990s; the British Critical Legal Conference and the creation of the journal *Law and Critique* in 1990. This point of connection led to interactions between the UK scholars and Australians and vice versa.[45] The second comes from the US law and literature/humanities, critical legal movement, coalescing around the influence of Richard Weisberg at Cardozo, James Boyd White at Michigan, Austin Sarat at Amherst College,[46] and Robert Cover, and through them, the founding law and popular culture/film/television figures in both the US and UK. Creating a field and a name in the 1970s for the dyads we have already described, the key journals in the US only took shape around the same time that the Australian field took shape. The third arc then comes from Australian socio-legal studies, and the Law and History movement that grew out of the Legal Studies Department at La Trobe University in Australia between 1972 and 1994, where, in Chris Tomlins' words, its

> multidisciplinary critical and theoretical perspectives on law – as substance, as professional practice, as field of academic inquiry – . . . [was] unrivalled in Australia or, with just a few exceptions, internationally.[47]

45 See MacNeil and Hutchings, above n 2.

46 See MacNeil and Hutchings, above n 2; Douzinas, above n 41; Sarat, Anderson and Frank, above n 12.

47 Christopher Tomlins, 'Law "and", Law "in", Law "as": The Definition, Rejection and Recuperation of the Socio-legal Enterprise' (2013) 29 *Law in Context* 137, 138.

Tomlins observed that a range of scholarly trajectories 'proliferated', including law and society, critical legal studies and feminist legal studies, which all melded and overlapped,[48] forming the conditions that would enable the multiple techniques that characterise cultural legal studies to emerge. The fourth arc of development will be traced to 1990, and to a series of individuals who were instrumental in bringing law and literature to Australia, and creating something new with it: Terry Threadgold, an English scholar originally from Sydney but who moved to Monash in Melbourne; Penny Pether, a lawyer who later undertook a PhD in English, who was the driving force behind the establishment of the first Law and Literature conference in Sydney in 1990;[49] and Joseph Pugliese, also an English PhD. It was the latter two who established *Law Text Culture* at the University of Wollongong in 1993, from the newly established Faculty of Law and the English Department.[50] Soon after the first issue of *Law Text Culture* was published in 1994, Penny Pether moved to Sydney Law School, and the journal moved to the Macquarie Law School, with Desmond Manderson as Managing Editor. The journal returned to Wollongong with Rick Mohr at the helm after Des Manderson moved first to Sydney Law School and then to Canada, in the early 2000s. The connections between individuals and places that marked the field in Australia took shape as well through the Law and Literature (later the Law Literature and Humanities) Association in Australia. Australian cultural legal scholars participated in the UK Critical Legal Conference, and the US Association for the Law Culture and Humanities conferences and journal, forming connections and building links that with Penny Pether's move to the US in 1997/98, Des Manderson's move to McGill in Canada, and Bill MacNeil's move to Australia in 1998, enabled a series of enfoldings and complections back out to the geographical north. This had the

48 Ibid, 139. Judy Grbich, Ian Duncanson and Margaret Thornton, all of whom were instrumental in creating the conditions for this scholarship and through them the creation of cultural legal studies, were forced to leave the institution as it rebranded itself as a conventional law school in the early 2000s.

49 Pether and Petch, above n 44: convened by Penny Pether and Simon Petch. The conference brought together academic presenters, practising lawyers and activists, and a keynote paper presented by the then President of the New South Wales Court of the Appeal, later High Court Justice, Michael Kirby: Joseph Pugliese, 'In Memoriam Penny Pether: For Friendship, Generosity, and Social Justice' (2014) 26 *Law & Literature* 259, 259. Thanks to Terry Threadgold and Joseph Pugliese for their recollections of the early years.

50 In 1993, the Faculty of Law at the University of Wollongong hosted the fourth Australian Law and Literature Association Conference, and this first issue of *Law Text Culture* was published a year later (the third, with some degree of controversy was published as a special issue of the *Australian Journal of Law and Society*, in 1993, including an article by Sue Turnbull (who has contributed Chapter 5 in this collection): 'Bodies of Knowledge: Pleasure and Anxiety in the Detective Fiction of Patricia D Cornwell', that had been presented at the 1992 Law and Society Conference): Peter Wilmshurst, 'Introduction: Literature and Law' (1993) 9 *Australian Journal of Law and Society* 1.

effect of taking the dyadic 'law and' coals back to Newcastle, but now shaped *through* cultural legal studies – returning to their place of origin in the north, but not quite as they left.[51]

Doing things differently

Coming from the geographic antipodes, it seems, was to do things differently and to do *something*. Speaking of Penny Pether, after her untimely death in 2013, Mark Sanders remarked: 'I could identify with the deep conviction recognizable among intellectuals from the dominions that ideas and arguments could, and ought to, make a positive difference in the world'.[52] It was, however, more than a geographic urge, but something that is antipodean in the sense that we have already remarked on, that of being to one side or beside, not in opposition necessarily, but to *do something*. This seems to be the abiding position in Penny's own clarion call after her move to the US from Australia in 1998 against what might be termed empty theory, or theory for its own sake, of the kind that she saw on display in the US legal academy:

> What I am interested in is the work that critical theory and interdisciplinary interventions in law can be made to do . . . the forensic impulse to work out what is going on . . . because it may reveal a node or pressure point where transformative work in law might be done.[53]

What she is describing is the form of *doing* – complection and enfolding that we argue marks out cultural legal studies. But there had been movements in that direction in the US, though tragically cut short by the early death of Robert Cover in 1986, at the age of 42. A founding member of the Law and Humanities Institute, with his close friend, Milner S Ball, an originator of the Law and Literature movement in the US,[54] Cover and Ball wanted to speak *through these fields* to the 'inter-relationships between law, theology and literature and a

51 Pugliese, above n 49. Joseph Pugliese makes it clear that Penny Pether was responsible for establishing law and humanities in Australia, and, moreover, exporting it, noting that in 1995, one year after we date the beginnings of cultural legal studies, she organised a 'major conference at the University of California, Berkeley, where she brought scholars from Australia, the UK, and the US together to initiate an international dialogue on law and the humanities'. The first Law, Culture and Humanities conference was held in Washington, DC, in 1998, after Penny had moved to the US.

52 Mark Sanders, 'Remembrance for Penny' (2014) 26 *Law & Literature* 257, 257.

53 Penny Pether, 'On Foreign Ground: Grand Narratives, Situated Specificities, and the Praxis of Critical Theory and Law?' (1999) 10 *Law and Critique* 211, 225.

54 Stephen Wizner, 'A Theology of Justice: Some Reflections on Milner Ball's Non-Religious Practice of Belief' (2006–2007) 41 *Georgia Law Review* 945.

passionate commitment to the struggle for social justice'.[55] This commitment spoke of a desire for 'law and literature' to engage with the realpolitik of law, through a history borne of civil rights movements (Cover himself, as a Princeton undergraduate, was jailed in Georgia while trying to effect change in the US south).[56] Wizner remarked of Cover that:

> to the extent that literature played a part in his jurisprudential thinking, it did so by presenting, dramatizing and illuminating through narrative the moral complexities imbedded in and reflected by individual and social behavior. To paraphrase Milner Ball, Cover took his law and his literature seriously and together . . . [57]

Cover is remembered more for his theory than his practice, for his narrative and nomos, and not for his demands of social justice through activism. But he also identified the forms of encounter, through a connection with lived experience, that we also find in cultural legal studies:

> Myth is the part of reality we create and choose to remember in order to *reenact.* It is intensely personal and committed. History is a countermove bringing us back to reality, requiring that we test the aspiration objectively and prudentially . . . Only myth tells us who we would become; only history can tell us how hard it will really be to become that.[58]

The complection that Ball and Cover sought was clearly articulated by Penny Pether over a decade later and it seems that this ability to connect dyads, theory and practice could really only come from this type of connection with reality that comes from experiencing the world as antipodean. Chris Tomlins, speaking of law and history scholars from Australia, notes that they are able to see things differently in a way that 'eludes most US legal history and much of the UK's . . . [which] expresses a peculiar willingness to think of law unblinkered.'[59] This difference is something that can only come from living at the bottom of the world, being imagined through the lens of a medieval cosmological antipodes

55 Ibid, 946.
56 Milner Ball, 'Special Editor's Introduction' A Commemorative Volume for Robert M. Cover (Spring/Summer, 1996) 8 *Cardozo Studies in Law and Literature* i, ii.
57 Stephen Wizner, 'Repairing the World through Law: A Reflection on Robert Cover's Social Activism' A Commemorative Volume for Robert M. Cover (Spring/ Summer, 1996) 8 *Cardozo Studies in Law and Literature* 1, 8.
58 Robert Cover, 'The Folktales of Justice' in Martha Minow, Michael Ryan and Austin Sarat (eds), *Narrative, Violence, and the Law: The Essays of Robert Cover* (The University of Michigan Press, 1992), 187.
59 Tomlins, above n 47, 146.

(with the belief that on the other side of the world, people's feet must inevitably grow from heads, in a world upturned). That heady image, though, is not so inapt. To come from the geographic antipodes means to be framed through material difference, through a constant need to explain (what or where is Wollongong?); to elucidate (no, the UK High Court might be an inferior court, but the Australian High Court is not); to an explanation of vowels and location (it is not that we speak English better than Germans because we are Austrians, but because we are Australians who are native English speakers). This constant need to explain means we are forever reminded of our physicality, which in turns asks us to do something deeply unnatural for theory – that we bodily respond to the existence of the theoretical, rather than conceiving of the theoretical as abstract and intellectual.[60] Being antipodean means that we might know who we are but no one else knows us, or at least not as we know ourselves. What Chris Tomlins observed; what Penny Pether knew; and what Robert Cover lived through his jailing, is that experience of being, and encounter comes not in the register of abstraction, but in real, lived, actualities. This experience, as Jeanne Gaakeer pointed out in 2014, grounds *phronèsis*: [61]

> What 'is' it that we actually see if we think of the influence of (popular) culture on the formation of the mental frames through which we perceive law and society, our local cultural imaginations, and scripts that are themselves narratives we live by?[62]

Law Text Culture Volume 1 (1994)

In her review article of Cornell, Rosenfeld and Carlson's 1992 collection, *Deconstruction and the Possibility of Justice*,[63] in the first issue of *Law Text Culture*, mental frames were in the forefront of Terry Threadgold's review which advances nothing less than a manifesto of the state of the Australian field that would be echoed by Penny Pether after her move to the US.[64] Noting that this US collection 'has a place in the chain of readings/rewritings . . . that constitute

60 Leiboff, above n 30, 35–36, used Brecht's *Verfremdungseffekte* as a cultural legal studies technique to estrange form and technique of analysis and of encounter between law and observer, reader and engagement.

61 Jeanne Gaakeer, 'Law and Literature Redux? Some Remarks on the Importance of the Legal Imagination' in Julen Etxabe and Gary Watt (eds), *Living in a Law Transformed: Encounters with the Works of James Boyd White* (Michigan Publishing, 2014). http://quod.lib.umich.edu/m/maize/12982987.0001.001

62 Ibid.

63 Terry Threadgold, 'Deconstruction and the Possibility of Justice: Critical and Cultural Difference' (1994) 1 *Law Text Culture* 140.

64 Pether, above n 53.

the field of . . . Australian work in Law and Literature and Critical Legal Studies',[65] it was extraordinarily different to the Australian work.[66] What was notable was its failure to include 'certain discourses, practices and trends that characterise comparable work in Australia . . . [which are] . . . all signs of a cultural difference which is as profound as it is socially and historically located'.[67] This difference between the approaches – empty theory and theory that took into account lived experience – and the uses that could be made of what we now call complecting and enfolding, sat behind Terry Threadgold's impatience.

The editors of *Law Text Culture* (Robin Handley, Penny Pether, Joseph Pugliese, and Maurice Scott), made it clear that their journal was not about empty theory, nor interesting dyadic connections between law and other disciplines without more. It was a journal committed to a praxis grounded in seeking justice and legal change through the:

> intersections of the law, textuality and all aspects of culture . . . *This differentiates Law Text Culture from other interdisciplinary journals devoted to the fields of law and the humanities and law and literature.*[68] (emphasis added)

In its articulation of 'the issues and development of the theories and practices generated by disciplinary crossings between fields and bodies of knowledge that have traditionally been seen as discrete and autonomous',[69] it offered spaces from which to write and speak about the law to people 'relegated to the minoritizing positions of "sub-" or "marginal" cultures'.[70] The editors wanted to 'acknowledge the often radical differences – linguistic, cultural, and political – that constitute contemporary Australian culture'.[71] This was praxis, but the journal named how it was going to take up this political stand. It did so using popular cultures and law to complect and enfold those fields into the creation of new approaches that would animate claims of justice. It is how the editors described this practice that we see their creation of what is nothing less than a blueprint of cultural legal studies. The 'new humanities' (cultural studies, communications/media studies, postcolonial studies, gender studies) would be used to think transformatively about law as a practice:

> The urgent need for the law to engage with other disciplines has been apparent from, for example, the changes in law, text(s) and culture generated by *Mabo v The State of Queensland*, and the media exposure of

65 Threadgold, above n 63, 140.
66 Ibid.
67 Ibid, 147.
68 Robin Handley, Penny Pether, Joseph Pugliese, Maurice Scott, J Robinson and C Hough, 'Introduction' (1994) 1 *Law Text Culture* 6, 6.
69 Ibid.
70 Ibid.
71 Ibid, 6.

> examples of judicial gender bias. Such changes exemplify the contemporary demands to reform Australian legal structures and practices in order to address criticisms of the limits to 'access to justice'.[72]

The radical demands of the journal (and so too cultural legal studies), was found in its claim to do something, to change law. It would do no less than connect 'theory and practice, academic debate and policy formation, the universities, legal institutions, and the larger cultural and political communities'.[73] Opening with Ruby Langford Ginibi's demands for Aboriginal law,[74] the first issue contained contributions from Richard Weisberg,[75] the crime novelist Sara Paretsky,[76] Nicholas Horn's encounter with titles – in and of law,[77] law and literature (Trollope and the nineteenth-century transformation of Law and the feminine,[78] and Billy Budd),[79] the politics and morality of the *Mabo* decision vis-à-vis the Australian community,[80] and the writing of the law.[81] True to its insistence on including other voices and other genres, the scholarly pieces were interspersed with poems and performance writing by Ruby Langford Ginibi, Kate Morris and Dean Kiley.[82] There were a number of book reviews.[83] Bill Priestley, a Justice of the NSW Court of Appeal,[84] reviewed Helena Kennedy's *Eve was Framed*,[85] while Robin Handley reviewed the collection of short stories, *I Took My Harp to a Party*,[86] by solicitor Alexandra Long. Lawyer Jonathan

72 Ibid, 6–7.
73 Ibid, 7.
74 Ruby Langford Ginibi, 'Aboriginal Traditional and Customary Law' (1994) 1 *Law Text Culture* 8.
75 Richard Weisberg, 'The Codification of Western Law & the Poetics of Disclosure' (1994) 1 *Law Text Culture* 28.
76 Sara Paretsky, 'Protocols of the Elders of Feminism' (1994) 1 *Law Text Culture* 14.
77 Nicholas Horn, 'Tityrus' (1994) 1 *Law Text Culture* 48.
78 Christine Higgins, '"The Woman Business": Mill, Trollope and the Law' (1994) 1 *Law Text Culture* 63.
79 Kieran Dolin, 'Sanctioned Irregularities: Martial Law in Billy Budd, Sailor' (1994) 1 *Law Text Culture* 129.
80 Tony Schirato, 'Mabo and the Politics of Community' (1994) 1 *Law Text Culture* 99.
81 Vince Robinson, 'Codes, Dooms, Constitutions and Statutes: The Emergence of the Legislative Form of Legal Writing' (1994) 1 *Law Text Culture* 106.
82 Ruby Langford Ginibi, 'Terra Nullius' (1994) 1 *Law Text Culture* 13; Kate Morris, 'In these Prisons' (1994) 1 *Law Text Culture* 40; Dean Kiley, 'I Panicked and Hit him with a Brick' (1994) 1 *Law Text Culture*, 81.
83 Liz Bradshaw, 'Writing (and) Crime Tunnel Vision: A V.I. Warshawski Novel' (1994) 1 *Law Text Culture* 151; Joelle Chenoweth, 'Not Asking the Law Question' (1994) 1 *Law Text Culture* 153; Yvette Christiansë, 'Clearing the Air – Eighteen Views of Capitol Hill' (1994) 1 *Law Text Culture* 155; Patricia Blazey-Ayoub, 'Nursing a Grievance' (1994) 1 *Law Text Culture* 161; Ben Ball, 'Dead Reckoning' (1994) 1 *Law Text Culture* 163.
84 Patron of the Law and Literature Association, and chair of the committee that would produce a set of minimum requirements for practice in Australia.
85 Bill Priestley, 'Eve was Framed' (1994) 1 *Law Text Culture* 148.
86 Robin Handley, 'Playing the System' (1994) 1 *Law Text Culture* 162.

Morrow reviewed the Australian crime TV drama *Janus*,[87] and its then novel improvisational style of TV filmmaking which 'aspires to the raw quality of documentary footage . . . [as] art imitating "reality TV"'[88] and *Four Corners*[89] style reconstruction.[90] Adding a touch of the popular cultural to the collection, this nod to *cinéma vérité* (art imitating life, illusion as reality or actuality and vice versa), wrapped up this first issue of *Law Text Culture* with an eye to the popular cultural as the prime site of cultural legal studies scholarship.

The pull to the antipodean was revealed throughout this first issue of *Law Text Culture* through its constant play of opposites and the act of being to one side: scholars from literature reviewed law; lawyers reviewed television drama; and a senior judge reviewed a book by a QC on the structural problems affecting women in law, his presence not just validating the field, but also stamping the project of cultural legal studies as central to law. Predecessors are acknowledged: Richard Weisberg, the founding editor of *Cardozo Studies in Law and Literature*, provides a sparkling piece of law and literature scholarship. But we can also see the new shape that the field is going to take. There are the transformative arguments where we see complection and enfolding of fields as they connect back to law, and an abiding reference to actuality and the materialities of being. The collection speaks to obligations and responsibility to law, place and people, breaking through the dyads to argue for changes to law that could only have happened in the geographic antipodes. It is in the contributions that are not legal, or scholarly articles, that we see this manifest itself strikingly. Ruby Langford Ginibi speaks twice as she must, insisting that we recognise Aboriginal Australia, its people, its law and understand what the lack of law means for the lives of Aboriginal people.[91] The body and the encounter, the lived experience, is central to her pieces and to the other poetry in the collection.

But it is in the piece contributed by US crime writer, Sara Paretsky, that we see something urgent, something unexpected about the role of law in making or shaping experience – and the experience of embodiment through the reach of history. With a degree in political science, and a PhD in history,[92] she is not

87 Jonathan Morrow, 'You've been Watching *LA Law* Again: *Janus*' (1994) 1 *Law Text Culture* 165.

88 In 1994, what we now know as reality TV did not exist. *Big Brother* had not yet been created, and so what this really meant was something like actuality television.

89 A long-running Australian investigative journalism program broadcast on the Australian Broadcasting Corporation (ABC), an institution in itself. *Four Corners* from time to time includes dramatic reconstructions of events in its exposés. The ABC is a publicly funded broadcaster, modelled on the BBC in the UK. It has no US equivalent.

90 Morrow, above n 87, 166.

91 Ginibi, above n 74, 8–12; Ginibi, above n 82.

92 http://en.wikipedia.org/wiki/Sara_Paretsky PhD from the University of Chicago on 'The Breakdown of Moral Philosophy in New England Before the Civil War'; Suzanne Goldenberg, 'Interview: Author Sara Paretsky, Life and style' *The Guardian* (21 March 2008). www.theguardian.com/lifeandstyle/2008/mar/22/familyandrelationships.crimebooks.

just the founder of Sisters in Crime, or the creator of VI Warshawski, but she is also deeply committed to social justice,[93] which speaks to the same issues that animated Robert Cover's demands of practice. In her contribution to that first issue, on the effect of speech and its consequences for women and other marginalised groups, she mentions something, almost as an aside, that is central to an understanding of what cultural legal studies, through its popular cultures, can do for law (while law is never mentioned, women are, and so are stories):

> Central to the problem is what it means to tell stories. The word fiction itself comes from the Latin 'fingere', meaning to mould, or form, by way of the Middle English 'feinen.' 'Fiction' means to 'fashion' or 'fann.' It gives – something – a shape. That is what stories do: they place a template over life experience and give it a shape. Women as constructors of fiction – women as shapers of experience – are relatively new.[94]

If fiction gives *shape*, then we can see with stunning clarity just how cultural legal studies, through complection and enfolding law with popular cultures, can give shape to a very different law. Law's shape had been formed through sets of lives, encounters, experiences that had not found space for *all lives*. Law's morphology, then, was ripe for transformation, as Penny Pether demanded.[95] And so to the latter part of our collection's subtitle, about which we have said very little so far. The *metamorphosis* – transformation, the changing of shape – of law is nothing more complex than observing that the shape of law can change through the insights that come from encounters with popular cultures, in all their forms. What the first issue of *Law Text Culture* did was create the possibilities of a set of encounters that could shape law differently, changing the shape of the encounter between legal theory, praxis, law and the dyads. There was still a fair bit of complection and enfolding still to happen, but the manifesto contained in the introduction, Terry Threadgold's irritations with bare theory, Jonathan Morrow's move to the popular cultural, and Ruby Langford Ginibi's articulation of the pain and violence that law has caused, created the template for cultural legal studies. By the late 1990s cultural legal studies had really moved into the multiple modes of engagement that now characterise the field. In short, it opened the door to reveal how law *could* be metamorphosed through popular cultures.

Metamorphosis and shapeshifting

How cultural legal studies metamorphoses law, then, is simply to think about law differently, to think about the shape it *could* take. But we can think of a

93 www.saraparetsky.com/biography/
94 Paretsky, above n 76, 19.
95 Pether, above n 53.

metamorphosis of law, also, through the popular cultures that permit the doing and the play that comes from the phrase cultural legal studies. In the first issue of *Law Text Culture*, we saw this in the tentative move towards television, and a realisation that the real – or in our terms, actuality – was not a stable concept through which to make claims of law, or indeed lived experience. The sources now drawn upon by cultural legal scholars have moved well beyond tentative steps out of literature, to their own lived experiences, to different forms of cultural forms and practices, and into new fields. Among our contributors to this collection, several scholars are founders in the field who have traced this journey, inspiring scholars of a new generation to value the lived experience of cultural legal studies – for example in crime-writing beyond borders (Sue Turnbull);[96] or the application of jurisprudence to popular film and television texts (William MacNeil); or the shift from screen to page and the role of the dramatic form (Peter Robson);[97] or even the (re)utilisation of law and film scholarship to move to the smallest of visual forms, the foetal ultrasound (Jessica Silbey).[98]

It is apparent that a multiplex cultural legal studies with its wealth of possibilities, is able to manifest all manner of possibilities for law, and justice, as the first issue of *Law Text Culture* revealed. The possibilities are endless, but we have organised the collection around three different modes of cultural legal studies – storytelling, technology and jurisprudence – all of which take one or more aspects of the intersectional practices of cultural legal studies and law in its popular cultural mode. It could have been different, as the shapes we have already remarked on reveal, perhaps organised around areas of law (crime, constitutionalism); or genres (film, tv, literature); or techniques (ethnography, interviews, narrative theory); global or local; myth or praxis; the variations and permutations abound. The contributions, with their diverse philosophical, disciplinary, methodological and theoretical approaches and subjects of examination and popular cultures, nevertheless all share the techniques, methodologies and practices of complection and/or enfolding. From the theoretical to the ethnographic, the descriptive to the critical, from praxis to actuality, the contributions reveal how a jurisprudence of materiality, embodiment and movement, of being in the world in its actualities and of the world, *through law's popular cultures*, can produce something that changes or transforms law. The mix of diversity and homogeneity are threaded together by an overarching theme – that we must take seriously an interrogation of law *as* culture and in its cultural form. That is, not asking 'how does a text *represent* law?', but instead 'how does the representational nature of both law and culture intersect?' and 'how does the *juridical* become visible in various cultural forms and their

96 See Chapter 5.
97 See Chapter 6.
98 See Chapter 7.

technological manifestations?' In short, we are questioning the manner in which law's popular cultures actively encounter, and then metamorphose law.

Encounter and metamorphosis is richly woven through each part of the collection. In Part 1, Marett Leiboff and Cassandra Sharp showcase the benefits of looking beyond the traditional borders of law to interpret and transform legal meaning. In particular, Leiboff asks us in Chapter 2 to think beyond our own borders, to encounter and code law differently by looking outside ourselves,[99] and in Chapter 3, Sharp demonstrates the need to appreciate a more nuanced methodological approach to an individual's encounter with law and justice. In both of these projects, there is an urgency to relate both method and story to the legal consciousness within which cultural legal studies thrives.

Part 2 picks up on this urgency by demonstrating the importance of storytelling for the metamorphosis of law. Ruby Langford Ginibi demanded that we listen and take responsibility 20 years ago. Honni van Rijswijk in Chapter 4, demonstrates how law still ignores Aboriginal people, and demands that we take responsibility for the misshapen form of life that law imposes on those who have suffered at its hands. She demands that we take responsibility not only through law but through national consciousness, using techniques drawn from the literary – genre and melodrama – to manifest social justice in contemporary Australia.[100] Sue Turnbull equally questions the shape of law on an international scale and places herself on the borders of law, both as a British subject resident in Australia, and by examining the expertly crafted Scandinavian television crime drama *The Bridge*. In Chapter 5, Turnbull encounters not only the jurisdictional limits (and challenges) to law, but also the misleading universality of law, which is seemingly able to traverse time and space to reach a globalised audience, yet will never really be fully translated.[101] Turnbull, in forcing the eye onto the place of borders in law, takes us from the cool of Scandicrime to the literal places in which law leaves its mark, keeping us within the world of criminal drama, a theme taken up by Peter Robson's return to drama. In Chapter 6, Robson reminds us of the Aristotelean virtues of time and place, inviting us to read the well-made play as ordering and reshaping the theatricality of law.[102]

What cultural legal studies reveals is the cultural formation of law, and the ability of law to be unshaped and unformed, as easily as it is reformed and reshaped. This is the theme that unites the contributions of Part 3 – a focus on the deployment of technology and images as cultural legal studies. The use of the image, to impose a conformity to a particular sense of morality, is

99 See Chapter 2.
100 See Chapter 4.
101 See Chapter 5.
102 See Chapter 6.

problematised by Jessica Silbey in Chapter 7, reminding us that the actuality of experience can be reformed, negatively, by the imposition of law as an actual practice,[103] while in Chapter 9, Karen Crawley so clearly reveals a metamorphosis in law's response to a photographic controversy involving partial nude images of older adolescents.[104] And of course Katherine Biber's Chapter 8 demonstrates that a cultural legal studies approach to photographs and archive now moves to the way we look, and the shape that law might take if we think differently about the ways we see, and the responsibilities we have when seeing.[105] Indeed, the demand to reshape and metamorphose is no better echoed than in the shapeshifting Time Lord, Doctor Who himself, who is the focus of attention for Kirsty Duncanson in Chapter 10. Utilising the well-known image of the immortal Doctor, Duncanson articulates questions about the shape that sovereignty takes in the British imaginary, and its resonances for the practices of law themselves. In combination, these chapters of Part 3 demonstrate that where law encounters new forms of seeing and encountering, we find a demand to alter the very shape of law itself.

Of course, where shapes exist, spaces are revealed. And so, returning to the changes in shape that can be rendered through sand, the new forms that can be created, and the accidental formations that occur through external forces, we need to acknowledge a mode of shaping that is negative, malevolent, a metamorphosis of law rendered darkly. In Part 4 of the collection, our contributions remind us to be alert to the shape that law can take, and what it can do by 'making strange' that which has been familiar. As we turn to the jurisprudential concerns of fictional drama in this Part, it is clear that the shifts in approaches to genres of film and television over the years, have also revealed shifts in concern about law's different manifestations and mechanisms through which metamorphosis takes place. Bill MacNeil's *lex populi* has shifted shape, as we see in Chapter 11, to now manifest a *lex vampirica*, a law of vampires,[106] and Tim Peters reveals in Chapter 12, the possibilities of a different account of law, not only within the boundaries of the legal and legality, but in the actions of finding way to change the shape of law itself.[107] It is here where we identify the gaps in the law that are visible in both the myth and theology that Ball and Cover were so keen to animate. In Chapter 13, Luis Gómez Romero demands again (using the *Harry Potter* series) that we understand that in a vanishing real, illusion speaks more clearly than reality itself. Gómez Romero makes visible the

103 See Chapter 7.
104 See Chapter 9.
105 See Chapter 8.
106 See Chapter 11.
107 See Chapter 12.

manifestation of a politics of law that is made clear through accounts in fiction in ways that cannot be revealed in the actuality.[108]

In total, these contributions demonstrate the value that can be taken from complection and enfolding, for this is the way that cultural legal studies does its thing now. We see it in van Rijswijk's call to literary theory, genre, and to melodrama,[109] or Tim Peters' call to Bertolt Brecht,[110] or Leiboff's theatricalisation,[111] and in the voices of those who lived with and through law in order to animate not only a call to justice but an improved sense of responsibility to law, and to life under law (see the Chapters of Biber, Silbey, Crawley, van Rijswijk and Sharp). Yet this entire project begs something of us, as interpreters, as scholars in different fields, who think about the shape of law, and the shape it might take. In keeping with the first issue of *Law Text Culture*, we are mindful that there is something to be said about connecting with originators, like MacNeil, Robson, Turnbull and Silbey, but there is also something that shapes the contributors to this collection, who are the next generation, who were able to build on the originators of the work of the first cultural legal scholars – Duncanson, whose own family connections with this scholarship and her doctoral supervisor, Alison Young – has moved her own work down different paths; Sharp, one of the first students in the Law School at Wollongong who was one of Penny Pether's students; Biber, who grew out of the milieu of the Macquarie Law School, where Desmond Manderson took *Law Text Culture*, before moving to Canada. There he supervised Karen Crawley's PhD, and Luis Gómez Romero worked with him as a postdoctoral fellow. Honni van Rijswijk followed in Penny Pether's footsteps, by undertaking a PhD in literature, rather than law in the US, returned to Australia, initially to Griffith, then UTS, where Katherine Biber had already moved. Crawley also moved to Griffith, where Tim Peters, one of Bill MacNeil's PhD graduates, was already working. Marett Leiboff, through her PhD at Griffith, came into contact with the Brit Crits in the mid-1990s, and eventually moved to Wollongong where Cassandra Sharp had returned early in her career, where Gómez Romero moved in 2013, soon after Desmond Manderson returned to Australia. Turnbull, though not in law, moved to Wollongong in 2011. The circle, as it were is complete, complected and enfolded, and perhaps slightly complicated, through the sticky connections that exist between us. The place of law matters enormously; but who we are matters even more, as we create and shape the law that each of us imagines and embodies. It is this metamorphosis of law that we wish to not only capture in this collection, but also to present as inspiration for the ongoing project of 'doing' law through cultural legal studies.

108 See Chapter 13.
109 See Chapter 4.
110 See Chapter 12.
111 See Chapter 2.

Bibliography

Asimow, Michael, Kathryn Brown and David Ray Papke (eds), *Law and Popular Culture: International Perspectives* (Cambridge Scholars Press, 2014)

Ball, Ben, 'Dead Reckoning' (1994) 1 *Law Text Culture* 163

Ball, Milner, 'Special Editor's Introduction' A Commemorative Volume for Robert M. Cover (1996) 8 *Cardozo Studies in Law and Literature* i

Barr,Olivia, 'A Moving Theory: Remembering the Office of Scholar' (2010) 14 *Law Text Culture* 40

Biber, Katherine, *Captive Images: Race, Crime, Photography* (Routledge-Cavendish, 2007)

Biber, Katherine and Trish Luker, 'Evidence and the Archive: Ethics, Aesthetics, and Emotion' (2014) 40 *Australian Feminist Law Journal* 1

Blazey-Ayoub, Patricia, 'Nursing a Grievance' (1994) 1 *Law Text Culture* 161

Bradshaw, Liz, 'Writing (and) Crime Tunnel Vision: A V.I. Warshawski Novel' (1994) 1 *Law Text Culture* 151

Braverman, Irus, Nicholas Blomley, David Delaney and Alexandre Keda, *The Expanding Spaces of Law: A Timely Legal Geography* (Stanford University Press, 2014)

Carpi, Daniela, 'Focus: Law, Literature and (Popular) Culture' (2014) 8 *Pólemos: Journal of Law, Literature and Culture* 1

Chenoweth, Joelle, 'Not Asking the Law Question' (1994) 1 *Law Text Culture* 153

Christiansë, Yvette, 'Clearing the Air – Eighteen Views of Capitol Hill' (1994) 1 *Law Text Culture* 155

Collis, Christy and Jason Bainbridge, 'Introduction—Popular Cultures and the *Law*' (2005) 19 *Continuum: Journal of Media and Cultural Studies* 159

Coombe, Rosemary J, 'Critical Cultural Legal Studies' (1998) 10 *Yale Journal of Law & the Humanities* 463

Coombe, Rosemary J, 'Is there a Cultural Studies of Law?' in Toby Miller (ed.), *A Companion to Cultural Studies* (Basil Blackwell, 2001) 36

Coombe, Rosemary J and Jonathan Cohen, 'Law and Late Modern Culture: Reflections on Between Facts and Norms from the Perspective of Critical Cultural Legal Studies' (1998–1999) 76 *Denver University Law Review* 1029

Cover, Robert, 'The Folktales of Justice' in Martha Minow, Michael Ryan and Austin Sarat (eds), *Narrative, Violence, and the Law: The Essays of Robert Cover* (The University of Michigan Press, 1992) 187

Dahlberg, Leif (ed.), *Visualising Law and Authority: Essays on Legal Aesthetics* (De Gruyter, 2012)

Davies, C and S Knox (eds), *Cultural Studies of Law* (Routledge, 2014)

Dolin, Kieran, 'Sanctioned Irregularities: Martial Law in Billy Budd, Sailor' (1994) 1 *Law Text Culture* 129

Dorsett, Shaunnagh and Shaun McVeigh, *Jurisdiction* (Routledge, 2012)

Douzinas, Costas, 'A Short History of the British Critical Legal Conference or, the Responsibility of the Critic' (2014) 25 *Law and Critique* 187

Douzinas, Costas and Linda Nead (eds), *Law and the Image: The Authority of Art and the Aesthetics of Law* (The University of Chicago Press, 1999)

Duncanson, Ian, 'Cultural Studies Encounters Legal Pluralism: Certain Objects of Order, Law and Culture' (1997) 12 *Canadian Journal of Law and Society* 115

Etxabe, Julen and Gary Watt (eds), *Living in a Law Transformed: Encounters with the Works of James Boyd White* (Michigan Publishing, 2014).

Gaakeer, Jeanne, 'Law and Literature Redux? Some Remarks on the Importance of the Legal Imagination' in Julen Etxabe and Gary Watt (eds), *Living in a Law Transformed: Encounters with the Works of James Boyd White* (Michigan Publishing, 2014)

Genovese, Ann, 'Critical Decision, 1982: Remembering *Koowarta v Bjelke-Petersen*' (2014) 23 *Griffith Law Review* 1

Ginibi, Ruby Langford, 'Aboriginal Traditional and Customary Law' (1994) 1 *Law Text Culture* 8

Ginibi, Ruby Langford, 'Terra Nullius' (1994) 1 *Law Text Culture* 13

Goldie, Matthew Boyd, *The Idea of the Antipodes: Place People and Voices* (Routledge, 2010)

Goldie, Matthew Boyd, 'Island Theory – The Antipodes' in Maeve McCusker and Anthony Soares (eds), *Islanded Identities: Constructions of Postcolonial Cultural Insularity* (Editions Rodopi, 2011) 1–40

Goodrich, Peter, 'Screening Law' (2009) 21 *Law & Literature* 1

Greenfield, Steve, Guy Osborn and Peter Robson, *Film and the Law* (Hart Publishing, 2nd edn, 2010)

Hall, Jerome, 'Open Letter Proposing a School of Cultural Legal Studies' (1951) 4 *Journal of Legal Education* 181

Handley, Robin, 'Playing the System' (1994) 1 *Law Text Culture* 162

Handley, Robin, Penny Pether, Joseph Pugliese, Maurice Scott, J Robinson and C Hough, 'Introduction' (1994) 1 *Law Text Culture* 6

Higgins, Christine, '"The Woman Business": Mill, Trollope and the Law' (1994) 1 *Law Text Culture* 63

Horn, Nicholas, 'Tityrus' (1994) 1 *Law Text Culture* 48.

Kahn, Paul W, *The Cultural Study of Law: Reconstructing Legal Scholarship* (University of Chicago Press, 1999)

Kamir, Orit, *Framed: Women in Law and Film* (Duke University Press, 2006)

Kiley, Dean, 'I Panicked and Hit him with a Brick' (1994) 1 *Law Text Culture* 81

Knox, Sara L and Cristyn Davies, 'The Force of Meaning' Special issue *The Force of Meaning: Cultural Studies of Law* (2013) 27 *Cultural Studies* 1

Leiboff, Marett, 'Of the Monstrous Regiment and the Family Jewels' (2005) 23 *Australian Feminist Law Journal* 33

Leiboff, Marett, 'Law, Muteness and the Theatrical' (2010) 14 *Law Text Culture* 384

Leiboff, Marett, 'Towards a Jurisprudence of the Embodied Mind – Sarah Lund, Forbrydelsen and the Mindful Body' in Hanne Petersen and Rubya Mehdi (eds), Special issue on 'Law and Art' Volume 2 (2015) 6 *NAVEIÑ REET: Nordic Journal of Law and Social Research*

Leiboff, Marett and Mark Thomas, *Legal Theories: Contexts and Practices* (Thomson Law Book Co, 2nd edn, 2014)

Leonard, Jerry and Marie Asche (eds), *Legal Studies As Cultural Studies: A Reader in (post) Modern Critical Theory* (State University of New York Press, 1995)

McCusker, Maeve and Anthony Soares (eds), *Islanded Identities: Constructions of Postcolonial Cultural Insularity* (Editions Rodopi, 2011)

MacNeil, William P, *Lex Populi: The Jurisprudence of Popular Culture* (Stanford University Press, 2007)

MacNeil, William P, *Novel Judgements: Legal Theory as Fiction* (Routledge-Cavendish, 2011)

MacNeil, William and Peter Hutchings, 'Law's Cultural Mediations: An Introduction by Way of Introduction' (2001) 10 *Griffith Law Review* 1

Manderson, Desmond (ed.), *Courting Death: the Law of Mortality* (Pluto Press, 1999)

Manderson, Desmond, *Songs Without Music: Aesthetic Dimensions Of Law and Justice* (University of California Press, 2000)
Manderson, Desmond, *Kangaroo Courts and the Rule of Law: The Legacy of Modernism* (Routledge, 2012)
Manderson, Desmond, 'Memory and Echo: Pop Cult, Hi Tech and the Irony of Tradition' (2013) 27 *Cultural Studies* 11
Mezey, Naomi, 'Law as Culture' (2001) 13 *Yale Journal of Law & the Humanities* 35.
Miller, Toby (ed.), *A Companion to Cultural Studies* (Basil Blackwell, 2001).
Minow, Martha, Michael Ryan and Austin Sarat (eds), *Narrative, Violence, and the Law: The Essays of Robert Cover* (The University of Michigan Press, 1992)
Mohr, Richard, 'Flesh and the Person' (2008) 29 *The Australian Feminist Law Journal* 31
Mohr, Richard, 'Signature and Illusion: Lessons from the Baroque for "Truth" in Law and the Humanities' (2012) 36 *The Australian Feminist Law Journal* 45
Moran, Leslie J, Emma Sandon, Elena Loizidou and Ian Christie (eds), *Law's Moving Image* (GlassHouse Press, 2004)
Morris, Kate, 'In these prisons' (1994) 1 *Law Text Culture* 40
Morrow, Jonathan, 'You've Been Watching *LA Law* Again: *Janus*' (1994) 1 *Law Text Culture* 165
Paretsky, Sara, 'Protocols of the Elders of Feminism' (1994) 1 *Law Text Culture* 14
Peters, Julie Stone, 'Law, Literature and the Vanishing Real: On the Future of the Interdisciplinary Illusion' (2005) 120(2) *PMLA* 442
Pether, Penny, 'On Foreign Ground: Grand Narratives, Situated Specificities, and the Praxis of Critical Theory and Law?' (1999) 10 *Law and Critique* 211
Pether, Penny and Simon Petch, 'Literature and Law' (1991) 7 *Australian Journal of Law and Society* 1
Philippopoulos-Mihalopoulos, Andreas, *Spatial Justice: Body, Lawscape, Atmosphere* (Routledge, 2015)
Priestley, Bill, 'Eve was Framed' (1994) 1 *Law Text Culture* 148
Pugliese, Joseph, 'In Memoriam Penny Pether: For Friendship, Generosity, and Social Justice' (2014) 26 *Law & Literature* 259
Redhead, Steve, *Unpopular Cultures: The Birth of Law and Popular Culture* (Manchester University Press, 1995)
Robinson, Vince, 'Codes, Dooms, Constitutions and Statutes: The Emergence of the Legislative Form of Legal Writing' (1994) 1 *Law Text Culture* 106
Robson, Peter and Jessica Silbey (eds), *Law and Justice on the Small Screen* (Hart, 2012)
Rush, Peter and Andrew Kenyon (eds), *Aesthetics of Law and Culture: Texts, Images, Screens* (Emerald Group Publishing Ltd, 2004)
Sanders, Mark, 'Remembrance for Penny' (2014) 26 *Law & Literature* 257
Sarat, Austin (ed.), *Imagining Legality: Where Law Meets Popular Culture* (University of Alabama Press, 2011)
Sarat, Austin, Matthew Anderson and Cathrine O Frank, *Law and the Humanities: An Introduction* (Cambridge University Press, 2010)
Sarat, Austin and Thomas R Kearns (eds), *Law in the Domains of Culture* (University of Michigan Press, 1997)
Sarat, Austin and Jonathan Simon, 'Beyond Legal Realism: Cultural Analysis, Cultural Studies, and the Situation of Legal Scholarship' 13 *Yale Journal of Law & Humanities* 3 (2001)

Sarat, Austin and Jonathan Simon (eds), *Cultural Analysis, Cultural Studies, and the Law: Moving Beyond Legal Realism* (Duke University Press, 2003)
Sarat, Austin and Martha Merrill Umphrey, 'Temporal Horizons: On the Possibilities of Law and Fatherhood in *To Kill a Mockingbird*' (2013) 27 *Cultural Studies* 30
Schirato, Tony, 'Mabo and the Politics of Community' (1994) 1 *Law Text Culture* 99
Schur, Anna, 'Flourishing or Perishing? Law and Literature Airbrushed' (2014) 26 *Law & Literature* 105
Seuffert, Nan, *Jurisprudence of National Identity: Kaleidoscopes of Imperialism And Globalisation from Aotearoa New Zealand* (Ashgate, 2006)
Sharp, Cassandra, 'Let's See How Far We've Come: The Role of Empirical Methodology in Exploring Television Audiences' in Peter Robson and Jessica Silbey (eds), *Law and Justice on the Small Screen* (Hart Publishing, 2012) 111
Sharp, Cassandra, 'Justice with a Vengeance – Retributive Desire in Popular Imagination' in Michael Asimow, Kathryn Brown and David Ray Papke (eds), *Law and Popular Culture: International Perspectives* (Cambridge Scholars Publishing, 2014) 153
Sherwin, Richard K, *When Law Goes Pop: The Vanishing Line Between Law and Popular Culture* (University of Chicago Press, 2000)
Sherwin, Richard K (ed.), *Popular Culture and Law* (Ashgate, 2008)
Sherwin, Richard K (ed.), 'Visualizing Law in the Digital Age' (2012–2013) 57 *New York Law School Review*
Stone, Matthew, Illan rua Wall and Costas Douzinas (eds), *New Critical Legal Thinking: Law and the Political* (Birkbeck Law Press, 2012).
Thornton, Margaret (ed.), *Romancing the Tomes: Popular Culture, Law and Feminism* (Cavendish, 2002)
Threadgold, Terry, 'Deconstruction and the Possibility of Justice: Critical and Cultural Difference' (1994) 1 *Law Text Culture* 140
Tomlins, Christopher, 'Law "and", Law "in", Law "as": The Definition, Rejection and Recuperation of the Socio-legal Enterprise' (2013) 29 *Law in Context* 137
Wagner, Anne and Richard K Sherwin (eds), *Law, Culture and Visual Studies* (Springer, 2014)
Weisberg, Richard, 'The Codification of Western Law & the Poetics of Disclosure' (1994) 1 *Law Text Culture* 28
Wilmshurst, Peter, 'Introduction: Literature and Law' (1993) 9 *Australian Journal of Law and Society* 1
Wizner, Stephen, 'Repairing the World through Law: A Reflection on Robert Cover's Social Activism' A Commemorative Volume for Robert M Cover (Spring/Summer, 1996) 8 *Cardozo Studies in Law and Literature* 1
Wizner, Stephen, 'A Theology of Justice: Some Reflections on Milner Ball's Non-Religious Practice of Belief' (2006–2007) 41 *Georgia Law Review* 945
Young, Alison, *Judging The Image: Art, Value, Law* (Routledge, 2005)
Young, Alison, *The Scene of Violence: Cinema, Crime, Affect* (Routledge, 2010)
Young, Alison, *Street Art, Public City: Law, Crime and the Urban Imagination* (Routledge, 2014)

Websites

Law and Popular Cultures. Legal Intersections Research Centre, University of Wollongong http://lha.uow.edu.au/law/LIRC/themes/UOW165568.html
Oxford English Dictionary, OED Online (Oxford University Press, December 2014)

Paretsky, Sara www.saraparetsky.com/biography/
Paretsky, Sara Wikipedia http://en.wikipedia.org/wiki/Sara_Paretsky
Popular Cultures Research Network, University of Leeds www.leeds.ac.uk/arts/info/40011/popular_cultures_research_network/1148/about

Media

Goldenberg, Suzanne, 'Interview: Author Sara Paretsky, Life and style' *The Guardian* (21 March 2008) www.theguardian.com/lifeandstyle/2008/mar/22/familyandrelationships.crimebooks

Chapter 2

Cultural legal studies as law's extraversion

Marett Leiboff

> We must get the relative roles of myth and history straight . . . Only myth tells us who we would become; only history can tell us how hard it will really be to become that.[1]

I start this chapter by reprising and adding to a quote from Robert Cover that has already appeared in this book.[2] Stripped back to a form of aphorism, or principle, these remaining words look like a formula that inevitably disregards the 'sacred stories/texts' of literature and tradition that Cover avers as law.[3] I realise that to not step into the story a little would be to frustrate, the desire to know what happened next appealing to most of us. But I have already distorted the narrative, for the aphorism does not begin Cover's tale, but sits smack in the middle.[4] While it will take me a little while to get to my point, I will let you know now that my use of Cover will not go in quite the direction that you might expect. My act of disruption is theatrical,[5] written to perturb the comfortable experience of following through an argument that has defined contours and

1 Robert Cover, 'The Folktales of Justice' in Martha Minow, Michael Ryan and Austin Sarat (eds), *Narrative, Violence, and the Law: The Essays of Robert Cover* (The University of Michigan Press, 1992), 187.
My thanks to Cassandra Sharp and Luis Gómez Romero for their challenges, support, suggestions, and very keen eyes.
2 Marett Leiboff and Cassandra Sharp, 'Cultural Legal Studies and Law's Popular Cultures' in Cassandra Sharp and Marett Leiboff (eds), *Cultural Legal Studies: Law's Popular Cultures and the Metamorphosis of Law* (Routledge, 2015).
3 Robert Cover, 'Foreword: Nomos and Narrative' (1983) 97 *Harvard Law Review* 4.
4 Cover, above n 1, 185.
5 Marett Leiboff, 'Towards a Jurisprudence of the Embodied Mind – Sarah Lund, Forbrydelsen and the Mindful Body' in Hanne Petersen and Rubya Mehdi (eds), Special issue on 'Law and Art' Volume 2 (2015) 6 *NAVEIÑ REET: Nordic Journal of Law and Social Research*.

patterns, as a form of Brechtian disruption,[6] a form of encounter that I hope will demand a response, though it must be through text rather than actual encounter. My use of one of Robert Cover's own sacred texts might have invoked a set of assumptions that are already playing out in your mind, that speak to what you think I might be about to say. It might have registered other myths of law,[7] or perhaps, in the register of the law and literature dyad, there is the pull of the story, what it will tell us of law and how the story will make us better lawyers. So to be brief. In *Folktales of Justice*, Cover takes a story from the *Talmud* that grounds the principle that kings should not be judged by law; marries its mythic status as a sacred text with an actual historical event recorded by Josephus; moves to its application in *Prohibitions del Roy* (you will remember that this is the decision where Coke LJ tells James I that he is bound by law, founding the principle that government must function according to law); and uses this to form a vision of courageous judging against power, through Nuremberg and Vietnam, and the pull to a utopian justice.

There you have it. Brief and near enough accurate as a surface level reading of 'what happened'. But it leaves out Cover's call to judicial courage and integrity in the exercise of jurisdiction (by which he means jurisdiction as the speaking or uttering of law).[8] That is what matters in *Folktales of Justice*, not stories for their own sake. The aphorism, the story, the call to courage, are all figured to speak to the present (though of course grounded in the past). In his sights are the judges who cosy up to government, who do not do their duty based on integrity to law. Integrity to law is 'prudential and principled,'[9] spoken as a commitment that needs to be understood within sacred texts and narratives, as bound up in the literatures and traditions that ground law.[10] For Cover, judging must maintain 'the vision that it is only that [integrity] which redeems which is law'.[11] In other words, an abiding commitment to a form of morality as utopian sits behind Cover's story, his parable, and that morality is law itself.

In its telling, Cover's story makes sense to us, because it reiterates. This, after all, is what myths and morality tales are designed to do, repeating and reminding us of what we already know. Myth is the story that becomes well known to us, and internalised in us, acting as the embodiment of abstract principle. Remembering and reiterating stories of Coke and James embeds the

6 Marett Leiboff, 'Of the Monstrous Regiment and the Family Jewels' (2005) 23 *The Australian Feminist Law Journal* 33, 35–36; see also Timothy Peters, 'Reading the Law Made Strange: Cultural Legal Studies, Theology and Speculative Fiction' in Sharp and Leiboff (eds), above n 2.

7 Peter Fitzpatrick, *The Mythology of Modern Law* (Routledge, 1992).

8 Cover above n 1, 185; Shaunnagh Dorsett and Shaun McVeigh, *Jurisdiction* (Routledge, 2012).

9 Cover, above n 1, 185.

10 Cover, above n 1, 177.

11 Ibid.

principle that government must operate under law more than simply an abstract idea. We remember the myths because they do something for us, otherwise there would be no point in remembering them.[12] Cover's approach towards myth is what I want to call *embodied abstraction*. For law, at least, this call to myth as embodied abstraction is easily digested, for it is law's practice to create abstractions, and it is an easy step for remnant words to form an empty principle as aphorism.

When reading *Folktales of Justice*, one thing becomes patently obvious. Cover cautions about *reality* in a range of different registers, despite its ability, through history, to function as a corrective of the ideal. The first of these cautions I will mention is played out in the register of reality and realpolitik. This is where he sees the dangers for law, where the courts: 'maintain the connection between law and reality . . . [and] risk losing law to the overpowering force of what is and what is dominant'.[13] Reality, the pull of the liberal democratic niceties of law, the politics and the politeness of legal form and encounter, is a dangerous supplement, for all the wrong reasons. The caution is registered through 'what is', or reality, and then emphasised by the call to 'what is dominant', or the register of power. Each form of reality lessens the pull to justice, the courage that is needed to manifest justice. In the second of Cover's cautions that I will mention, reality is something that needs to be repudiated for utopian purposes. Law needs to function as a 'bridge from *reality* to a new world'.[14] So when Cover avers to history, he does so with his eye firmly on myth, for history – as reality – is both secondary to myth, and potentially obfuscating for the abstract ideals they contain.

The idea that resides in this assumption is that realities of this kind are the reserve position, a slightly soiled or stained or compromised supplement of the ideal. This conflicts, inevitably, with the assumptions found in cultural legal studies, which treats the materialities or realities as part of the mix, rather than something to one side. Cover's formula, to place reality or actuality, hierarchically below the ideals contained in the embodied abstraction of myth, is familiar to law and it is familiar to the abstracted form of theory that frustrated both Penny Pether and Terry Threadgold.[15] This investment of reality as an inferior state of being is a familiar tale of the theoretical, also represents a mistrust of the empirical of a source of experience. In similar terms to those expressed by Cover 30 years ago, Costas Douzinas recently remarked:

12 Cover, above n 1, 187.

13 Cover, above n 1, 201.

14 Cover, above n 1, 188; also see Sue Turnbull, 'Border Crossings: The Transnational Career of the Television Crime Drama' in Sharp and Leiboff (eds), above n 2.

15 See discussion in Leiboff and Sharp, above n 2.

> Courage does not call for empirical knowledge but for moral knowledge of self, of the good and beautiful and it is disclosed by *parrhesia*—fearless speech. It sets the natural ends of action and frees man from natural and social fears.[16]

I want to perturb the idea that moral knowledge is in the gift of an abstract interiority, or principle, or even the embodied abstraction of myth. I will now catch up with my brief references to the theatrical, because it is through experience and encounter that I want to question what we make of reality (or actuality). Does encounter and experience – those seeming external or exogenous parts of our being – affect how the self carries out the process of recognising when there is a need to act, when there is a legal wrong, or animate the courage to do justice? Put another way, if we have lived *without* the impetus or imperative that alerts to the need for courage, that is, something which gives form to and animates the moral self to act and respond, do stories in the abstract prompt without more? Or is the moral self able to act of its own accord, that is, as a self-animating subject absent anything other than an abstract ideal? This latter position makes all the sense in the world to a law, a discipline that bears all the hallmarks of Jungian introversion.[17] The former position, which bears the hallmarks of Jungian extraversion, is cultural legal studies' wont. Rather than being external to a self, encounter and experience becomes embodied in us, and prompts us to respond. Without that animating force, what can we notice of law and justice, or particularly, law and injustice?

The past is never dead. It's not even past.[18]

I will pick up this thread later in this chapter, but let me agitate a little, in a form that will be comfortable to Jungian extraverts, but less so, or not at all, to introverts. Let me start with David Seymour's position that there is a marked difference between the material conditions of the Holocaust and its reframing through abstracted categories in place of the real lives and existences of those who experienced the actual, rather than an abstracted Holocaust.[19] If it seems

16 Costas Douzinas, 'A Short History of the British Critical Legal Conference or, the Responsibility of the Critic' (2014) 25 *Law and Critique* 187, 196.

17 Marett Leiboff, '"DITTO": Law, Pop Culture and Humanities and the Impact of Intergenerational Interpretative Dissonance' (2012) 36 *The Australian Feminist Law Journal* 145, 152–153; Marett Leiboff and Mark Thomas, *Legal Theories: Contexts and Practices* (Thomson Law Book Co, 2nd edn, 2014).

18 William Faulkner, *Requiem for a Nun* 1950, quoted in Robert W Hamblin and Charles A Peek (eds), *A William Faulkner Encyclopaedia* (Greenwood Press, 1999), 326.

19 David M Seymour, *Law, Antisemitism and the Holocaust* (Routledge-Cavendish, 2007); cf Costas Douzinas, 'History Trials: Can Law Decide History?' (2012) 8 *Annual Review of Law and Social Science* 273.

preferable or more appropriate to ignore or avoid descriptions of the real experiences of people in death camps in favour of an idealised or universal image or representation of suffering as a form of theoretical positioning, then it will be immediately apparent that the starting point of extraversion will be uncomfortable, if not unnerving. So to step in a little deeper, I will suggest that though neither acknowledges it, Cover and Douzinas are deeply enmeshed in animating realities, which are fundamental to, and instrumental in grounding the ideals and modes of abstraction contained within their work. If we look, we can find animating concepts, triggers, pressure points. Robert Cover's Jewishness is everywhere in his work, found in his use of materials and sources, his choice of stories, his framing conceits. Born at the end of World War Two, he was a student during the Vietnam War, and was jailed in the US South, during the 1960s civil rights movement (for his part in actively supporting African American equality).[20] In *Folktales*, we have references to the Nuremberg trials and Vietnam, the latter a site of actual encounter, the former a memory that is impossible to excise. He writes *Folktales* on the cusp of Ronald Reagan's second presidency, with an extant USSR still firmly in place, and though it is published in 1985, the piece had formed the basis of a speech given in 1984 at Capital University Law School. *Nineteen Eighty-Four*, of course, was a year and a promise, the title of George Orwell's 1949 dystopian novel penned at the outset of the Cold War. Its representation of the loss of the democratic spirit, marked by perpetual war, the removal of freedom and the imposition of a government for its own sake, was both fiction and reality. The stand-off between the USA and the Soviet government meant the threat of nuclear war was ever present.

Folktales looks different when it is read through its time and place. The abstract argument for law as utopian agent is enriched. It is informed by a politics and through a politics, and the experiences and encounters that inevitably shaped Robert Cover. Its realities, its actualities are present, but read time out of mind, without those snippets of knowledge in place, it reads as a plea to a form of utopia in the abstract. Being in a time and place cannot be reiterated. How *Folktales* is read now can never be the same as how *Folktales* was read in 1984 or 1985. Even those who read it then can never go back, can't read it the same way now. It is impossible to return to a moment that has been.[21] We can get a sense of a time, but it is not the same as being there. Listen to and have a look

To abstract removes the human or the event, inserting A, B and C or Blackacre or Whiteacre in its place, and in their absence, a reframing of actuality through principle. Kristen Rundle, 'The Impossibility of an Exterminatory Legality: Law and the Holocaust' (2009) 59 *University of Toronto Law Journal* 65; Kristen Rundle, 'Law and Daily Life: Questions for Legal Philosophy from 1938' (2012) 3 *Jurisprudence* 429.

20 Stephen Wizner, 'A Theology of Justice: Some Reflections on Milner Ball's Non-Religious Practice of Belief' (2006–2007) 41 *Georgia Law Review* 945.

21 Leiboff, above n 17, 163.

at the video of *Two Tribes*,[22] created by the UK band, Frankie Goes to Hollywood. It was released internationally in 1984, the same year that *Folktales* was presented to an audience prior to publication. An early piece of dance music, its serious remit was made clear in its video, where we see Ronald Reagan wrestling the leader of the USSR (Chernenko), and the endgame, nuclear destruction. What is left behind is a now pretty unsophisticated, grainy looking video, in old format. At the time it was a pretty exciting video (you have to trust me on this). Like *Folktales*, this piece was created by someone in a particular time and place, capturing a moment in time. Now, if you are interested, find the lyrics of the *Two Tribes* (trust me on this as well, it is impossible to understand most of them as music). The lyrics, on their own, mean very little at all. But if you were there, at the time, there was no doubt what the song was about, because there was an ever-present threat of all-out war between the USA and the USSR.

I have known Costas Douzinas for a long time, but like most people we come to know through networks and connections, I don't know much about his background. I know he was born in Greece, and that he'd lived in England for a considerable length of time. But like Robert Cover, it is possible to find out something about Costas through published material – Wikipedia, university biographies, and perhaps, through scholarship. These materials leave gaps waiting to be filled, and I have chosen not to fill them. Born six years after the end of World War Two, he was a student in Athens at the time of the student resistance to the Colonels' Dictatorship (1967–1974).[23] His biography reveals that he holds an LLB (Athens), and he joined the student resistance while studying in Athens. He left Greece in 1974, and continued studying in London (obtaining an LLM and PhD from the LSE). There is silence in the biographical materials, but there is something more to be uncovered. By way of background, the Colonels' Dictatorship was formed through a military *coup d'état* in the late 1960s. Dictatorship meant that – autocracy and military rule. It ended in 1974, following a brutally suppressed uprising at the Athens Polytechnic in 1973. That event itself had a prelude, and that was a strike of law students, who, on 21 February 1973, barricaded themselves in the building of the Law School of the University of Athens. In one of his pieces, we see vivid descriptions of the forms of torture conducted by the military against their opponents, in engaging with the pull to a Lacanian psychoanalytic jurisprudence.[24] Absences in the texts are either telling or have no import. We can read between the lines, or read into the gaps in ways that might fill out his story, or that might distort it.

22 Frankie Goes to Hollywood, *Two Tribes* www.youtube.com/watch?v=K2QAMqTgPKI. The song 'Russians' by Sting http://en.wikipedia.org/wiki/Russians_%28song%29 was released in 1985 and touches on similar themes www.youtube.com/watch?v=wHylQRVN2Qs.

23 Costas Douzinas, Director, Biography, *The Birkbeck Institute for the Humanities* www.bbk.ac/bih/about; www.bbk.ac.uk/law/our-staff/ft-academic/douzinas/biog.

24 Costas Douzinas, 'Human Rights and Postmodern Utopia' (2000) 11 *Law and Critique* 219, 228–229.

Courage may be grounded in the ideal of the 'moral knowledge of self',[25] but what is left behind is a question that goes begging. Has this moral sense, the ideal, been animated by experience, or was experience animated through self-awareness? Is the abstract shaped, or a sense of awareness triggered through encounter and experience, prompting in us a form of conduct, to know that a military dictatorship is wrong, to become aware that rights are traduced, that a piece of legislation goes too far? Conversely, what goes unnoticed without the pull of encounter and experience? Can an engaged retelling reiterate and alert? I will get to where this is taking me soon, but I do want to observe that Shaun McVeigh, building on Peter Rush's work, has remarked that external reality and internal qualities are *both* required to manifest the 'ethic of office' held by the jurist which:

> engages the responsibility of the jurist to create and maintain some form of 'interiority' to law—an interiority or experience of law adequate to sustain conscience and judgment. It is an ethic of responsibility that is framed in terms of finding the appropriate *internal qualities to meet external realities*.[26]

This move towards a rapprochement, between the internal and external, only goes so far, that there is an interior life that can see what is wrong with external realities. What this chapter is asking, through embodied encounter, or as much of it as is possible through words rather than actual encounter, is how that interior life is shaped by external realities. Reality is formative of the self that is constantly reiterated and reframed against experience, created or formed *through our encounters with the world*, and through the cultural artefacts like literature, music, history, and so on that create the conditions for being,[27] as we see in Cover's and Douzinas' biographies.

I draw on Jungian introversion and extraversion to think more about this, and why cultural legal scholarship is able to turn the question around, to pose a different methodological arrangement that does not privilege myth over history, or history over myth, why we do not think it is wrong to undertake empirical work and blend it with the theoretical and the legal, why we use it to move

25 Douzinas, above n 16.

26 Shaun McVeigh, 'Law As (More or Less) Itself: On Some Not Very Reflective Elements of Law' (2014) 4 *University of California Irvine Law Review* 471 (emphasis added, footnotes removed); references are to Peter Rush, 'An Altered Jurisdiction: Corporeal Traces of Law' (1998) 6 *Griffith Law Review* 144, 149; Peter Rush, 'Dirty War Crimes: Jurisdictions of Memory and International Criminal Law' in Kevin Jon Heller and Gerry Simpson (eds), *The Hidden Histories of War Crimes Trials* (Oxford University Press, 2013), 367.

27 Heidegger, Gadamer, and Ricoeur: Bjørn Ramberg and Kristin Gjesdal, 'Hermeneutics', *The Stanford Encyclopedia of Philosophy* (Summer 2013 Edition), Edward N Zalta (ed.), http://plato.stanford.edu/archives/sum2013/entries/hermeneutics/; cf Julen Etxabe, *The Experience of Tragic Judgment* (Routledge, 2013).

beyond our own frame of reference, not as empty empiricism, but as a form of encounter that tells us something that we cannot find through our own resources. Cultural legal studies asks us if there is something to be gained by moving beyond what we already assume we know of the world, what we already hold internal to ourselves. We need to look *outside* ourselves to enjoin the promise of cultural legal studies, [28] and I will play a small game shortly, theatricalising what we know, using Robert Cover's myth and history, in a small gesture of disruption, which has nothing to do with his argument or with his article at all.

You achieve balance, however, only if you nurture your opposite. But that is hateful to you in your inner most core . . .[29]

In a number of places in this chapter so far, I have used the words encounter and experience. Each is theatrical, that is, encounter and experience each function in the register of *embodied response and reaction*, rather than the embodied abstraction, say, of story or myth. Embodied response is equivocal, accepting imperfectability; embodied abstraction is unequivocal, assuming that what can be known *is* known, as ideal and as perfection. The former is exemplary of the characteristics of the Jungian attitude of *extraversion*,[30] a mode of conduct that is 'outward turning' from the self, drawing energy and ideas from the external world. Its opposite, of course, is to be 'inward turning' to the self, or the Jungian attitude of *introversion*. Or as Casement, a Jungian expert describes it: 'The extraverted attitude depicts a movement of interest outwards towards the object; the introverted attitude, on the other hand, results in a movement of interest inwards towards the subject'.[31]

A simple way to think of the differences can be found in the assumptions you might have drawn from my references to theatre in this chapter so far. To think of theatre as a place where literature is represented on stage is introvert; to think of theatre as a place where the unknown happens to an audience is extravert. If you have construed my references to the theatrical in this chapter as referring to playtexts or drama, you are registering an introvert response, 'by moving interest inwards towards the subject'. Theatre, as a place of encounter and experience, is the place par excellence of embodied response and reaction. To

28 Jeanne Gaakeer, 'Reverent Rites of Legal Theory: Unity–Diversity–Interdisciplinarity' (2012) 36 *Australian Feminist Law Journal* 19; Jeanne Gaakeer, 'European Law and Literature Forever Young. The Nomad Concurs' in Helle Porsdam and Thomas Elholm (eds), *Law and Literature: Dialogues on Justice: European Perspectives on Law and Humanities* (Walter de Gruyter, 2012).

29 C G Jung, cited in Steven Galipeau, 'The Red Book and Jung's Typology' (2013) 56 *Psychological Perspectives: A Quarterly Journal of Jungian Thought* 34, 40.

30 Carl G Jung, *Psychological Types* (Routledge, 1971).

31 Ann Casement, *Carl Gustav Jung* (Sage, 2011), 68.

interpolate embodied abstraction in its place, that is, to expect what is already there in the form of what is already known, is the mark of introversion. A well-known Australian social researcher complained that when he went to the theatre he expected to see the play, and to not be irritated by actors who moved around in the aisles or engaged with individual audience members. It is introvert to know what to expect in theatre, it is extravert to go along for the ride.

Now to turn for a moment to Jung's attitudes and (and the qualifying typologies), for they are mired in misconception and misunderstanding. Even Jung had to correct misapprehensions soon after the publication in 1921 of the first edition of his book, *Psychological Types* – that he was seeking to shoe-horn people into types.[32] These two Jungian *attitudes* – introversion and extraversion – represent the two antonymic means by which individuals respond to the world around them.[33] Despite this, all of us have introvert and extravert characteristics, with one predominant to a greater or lesser degree (as expressed through other preferences of thinking, feeling, sensation or intuition). An introvert thinking type will be very different from an extravert thinking type, and so on.[34] The dyads of extraversion and introversion are the foundational philosophical conceits that sit behind Jung's theory of types, and one of these was foundational to law, its practices, dogmas, doctrines, and it has to be said, its theories, and that is introversion.[35] For introversion is law's orthodoxy (abstraction, principle, known texts),[36] while extraversion its aberrant subaltern (the real, encounter, engagement, the unknown). This prioritising is not Jung's, but mine. It is obvious, really. Law itself is introvert because lawyers, by and large, are introvert,[37] so it is inevitable that law will build up techniques, methods and practices that speak to what it and its selves know best. Chicken and egg, law reiterates its own kind.

Although Julius Stone once remarked that jurisprudence is law's extraversion, because it obtained its modes of thinking from 'knowledge in disciplines other than law',[38] this is a one-dimensional conception of how the Jungian attitudes

32 Jung cited in Galipeau, above n 29, 37.

33 Jung uses the moniker 'attitude' to these two forms of being and delineates between conscious and unconscious version of the attitudes, and 'typology' to sensation, feeling, thinking, intuition.

34 Eight types exist in Jung's schema. Isabel Myers and Katharine Briggs applied the theory to create their Type Indicator Instrument based on Jung's theory of psychological type, and expanded the types to sixteen from his eight. See generally Larry Richard, 'The Lawyer Types' (1993) 79 *ABA Journal* 74; Mary H McCaulley and Charles R Martin, 'Career Assessment and the Myers-Briggs Type Indicator' (1995) 3 *Journal of Career Assessment* 219.

35 Leiboff and Sharp, above n 2.

36 Richard, above n 34; McCaulley and Martin, above n 34, 230–231.

37 Richard, above n 34.

38 Julius Stone, 'The Province of Jurisprudence Redetermined (Concluded)' (1943–1944) 7 *Modern Law Review* 177, 178; Julius Stone, *Legal System and Lawyers' Reasonings* (Stanford University Press, 1964), 16. Different spellings exist: extr*o*version is used in the *Modern Law Review* article and extr*a*version in the 1964 book.

of introversion and extraversion function. Scholarship is introvert in a Jungian sense when it demarcates and contains, when it is sceptical of the use of its own conception of subaltern fields. This means that critical approaches to law can also be introvert. Scholarly work is characteristically introvert when it, too, 'moves interest inwards towards the subject'. That is, the ideal is able to function in the absence of any consideration of realities/actualities.[39] The complection and enfolding of cultural legal studies, on the other hand, needs both introversion and extraversion, to achieve a Jungian balance, and to 'nurture your opposite'.

This chapter has resulted from research that 'nurtured the opposite', by complecting and enfolding techniques drawn from the social sciences, history, pop culture, legal interpretation, claims to theory, with an eye to what this all means for the formation of lawyers.[40] It has an eye to other work I carried out complecting and enfolding archives, biography, history and the jurisprudence of the mask.[41] But all of it, in its own way, sits against the backdrop of how conscience and judgment, and the ethic of responsibility is formed and created in the legal self,[42] and how the legal self responds to challenges to what it knows, and what it assumes. How might it react to being asked to move beyond introversion? How might it react to being asked to look 'outside', to challenge what is already embedded into the 'patterns of existence'? This cultural legal studies work uses techniques that are extravert to think differently and to challenge, to perturb what we do and how we do it. But these techniques also work to unmask the legal self, to try to find out something about how they animate their sense of responsibility to law. Of course, these practices also reveal quite a lot about me, even though I have not once said that I am not an introvert. The choice of the double negative is not accidental. If you thought that I am an introvert . . . I will rewind . . . if *you* are an introvert, it is more likely than not that you will have already assumed that most of what is included in this chapter is irrelevant, has diverged from accepted positions, but even worse, has barely paid attention, explicitly, to all that much theory (don't take this to heart, I am wanting to get an embodied response from you). But there is a serious side to this jape. Methodologically, there is a gaping maw between those of us who adopt extravert practices, and those who don't. Introverts will look for the principle, and the ideal, and strip away the stories, the complection, the enfolding. At the 'get-go' in law school, extraverts had to learn to work with techniques and methods that are not their own, and accidently found a way to overcome that which is 'most hateful to their inner core', otherwise they could never have

39 Desmond Manderson and Richard Mohr, 'From Oxymoron to Intersection: An Epidemiology of Legal Research' (2002) 6 *Law Text Culture* 159.

40 Leiboff, above n 17.

41 Marett Leiboff, '"The main thing is to shut them out" The Deployment of Law and the Arrival of Russians in Australia 1913–1925: An histoire' (2011) 15 *Law Text Culture* 233.

42 McVeigh, above n 26.

come out the other side. That means that extraverts have already had to find a way to achieve a (kind of) balance.

Middle eight

That we haven't thought much about what this means for us as theorists is curious. For the most part, there are sets of positions that are unable to be breached. In 2012, when writing about a project that used social science techniques in a piece of law and humanities/cultural legal studies scholarship, I masked my discomfit at using *infra dig* techniques and practices – Bourdieu's empirical practices, as well as his theory.[43] Now that we have accounted for complection and enfolding,[44] the move beyond interiority into the realm of the exterior as formative of the legal self might not seem to require an explanation, to hedge a little, to hesitate and be tentative, to apologise for:

> a step into a liminal space . . . [which is] antithetical to the ethic of the humanities . . . to enrich what has long been theorised . . . We can surmise intellectually . . . but finding out what people actually do enriches the theory, and expands upon and perhaps corrects what we imagine.[45]

In 2014, two years later, a pair of review essays appeared back to back in the pages of the journal *Law and Humanities*, in which two leaders of cultural legal studies, people I have known for a long time and are good friends of mine (and who know each other well), stake very different positions in the ground about the character of the work in the field. Though framed within law and humanities, what matters for a dyadic law and humanities inevitably crosses over to the interests of cultural legal studies. One of these positions is introvert, and the other extravert. One favours complection and enfolding across the *attitudes* of extraversion and introversion. The other does not. You decide.

In the first of the two pieces, in reviewing a piece of socio-legal scholarship that touches on the humanities, Des Manderson argues that law and humanities and law and society or sociological research functions in different registers, with different methods, with different purposes.[46] Though located in a review essay, it is manifesto and polemic, position statement and charter, of law and

43 Pierre Bourdieu, *Distinction: A Social Critique of the Judgement of Taste* (Richard Nice trans, Routledge & Kegan Paul, London, 1986) [trans of: *La distinction: critique sociale du jugement* (first published 1979)].

44 Leiboff and Sharp, above n 2.

45 Leiboff, above n 17, 150–151.

46 Desmond Manderson, 'AD 2014: A Review of Eve Darian-Smith, Laws and Societies in Global Contexts – Contemporary Approaches (Cambridge University Press, 2013)' (2014) 8 *Law and Humanities* 77.

humanities and how strongly it diverges from law and society or sociologically based research. He sticks his neck out,[47] as he says. This 'neck sticking' is in aid of keeping the fields distinct. Law and the humanities is oriented towards discourse, rather than institutions, in 'representations' not effects, diagnosing the condition of law, not prescribing reforms, methodologically and temperamentally distinct.[48] Law is 'object' for the social science, 'a lived reality' 'whose effects can be measured, often through empirical methods'.[49] How law constitutes us through discursive practices that can be examined, essentially through hermeneutic method, are the mark of law and humanities scholarship, using 'singular representations of law' to find out something about 'legal consciousness, ideology, norms or assumptions'.[50] There is more, but I will leave it to one side.

The second piece concerns a legal aesthetics collection reviewed by Les Moran.[51] He turns his attention to 'law and humanities', its methods, approaches, and what it could learn from social science-based scholarship. In his sights is the emphasis in the field on 'representations'. He throws down a gauntlet,[52] (rather than sticking his neck out), to advocate for the use of social science methods in law and humanities scholarship, to challenge the 'familiar and comfortable'[53] 'dominant method' found in it,[54] which 'coincides a little too neatly with long-standing legal scholarly (traditional and progressive) preoccupations with and assumptions attached to methods that focus on textual analysis'.[55] He draws on Catherine Soussloff's term, the 'illusion of immanence',[56] a criticism of the assumption that it is possible to read the text or object within the frame. Reading and interpreting within these confines disregards 'the social, political and cultural context', and the significance of the interaction between object and subject. Moving beyond the frame (specifically to a blurb on a back cover of a book), he refers to recent work in media studies, or specifically, reality TV. This work does not ask: 'how the reality television genre is interpreted as text or representation [instead] the authors investigate the politics of viewer encounters as interventions, evocations and more generally mediated social relations'.[57] Again there is more, but I will leave it to one side.

47 Ibid, 81.
48 Ibid.
49 Ibid, 81–82.
50 Ibid.
51 Leslie J 'Moran, 'Visual Law: A Review of Leif Dahlberg (ed.), Visualising Law and Authority: Essays on Legal Aesthetics (De Gruyter, 2012)' (2014) 8 *Law and Humanities* 88, 94.
52 Ibid, 95.
53 Ibid.
54 Ibid, 94.
55 Ibid.
56 Catherine Soussloff, *The Subject in Art: Portraiture and the Birth of the Modern* (Duke University Press, 2006) 5, cited in Moran, above n 51.
57 Beverley Skeggs and Helen Wood, *Reacting to Reality Television: Performance, Audience and Value* (Routledge, 2012), cited in Moran, above n 51.

The middle eight of a song is the part where its melody, tone and perhaps its key, changes. You can hear it shift. It sounds different. It takes a different turn from the sound of the song up to that point, changes direction, and once it is finished, it then returns to the sound and melody of the rest of the song.[58] It can be used to bridge a song, and is sometimes called a bridge. These three sets of thoughts are a middle eight in this piece, a bridge between parts. I leave them unremarked, though I have perhaps already said too much through my own framing of each of the pieces, what I included, what I excluded. This is a bridge that goes nowhere. It is a bridge that alters the tone with its different calls to a method and practice. For Jung, bridges were intended to resolve conflicts between opposites, as exemplified in the conflict of the opposites depicted in Goethe's *Faust*, and resolved, in Jung, by 'The Trickster, the symbolic bearer of an attempt to resolve the conflict of opposites between Prometheus/Epimetheus; Apollo/Dionysus; Faust/Mephistopheles; conscious/unconscious'.[59] I now return to where I left off, to introversion and extraversion, redux, Jung's, and Robert Cover's, use of myth and history.

Systoles and diastoles, myths and histories

Introversion and extraversion represent the polarities that mark the form of encounter between self and object, or object and self as subject. Jung adapted Goethe's polarities of systole and diastole to conceive or explain the differences between introversion and extraversion.[60] These were not Goethe's terms, but come to us from the ancient Greek. Systole is a contraction; diastole is dilation. This literary and cultural terminology also speaks to the knowledge of the medically trained Jung (with its references to the heart and blood pressure). The systole moves away from object back to the self; the diastole moves away from the self and towards object.[61] The systole (introvert) contracts, and detaches energy from the object or external world; the diastole (extravert) dilates, and seizes the object or external world to obtain energy.[62] Jung draws on myriad sources to then explain, characterise and individuate from these two attitudes. He is inspired, but unconvinced, by the pragmatist philosopher William James' 'tender-minded rationalist' (characterised as principled, intellectual, abstract, ideal, dogmatic) and 'tough-minded empiricist' (characterised as going by facts, sensationalistic, materialistic, sceptical).[63] He turned to myth, history, literature

58 Will Byers, 'School of Rock: Figuring out the Middle Eight' *The Guardian Online* (9 July 2008) www.theguardian.com/music/musicblog/2008/jul/08/schoolofrockletshearitfo.
59 Casement, above n 31, 72.
60 Paul Bishop, *Carl Jung* (Reaktion Books, 2014) 136.
61 Ibid.
62 Ibid.
63 Casement, above n 31, 68–69.

and philosophy: Schiller, the Indian Vedas, Taoism, poetry, medieval Christianity, symbolism.[64] In two early Church fathers he found thinking modifiers of introversion and extraversion –Tertullian (thinking introvert) and Origen (thinking extravert), that represent sacrifice,[65] and a one-sided attitude (the former gives up hedonism, the latter is said to have been castrated, in order to serve).[66] There is Prometheus (the introvert, forward thinker) and Epimetheus (the extravert backward thinker).[67] In Nietzsche's *Birth of Tragedy*, Jung finds that the oppositions of the Apollonian (introvert) and Dionysian (extravert) operate as a form of reconciliation that results in Greek civilisation.[68]

Crellin observes that Jung appears to be creating a lineage, to create an impression of a long process of thinking from which the theory was derived logically and rationally. She suggests that this is 'encrypted' Jung, that concealed the personal and experiential origins of his psychology, in a wealth of comparative literature.[69] That is, she argues that Jung created his theory out of his own experiences, concealing the source of his ideas, because a theory built out of personal experience would not be accepted by a scientific community, because it was not 'valid empirical evidence'.[70] If Crellin is right, then he is doing what we expect of the scholar, the distancing through sources, the denial of the personal, the discomfit with the intrusion of the self into the text. The removal of the self from the work of scholarship is not just a mark of discomfit; it is also the mark of introversion. Looking outside the frame perturbs.

So let me return to the beginning now, and the theatrical game I want to play with Cover's use of myth and history. As you will see, it has nothing to do with the piece itself, as I foreshadowed earlier. The concepts that Cover uses make sense to all of us, even in the abstract, even or especially in the form that I have represented it at the beginning of this chapter, that is, as principle and aphorism. It is the mark of introversion to bring those words to the self and impose meaning. Extraversion will be dissatisfied and uncomfortable because there is nothing that grounds the words externally. But regardless, even if we only look at the nouns involved, they make sense to all of us, even if the principle or aphorism does not. Most of us will draw on what we know, ourselves, of myth and history: Barthes' 'myth today',[71] ancient Greek myth, Fitzpatrick's

64 Clare Crellin, *Jung's Theory of Personality: A Modern Reappraisal* (Routledge, 2014) 39–49.
65 Marilyn Nagy, *Philosophical Issues in the Psychology of C G Jung* (State University of New York Press, 1991) 75.
66 Ibid, 40.
67 Ibid, 44–45.
68 Casement, above n 31, 69–71.
69 Crellin, above n 64, 40–41.
70 Ibid, 41.
71 Roland Barthes, 'Myth Today' in *Mythologies* (Annette Lavers trans, Jonathan Cape, 1972), 109–159 [trans of *Mythologies* (first published 1957)].

mythology of modern law,[72] if we know anything of Cover, there is likely to be large amounts of Jewish myth in play.[73] We have coded myth, and we will have decided what it means and how it is used.[74]

Myth is ancient, right?[75] Of course, the ancient concepts are longstanding, but the *English word* 'myth', that we take for granted, did not enter the language until 1840.[76] There are older words. 'Mythus' just edged 'myth' into usage in 1825.[77] 'Mythos' comes from the eighteenth century,[78] while 'mythic', the splendid 'mythologer', and 'mythological' are traced to the seventeenth century,[79] and 'mythology' to the fifteenth century.[80] They are not the same as myth, though. Obsolete forms of the word 'myth', of Scandinavian etymological origins, have a much longer pull on English. But they don't mean the same as the 'myth' we all now know. It meant 'To show, reveal, demonstrate' or 'To observe, notice' (eleventh century);[81] 'gentle, modest' (fifteenth century);[82] 'to measure, to reckon' (sixteenth century).[83] Myth, as Cover remarked,[84] may tell us who we would become, but history can, with a thud, unpack and unmask the very foundations of what we think of as myth. While we all understand what myths are, we read the past incorrectly if we read myth where there was no myth at all. The history of 'myth' as reality is a world away from the myth of myth. So anything we read from before 1840 that refers to myth is not 'myth' at all, or not the myth we think it is. There is something to be said for looking outside the frame.

Foreign ground

Cultural legal studies provides a technique and method of encounter that plays out through embodied action and movement – of law, its scholars and sites of engagement and encounter. In thinking of cultural legal studies as law's extraversion, this chapter turned itself back to 'us' or 'we', or 'I', to ask us to think about our role as the interpretative actor. Jerome Frank demanded this

72 Fitzpatrick, above n 7.
73 Cover, above n 1; Cover, above n 3; Wizner, above n 20.
74 Barthes, above n 71.
75 Andrew Von Hendy, *The Modern Construction of Myth* (Indiana University Press, 2002); Fitzpatrick, above n 7, 17–18.
76 'myth, n.', *OED Online* (Oxford University Press, December 2014) (accessed 16 January 2015).
77 'mythus, n.', *OED Online*, above n 76.
78 'mythos, n.', *OED Online*, above n 76.
79 'mythic, adj.', *OED Online*, above n 76.
80 'mythology, n.', *OED Online*, above n 76.
81 '† myth, v.1', *OED Online*, above n 76.
82 '† myth, adj.', *OED Online*, above n 76.
83 '† myth, v.2', *OED Online*, above n 76.
84 Cover, above n 1.

of lawyers; the Frankfurt School before him demanded it of its scholars.[85] In returning to the 'I', I have also returned to Brecht and his process of theatrical displacement, as a small device that might help us think outside the frame, through an actual displacement, of sorts. We are displaced when we move to foreign ground, to a place that is not our own. We are forced to see things differently, and we have to explain ourselves. We are able, then, even in a small way, to think beyond what is obvious. In speaking of Penny Pether, Peter Goodrich remarks on the effect of being on foreign ground, he *mos britannicus*, and she *mos austrialiacus*.[86] An Australian in the US, an Englishman in New York, they were 'exiled from a tradition and so *in partibus infidelium*',[87] in the lands of the unbelievers. For Penny, this meant:

> The absence of context, body, situation and contact, the abandonment of the personal archive and its commitments, is in other words the norm from which she starts, the familiarity that being on foreign ground, the ontology of peregrination, will challenge.[88]

What Peter describes here is an experience and encounter of estrangement, the technique of Brechtian *verfremdungseffekte*, designed to discomfort, through an active process of disrupting. Disruption can be captured, imaginatively, by remembering what it is like to be on foreign ground. An accent misunderstood, unfamiliar words for familiar objects, walking or driving on the wrong side of the road. These are physical encounters in the external world that we all must negotiate, respond to, and work with. It is precisely these forms of encounter that can be used to think differently, to ask other questions.

Jung understood that the weaving together of different energies creates a dynamic and transformative process of understanding individuation,[89] and the same can be said for energies that reside in the techniques and methods of cultural legal studies. Complection and enfolding creates the possibilities of dynamic and transformative modes of thinking that can enrich the assumptions of theory. To enfold history, myth, law, ideal and the self can do more as the sum than as parts on their own, that gives us different positions from which to 'reveal a node or pressure point where transformative work in law might be done'.[90] Cultural legal studies is not just theory, but a form of practice, that looks to the

85 Deborah Cook, *Theodor Adorno: Key Concepts* (Acumen, 2008).
86 Peter Goodrich, '*Mos americanus*; or common law *in partibus infidelium*' (2015) 60 (3) *Villanova Law Review* (forthcoming).
87 Ibid.
88 Ibid.
89 Crellin, above n 64, 41.
90 Penny Pether, 'On Foreign Ground: Grand Narratives, Situated Specificities, and the Praxis of Critical Theory and Law?' (1999) 10 *Law and Critique* 211, 225.

modes of how law is done. It reveals that to negate the role that extraversion plays in the formation of self is to negate a responsibility for law, as much as a negation of the moral self is a danger for law.

And now to end, with two snippets, with a little bit of myth and little bit of history. A form of practice that registers just how unreliable our introvert practices can be. To end without ending, because this is fundamental to extraversion, to keep looking beyond, to see what happens when one is placed on foreign ground.

It is fair to say that the Romans have had a considerable influence on law. But not all Romans, it seems, are equal. This exchange that occurred in an application for special leave to appeal to the Australian High Court (the ultimate court in the Australian legal hierarchy):

HAYNE J: It is rather like, 'What have the Romans ever done for us?', is it not, Mr Hastings?
MR HASTINGS: Not quite, your Honour.
HAYNE J: It depends upon your familiarity with Monty Python, does it not? [91]

It was one of those awkward moments. A little judicial jest that seemed harmless enough, and Hayne J did at least explain what he meant to the heroic Mr Hastings. In 2001, it might have seemed obvious that one of the most memorable and ironic lines in the 1979 film, *The Life of Brian* would have been common knowledge: 'All right, but apart from the sanitation, medicine, education, wine, public order, irrigation, roads, the fresh water system and public health, what have the Romans ever done for us?' Was that what Mr Hastings was thinking? Within a confined conception of the Rome of law – of Justinian, Cicero, *res* and *jus*, an unknown doctrine or principle? One might imagine that an eminent silk might be thinking too hard, looking for the right answer within the toolkit, the law as law. To imagine that there might be something to be had in looking beyond the expected, was a step too far. Mr Hastings is seeing too much in the quip, but what he is seeing is confined within law itself. We could all make this mistake. This is harmless enough, not representing a moral failure.

I now take you to 1997, to the outskirts of Brisbane, the capital city of the state of Queensland in Australia. To be in the north in Australia is to be in the hotter, wetter, more humid climes. Queensland has also had a somewhat interesting political history. In the 1970s, its government banned political street-marches, a ban which was only overturned in the latter part of the 1980s.[92] Within a few years of the repeal of the ban, a group of people was arrested and charged with trespass. The protestors attempted to push over a fence at an army

91 *Conway v The Queen* C11/2001 [2001] HCATrans 486.
92 Raymond Evans and Carole Ferrier, *Radical Brisbane: An Unruly History* (The Vulgar Press, 2004) 277–284.

camp. The six peace protesters were young, and mostly women. The fence was flimsy, and they were successful. The Magistrate Sheryl Cornack SM found them guilty of trespass but did not record convictions. In her remarks, her Worship made a number of observations: that 'protest is an important part of our community';[93] Australia had a 'long history of protests to bring about social change';[94] that 'there are some people who hold moral beliefs so passionately that they are prepared to break the law to bring about social change', and that she acknowledged 'the sincerely held beliefs by each of the persons charged'.[95]

To read these words in the abstract is a dangerous activity; to read it out of time even more so. I chose to write its place in time at the outset. The years matter. It is a few years after street marches have been permitted in Queensland. The previous bans, and their consequences hangs heavily. I have used this extract for many years, too many years, with law students in and out of Queensland. When I first began to use it, there was some political opposition to the decision, and maybe some remarks about the politics of the magistrate, or the legality of her decision to not record sentences. The usual stuff expected of law students, based in politics, perhaps based in gender. There was some amusement that the army could not defend its own camp, that its fence was so flimsy that even girls could push it over. A few years later, the responses changed a little, and then a lot. It took me a while to register what the new responses represented. The focus of attention was now on the fence, and horror and disgust that anyone would try to harm the military. These were now dangerous actions, carried out by a group of terrorists. The references to peace protestors disappeared, the references to a trespass vacated. And the magistrate acted illegally in letting them off.

It is an act of introversion to read a text like this, not the other way around, the inner impression forming reality.[96] Look at what has happened to the text. Even if the year is ignored (ie pre 9/11), the words 'peace' and 'social change', 'history', and 'moral' are also ignored as well. Our moral interiority, our moral knowledge of self cannot function on its own. Embodied abstraction of principle and aphorism is not vouchsafed. It also needs the gift that is found in an empirical awareness of being beyond your own self, remembering the past for the present, to ground an ethic of responsibility for law.

Bibliography

Barthes, Roland, *Mythologies* (Annette Lavers trans, Jonathan Cape, 1972), 109–159 [trans of *Mythologies* (first published 1957)]

Bishop, Paul, *Carl Jung* (Reaktion Books, 2014)

93 *The Courier Mail* (Brisbane), 2 December 1997, 3.
94 Ibid.
95 Ibid.
96 Casement, above n 31, 76.

Bourdieu, Pierre, *Distinction: A Social Critique of the Judgement of Taste* (Richard Nice trans, Routledge & Kegan Paul, London, 1986) [trans of: *La distinction: critique sociale du jugement* (first published 1979)]
Casement, Ann, *Carl Gustav Jung* (Sage, 2011)
Cook, Deborah, *Theodor Adorno: Key Concepts* (Acumen, 2008)
Cover, Robert, 'Foreword: Nomos and Narrative' (1983) 97 *Harvard Law Review* 4
Cover, Robert, 'The Folktales of Justice' in Martha Minow, Michael Ryan and Austin Sarat (eds), *Narrative, Violence, and the Law: The Essays of Robert Cover* (The University of Michigan Press, 1992) 187
Crellin, Clare, *Jung's Theory of Personality: A Modern Reappraisal* (Routledge, 2014)
Dorsett, Shaunnagh and Shaun McVeigh, *Jurisdiction* (Routledge, 2012)
Douzinas, Costas, 'Human Rights and Postmodern Utopia' (2000) 11 *Law and Critique* 219
Douzinas, Costas, 'History Trials: Can Law Decide History?' (2012) 8 *Annual Review of Law and Social Science* 273
Douzinas, Costas, 'A Short History of the British Critical Legal Conference or, the Responsibility of the Critic' (2014) 25 *Law and Critique* 187
Etxabe, Julen, *The Experience of Tragic Judgment* (Routledge, 2013)
Evans, Raymond and Carole Ferrier, *Radical Brisbane: An Unruly History* (The Vulgar Press, 2004)
Faulkner, William, *Requiem for a Nun* 1950, in Robert W Hamblin and Charles A Peek (eds), *A William Faulkner Encyclopaedia* (Greenwood Press, 1999) 326
Fitzpatrick, Peter, *The Mythology of Modern Law* (Routledge, 1992)
Gaakeer, Jeanne, 'Reverent Rites of Legal Theory: Unity–Diversity–Interdisciplinarity' (2012) 36 *Australian Feminist Law Journal* 19
Gaakeer, Jeanne, 'European Law and Literature: Forever Young. The Nomad Concurs' in Helle Porsdam and Thomas Elholm (eds), *Law and Literature: Dialogues on Justice: European Perspectives on Law and Humanities* (Walter de Gruyter, 2012)
Galipeau, Steven, 'The Red Book and Jung's Typology' (2013) 56 *Psychological Perspectives: A Quarterly Journal of Jungian Thought* 34
Goodrich, Peter, '*Mos americanus*; or common law *in partibus infidelium*' (2015) 60 (3) *Villanova Law Review* (forthcoming)
Hamblin, Robert W and Charles A Peek (eds), *A William Faulkner Encyclopaedia* (Greenwood Press, 1999)
Heller, Kevin Jon and Gerry Simpson (eds), *The Hidden Histories of War Crimes Trials* (Oxford University Press, 2013)
Jung, Carl G, *Psychological Types* (Routledge, 1971)
Leiboff, Marett, 'Of the Monstrous Regiment and the Family Jewels' (2005) 23 *The Australian Feminist Law Journal* 33
Leiboff, Marett, '"The Main Thing is to Shut Them Out" The Deployment of Law and the Arrival of Russians in Australia 1913–1925: An Histoire' (2011) 15 *Law Text Culture* 233
Leiboff, Marett, '"DITTO": Law, Pop Culture and Humanities and the Impact of Intergenerational Interpretative Dissonance' (2012) 36 *The Australian Feminist Law Journal* 145
Leiboff, Marett, 'Towards a Jurisprudence of the Embodied Mind – Sarah Lund, Forbrydelsen and the Mindful Body' in Hanne Petersen and Rubya Mehdi (eds), *Special issue on 'Law and Art' Volume 2* (2015) 6 *NAVEIÑ REET: Nordic Journal of Law and Social Research*

Leiboff, Marett and Cassandra Sharp, 'Cultural Legal Studies and Law's Popular Cultures' in Cassandra Sharp and Marett Leiboff (eds), *Cultural Legal Studies: Law's Popular Cultures and the Metamorphosis of Law* (Routledge, 2015)
Leiboff, Marett and Mark Thomas, *Legal Theories: Contexts and Practices* (Thomson Law Book Co, 2nd edn, 2014)
McCaulley, Mary H and Charles R Martin, 'Career Assessment and the Myers-Briggs Type Indicator' (1995) 3 *Journal of Career Assessment* 219
McVeigh, Shaun, 'Law As (More or Less) Itself: On Some Not Very Reflective Elements of Law' (2014) 4 *University of California Irvine Law Review* 471
Manderson, Desmond, 'AD 2014: A Review of Eve Darian-Smith, Laws and Societies in Global Contexts—Contemporary Approaches (Cambridge University Press, 2013)' (2014) 8 *Law and Humanities* 77
Manderson, Desmond and Richard Mohr, 'From Oxymoron to Intersection: An Epidemiology of Legal Research' (2002) 6 *Law Text Culture* 159
Minow, Martha, Michael Ryan and Austin Sarat (eds), *Narrative, Violence, and the Law: The Essays of Robert Cover* (The University of Michigan Press, 1992)
Moran, Leslie J, 'Visual Law: A Review of Leif Dahlberg (ed.), Visualising Law and Authority: Essays on Legal Aesthetics (De Gruyter, 2012)' (2014) 8 *Law and Humanities* 88
Nagy, Marilyn, *Philosophical Issues in the Psychology of C G Jung* (State University of New York Press, 1991)
OED Online (Oxford University Press, December 2014) (accessed 16 January 2015).
Peters, Timothy, 'Reading the Law Made Strange: Cultural Legal Studies, Theology and Speculative Fiction' in Cassandra Sharp and Marett Leiboff (eds), *Cultural Legal Studies: Law's Popular Cultures and the Metamorphosis of Law* (Routledge, 2015) 252
Petersen, Hanne and Rubya Mehdi (eds), *Special issue on 'Law and Art' Volume 2* (2015) 6 *NAVEIÑ REET: Nordic Journal of Law and Social Research.*
Pether, Penny, 'On Foreign Ground: Grand Narratives, Situated Specificities, and the Praxis of Critical Theory and Law?' (1999) 10 *Law and Critique* 211
Porsdam, Helle and Thomas Elholm (eds), *Law and Literature: Dialogues on Justice: European Perspectives on Law and Humanities* (Walter de Gruyter, 2012)
Ramberg, Bjørn and Kristin Gjesdal, 'Hermeneutics', *The Stanford Encyclopedia of Philosophy* (Summer 2013 Edition), Edward N Zalta (ed.), URL = http://plato.stanford.edu/archives/sum2013/entries/hermeneutics
Richard, Larry, 'The Lawyer Types' (1993) 79 *ABA Journal* 74
Rundle, Kristen, 'The Impossibility of an Exterminatory Legality: Law and the Holocaust' (2009) 59 *University of Toronto Law Journal* 65
Rundle, Kristen, 'Law and Daily Life: Questions for Legal Philosophy from 1938' (2012) 3 *Jurisprudence* 429
Rush, Peter, 'An Altered Jurisdiction: Corporeal Traces of Law' (1998) 6 *Griffith Law Review* 144
Rush, Peter, 'Dirty War Crimes: Jurisdictions of Memory and International Criminal Law' in Kevin Jon Heller and Gerry Simpson (eds), *The Hidden Histories of War Crimes Trials* (Oxford University Press, 2013) 367
Seymour, David M, *Law, Antisemitism and the Holocaust* (Routledge-Cavendish, 2007)
Sharp, Cassandra and Marett Leiboff (eds), *Cultural Legal Studies: Law's Popular Cultures and the Metamorphosis of Law* (Routledge, 2015)

Skeggs, Beverley and Helen Wood, *Reacting to Reality Television: Performance, Audience and Value* (Routledge, 2012)
Soussloff, Catherine, *The Subject in Art: Portraiture and the Birth of the Modern* (Duke University Press, 2006)
Stone, Julius, 'The Province of Jurisprudence Redetermined (Concluded)' (1943–1944) 7 *Modern Law Review* 177
Stone, Julius, *Legal System and Lawyers' Reasonings* (Stanford University Press, 1964)
Turnbull, Sue, 'Border Crossings: The Transnational Career of the Television Crime Drama' in Cassandra Sharp and Marett Leiboff (eds), *Cultural Legal Studies: Law's Popular Cultures and the Metamorphosis of Law* (Routledge, 2015)
Von Hendy, Andrew, *The Modern Construction of Myth* (Indiana University Press, 2002)
Wizner, Stephen, 'A Theology of Justice: Some Reflections on Milner Ball's Non-Religious Practice of Belief' (2006–2007) 41 *Georgia Law Review* 945

Media

Byers, Will, 'School of Rock: Figuring Out the Middle Eight' *The Guardian Online* (9 July 2008) www.theguardian.com/music/musicblog/2008/jul/08/schoolofrockletshearitfo.
Douzinas, Costas, Director, Biography, *The Birkbeck Institute for the Humanities* www.bbk.ac/bih/about; www.bbk.ac.uk/law/our-staff/ft-academic/douzinas/biog
Frankie Goes to Hollywood, *Two Tribes* www.youtube.com/watch?v=K2QAMqTgPKI.
Sting, *Russians* http://en.wikipedia.org/wiki/Russians_%28song%29; www.youtube.com/watch?v=wHylQRVN2Qs.
The Courier Mail (Brisbane), 2 December 1997, 3

Transcript

Conway v The Queen C11/2001 [2001] HCATrans 486

Chapter 3

Finding stories of justice in the art of conversation

Ethnography in cultural legal studies

Cassandra Sharp[1]

Storytelling is one way in which the imagination is put to practical effect, and it is an effective stimulant and vehicle for connecting and transforming meaning and desire in relation to issues of law and justice. This is no more evident than in stories of justice as presented in media reports, which play an important role in provoking responses to issues such as ethics, crime, punishment and social responsibility. Because stories 'mediate the inner subjective world and the outer, objective world, the private and public aspects of our lives',[2] it has been my consistent argument that not only do individuals use stories to frame and contextualise normative expectations of the legal system,[3] but that they also concomitantly participate in the embodiment of law. That is, in the (re)telling of justice stories, individuals verbalise and render apparent that which is often omitted from traditional accounts of law, 'such as the feelings, desires, conflicting impulses and wishes that circulate within the law'.[4] Stories are essential to this experience of being human[5] – to the ways we communicate, learn and reflectively make sense of the world, and as such they are a useful tool for evaluating and critiquing law as deeply constituted in culture. While traditional law and media research has been often dominated by concerns with the 'effects'

1 This chapter was made possible by a grant from the *Legal Intersections Research Centre* (LIRC) UOW.

2 Julian Webb, 'Ethics for Lawyers or Ethics for Citizens? New Directions for Legal Education' (1998) 25 *Journal of Law and Society* 134, 143.

3 Cassandra Sharp, '"Represent a Murderer . . . I'd Never do That!" How Students use Stories to Link Ethical Development and Identity Construction' in Michael Robertson *et al.* (eds), *The Ethics Project in Legal Education* (Routledge, 2011) 33; Cassandra Sharp, 'The "Extreme Makeover" Effect of Law School: Students being Transformed by Stories' (2005) 12(1) *Texas Wesleyan Law Review* 233.

4 Richard Sherwin, 'Symposium: Introduction: Picturing Justice: Images of Law and Lawyers in the Visual Media' (1996) 30 (Summer) *University of San Francisco Law Review* 891.

5 Bret Rappaport, 'Tapping the Human Adaptive Origins of Storytelling by Requiring Legal Writing Students to Read a Novel in Order to Appreciate How Character, Setting, Plot, Theme, and Tone (CSPTT) are as Important as IRAC' (2008) 25 *T M Cooley Law Review* 267, 268.

of various media on individuals, this chapter focuses on the 'use' individuals make of media stories, and highlights the utility of ethnographic methodology designed to interrogate and challenge law as expressed in 'justice conversations'. Rather than following the media effects tradition which focuses on the ways in which media reporting of criminal sentencing influence an audience, this chapter describes a methodology that goes beyond mere examination of texts, to acknowledging that individuals are active in their interpretation, transformation and construction of legal meaning from the cultural text. Within such an approach that is uniquely cultural legal studies in nature, this chapter shines the spotlight on the cultural (re)imaginings of law and justice that are socially constructed and transformed among individuals, and expressed by focus group participants.

The research discussed in this chapter represents the second phase of analysis from a larger ongoing project that I have designed to (i) provide more information about the form and substance of public rhetoric surrounding issues of law and justice, and (ii) to pursue the symbiotic connection between news media and the transformation and (re)construction of popular understandings of law and justice.[6] This long research trajectory has primarily sought to get to the heart of what individuals think and feel about what 'justice' is and how it (dis)connects with law – especially from the point of view of punishment. Elsewhere I have described the first phase of analysis in this project, which concluded that retributive justice is a preoccupation of both the public imagination and texts of media and popular fiction.[7] The second phase described in this chapter takes the analysis even further by arguing that media stories of ineffectual criminal sanctions are actually driven by an expectation of public desire for retributive justice. Using this analysis I argue that a cultural legal studies approach to public perception of issues of justice, crime and punishment is vitally important if we want to access and explore the active participation and involvement of individuals in the constitutive practices of law.

Because the primary concern of this research project has been the ways in which popular stories about justice in the media capture the public imagination and contribute to normative understandings about the operation of law, the focus has been on how individuals use media stories to produce expectations of

6 One aspect of this larger research project incorporated an evaluation of the superhero genre as an antidote to law's perceived failings, see: Cassandra Sharp, 'Riddle Me This . . . ? Would the World Need Superheroes if the Law Could Actually Deliver "Justice"?' (2012) 16 *Law Text Culture* 353.

7 Cassandra Sharp, 'Justice with a Vengeance – Retributive Desire in Popular Imagination' in Michael Asimow, Kathryn Brown and David Ray Papke (eds), *Law and Popular Culture: International Perspectives* (Cambridge Scholars Publishing, 2014). See also Cassandra Sharp, 'Riddle Me This . . . ? Would the World Need Superheroes if the Law Could Actually Deliver "Justice"?' (2012) 16 *Law Text Culture* 353.

law in relation to standards of justice. To this end discussion was facilitated around a series of open-ended questions in a pilot study of four different demographics – young adults, retirees, academics and mothers.[8] Through an interrogation of the way the concept of 'justice' is articulated, negotiated, shared and transformed in and through these focus group discussions, the chapter argues that media stories act as a unique locus of legal storytelling that the popular imagination simultaneously accepts and challenges. The analysis will show that while on the one hand participants implicitly accept and use media stories to contest law's limits in achieving justice, on the other hand they simultaneously challenge and critique the manipulation of individual emotions by the media, and recognise the stories as simply a stimulus for, and vehicle of, the maintenance of retributive desire. Along these lines, the chapter will first briefly provide some context for the cultural legal studies approach to this research and second, showcase some analysis from focus group discussions that will demonstrate not only the dichotomous response from the participants in relation to media reporting of criminal sentencing, but also the active participation of individuals in the transformation of legal meaning.

Ethnography as cultural legal studies methodology

We live in an era where the public is extremely active in the process of consuming stories as one stimulant to the production, transformation and perpetuation of meaning and desire in relation to issues of law and justice. No longer are individuals regarded as passively or blindly 'affected' by media, but rather they are seen as active producers of meaning who themselves use media to not only construct that meaning, but also I argue, to participate in the (re)construction of legal knowledge. For this reason, I have adapted ethnography, an empirical and theoretical inheritance from anthropology, as a useful methodology for my research. As noted in Chapter 1 of this collection, cultural legal studies facilitates the exploration of active and embodied connections of legal meaning, and the qualitative concern of ethnography is concentrated on details of life while connecting them to wider cultural processes and existence. This has meant that an ethnographical methodology is well suited to the 'sticky embraces'[9] of the ambiguities, uncertainties and contradictions inherent within a study of legal culture. While in the context of media-oriented cultural studies, 'ethnography has become a code-word for a range of qualitative methods, including participant observation, in-depth interviews and focus groups',[10] it is the qualitative

8 These focus groups were conducted in 2010 and were conducted as part of a project made possible by a grant from the University of Wollongong's Research Council (URC) Small Grant Scheme. UOW Ethics approval ID: HE09/109.

9 See Chapter 1.

10 Chris Barker, *Cultural Studies: Theory and Practice* (Sage Publications, 2000) 28.

understanding of cultural activity in context that is the key 'spirit' of ethnography,[11] and that which is of value to cultural legal studies. In my research I have developed and deployed a hybrid form of ethnography and critical jurisprudence in order to access the rich and complex processes that comprise an individual's lived experience as expressed through the (re)telling of stories. To me it has been 'less an expedition in search of "the facts" and more a conversation between participants',[12] less a focus on exegeting legal texts, and more on accessing personal, social and cultural encounters with the law, that are active and interrogatory, nuanced and complicated. In utilising this unique cultural legal studies methodology in several projects over the last decade or so, I have been able to explore the ways in which different groups of individuals actively interpret, challenge, construct and embody legal meaning – particularly in response to popular cultural resources.[13]

This embodiment of legal meaning is one aspect of what Cover conceptualised in his idea of the 'nomos', a cultural world of law that includes what people believe law is and the stories they tell about it.[14] Sherwin *et al.* argue in relation to the 'nomos' that:

> no set of legal institutions or prescriptions exists apart from the narratives that locate it and give it meaning. . . . Once understood in the context of the narratives that give it meaning, law becomes not merely a system of rules. Law is a world in which we live.[15]

Law then is viewed as 'inseparable from the interests, goals, and understandings that deeply shape or comprise social life,'[16] and so it seems entirely appropriate to appreciate how individuals produce, interpret, transform and exchange meanings about law through popular stories (both circulating within

11 Ibid.

12 Chris Barker and Dariusz Galasinski, *Cultural Studies and Discourse Analysis: A Dialogue on Language and Identity* (Sage, 2001) 29.

13 Cassandra Sharp, 'Changing the Channel: What to Do with the Critical Abilities of Law Students as Viewers?' (2004) 13(2) *Griffith Law Review* 185; Cassandra Sharp, '"Represent a Murderer . . . I'd Never do That!" How Students Use Stories to Link Ethical Development and Identity Construction' in Michael Robertson *et al.* (eds), above n 3; Cassandra Sharp, 'Let's See How Far We've Come: The Role of Empirical Methodology in Exploring Television Audiences' in Peter Robson and Jessica Silbey (eds), *Law and Justice on the Small Screen* (Hart Publishing, 2012).

14 Robert M Cover, 'Nomos and Narrative' (1983) 97 *Harvard Law Review* 4.

15 Richard Sherwin, Neal Feigenson and Christina Spiesel, 'Law in the Digital Age: How Visual Communication Technologies are Transforming the Practice, Theory and Teaching of Law' (2006) 12 *Boston University Journal of Science and Technology Law* 227, 258.

16 Austin Sarat and Thomas Kearns, *Law in the Domains of Culture* (Ann Arbor: University of Michigan Press, 1998) 6.

cultural texts and those (re)told in conversation). This chapter proceeds on the basis that it is through everyday stories that perceptions of law and justice are formed and maintained, and it adopts a constitutive perspective that 'firmly situates the law at the heart of everyday life.'[17] This approach is what many scholars have termed 'legal consciousness', and as an integral aspect to cultural legal studies, it is key to recognising the interpretive nature of responding to popular cultural texts:

> Cultural legal studies adopts this focus, seeking to go beyond appellate case law, statutory interpretation, and social policy, the dominant topics of law teaching and academic writing, in order to more broadly encompass legal meaning making practices throughout society.[18]

In this way, the methodological techniques of ethnography, within a framework of cultural legal studies, do so much more than simply summarising a person's attitudes and opinions about law and the legal system. Instead they can reveal the deeply imbricated account of legality deployed by individuals and groups within these meaning-making practices. Because the 'ethnographic tradition of law in everyday life, which clearly adopts a constitutive approach, regards law as something that is deeply embedded in people's consciousness',[19] it is consciousness (rather than knowledge per se) that is the focus of this methodology. And so, the choice of using focus groups in this research under the broad banner of ethnography was therefore based firmly on the rationale that a rich exploration into understandings and expectations could not be adequately achieved through simply the 'snapshot' approach provided by quantitative surveys or questionnaires. Instead, the complexity of an individual's meaning-making process demanded an in-depth approach that would allow exploration of the various cultural discourses that bring the law into being as meaningful. Focus groups provide a mechanism for story articulation and development in a mutually stimulative and spontaneously reactive environment, and this in turn generates an extremely fertile ground of analysis.[20] As described above, the research discussed in this chapter was garnered from a pilot study of four demographically diverse focus groups, and they were conducted with two central objectives: (i) to present opportunities for individuals to talk informally about issues of justice and to explore from their perspective what role the law plays in maintaining justice; and (ii) to delve into the nuanced ways

17 Lieve Gies, 'The Media and Public Understanding of the Law' in Steve Greenfield and Guy Osborn (eds), *Readings in Law and Popular Culture* (Routledge-Cavendish, 2008) 74.

18 Sherwin *et al.*, above n 15, 259.

19 Gies, above n 17, 75.

20 For other focus group methodology, see Chris Barker and Julie Andre, 'Did You See? Soaps, Teenage Talk and Gendered Identity' (1996) 4(4) *Young: Nordic Journal of Youth Research* 23.

legal discourse is constituted in and challenged by individuals as they talk about issues of law and justice and (re)tell stories of how they perceive the legal world.

When individuals made comments on the activity and competence of the legal system in relation to justice, the group was then able to explore together the ideas that inform their views on the efficacy of law and justice. That is, by discussing their responses to media reporting about sentencing, participants provided insight into the uses they make of such stories to actively respond to law.[21] The transcripts were therefore analysed using an interpretive literary method, where the discussion or 'talk' became the 'text' from which to unpack participant understandings. The goal of the analysis was to acknowledge that what is important is not what people know about the law, but how they use it to construct, transform and challenge legal meaning.

Analysis – stories hidden in conversation

By constructing meaning about law through stories, both heard in the media and then retold, individuals imagine what they believe the law should be and how law should function in society. To better understand the 'legal consciousness' through these focus group interactions, the 'talk' of the participants was coded and analysed in line with an acknowledgement that readers/viewers have distinct patterns of involvement with popular stories – primarily in what is termed the critical and referential realms.[22] That is, an individual may use the text referentially as a connection to real life (including their own), utilising it to form expectations and ideas about certain aspects of their lives; or, they may use it more critically by showing an awareness of the text as a construction of reality and subsequently concerning themselves with the impact of that construction. Of course, 'a sophisticated viewer should be seen as a commuter between the referential and the critical'.[23] Indeed, this section will use examples from the focus groups to demonstrate that participants constantly commute between the two realms. The analysis will show that: (i) the media construction of crime stories function as a stimulant to the acceptance, transformation and perpetuation of retributive desire evident in these participants, and (ii) almost paradoxically, that the participants also recognise the constructed nature of media justice stories and actively make efforts to resist the dominant representation.

21 It is in narrative, which 'suggests a whole world of experience', that we learn these things: James Elkins, 'On the Emergence of Narrative Jurisprudence: The Humanistic Perspective Finds a New Path' (1985) 9 *Legal Studies Forum* 123, 135.

22 In the context of comparing cross-cultural readings of *Dallas*, Liebes and Katz in the late 1980s argued that viewers may use a television program referentially or critically. See Tamar Liebes and Elihu Katz, 'On the Critical Abilities of Television Viewers' in eds Ellen Seiter *et al.*, *Remote Control: Television Audiences and Cultural Power* (Routledge, 1989) at 209, and Tamar Liebes and Elihu Katz, *The Export of Meaning: Cross-Cultural Readings of Dallas* (Wiley Publishing, 1993) at 100.

23 Liebes and Katz (1989) ibid.

Acceptance of media construction – we know 'justice' because of the 'injustice'

As I have described in relation to the first phase of this project, the initial analysis from these discussions was predictable in relation to the difficulty participants expressed at defining and explaining their understanding of 'justice,' and how it actually 'works' with law.[24] Furthermore, despite their definitional uncertainty, this early analysis also demonstrated a consistent shared belief that the function of law actually is to provide justice,[25] and thus believing this to be the promise of law, participants were often quick to suggest that the law in fact does not deliver or live up to this promise in the retributive sense. It was retribution's underlying philosophy of an 'eye for an eye', whereby offenders deserve to be punished in proportion to the severity of the offending conduct, that was prominent in the participants' intuitive response to media stories and their subsequent critique of the law.[26]

Taking the analysis deeper in this second phase, it became clear that not only were participants viewing retributive measures as the primary determiner of an effective criminal justice system, but they also accepted that every time a media story bemoaned an absence of punishment it would signify a corresponding absence of justice.[27] Numerous participant comments indicated that it is only when the guilty are actually punished that justice is seen to be done, and as a corollary, justice must be absent if the penalties are insufficient or non-existent. In several comments it was clear that the participants were using the news stories in this negative sense – not helping them to define what 'justice' is, but instead enabling them to identify what 'justice' is not. Take for example these comments:

24 For some early analysis of this research which demonstrates a public dissatisfaction with the law, see Cassandra Sharp (2012), above n 7, 353.

25 For example: Emily: ' . . . the justice system is upholding the law because then it says: "look you've broken this law and so then you face these consequences".' Focus Group 2, page 8. Hereafter Focus Groups are referred to by number of group (FG #) and then the corresponding page number of the quote. Transcripts on file with the author. For more on this line of analysis see: Cassandra Sharp (2014), above n 7.

26 Indeed theories of human behaviour in psychology have long 'identified justice as a core need for people' because we have a 'strong desire to live in a fair world where people get what they deserve and deserve what they get.' Dena M Gromet and John M Darley, 'Retributive and Restorative Justice: Importance of Crime Severity and Shared Identity in People's Justice Responses' (2009) 61(1) *Australian Journal of Psychology* 51.

27 Interestingly, the participants often described their awareness of 'justice' by adopting this Kantian-like philosophy of concluding that punishment equates with justice. Research has shown that people often equate punishment with justice. Andrew Welsh, Thomas Fleming and Kenneth Dowler, 'Constructing Crime and Justice on Film: Meaning and Message in Cinema' (2011) 14 (4) *Contemporary Justice Review: Issues in Criminal, Social and Restorative Justice* 457, 460.

JUSTIN: I think it's a lot easier to know when [justice] hasn't been achieved because we have this inbuilt capacity to recognise there's an action and there needs to be a consequence and when the consequence doesn't fit the action that's when there is injustice.[28]

JONATHON: So people equate that with injustice – when the punishment isn't fitting the crime.[29]

PHOEBE: I guess it's probably something that we just expect and if it happens we don't necessarily notice because we think it's what should happen . . . but if justice isn't done, we're more likely to notice.[30]

JONATHON: Well that's where the injustice comes in, a life is taken and if it's a manslaughter charge, then they're probably only going to get 2 or 3 years maybe and they might even be out quicker than that. So their life is back on track but the other person is devastated by it . . .[31]

In each of these comments, the participants describe their understanding of 'justice' by a reference to what is lacking. Correlating nicely with the research of Gromet and Darley who 'suggest that the desire for retribution is people's initial, intuitive response to crimes,'[32] focus group members were consistent in this negative collocation of ineffective criminal justice and an absent justice. The comments resonate clearly with the retributive rhetoric associated with many media reports that demand punishment as the only form of acceptable justice in response to the crime, and they indicate that while media viewers/readers[33] utilise these reports to help them determine the substance and form of justice, they do so primarily in reference to an absence or lack. Given that research has recently demonstrated that, 'viewers are attracted to media sources that contain justice-oriented themes'[34] and that individuals 'exhibit a preference for narrative structures that equate punishment or retribution with justice',[35] it is argued that such a single-minded preoccupation of the public imagination to seek retribution over and above anything else is exactly what media stories covet, and then use to great effect. This of course, is mirrored in portrayals on the small screen. A quick survey of popular fiction airing on free-to-air Australian television screens in any given week shows a high level of preoccupation with bringing offenders

28 FG 2, 9–11.
29 FG 4, 4.
30 FG 2, 2.
31 FG 4, 11.
32 Gromet and Darley, above n 26.
33 For the purposes of this chapter it is assumed that participants are either viewers or readers of different textual forms within the broad genre of news media, and hereafter an audience member will be referred to as a 'reader'.
34 Andrew Welsh *et al.*, above n 27, 460.
35 Ibid, 458.

to retributive justice. For example, in series showing on major free Network television stations in Australia across the month of November 2014 (such as *NCIS*, *Arrow*, *Elementary*, *Blacklist*, *CSI*, *Revenge* and *The Mentalist*) the singular emphasis of the narrative is to ensure offenders are caught and punished so that 'justice' can be done.

It is interesting to note in the extracts above that Phoebe's statement concerning our awareness of injustice is linked to this dominant focus of media reporting – of course we are more likely to notice injustice if that is the pre-occupation of what is considered newsworthy by a media seeking to capitalise on public retributive desire. It would seem that these comments then reflect a public acceptance of a retributive media rhetoric that criticises penal policies on the grounds that they perpetuate injustice. As the examples above demonstrate, this public acceptance of the retributive rhetoric is constituted in the instinctive public responses and the (re)telling of those particular news stories that decry dissatisfaction in the penal sanctions accorded to particular crimes.

Of course one might argue that this is effective news 'framing'. The idea of news frames is prevalent within media studies scholarship and refers to the 'interpretive structures that journalists use' to 'simplify, prioritise and structure the narrative flow of events'.[36] Effective news framing therefore contributes to the positioning of public knowledge and opinion of criminal justice to be 'based upon collective representations rather than accurate information'.[37] Moreover, given that news media not only reflects a version of social reality, but also negotiates, develops and contributes to the way we respond to issues of justice,[38] the concept of 'framing' provides a useful method for news reporting to contribute to common sense understandings about key processes and institutions.[39] It is argued that news reporting understands and portrays penal policy and criminal sentencing through the 'framing' of 'injustice'. That is, news frames about penal sanctions will 'bundle key concepts, stock phrases, and iconic images'[40] relating to the attainment of justice, in order to reinforce certain ways of interpreting and responding to criminal sentencing. The news frame of 'injustice' thus contributes to widespread audience acceptance of the retributive rhetoric that

36 Pippa Norris, Montague Kern and Marion Just, *Framing Terrorism: The News Media, The Government and The Public* (Routledge, 2003) 10.

37 David Garland, *The Culture of Control* (Oxford University Press, 2001) quoted in Neil Hutton, 'Beyond Populist Punitiveness?' (2005) 7 *Punishment & Society* 243, 247.

38 'The role of media in public perceptions and understandings of crime and justice issues cannot be underestimated. Far from the objective lens of events, the media are platforms wherein our social reality is not only reflected but to some extent negotiated and developed.' Welsh *et al.*, above n 27, 471; Nicole Hahn Rafter, *Shots in the Mirror: Crime Films and Society* (Oxford University Press, 2006) 3.

39 Welsh *et al.* further argue that the media significantly shapes our socially constructed 'expectations about justice and appropriate responses to crime.' Welsh *et al.*, above n 27

40 Norris *et al.*, above n 36.

cries foul in the face of possible injustice. The focus group conversations indicate that through an effective framing of 'injustice' public retributive desire is not only reflected in the stories, but can also be fuelled by them. This can be demonstrated in the following participant responses in relation to the crime of rape – Chris and Justin together respond to the generic tendency of media reports to describe unsatisfactory sentences; while Isabelle questions the level of justice in the procuring of a victim's testimony:

CHRIS: [in some reports] you could see someone getting let off for rape and that's unjust . . .

JUSTIN: I think OK, the guy who raped somebody needs, has to, you know, go to gaol, or there has to be some kind of . . . punishment paid for him to have met justice . . . I think we still have this inbuilt capacity to go, yeah, that's not just, there's a lack there.[41]

ISABELLE: when you hear about for instance rape and the victims are dragged through the courts to have to give testimony, that to me is unjust, . . . so when you're questioned and portrayed as enticing rape and whatever, its extremely unjust, especially when the offender gets off lightly.[42]

When participants become aware of a lack in the criminal justice system they are spurred on to retributive desire, and so because news frames 'draw on reservoirs of familiar stories to cue readers'[43] (eg the story of a victim's family aghast at the sentence handed to the perpetrator), the media reports become the barometer of justice. The participants in the comments above and in the ones to follow referentially utilise and then redeploy media stories in order to connect them with personal and real expectations of the criminal justice system. It is in discussing these stories referentially that participants spontaneously use the news report as a springboard for relating to emotional and personal attitudes and values. 'Vengeance and punishment for wrongdoings and their association with justice, are common narrative themes'[44] in popular media precisely because they tap into our individual emotive evaluation of what deserves punishment.

In particular, embodied in this framing of injustice within crime stories is an emotional association with the victim. In using familiar storytelling conventions that particularly focus on the victim's encounters with crime, these popular news

41 FG 2, 2. See further Sharp (2014), above n 7, where Justin's comment was also discussed in reference to the kantian-like response of participants to the notion of injustice.

42 FG 1, 8.

43 'The essence of framing is selection to prioritise some facts, images and developments over others, thereby unconsciously promoting one particular interpretation of events . . .' Norris *et al.*, above n 36.

44 Welsh *et al.*, above n 27, 460.

reports depend on the viewer/reader's emotional identification with the victim to convert those responses into a critique of law's ability to provide an appropriate retributive measure against crime. It has been argued that individuals will endorse a retributive response to justice when they see themselves as sharing identity with the victim,[45] and Isabelle's comment above seems to confirm this. As mentioned earlier, a viewer/reader will often relate stories to their own lives or to the lives of other real people,[46] and in turn respond emotionally to them.[47] Note particularly Isabelle's subconscious use of language that belies her retributive desire. She uses the second person pronoun 'you' to not only associate herself with the victim, but to imagine herself in that situation and to envisage the justice she might desire if she was the victim. In this way, Isabelle is then able to easily accept and reproduce the retributive rhetoric that is utilised by media reports to emotively 'frame' injustice via the image of the guilty going unpunished.

In the comments below we can again see the participants identifying what is 'just' by using the negative marker of injustice, but this time adding the more complex layer of intuitive emotion as an indicative response to hearing of injustice in the media:

PHOEBE: I think [injustice] is more likely to provoke an emotional reaction in you, if it makes me angry then it's probably not just . . .

JEMMA: I do understand that – like you feel kind of outraged when you have been done, when wrong has been done, so that is part of it.[48]

LAUREN: Say if they got fifteen years for running me over with a car, then I don't think that's good enough, because I'd want them to die if they ran me over, or live in gaol forever . . . [49]

In trying to explain how one might know if justice has been achieved, Phoebe and Jemma seem to agree that we know injustice because we have an instinctive emotional reaction, and Lauren uses very expressive second person pronoun language to describe her responsive retributive stance. In each of the focus groups, the participants consistently articulated this shared retributive perspective that is based on an intuitive emotional acceptance of news reports that 'frame' injustice. Yet, as the next section will show, participants in their discussions also simultaneously seek to actively challenge this 'framing'.

45 Gromet and Darley, above n 26, 52.
46 Liebes and Katz (1993), above n 22, 32.
47 Liebes and Katz (1993), above n 22, 100.
48 FG 2, 10.
49 FG 3, 1–2.

Challenge of media construction – pragmatic criticism

Despite at times accepting the retributive rhetoric reproduced in the news, participants in this research also exhibit critical ability in the syntactic domain – that is, they reveal an understanding of the component elements of the genre of media news framing and its dramatic function. Liebes and Katz have argued that when viewing popular stories, a critical reading involves (a) an ability to discuss programs as aesthetic constructions[50] by recognising narrative elements of genre, formulaic conventions,[51] and theme and messaging;[52] and (b) a 'pragmatic awareness' of the text by their cognitive, affective and social self. The participants of these focus groups spent considerable time critically reflecting on the constructed nature of news reporting, and interchangeably acknowledging the way these constructions impact on their perceptions.

Take for example, Isabelle's comment below as she points out that the inherent interests behind news production will ensure a skewed version of reality is presented (which is therefore not to be trusted):

> ISABELLE: . . . often media has an underlying interest in exposure and getting as much publicity as possible by any means possible, so their views are fairly skewed and biased I would say . . . yeah, I think it has to be taken with a grain of salt.[53]

Critical viewers are able to reflect on the 'type' or 'version' of reality that is constructed within the texts, and in these focus groups, the participants recognise the genre of news reporting as a serial offender in the manipulation of 'reality'. For example in one group Stuart points out that various news reports 'manipulate our senses of what's right and wrong by omission'.[54] Equally, in another group, James argues that the 'way certain stories are covered and the issues that are emphasised can be entirely inconsistent with the truth' making both the media and public opinion 'fickle'.[55] By ascribing manipulative intent in this way to the production of news, participants are challenging the message that news reports comprise a truthful repository of facts.

Interestingly, the constructed nature of news production was often the focus of many group conversations and the participants would jointly spur each other on to challenge the seemingly natural public acceptance of news reports as fact. In the following extract, note the mutually aiding interaction among the group

50 Liebes and Katz (1993), above n 22, 32.
51 Liebes and Katz (1989), above n 22, 204–205.
52 Ibid.
53 FG 1, 5.
54 FG 4, 34.
55 FG 1, 11.

as they identify the role of the media together, starting with Justin's duplicated reference to the way media 'frames' its own version of justice:

JUSTIN: there are issues in the way the media frames people, . . . [the media] definitely has its own brand of justice. So, it can paint hugely negative pictures of people and crimes using sort of framing in language.

EMILY: yeah, often with minimal evidence . . . well, because it makes a good story, it will sell papers.

JUSTIN: yeah, so they have to put in the obligatory 'accused' . . . but in our minds we're reading it and we're saying, 'oh he's the only one they've found in connection with this case and so he must have done it' and . . . yeah, I think there's a big influence on how the media shapes its own brand of justice.

PHOEBE: I don't know if it necessarily shows us what's normal, because any things that are newsworthy are things that are going to make us pay attention and watch what's going on. Like, if there was a news programme saying 'yes, there was a court case today and paperwork was filed effectively and according to procedure' . . . (laughter) No-one would watch that segment of the news and then turn it off and there'd be no advertising watched and so on . . .

EMILY: yeah that's true. Like everyday many cases are brought and they're cleared or completed and tied up successfully and, but it's the extreme ones or the ones where there's emotional reactions to the injustice . . .

PHOEBE: it's the ones that have gone wrong

EMILY: . . . yeah, ones that have gone wrong.[56]

By critically evaluating the formula of news reporting and the various elements of dramatic function, the participants are together identifying the role of media as a subjective definer of the cultural product of 'justice'. In an almost derisive tone, the participants in the discussion above are critical of the 'reality' portrayed by news reports, because they argue that economics is a key motivator in news production necessitating only that which produces drama, excitement and tension. It is a naturalist approach to realism where the participants use their own judgment to determine whether a given activity does and will occur in 'real life'.[57]

Notice here how the members of the group are finishing each other's sentences and feeding off each other to share an understanding or interpretation about

56 FG 2, 13–14.

57 Naturalism or literal realism is one use of the concept of realism that Barker and Andre identified in their work on the role of soap opera in teenagers' identity projects. Naturalism involves questioning the appearance of reality and the plausibility of action and linear construction in terms of everyday life. Barker and Andre, above n 20, 33.

how the criminal justice system must work in 'reality'. In acknowledging dramatic function and formulaic aspects of news media, the participants in this interaction believe that because news reports do not show the mundane aspects of criminal justice, what is missing must be the reality. In acknowledging the requisite dramatic function and narrativity within news reports, the participants reveal that despite their retributive stance described earlier, they do believe that media stories only hype up those controversial cases that will heighten emotional responses, and in their hurry to completely separate reality from fiction, they reveal a somewhat contradictory recognition of the legal system as generally effective. It is contradictory because on the one hand (as I've argued in the first section) the participants accept and use news reports to critique the efficacy of the criminal justice system. Yet on the other hand, they clearly challenge the news reports on the basis that they must be misleading.

As participants attempt to challenge the role of media as truth-teller, there is still some confusion among them as to what extent the media can be trusted, and particularly the level at which it actually occupies their imagination. This can be seen in the pragmatism evident in Justin's comment above when he demonstrated the way the news reports play on our thinking: 'in our minds we're reading it and we're saying . . .'. In challenging various aspects of crime news reporting, the participants exhibited a substantial capacity for this type of pragmatic criticism. As stated earlier, a critical audience member not only exhibits a manifest awareness of the constructedness of the program but also is aware of the audience experience of it.[58] That is, the reader is critically aware if they are cognisant of the 'ways in which the structure of the [text] captures and occupies their imagination'.[59]

The participants in this study frequently referred to the pragmatic uses we should make of news reports. In this next extract, the participants take part in a referential forum in which you can see an implicit recognition that news reporting has implications for their affective selves on their reflections on 'just how true' news reporting is:

CHRIS: but again, it's the media influencing what I know. . . . I mean, like we tell, Ok we're still a culture that communicates information through stories, I mean, no one, like no one, no, very few people would enjoy sitting down and reading court transcripts to kind of figure out what the law is, but, if it's a story, then people can sit down, read it and engage with it, and while it may be slightly skewed point of view, you can stick with it and understand, oh OK, this is what's happened.

58 Liebes and Katz (1993), above n 22, 32.
59 Liebes and Katz (1989), above n 22, 216.

EMILY: but not all journalists are, I've been really cynical about them tonight, but not all journalists are necessarily biased.

CHRIS: well, yeah.

EMILY: Like some of them try really hard to be objective and to get both sides of the case so, there's I guess, a role in which media are really helpful in informing us and giving us that sense of what's happening in our country and where we're getting these things from.

JUSTIN: I still think it's too dangerous to lump our perceptions or filter our perceptions of justice through the media . . . 'cause ultimately the media is made up of people working for other people who have agendas. I know that sounds really cynical, but it's true.

EMILY: Right.

JUSTIN: So there's this huge idea that you can be very influenced, poorly, through the media. So, in my idea, you'd have to have a huge base of competing and different media sources. So, I think we're just too, I think information just flows through too narrow channel.[60]

In acknowledging the formulaic element of news production, the participants challenge themselves and each other to question the representation in light of their own assumptions about reality. Interestingly, Chris starts the discussion by commenting that it is the media that makes the law interesting and entertaining through storytelling. Emily responds by articulating that media reporting does have altruistic motivations and effects, yet this is refuted by Justin, who argues that it is dangerous to believe in the media because any such altruistic goals are overtaken by political agendas and media motivations.

In this way it might be argued that while participants recognise the constructed nature of news reporting, there is a still a sense in which they rely on it as a referential filter for the truth. That is, lying beneath the participants' active challenges to media construction was an almost reluctant simultaneous acceptance of news reporting as an effective vehicle for disseminating information about the criminal justice system. See for example this next extract, where underneath the participants' critique of manipulative media intent is a lingering question as to how factual the crime reports could actually be:

LAUREN: They [media] only tell us the victim's side.

ANNA: I reckon they tell us what sells. In most cases, I think whatever sells, whatever's going to sell, they pay for.

JUSTINE: they'll always exaggerate it.

ANNA: yeh, so that they can sell. 'Cos if they're going to put the facts, the true facts of most cases, they probably wouldn't be that interested, but if they pick out that one thing . . . it's how they make their money and if it was

60 FG 2, 26–28.

your business you'd probably do the same 'cos they're trying to make their money unfortunately, as much as we don't like it.

LAUREN: Well, they suck you in. It's like when they show you all the funny bits of a movie and you go and watch it and they were the only funny bits there.

JUSTINE: That's a great way of explaining it . . . not very technical but, yeah, It makes sense (laughter)

ANNA: I think to a certain degree you do believe [the media] 'cos you have, well I do have, in the back of my mind the fact that I mean surely they couldn't be telling that big of a lie when it's such an important case, but I suppose there's always more to it.

LAUREN: but it wouldn't exactly be a lie it just would be

JUSTINE: a fabrication (laughs).[61]

Here, the participants are acknowledging the role of news reporting in affecting public consciousness, including their own. Again, there is the critique that only the dramatic elements are included as a way of manipulating audiences, and yet Anna's comment referentially concedes the impact on individual perception of a general assumption that media reports must be rooted somewhere in truth. This is powerful pragmatism because it allows participants to convince themselves that they are able to sift the truth from the lies within what is reported. In this way, while recognising the constructed nature of the text, the participants use the news reports to at first gain some insight into the criminal justice system and its activity, and then subsequently assess its efficacy. As Dorothy commented:

DOROTHY: We're relying on media to perfect our opinion of the law or what's going on because how else can you know except you go and sit in every case, study every case minutely and know the law that applies to that specifically.[62]

Despite the participants' critical recognition that news reporting often has a one-sided connection with reality, these few examples have demonstrated that they nevertheless consistently utilise the content of news reports to construct expectations of both the criminal justice system, and the media as a (re)production of news.

Conclusion

Media reports and public conversation each deploy the power of storytelling to provoke, engage and animate imagination in relation to expectations of the law, the criminal justice system and of media outlets. This chapter has commended

61 FG 3, 16–17.
62 FG 4, 17.

the further utilisation of these stories as a dynamic window into the popular cultural scripts at play within an individual response to crime stories. It has demonstrated the value and importance of a cultural legal studies approach to researching the complexities inherent in public perception of the criminal justice system. Moreover, the ethnographical methodology deployed here has demonstrated the socially constitutive nature of public ideas about justice and the cyclical rhythm of retributive desire within the stories of both news reporting, and conversation. There is still so much about the transformation, challenge and embodiment of legal meaning within popular imagination to be explored, and this chapter seeks to commend the further utilisation of conversation as a fruitful window into the nuanced ways individuals participate in, and embody law and justice.

Bibliography

Asimow, Michael, Kathryn Brown and David Ray Papke (eds), *Law and Popular Culture: International Perspectives* (Cambridge Scholars Publishing, 2014)

Barker, Chris, *Cultural Studies: Theory and Practice* (Sage Publications, 2000)

Barker, Chris and Julie Andre, 'Did You See? Soaps, Teenage Talk and Gendered Identity' (1996) 4(4) *Young: Nordic Journal of Youth Research* 23

Barker, Chris and Dariusz Galasinski, *Cultural Studies and Discourse Analysis: A Dialogue on Language and Identity* (Sage, 2001)

Cover, Robert M, 'Nomos and Narrative' (1983) 97 *Harvard Law Review* 4

Elkins, James, 'On the Emergence of Narrative Jurisprudence: The Humanistic Perspective Finds a New Path' (1985) 9 *Legal Studies Forum* 123

Garland, David, *The Culture of Control* (Oxford University Press, 2001) quoted in Neil Hutton, 'Beyond Populist Punitiveness?' (2005) 7 *Punishment & Society* 243

Gies, Lieve, 'The Media and Public Understanding of the Law' in Steve Greenfield and Guy Osborn (eds), *Readings in Law and Popular Culture* (Routledge-Cavendish, 2008)

Greenfield, Steve and Guy Osborn (eds), *Readings in Law and Popular Culture* (Routledge, 2008)

Gromet, Dena M and John M Darley, 'Retributive and Restorative Justice: Importance of Crime Severity and Shared Identity in People's Justice Responses' (2009) 61(1) *Australian Journal of Psychology* 51

Liebes, Tamar and Elihu Katz, 'On the Critical Abilities of Television Viewers' in Ellen Seiter, Hans Borchers, Gabriele Kreutzner and Eva-Maria Warth (eds), *Remote Control: Television Audiences and Cultural Power* (Routledge, 1989)

Liebes, Tamar and Elihu Katz, *The Export of Meaning: Cross-Cultural Readings of Dallas* (Wiley Publishing, 1993)

Norris, Pippa, Montague Kern and Marion Just, *Framing Terrorism: The News Media, The Government and The Public* (Routledge, 2003)

Rafter, Nicole Hahn, *Shots in the Mirror: Crime Films and Society* (Oxford University Press, 2006)

Rappaport, Bret, 'Tapping the Human Adaptive Origins of Storytelling by Requiring Legal Writing Students to Read a Novel in Order to Appreciate How Character, Setting, Plot, Theme, and Tone (CSPTT) are as Important as IRAC' (2008) 25 *T M Cooley Law Review* 267

Robertson, Michael, Lillian Corbin, Kieran Tranter and Francesca Bartlett, *The Ethics Project in Legal Education* (Routledge, 2011)
Robson, Peter and Jessica Silbey, *Law and Justice on the Small Screen* (Hart Publishing, 2012)
Sarat, Austin and Thomas Kearns, *Law in the Domains of Culture* (Ann Arbor: University of Michigan Press, 1998)
Seiter, Ellen, Hans Borchers, Gabriele Kreutzner and Eva-Maria Warth, *Remote Control: Television Audiences and Cultural Power* (Routledge, 1989)
Sharp, Cassandra, 'Changing the Channel: What to Do with the Critical Abilities of Law Students as Viewers?' (2004) 13(2) *Griffith Law Review* 185
Sharp, Cassandra, 'The "Extreme Makeover" Effect of Law School: Students being Transformed by Stories' (2005) 12(1) *Texas Wesleyan Law Review* 233
Sharp, Cassandra, '"Represent a Murderer . . . I'd Never do That!" How Students use Stories to Link Ethical Development and Identity Construction' in Michael Robertson, Lillian Corbin, Kieran Tranter and Francesca Bartlett (eds), *The Ethics Project in Legal Education* (Routledge, 2011)
Sharp, Cassandra, 'Let's See How Far We've Come: The Role of Empirical Methodology in Exploring Television Audiences' in Peter Robson and Jessica Silbey (eds), *Law and Justice on the Small Screen* (Hart Publishing, 2012)
Sharp, Cassandra, 'Riddle Me This . . . ? Would the World Need Superheroes if the Law Could Actually Deliver "Justice"?' (2012) 16 *Law Text Culture* 353
Sharp, Cassandra, 'Justice with a Vengeance – Retributive Desire in Popular Imagination' in Michael Asimow, Kathryn Brown and David Ray Papke (eds), *Law and Popular Culture: International Perspectives* (Cambridge Scholars Publishing, 2014)
Sherwin, Richard, 'Symposium: Introduction: Picturing Justice: Images of Law and Lawyers in the Visual Media' (1996) 30 (Summer) *University of San Francisco Law Review* 891
Sherwin, Richard, Neal Feigenson and Christina Spiesel, 'Law in the Digital Age: How Visual Communication Technologies are Transforming the Practice, Theory and Teaching of Law' (2006) 12 *Boston University Journal of Science and Technology Law* 227, 258
Webb, Julian, 'Ethics for Lawyers or Ethics for Citizens? New Directions for Legal Education' (1998) 25 *Journal of Law and Society* 134
Welsh, Andrew, Thomas Fleming and Kenneth Dowler, 'Constructing Crime and Justice on Film: Meaning and Message in Cinema' (2011) 14 (4) *Contemporary Justice Review: Issues in Criminal, Social and Restorative Justice* 457

Part II

Cultural legal studies as legal storytelling

Chapter 4

Interventions into the feeling of popular justice

Australia's Stolen Generations, the problem of sentimentality, and re-encountering the testimonial form

Honni van Rijswijk

Introduction: sentimental encounters

2017 will mark the twentieth anniversary of *Bringing Them Home*,[1] and 13 February 2018 will be the tenth anniversary of former Prime Minister Kevin Rudd's 'Apology to Australia's Indigenous People'.[2] Looking ahead to these anniversaries, we need to evaluate the ways in which Stolen Generations' narratives and testimonies have circulated in the Australian public sphere, and pre-empt the shaping of these anniversaries by both state and public. This chapter considers the significance of Stolen Generations' testimonies to the Australian imaginary – especially the relationship of the public's encounters with testimonies to the political and juridical claims of the Stolen Generations. I focus on the role of non-Aboriginal readers of Stolen Generations testimony, and argue that public Stolen Generations projects need to be reframed in ways that encourage their audiences to move beyond the position of compassionate bystanders. The chapter begins with the *Bringing Them Home* Inquiry and Report of the late 1990s, reviewing criticism of the ways in which Stolen Generations' testimonies have been framed and instrumentalised as part of wider state and cultural myths. I will then turn to where we are now, eighteen years after *Bringing Them Home*, by examining recent testimonies that have been published online as *The Stolen Generations Testimonies Project*.[3] I will consider what can be done to intervene in

1 Commonwealth, National Inquiry into the Separation of Aboriginal and Torres Strait Islander Children from Their Families, *Bringing Them Home: Report of the National Inquiry into the Separation of Aboriginal and Torres Strait Islander Children from Their Families* (1997) ('*Bringing Them Home*').
2 Commonwealth, *Parliamentary Debates*, House of Representatives, 13 February 2008, 167 (Kevin Rudd, Prime Minister). Hereafter 'the Apology'.
3 *Stolen Generations' Testimonies*, Stolen Generations' Testimonies Foundation http://stolengenerationstestimonies.com

the history of the Australian public's problematic encounters with Stolen Generations' testimonies, since this history shapes contemporary encounters. In order to explain the problem of encounter, and suggest methods of intervention, I will consider the different iterations of Stolen Generations' testimonies using the framework of genre.[4]

Stolen Generations' testimonies are one of the main domains through which the Australian public has encountered the history of the Stolen Generations, and through which the public has made sense of the political and juridical claims that arise from the Stolen Generations' experiences. But as a number of scholars have noted, these encounters tend to occur in the sentimental register, and even, in Robert Meister's terms,[5] through the genre of 'melodrama'.[6] The consequence of the public encountering these testimonies in the sentimental mode is that the political and juridical claims of the testimonies are thereby significantly weakened: people encounter the testimonies in a 'bystander' role, rather than as responsible actors.[7] However, this chapter will argue that these testimonies tell many different stories, and that the ways in which they are encountered need not be overdetermined. Often, the sentimental encounter has dominated because fragments from testimonies have been selected and instrumentalised in public meta-narratives that emphasise particular elements of the Stolen Generations' experiences. Encountered in their entirety, I argue, these testimonies tell a number of stories, and contain a number of different figures, tones, registers and demands – stories of critique and claim, as well as of sentiment. Much depends on the framing and contextualisation of the testimonies, and of bringing out themes that are already strong in the testimonies, but which have not been previously emphasised. The problems of encounter are not insurmountable and can be redressed by educating readers in the history of the production of these testimonies, as well as encouraging reading practices that include paying attention to context.

4 A number of legal scholars, including Mark Antaki, Stewart Motha and Karin van Marle, have recently turned their attention to the potential of genre to offer insights into the 'the liminal space of critique at the intersection of law, aesthetics and politics.' (Stewart Motha and Karin Van Marle, 'Introduction' in Karin Van Marle and Stewart Motha (eds), *Genres of Critique* (Sun Press, 2013) 17).

5 Robert Meister, *After Evil: A Politics of Human Rights* (Columbia University Press, 2011) 63–64.

6 See also Rosanne Kennedy, 'An Australian Archive of Feelings' (2011) 26 *Australian Feminist Studies* 257; Anne Orford, 'Commissioning the Truth' (2006) 15 *Columbia Journal of Gender and Law* 851; Trish Luker, '"Postcolonising" Amnesia in the Discourse of Reconciliation: The Void in the Law's Response to the Stolen Generations' (2005) 22 *Australian Feminist Law Journal* 67.

7 Robert Meister, above n 5.

From *Bringing Them Home* to online testimonies: the continuing significance of Stolen Generations' testimonies as a domain of popular justice

Between 1995 and 1997, an Australian federal government agency, the Human Rights and Equal Opportunity Commission (HREOC), conducted an inquiry into the removal of Aboriginal children from their communities during the twentieth century. HREOC's final report, *Bringing Them Home*, published in 1997, found that from approximately 1910 to 1970, between one and three of every ten Aboriginal children had been forcibly removed from their families, and that this had led to ongoing physical and psychological harms.[8] *Bringing Them Home* is a didactic text – one of its main purposes was to educate the mainstream public regarding the experiences of the Stolen Generations, and the responsibilities that arose through this suffering. It was clearly aimed at eliciting empathic responses from the public in ways that were compatible with a broader narrative of healing and reconciliation. But significantly, *Bringing Them Home* also made strong political and legal claims. The Report concluded that the forcible removal of Aboriginal children constituted cultural genocide under the United Nations Genocide Convention 1948 (ratified by Australia in 1949) and customary international law.[9] It recommended the use of the United Nations' van Boven Principles for Victims of Gross Violations of Human Rights, including a full range of reparation measures, such as restitution, compensation, rehabilitation, satisfaction and guarantees of not-repetition.[10] The Report also recommended that a reparations scheme be adopted to deal with compensation arising from harms suffered by the Stolen Generations, and that there be a national apology.[11] The Inquiry and Report thereby did important work in documenting 'the everydayness and bureaucratization of genocide and of massive human rights violations in the liberal democratic state'.[12] In tracing the past 'laws, practices and policies' that produced the Stolen Generations,[13] it made a significant intervention into the silence of both the legal domain and the public sphere of that time.

The significance of *Bringing Them Home* needs to be understood in the context of the failure of the common law to become a site of redress for the harms suffered by the Stolen Generations. There have only been a handful of cases

8 National Inquiry into the Separation of Aboriginal and Torres Strait Islander Children from Their Families, above n 1, 308 et seq.
9 Ibid, 308–309.
10 Ibid.
11 Ibid.
12 Anne Orford, 'Commissioning the Truth' (2006) 15 *Columbia Journal of Gender and Law* 851.
13 National Inquiry into the Separation of Aboriginal and Torres Strait Islander Children from Their Families, above n 1, 3.

dealing with compensation for members of the Stolen Generations.[14] Only one of these claims, set out in the *Trevorrow* Cases, has been successful, and this case was decided as late as 2010. One of the greatest obstacles to the success of Stolen Generations' cases has been the courts' practice of preferring documentary records (usually produced by government or defendant agencies) over oral testimony (usually provided by Aboriginal applicants). The most notorious of the earlier cases is *Cubillo v Commonwealth*,[15] where Justice O'Loughlin spoke of the 'huge void' created by the absence of documentary evidence as a key explanation for the applicants' failure to prove their case, despite the availability of significant oral testimony – judicial reasoning that has been the subject of significant criticism.[16]

Despite the efforts of *Bringing Them Home*, Australian law and politics have largely failed the Stolen Generations. The Report's political and legal elements have subsequently been left behind, so that the primary way in which the Stolen Generations are encountered in the Australian public sphere is through an affective mode of engagement. The Prime Minister at the time of publication of *Bringing Them Home*, John Howard, refused to apologise to the Stolen Generations, on the basis that 'Australians of this generation should not be required to accept guilt and blame for past actions and policies over which they had no control'.[17] Prime Minister Kevin Rudd's later 'Apology to Australia's Indigenous People,' on 13 February 2008, was a momentous event in the national Australia imaginary. But as will be discussed later, its emphasis on reconciliation

14 The Federal Court denied claims for compensation in *Kruger v Commonwealth* (1997) 190 CLR 1, and in *Cubillo v The Commonwealth* (2000) 103 FCR 1 and *Cubillo v The Commonwealth [No 2]* (2001) 112 FCR 1 ('*Cubillo*'). *South Australia v Lampard-Trevorrow* (2010) 106 SASR 331 (*'Lampard-Trevorrow')*, where the court dismissed the State's appeal against the decision of Gray J in *Trevorrow v South Australia [No 5]* (2007) 98 SASR 136 (*'Trevorrow')*, has been the only successful Stolen Generations case. See, Honni Van Rijswijk and Thalia Anthony, 'Can the Common Law Adjudicate Historical Suffering?' (2012) 36 *Melbourne University Law Review* 618. The Western Australian Supreme Court recently denied a claim for compensation in *Collard v The State of Western Australia [No 4]* (2013) WASC 455.

15 *Cubillo v Commonwealth* (2000) 103 FCR 1. A number of aspects in the trial case favourable to the applicants were reversed on appeal, but all adverse findings were affirmed: *Cubillo v Commonwealth* (2001) 112 FCR 455 ('*Cubillo (Appeal)*').

16 See especially Trish Luker, '"Postcolonising" Amnesia in the Discourse of Reconciliation: The Void in the Law's Response to the Stolen Generations' (2005) 22 *Australian Feminist Law Journal* 67; see Chris Cunneen and Julia Grix, 'The Limitations of Litigation in Stolen Generations Cases' (Research Discussion Paper No 15, Australian Institute of Aboriginal and Torres Strait Islander Studies, 2004). There are a number of critical historians and legal scholars working in this area, including Thalia Anthony, Larissa Behrendt, Tony Birch, Ann Curthoys, Ann Genovese, Ben Golder, Trish Luker, Rosanne Kennedy, Ann McGrath, Stewart Motha, Peter Read, Alexander Reilly and Patrick Wolfe.

17 John Howard, 'Practical Reconciliation' in Michelle Grattan (ed.), *Reconciliation: Essays in Australia Reconciliation* (Bookman Press, 2000) 90.

promoted the public's affective, sentimental engagement with the Stolen Generations, at the expense of political and legal remedies. In defiance of the recommendations of *Bringing Them Home*, there is still no federal reparations scheme.

As this chapter will explore, Stolen Generations' testimonies potentially offer a powerful resistance to legal and political failures in relation to the Stolen Generations' experiences – not only to the gaps and absences of political and legal realms, but also to the problematic myths that have arisen concerning the Stolen Generations. However, alongside the potential of these testimonies, scholars have rightly pointed out the risks when testimonies are captured as part of wider meta-narratives, in particular the ways in which the state has mediated the public's encounters with the Stolen Generations.[18] Rosanne Kennedy argues that a didactic training of the Australian public began with the Council for Reconciliation, and continued through the inquiry by HREOC, and its subsequent report, *Bringing Them Home*, as well as through the activities of the National Sorry Day Committee.[19] Kennedy describes the Sorry Books Campaign of the late 1990s as 'a popular reconciliation movement',[20] and argues that, far from Australians' responses of personal apology being spontaneous or 'intuitive', the Sorry Books were the effect of a didactic movement that 'educated' ordinary Australians on their moral obligation to respond – and on the forms their response should take.[21] Kennedy compares this response to what Lauren Berlant has written about,[22] in the context of the United States, as 'a popular belief in national sentimentality, a rhetoric of promise that a nation can be built across fields of social difference through channels of affective identification and empathy'. Berlant argues that sentimentality:

> . . . is the means by which mass subaltern pain is advanced in the dominant public sphere, as the true core of national collectivity. It operates when the pain of intimate others blurs into the consciousness of classically privileged

18 See, e.g., Bain Attwood, 'The Stolen Generations and Genocide: Robert Manne's *In Denial: The Stolen Generations and the Right*' (2001) 25 *Aboriginal History* 163; Anne Orford, 'Commissioning the Truth' (2006) 15 *Columbia Journal of Gender and Law* 851; Anna Haebich, *Broken Circles: Fragmenting Indigenous Families, 1800–2000* (Fremantle Arts Centre Press, 2000); Rosanne Kennedy, Lynee Bell and Julia Emberley, 'Decolonising Testimony: On the Possibilities and Limits of Witnessing' (2009) 15 *Humanities Research* 1; Rosanne Kennedy, 'Subversive Witnessing: Mediating Indigenous Testimony in Australian Cultural and Legal Institutions' (2008) 36 *Women's Studies Quarterly* 58.

19 Rosanne Kennedy, 'An Australian Archive of Feelings' (2011) 26 *Australian Feminist Studies* 257.

20 Ibid.

21 Ibid, 265.

22 Lauren Berlant, 'The Subject of True Feeling: Pain, Privacy and Politics' in Austin Sarat and Thomas Kearns (eds), *Cultural Pluralism, Identity Politics and the Law* (University of Michigan Press, 2000) 49, 53.

national subjects, in such a fashion that they feel the pain of flawed or denied citizenship as their pain.[23]

A certain affect or empathy is felt, without the experience of the material conditions that cause the pain. *Bringing Them Home* was the medium through which testimonies of suffering circulated, prompting their audience to identify empathically with that suffering.[24] Encountered in this way, the testimonies became a form of nation-building that has little to do with the material experiences of suffering, past or present.[25]

Stolen Generations' testimonies clearly have the potential to promote popular justice – not only to elicit empathy from the Australian public, but also to articulate political and juridical claims. The continuing interest and potential of the testimonies is evidenced by a new iteration of testimonies, *The Stolen Generations Testimonies Project*, which is funded through both state and private resources,[26] and which currently includes over thirty personal testimonies of survivors online, with more testimonies currently being produced.[27] On its website, the Stolen Generations' Testimonies Foundation states that '[b]y allowing Australians to listen to the Survivors' stories with open hearts and without judgment, the foundation hopes more people will be engaged in the healing process'.[28] The hope of the Foundation is that the online project opens up multiple possibilities of encounter, and that those encounters facilitate healing and social justice. Debra Hocking, a Stolen Generations survivor, says:

> There's nothing more powerful than the personal story. For people to understand, we have to open ourselves up. It's hard to tell our personal stories but we are doing this to educate people. For us to heal as a country these are the stories we need to share. They're sad stories but they're important stories . . . . . . For those people who do feel challenged about the 'Stolen Generations', we ask you to listen to just one of these testimonies to see if you still feel the same. That's all we ask.[29]

23 Ibid.
24 Rosanne Kennedy, above n 19, 259.
25 See also Trish Luker, '"Postcolonising" Amnesia in the Discourse of Reconciliation: The Void in the Law's Response to the Stolen Generations' (2005) 22 *Australian Feminist Law Journal* 67.
26 The project is an initiative of the Stolen Generations Foundation, which acknowledges the support of Department of Families, Housing, Community Services and Indigenous Affairs, the Hunt Foundation and the Rio Tinto Aboriginal Foundation.
27 Stolen Generations' Testimonies Foundation, above n 3.
28 About This Project, Stolen Generations' Testimonies Foundation http://stolengenerations testimonies.com/about_stolent_generations/html.
29 Ibid.

This latest iteration of Stolen Generations' testimonies raises key questions of encounter and engagement: On what terms can testimony be a domain of critical intervention in legal and political problems? Can the testimonial form itself offer a way out of, or through, problematic meta-narratives of reconciliation, redemption and apology, which have worked to close down juridical and political demands? Given the history of the framing of Stolen Generations' testimonies, and the nature of contemporary social and political imaginaries, can the hopes of the Stolen Generations' Testimonies Board – and especially of those providing the testimonies – be realised? Most important, what can be done to reframe these kinds of testimonial projects in ways that acknowledge the problematic historical relation between testimony and the state, and which encourage audiences to encounter testimonies in new, critical ways?

These problems are not insurmountable, but I will draw attention to two practices, in particular, that need to be encouraged when the Australian public encounters Stolen Generations' testimonies. First, I suggest that the histories of the testimonial form and its relation to state projects needs to be explained and highlighted in the framing of testimonies. Second, the *genre* of the Stolen Generations' testimonies needs to be thematised in the encounter – brought explicitly to the mind of people watching and listening to the testimonies – if these testimonies are to be brought out of the sentimental register and experienced as sites of political and juridical claiming. Non-Aboriginal audiences need to be educated as to what is at stake in the genre of popular justice. Participants in encounters need to be encouraged to take up a position of readerly responsibility with respect to their encounters with Stolen Generations' testimonies, so that they move away from the position of mere bystanders into a place of responsibility. Contemporary audiences need to become self-conscious about how they encounter these testimonies, and to engage critically with the framing narratives used. The focus is to shift the framing of Stolen Generations' testimonies from a sentimental genre to a genre of critique; a shift from an emphasis on suffering to one of responsibility. This chapter suggests that the histories of the testimonial form and of the genre of the Stolen Generations' testimonies both need to be thematised in the encounter if these testimonies are to be brought out of the sentimental register and experienced as sites of political and juridical claiming.

The significance of genre

In his 2011 book *After Evil: A Politics of Human Rights*, Robert Meister argues that transitional justice processes, such as Australia's responses to the Stolen Generations, and Reconciliation movements more generally,are processes that *essentially* structure participants' engagement as aesthetic and affective, rather than as political. Meister argues that transitional justice should be understood as a genre in which participants engage as an audience, rather than as a political process with which participants engage as political beings. For Meister,[30] this form of encounter is part of a wider historical process in which the political domain of action has been undermined – the effect of a turn to a certain kind of self-focused ethics, which is evidenced as sentimentality. The power in this argument lies in its analysis of the vesting of authority: Meister argues that participants are vested with authority essentially through encounters of readership, which means that these discourses are not only eliciting a certain kind of substantive response, but a particular *mode* of response – turning politics into affective experience. This turn, based on sentimental identification, blocks the achievement of social justice, while at the same time disguising this fact.

At the same time that Stolen Generations' testimonies have been part of important projects to address the gaps and refusals of law and public life, the testimonies have also been instrumentalised by state narratives that are counter-productive to the achievement of justice for the Stolen Generations. The Apology made by Prime Minister Rudd in 2008 only went so far – it did not acknowledge the full degree of the damage caused by removal policies to individuals and to Aboriginal communities through the destruction of Aboriginal cultural identity and language, and Rudd did not commit to a federal reparations or compensation scheme, as had been recommended by *Bringing Them Home*. The Apology was the ideal moment when a federal reparations scheme should have been implemented. Instead, the Apology emphasised the discursive justice aspect of responses to the Stolen Generations, and implied that the state's apology signified closure of past injustices, and a shift to a focus on the future. Most significant, Prime Minister Rudd's Apology provided a powerful lesson from state to public in how to interpret the Stolen Generations' experiences. In his speech preceding the Apology, Rudd drew on the testimony of a member of the Stolen Generations, instrumentalising select elements of her life story so that it corresponded to the framework of Reconciliation, and fit within a sentimental, resolvable narrative.[31]

Stating that Nanna Nungala Fejo's story was one of many thousands of stories of forced separation, Rudd emphasised the role of suffering in grounding the need for a response:

> There is something terribly primal about these firsthand accounts. The pain is searing; it screams from the pages. The hurt, the humiliation, the

30 Robert Meister, *After Evil: A Politics of Human Rights* (Columbia University Press, 2011) (see especially 'Preface' and 'Chapter 1').

31 See also John Frow, 'Discursive Justice' (2001) 100 *The South Atlantic Quarterly* 331; Alex Reilly, 'How Sorry Are We? The Limits of the Apology to the Stolen Generation' (2009) 34 *Alternative Law Journal* 97; Nayanika Mookherjee *et al.*, 'The Ethics of Apology: A Set of Commentaries' (2009) 29 *Critique of Anthropology* 345.

> degradation and the sheer brutality of the act of physically separating a mother from her children is a deep assault on our senses and on our most elemental humanity. . . . These stories cry out to be heard; they cry out for an apology. Instead, from the nation's parliament there has been a stony and stubborn and deafening silence for more than a decade.[32]

Rudd then proceeded to tell her story, recalling Nanna Fejo's earliest childhood days in the late 1920s, living with her family and her community in a bush camp just outside Tennant Creek in the Northern Territory. Rudd deploys the subjective third person point of view in his retelling of Nanna Nungala Fejo's story. Focalising his speech through a childlike point of view, and using short sentences and simple vocabulary to evoke a child's experience, Rudd recounts Nanna Fejo's early life, before her removal, taking on a position of innocence and naivety:

> She remembers her earliest childhood days living with her family and her community in a bush camp just outside Tennant Creek. She remembers the love and the warmth and the kinship of those days long ago, including traditional dancing around the campfire at night. She loved the dancing. She remembers once getting into strife when, as a four-year-old girl, she insisted on dancing with the male tribal elders rather than just sitting and watching the men, as the girls were supposed to do.[33]

Rudd then relates the scene of removal, again using short sentences and simple words to evoke the point of view of a child:

> But then, sometime around 1932, when she was about four, she remembers the coming of the welfare men. Her family had feared that day and had dug holes in the creek bank where the children could run and hide. What they had not expected was that the white welfare men did not come alone. They brought a truck, two white men and an Aboriginal stockman on horseback cracking his stockwhip. The kids were found; they ran for their mothers, screaming, but they could not get away. They were herded and piled onto the back of the truck. Tears flowing, her mum tried clinging to the sides of the truck as her children were taken away to the Bungalow in Alice, all in the name of protection.[34]

32 Commonwealth, *Parliamentary Debates*, House of Representatives, 13 February 2008, 167 (Kevin Rudd, Prime Minister).

33 Ibid.

34 Ibid.

She was taken to a mission, and Prime Minister Rudd takes up her story there:

> She stayed at the mission until after the war, when she was allowed to leave for a prearranged job as a domestic in Darwin. She was 16. Nanna Fejo never saw her mum again. After she left the mission, her brother let her know that her mum had died years before, a broken woman fretting for the children that had literally been ripped away from her.

Rudd says:

> As I left, later on, Nanna Fejo took one of my staff aside, wanting to make sure that I was not too hard on the Aboriginal stockman who had hunted those kids down all those years ago. The stockman had found her again decades later, this time himself to say, 'Sorry.' And remarkably, extraordinarily, she had forgiven him.[35]

In this recounting, Nanna Fejo's particular experience becomes an allegory for the Reconciliation of the nation – all losses are remedied by the return to family, all losses are now in the past, and most important, there has been forgiveness and resolution. The stockman's apology is graciously accepted, anticipating and modelling the response that Rudd hopes for his own, national Apology. This is a familiar pattern in the shaping of testimonies – writing of *Bringing Them Home*, Orford argues that the Report's narrative begins with the transgressions of violence and removal, and ends with the resolution of obligations, and with stable families, 'where all are sorted back into their proper places and all debts are paid'.[36] She notes that many people found that there was no home to return to, and that they could not recover their old identity or community, so that 'the text is haunted by the stories of children who cannot go home'.[37] These losses that cannot be recovered are present in the testimonies, but are not prominent in the Report's final recommendations[38] – and indeed, the genocidal practices, and colonisation in general, have set in motion losses that can never be recovered.

In the Apology, these losses are also ignored – but the move is more extreme, in comparison to *Bringing Them Home*, because the testimonies of these unresolved losses are not included in the Apology. The fragments drawn from Nanna Fejo's story shape an account of past injustice and violence that puts this violence firmly in the past, makes a break with it, and then looks to the future. Indeed,

35 Ibid.
36 Anne Orford, above n 12, 870–871.
37 Ibid, 871.
38 Ibid, 872.

Rudd's Apology proceeds to describe a future that 'embraces all Australians'.[39] It flattens out history, and asserts that Aboriginal and non-indigenous Australians hold equal positions with respect to both the past and the future. A number of clauses in the Apology open with reference to 'a future', and there are a number of statements that gesture towards the closing of the past, symbolically, with the discursive act of Apology. Rudd says, 'The time has now come for the nation to turn a new page in Australia's history by righting the wrongs of the past and so moving forward with confidence to the future.'[40] By 'righting the wrongs of the past', Rudd refers to the Apology itself – a discursive response that is not supported by a reparations scheme. Rudd proceeds to say that a 'new page in the history of our great continent can now be written', a future in which 'all Australians' determine to 'close the gap' between Indigenous and non-Indigenous Australians, a future based on 'mutual responsibility'. 'Doing justice' means empathising, apologising, and focusing on the future.

What we see in the Australian imaginary is an emphasis not on entire testimonies but on myths that instrumentalise fragments of testimonies into larger narratives. Stolen Generations' testimonies have had the paradoxical characteristic of being essentially concerned with the expression of the particular experience of the testimonial subject, while, at the same time, they have been framed by meta-narratives that generalise these particularities. The individual testimonies actually tell multiple stories, and challenge state, legal and cultural narratives in a number of ways, but they have been framed as part of larger stories that follow much more limited paths, and which encourage the audience to respond in prescribed ways. In these contexts, the testimonies are no longer encountered as testimonies of particular experience, strictly *as* testimony, but as captured fragments that are instrumentalised for state (and other) purposes.

The consequences of misreading genre: the emergent figure of the bystander

Most public encounters with Stolen Generations projects break the laws of genre – political and legal relations become sentimental fantasies. In his book *The Beast and the Sovereign*, Derrida writes of the dangerous consequences of this kind of category misrecognition:

> in the prevalent or hegemonic tradition of the political, a political discourse, and above all a political action, should in no case come under the category of the fabular, of that type of simulacrum called fabular . . . For, as its Latin name indicates, a fable is always and before all else speech – *for, fari*, is to

39 Kevin Rudd, above n 32.
40 Ibid.

> speak, to say, to celebrate . . . *fabula* is first of all something said, a familiar piece of speech, a conversation, and then a mythical narrative without historical knowledge . . . in any case a fiction that claims to teach us something . . . a pretend knowing, a false knowing, a simulacrum of knowing, a mask of knowing.[41]

And so, Derrida asks, what happens at these moments of failure to read properly, in which politics is 'constituted or even instituted by something fabular . . . by that fictive modality of "storytelling"?'[42] He replies that the effects are devastating, and go beyond 'discursive operations' to 'determine the political actions, military operations, killings, so-called acts of war or of terrorism . . .'[43]

The problem with the public's connection to Stolen Generations' harms is that not only do we live with troubling myths, but we also have a troubled relation to those myths. We live within an ideological structure that Derrida describes as an 'empire of the fable'[44] – where politics and laws are animated by specific imaginaries, but where these processes are disguised, along with their animating powers. These representational habits have produced the 'becoming-fabulous of political action and discourse'.[45] One effect is that 'Death and suffering, which are not fabular, are yet carried off and inscribed in the affabulatory score'.[46] We relate affectively to suffering, but there is a sense of unreality to this encounter. What is needed are interventions to transform these encounters to those that would have political and legal effects – to transform the encounter from one of fantasy to one that is engaged with the material suffering of survivors.

Significantly, the sentimental genre disciplines the audience into a particular *mode* of response: these testimonies are experienced as 'scenes of suffering' rather than as 'scenes of injustice',[47] thereby foreclosing legal and political interventions. According to Meister,[48] making pain readable through melodrama protects beneficiaries by 'neutralizing' the threat posed by victims: 'the victim's grief is now disconnected from their sense of grievance'.[49] Meister argues that previously, when suffering registered in the political domain, the dominant narrative was that of a struggle for justice against perpetrators, with the idea that this fight would continue until the perpetrators were vanquished.[50] But in the melodrama, it is neither the victim nor the perpetrator but rather the *beneficiary* who becomes

41 Jacques Derrida, *The Beast and the Sovereign* (University of Chicago Press, 2009) 35.
42 Ibid.
43 Ibid.
44 Ibid, 5.
45 Ibid, 36.
46 Ibid.
47 Rosanne Kennedy, above n 19, 270.
48 Robert Meister, above n 30, 66–67.
49 Robert Meister, above n 30, 70.
50 Ibid, 8–30.

the main figure who is addressed and interpellated through the melodrama, who 'can understand themselves as bystanders who are capable of feeling compassion without fear'.[51] The role of the audience is to feel, and to feel that what they are feeling is right, without being confronted in any significant way, such as by experiencing a sense of complicity in an act of injustice.[52] Reconciliation is aimed at ending violence, rather than encouraging a struggle for justice. Applying Meister's analysis to the Australian context, these aesthetic relations produce the Australian nation as a community of bystanders and beneficiaries regarding the harms of the past, with non-Aboriginal Australians interpellated into a relationship with Aboriginal Australians through their demonstrations of bystander compassion, rather than through responsible and responsive action.

The melodrama genre also determines the temporality of the justice offered. Meister argues that the logic of the melodrama is one of 'buying more time' for beneficiaries, buying more time for them 'after evil' but 'before justice'.[53] In the Australian context, the narrative arc of the removal of Aboriginal children ends in reconciliation and closure, with the painful effects, along with responsibility, located in the past. Orford contends that transitional justice processes such as *Bringing Them Home* are '*centrally* concerned with temporality' and how this temporality relates to questions of responsibility.[54] *Bringing Them Home*'s narrative of tracing a journey home, suggesting that all journeys and losses return to the same place, imposes closure on a process that necessarily cannot (and should not) be closed.[55] This temporality is reinforced through the emphasis upon the figure of the child, which tends to be focused upon in the sections of Stolen Generations' testimonies that are taken up in the public sphere, such as Rudd's use of Nanna Nungala Fejo's story in the Apology speech, at the expense of narratives of the present-day suffering of adult survivors. Suffering is perceived to attach to the child who suffered in the past, whose experiences are foregrounded at the expense of the adult who suffers in the present, and whose present suffering would otherwise support a claim for present responsibility.

Reading against the grain of sentimentality

Reading testimony as genre is helpful in thinking through the ways in which, since *Bringing Them Home*,[56] certain HREOC recommendations have been taken up in the public sphere, (such as the National Apology, and discourses of healing),

51 Ibid, 63–64.
52 Ibid, 70.
53 Ibid, 13.
54 Anne Orford, above n 12, 880 (emphasis added).
55 Ibid, 883.
56 National Inquiry into the Separation of Aboriginal and Torres Strait Islander Children from Their Families, above n 1, 308–309.

while other, more political and rights-based approaches have fallen away (such as a national reparations scheme and human rights-based discourses). In response, we need to promote new literacies of public engagement, especially literacies in genre and form. We need to promote the public's understanding of the ways in which these forms ultimately determine questions of politics and justice. The problem of sentimental reading is thereby turned back productively against itself – through a reading against its grain.

We have seen, above, how sentimental readers experience a certain kind of authority when encountering testimonies – an authority which obscures the political and juridical claims of Stolen Generations' testimonies, and vests the reader with perceived moral benefits. Each reading experience further reinforces this authority, strengthening the reader's position as both beneficiary and bystander. The claim of this chapter is that more attention needs to be paid to the practices people engage in their encounters with legal and political processes. More specifically, the claim is that closer attention needs to be paid to genre, and the ways in which certain public, aesthetic projects interpellate audiences towards affective engagements, at the expense of legal and political engagements. The nature of the public's encounter with testimony can be changed by encouraging people to encounter testimonies in new ways: training the public to be aware of the effects of genre, and of category misrecognition, and encouraging an understanding of the different effects and claims of affective, political and legal domains. In particular, this practice would foreground the role of the reader as the beneficiary of political, social and economic benefits, and the ways in which particular reading experiences reinforce, rather than challenge, this position. In the context of Stolen Generations' testimonies, this involves bringing out aspects of the testimonies that have not been foregrounded in state myths and public projects: in particular, the evidence of state practices, and of structural and systemic racism. A significant intervention can be made by focusing on those aspects of testimonies that describe the creation of documentary state archives and the pursuit of policies that were designed to assimilate Indigenous subjects, rather than stories that focus on the scenes and experiences of removal and suffering.

The framing narratives in *Bringing Them Home* focus on the scene of removal, whose significance depends upon subsequent legal or social recognition.[57] This has the effect of separating the event of removal from its ongoing context, and creates a false distance between removal and the wider policies of past and present. Policies regarding the Stolen Generations are better understood as a series of ongoing practices.[58] Narratives of the continuing rupture of Aboriginal lives are important – narratives that show the ways in which this suffering is

57 Anne Orford, above n 12, 870–871.

58 See Anne Orford, above n 12; Anna Haebich, above n 18.

not 'historical' for those who have survived, but present-day, and interrelated with current structural racism and gendered harms.

The new *The Stolen Generations' Testimonies* website provides an opportunity to shape encounters that encourage these new literacies – and these new literacies should also be encouraged in projects leading up the anniversaries of *Bringing Them Home* and the Apology. I would like to outline here a number of ways in which the careful framing of these online testimonies could encourage different encounters not only with the testimonies themselves, but with the history of the Stolen Generations' meta-narratives and myths that have arisen through and around the testimonies. These layered encounters could encourage the public's understanding of the history and politics of the framing narratives within which testimonies have been received, and perhaps, also, the conscious development of new meta-narratives as a strategy of intervention – meta-narratives that thematise the relationship of oral testimony to the states' documentary archives, and which bring out the roles that state archives have played in the historical and contemporary lives of Aboriginal people. There is a need to bring out and emphasise narratives within the testimonies that speak to the significance of oral testimony as against the historical privileging of the documentary record – that this is not merely a technical issue, but one concerned with justice.

As will be described below, testimonies of encounter with the government file, and the life of the file in the lives of Aboriginal survivors, are important in generating a meta-narrative of responsibility. These narratives tell the story of state power, state coercion and duplicity, and the importance of testimony in the face of the documentary record. They tell of the agency of the documentary record and its 'doubly wicked' effects: first, the role of the record in falsely documenting the occasion for removal (such as neglect or parental consent), and then subsequently at the moment of judgment in the courts, creating a barrier to challenging the reasons for removal.[59]

Another intervention made possible by this emphasis on the government file concerns the law's role in affirming problematic stories of removal. One of the issues considered by the court in *Cubillo* was the role of the consent by the mother of Peter Gunner, one of the applicants. Essentially, the Commonwealth sought to re-characterise the act of removal as consensual and authorised by the mother. The government presented a document with a thumbprint on it, purportedly that of Peter Gunner's mother, as evidence that Gunner's mother had consented to his removal. O'Loughlin J found that the documents reflected Gunner's mother's informed consent. In doing so, O'Loughlin J failed to adequately acknowledge the power disparity between the government agency and Aboriginal persons as well as the wider historical and social context in which many Aboriginal parents, such as Topsy Gunner, were not literate in

59 See Honni Van Rijswijk and Thalia Anthony, above n 14.

English,[60] and were therefore unlikely to have understood the content and implications of the form on which her thumbprint appears. The case perpetuates a harmful story: that mothers consented to the removal of their children.

By contrast, in the *Trevorrow* Cases, the South Australian courts expressed a distrust of the documentary record relating to parental consent. The Court noted:

> when necessary, in the perceived interests of a child, the APB [Aborigines Protection Board] would place a child in an institution or with a foster family without parental consent, using a pretence of power (which undoubtedly would have been effective) and, if appropriate, using an element of bluff or deception.[61]

Such findings would seem to be good news for survivors of the Stolen Generations, and would seem to indicate that courts in the future might look carefully and properly (contextually) at documentary archives. But the success of Bruce Trevorrow's case in 2010 has not led to numbers of claims on behalf of members of the Stolen Generations, and indeed, the latest claim since *Trevorrow*, heard in Western Australia in 2013, has failed.[62] The problem is that Bruce Trevorrow's case is unique, in that no document was found in his records that indicated his parent's formal consent, and the file also provided evidence that his mother, Thora Karpany, did not consent to his removal (including letters in which she requested Bruce's return). This documentary support is not available where parents signed documents prior to removal (such as in Topsy Gunner's case) but might not have understood what they were signing, or did so under duress, or as a result of the processes of 'bluff or deception' noted by the court in *Trevorrow*. While *Trevorrow* preferred the claimant's evidence where the documentary record was not contradicted by oral evidence (and even supported by his mother's letters), there has not yet been a case in which the court has preferred a claimant's oral evidence where that has come into conflict with the documentary record – where, for example, there has been formal consent, but this consent was made under duress, or in situations where the parent did not understand what they were consenting to.

The online project includes a number of testimonies that do the work of countering these problematic narratives that have circulated in the legal cases, and which speak to the role of the government record. These sections of the testimonies could be further brought out and thematised through new framing narratives within the online archive. Eileen Moseley relates in her testimony how she and her mother were taken to the welfare office and her mother was

60 Chris Cunneen and Julia Grix, above n 16, 14.

61 *South Australia v Lampard-Trevorrow* (2010) 106 SASR 331, 362, [133].(Doyle CJ, Duggan and White JJ).

62 *Collard v The State of Western Australia [No 4]* (2013) WASC 455.

made to 'sign a lot of papers'.[63] Her mother was illiterate, and didn't know what she was signing, but they made her put a 'cross' on all the papers. Then they took Eileen to St Mary's. So far, the courts have not dealt well with these kinds of cases, and have shown an inability to look behind the formal records of government archives, to critically examine the circumstances in which consent was given.

The online project documents the fact that mothers often wrote to the authorities to beg for the return of their children, but these letters were ignored or responded to with threats. Lester Maher,[64] Vince Wenberg[65] and Gus Wenberg,[66] all speak of finding letters in their files, from their mothers, fathers and grandparents, begging for the return of the children. After her children were taken, Debra Hocking's mother Jean wrote again and again to ask for them to be returned:

> Dear sir, I am writing once again for you to consider letting me have my babies. Please sir if there's anything else I have to do to prove myself could you tell me what it is. I'm just waiting to give my whole life in making up to my babies for the past but sir the waiting is almost unbearable. I have paid dearly for my mistakes a hundred times over by being parted from my children . . . [67]

Jean Hocking's letter had no effect.

In her online testimony, Debra Hocking recounts that her mother's attempts to try to preserve her Aboriginal heritage were coded as 'neglect'. Her Aboriginality, and attempts to preserve her Aboriginal culture, were at the heart of the reasons behind the removal of her children. Debra Hocking says:

> I look at my Government file and look at how it all happened and how tragic it must've been for her and how she wanted to continue her culture and the authorities said no, you actually can't do that because if you do – if you continue to, you know, raise your children in this way we'd say it's neglect.[68]

63 Eileen Moseley, *Testimony*, Stolen Generation Testimonies http://stolengenerationstestimonies.com/index.php/testimonies/1015.html.

64 Lester Maher, *Testimony*, Stolen Generation Testimonies http://stolengenerationstestimonies.com/index.php/testimonies/983.html.

65 Vince Wenberg, *Testimony*, Stolen Generation Testimonies http://stolengenerationstestimonies.com/index.php/testimonies/1000.html.

66 Gus Wenberg, *Testimony*, Stolen Generation Testimonies http://stolengenerationstestimonies.com/index.php/testimonies/999.html.

67 Debra Hocking, *Testimony*, Stolen Generation Testimonies http://stolengenerationstestimonies.com/index.php/testimonies/973.html.

68 Ibid.

Hocking's mother Jean tried to raise her family under constant monitoring, and amidst threats of the children being taken away:

> My older sister said, she said 'Oh it was just awful,' because, you know, there'd be – they had to keep all the curtains open and the minute they saw a car pull up, you know, she said she'd run around and she'd try and make sure that everything – there was always something that she hadn't done. She was so scared because she knew they found anything, anything – a box of matches in the wrong place. 'What happens if the kids get hold of them?! You know Jean. You've been told about this. You know you've got to put that away. You know you've got to have more food in your cupboard. Otherwise we're going to have to take your children you know.' Poor Jean. There she was. Poor old mum, you know, running around. Making sure everything was alright.[69]

The experiences and policies behind the Stolen Generations, and the ways in which government and social policies have determined what counts as history, are important questions of social justice. A significant source of trouble has been what counts as the evidence upon which the past is judged. The removal policies generated their own documentary trail, often found to be problematic, and which is contradicted by the oral testimony of a number of survivors and their families.[70] There is a way in which the government's documentary archives have generated their own force, their own law, their own version of the truth, and this in turn has put harmful stories into circulation. These stories are taken up by the law, which not only judges claimants negatively against these stories, but in turn puts into the public sphere problematic representations of the Stolen Generations. The documentary archive is a force that survivors of the Stolen Generations have had to deal with, and these online testimonies not only counter the narratives of the documentary archive, but they also provide moments of meta-awareness, through their narration of encounters with the state's documentary records. These moments re-situate the documentary archive within a wider, more critical, context of meaning.

Temporality and responsibility

The *temporality* of the encounter with testimonies also needs to be foregrounded. The framing narratives of Stolen Generations' experiences need to connect the

69 Ibid.

70 See Honni Van Rijswijk and Thalia Anthony, above n 14; Ann Genovese, 'Metaphor of Redemption, Myths of State: Historical Accountability in Luhrmann's *Australia* and *Trevorrow v South Australia*' (2011) 20 *Griffith Law Review* 67.

practices that led to the Stolen Generations with ongoing, contemporary political and legal relations. These testimonies need to be connected to questions of Aboriginal sovereignty, and Aboriginal law, since the project of assimilation in a very deep sense, constituted breaches of Aboriginal sovereignty, authority and laws.

The Stolen Generations' testimonies have a different meaning now from what they held before 2008, which saw not only the Apology but also the Labor government's continuation of the Northern Territory National Emergency Response Intervention.[71] Framing narratives are needed to read these testimonies in the context of the Northern Territory Intervention. The Intervention was initially implemented in 2007 by the Conservative Howard government, through a set of laws that permitted the seizure of local community land leases by the federal government, the deployment of the army into Northern Territory communities, the use of extra police powers, and the quarantining of welfare benefits. This regime ended in 2012, when it was replaced by a similar set of laws implemented by the Labor government.[72] The occasion for the Intervention was the publication of the *Little Children are Sacred Report*,[73] which followed an Inquiry commissioned by the Territory's Inquiries Act. The Board of Inquiry's task was to, among other things, 'Examine the extent, nature and factors contributing to sexual abuse of Aboriginal children, with a particular focus on unreported incidents of such abuse',[74] and to 'Consider how the NT Government

71 *Northern Territory National Emergency Response Act 2007* (Cth) ('NTNERA'); *Family, Community Services, Indigenous Affairs and Other Legislation Amendment (Northern Territory National Emergency Response and Other Measures) Act 2007* (Cth); *Social Security and Other Legislation Amendment (Welfare Payment Reform) Act 2007* (Cth); *Families, Community Services and Indigenous Affairs and Other Legislation Amendment (Northern Territory National Emergency Response and Other Measures) Act 2007* (Cth); *Appropriation (Northern Territory National Emergency Response) Act (No. 1) 2007* (Cth) *and Appropriation (Northern Territory National Emergency Response) Act (No. 2) 2007* (Cth). I use the phrase 'the Northern Territory Intervention' or 'the Intervention' to refer to this regime.

72 When the Northern Territory Intervention came to the end of its five-year period in July 2012, it was immediately replaced by the *Stronger Futures in the Northern Territory Act 2012* (Cth) and related laws: *Stronger Futures in the Northern Territory Act 2013* (Cth); *Social Security Legislation Amendment Act 2012* (Cth). These laws will operate for a ten-year period: *Stronger Futures* s118. Stronger Futures is broken up into a number of Parts that administer aspects of the lives of Aboriginal citizens in the Northern Territory. 'Tackling alcohol abuse' (Part 2) is aimed at 'reducing alcohol-related harm to those Aboriginal people'; 'Land reform' (Part 3), is 'aimed at facilitating the granting of rights and interests, and promoting economic development'; 'Food security' (Part 4), and some miscellaneous matters (Part 5) are also covered. The legislation includes income management schemes, and provisions for the suspension of parents' welfare payments if children's attendance rate at school is considered unacceptable (*Social Security Legislation Amendment Act 2012* (Cth) (Sch 2)). I use the term 'Stronger Futures' to refer to this regime.

73 Board of Inquiry into the Protection of Aboriginal Children from Sexual Abuse, Government of the Northern Territory, *Ampe Akelyernemane Meke Mekarle 'Little Children are Sacred'* (2007).

74 Ibid.

can help support communities to effectively prevent and tackle child sexual abuse'.[75] The subsequent report did not express the problem as an 'emergency', but it did find that child sexual abuse was an issue that required urgent action. A number of earlier reports had also documented child abuse and violence against women as being significant problems in Aboriginal communities in the Northern Territory – communities that were also dealing with poverty, poor health, alcoholism and racism.[76] However, the Northern Territory Intervention and Stronger Futures legislation introduced measures that went well beyond the issue of child abuse, to affect land rights, welfare benefits and access to services. The Inquiry's ninety-seven recommendations included an emphasis on community consultation, family support services, education, employment and housing but most of these recommendations were not implemented in the subsequent legislation. The Intervention has been the subject of criticism from a number of human rights organisations, including the United Nations.[77] It is also worth noting that levels of the sexual abuse of children are in fact higher in several other Australian jurisdictions than in the Northern Territory.[78] In *Little Children Are Sacred*, there is an eerie but repressed evocation of the state's actions that were documented ten years earlier in *Bringing Them Home*.

75 Ibid.

76 See Chris Cunneen and Terri Libesman, *A Review of International Models for Indigenous Child Protection* (2002) NSW Department of Community Services; Aboriginal and Torres Strait Islander Social Justice Commissioner, 'Ending Violence and Abuse in Aboriginal and Torres Strait Islander Communities – Key Issues' (Overview Paper, Human Rights and Equal Opportunities Commission ('HREOC'), June 2006); NSW Aboriginal Child Sexual Assault Taskforce, 2006, 'Breaking the Silence: Creating the Future, Addressing Child Sexual Assault in Aboriginal Communities in NSW' (Report, NSW Premier's Department, 2006); Queensland Crime Commission and Queensland Police Service, 2000, 'Child Sexual Abuse in Queensland: The Nature and Extent: Volume 1. Project Axis' (Report, Queensland Crime Commission and Queensland Police Service, June 2000); Sue Gordon, Kay Hallahan and Darrell Henry, 'Putting the Picture Together, Inquiry into the Response by Government Agencies into Complaints of Family Violence and Child Abuse in Aboriginal Communities' (Report, Department of the Premier and Cabinet Western Australia, 31 July 2002).

77 See, e.g., Amnesty International, *Discriminatory Aspects of the NTER Yet to be Addressed* (4 February 2009) www.amnesty.org.au/news/comments/20169; Intervention Rollback Action Group, 'Rollback the Intervention' (2009) http://rollbacktheintervention.wordpress.com; James Anaya, 'Observations on the Northern Territory Emergency Response in Australia' *Report by the United Nations Special Rapporteur on the Situation of Human Rights and Fundamental Freedoms of Indigenous People* (United Nations Human Rights Council, 2010). For a feminist analysis of the Intervention, and an historical contextualisation of its provisions in comparison to the earlier *Aborigines Protection Acts*, see Nicole Watson, 'The Northern Territory Emergency Response – Has It Really Improved the Lives of Aboriginal Women and Children?' (2011) 35 *Australian Feminist Law Journal* 147.

78 See Australian Institute for Health and Welfare, *Australia's Health No 10* (Government Printer, 2006) cited in Desmond Manderson, 'Not Yet: Aboriginal People and the Deferral of the Rule of Law' (2008) 29 *ARENA Journal* 219. See especially, Manderson, 241.

The Intervention policies that make living conditions more difficult for Aboriginal people, are supported by a narrative of harm-prevention, of protecting Indigenous people from themselves – fables that resonate with the policies documented in *Bringing Them Home*.

In their recent, detailed analysis of the Intervention, Jon Altman and Susie Russell note that 'it is impossible to say' whether the results of the Intervention have been positive, negative or mixed.[79] They argue that 'the Intervention had no foundational, evidence-based policy logic, and no baseline against which to measure improvements',[80]and that, despite 'extraordinary levels of monitoring, review and evaluation . . . the absence of an overarching evaluation strategy has resulted in a fragmented and confused approach'.[81] In fact, they conclude that the evaluations of the Intervention themselves seem to act as another state technique for the administration of Aboriginal people.[82] As Irene Watson argues (2009, p.1), past and present violence against Aboriginal people has been read as 'beneficial', as acts of 'saving them from themselves'. We therefore need techniques to promote public awareness of the particularity of state law's assertions of authority, of its ever-changing and mobile strategies. One way of fulfilling this responsibility and responsiveness is through the development of the public's critical reading practices that focus on the role of the representation of violence in the production of sovereignties and legalities – an awareness that could be promoted by connecting the Stolen Generations' testimonies explicitly with the Northern Territory Intervention, in framing narratives that contextualise the testimonies regarding past practices with those of the present.

The responsibility here is to re-animate legal and state archives, to parse legal and state imaginaries, and to re-imagine, even re-script meta-narratives of responsibility and politics. In the case of the Stolen Generations' testimonies, this would mean a project of bringing the testimonies in conversation with, and in confrontation with, the documentary government archive, to produce a meta-narrative of responsibility and accountability that is present-time and continuing. The task is to re-train public sensibilities and reading practices to change the nature of the encounter, and embed testimonies in counter-narratives that thematise not only the stories of removal and its effects, but the history and politics of the testimonial form itself – and its capture into grand, sentimental national narratives. The task would be to bring out narratives in the testimonies

79 Jon Altman and Susie Russell, 'Too Much "Dreaming": Evaluations of the Northern Territory National Emergency Response Intervention 2007–2012' (2012) 3 *Evidence Base* 1, 3.

80 Ibid, 18.

81 Ibid, 1.

82 Ibid, 1. See also Jon Altman's detailed analysis of the Intervention, spanning over 150 pages, in which he documents results that include an increase in violence, malnutrition and truancy in particular communities following the Intervention: Jon Altman, 'Arguing the Intervention' (2013) 14 *Journal of Indigenous Policy*, see especially 79.

beyond scenes of child removal, to emphasise narratives of encounter with the government file, and the life of the file in the lives of Aboriginal survivors. Read this way, the testimonies reveal contemporary politics and relations to social justice projects, rather than being relegated to questions of the past.

Testimonies have been captured as part of state archival practices, but they can be recovered and reclaimed through certain practices and encounters. This chapter has outlined the ethics and politics of such an encounter, describing ways to promote awareness of form and temporality that are important in drawing attention to the politics of testimony, and its significant role in the limited justice that has been provided to survivors of the Stolen Generations. This critical intervention arises through the deployment of reading and interpretive techniques that draw attention to the ways in which the Stolen Generations' testimonies have interpellated non-Aboriginal subjects into positions of non-responsibility. The goal is to find ways of re-framing the testimonies, of drawing attention to the means of production of testimonies, as well as to the experience of encountering them. These techniques seek to provide a way to re-make the public's ethical and aesthetic relations into modes of political encounter, and to develop those relations so that they promote the goal of social justice.

Bibliography

Aboriginal and Torres Strait Islander Social Justice Commissioner, 'Ending Violence and Abuse in Aboriginal and Torres Strait Islander Communities — Key Issues' (Overview Paper, Human Rights and Equal Opportunities Commission ('HREOC'), June 2006)

Altman, Jon, 'Arguing the Intervention' (2013) 14 *Journal of Indigenous Policy*

Altman, Jon and Susie Russell, 'Too Much "Dreaming": Evaluations of the Northern Territory National Emergency Response Intervention 2007–2012' (2012) 3 *Evidence Base* 1

Amnesty International, *Discriminatory Aspects of the NTER Yet to be Addressed* (4 February 2009) www.amnesty.org.au/news/comments/20169

Anaya, James, 'Observations on the Northern Territory Emergency Response in Australia', *Report by the United Nations Special Rapporteur on the Situation of Human Rights and Fundamental Freedoms of Indigenous People* (United Nations Human Rights Council, 2010).

Attwood, Bain, 'The Stolen Generations and Genocide: Robert Manne's In Denial: The Stolen Generations and the Right' (2001) 25 *Aboriginal History* 163

Australian Institute for Health and Welfare, *Australia's Health No 10* (Government Printer, 2006) cited in Desmond Manderson, 'Not Yet: Aboriginal People and the Deferral of the Rule of Law' (2008) 29 *ARENA Journal* 219

Berlant, Lauren, 'The Subject of True Feeling: Pain, Privacy and Politics' in Austin Sarat and Thomas Kearns (eds), *Cultural Pluralism, Identity Politics and the Law* (University of Michigan Press, 2000) 49

Board of Inquiry into the Protection of Aboriginal Children from Sexual Abuse, Government of the Northern Territory, *Ampe Akelyernemane Meke Mekarle 'Little Children are Sacred'* (2007)

Commonwealth, National Inquiry into the Separation of Aboriginal and Torres Strait Islander Children from Their Families, *Bringing Them Home: Report of the National Inquiry into the Separation of Aboriginal and Torres Strait Islander Children from Their Families* (1997) ('*Bringing Them Home*')

Commonwealth, *Parliamentary Debates*, House of Representatives, 13 February 2008, 167 (Kevin Rudd, Prime Minister)

Cunneen, Chris and Julia Grix, 'The Limitations of Litigation in Stolen Generations Cases' (Research Discussion Paper No 15, Australian Institute of Aboriginal and Torres Strait Islander Studies, 2004)

Cunneen, Chris and Terri Libesman, *A Review of International Models for Indigenous Child Protection* (2002) NSW Department of Community Services

Derrida, Jacques, *The Beast and the Sovereign* (University of Chicago Press, 2009)

Frow, John, 'Discursive Justice' (2001) 100 *The South Atlantic Quarterly* 331

Genovese, Ann, 'Metaphor of Redemption, Myths of State: Historical Accountability in Luhrmann's *Australia* and *Trevorrow v South Australia*' (2011) 20 *Griffith Law Review* 67

Gordon, Sue, Kay Hallahan and Darrell Henry, 'Putting the Picture Together, Inquiry into the Response by Government Agencies into Complaints of Family Violence and Child Abuse in Aboriginal Communities' (Report, Department of the Premier and Cabinet Western Australia, 31 July 2002)

Haebich, Anna, *Broken Circles: Fragmenting Indigenous Families, 1800 – 2000* (Fremantle Arts Centre Press, 2000)

Howard, John, 'Practical Reconciliation' in Michelle Grattan (ed.), *Reconciliation: Essays in Australia Reconciliation* (Bookman Press, 2000) 90

Intervention Rollback Action Group, 'Rollback the Intervention' (2009) http://rollbacktheintervention.wordpress.com

Kennedy, Rosanne, 'Subversive Witnessing: Mediating Indigenous Testimony in Australian Cultural and Legal Institutions' (2008) 36 *Women's Studies Quarterly* 58

Kennedy, Rosanne, 'An Australian Archive of Feelings' (2011) 26 *Australian Feminist Studies* 257

Kennedy, Rosanne, Lynee Bell and Julia Emberley, 'Decolonising Testimony: On the Possibilities and Limits of Witnessing' (2009) 15 *Humanities Research* 1

Luker, Trish, '"Postcolonising" Amnesia in the Discourse of Reconciliation: The Void in the Law's Response to the Stolen Generations' (2005) 22 *Australian Feminist Law Journal* 67

Meister, Robert, *After Evil: A Politics of Human Rights* (Columbia University Press, 2011)

Mookherjee, Nayanika, Nigel Rappert, Lisette Josephides, Ghassan Hage, Lindi Renier Todd and Gillian Cowlishaw, 'The Ethics of Apology: A Set of Commentaries' (2009) 29 *Critique of Anthropology* 345

Motha, Stewart and Karin Van Marle, 'Introduction' in Karin Van Marle and Stewart Motha (eds), *Genres of Critique*, (Sun Press, 2013) 17

NSW Aboriginal Child Sexual Assault Taskforce, 2006, 'Breaking the Silence: Creating the Future, Addressing Child Sexual Assault in Aboriginal Communities in NSW' (Report, NSW Premier's Department, 2006)

Orford, Anne, 'Commissioning the Truth' (2006) 15 *Columbia Journal of Gender and Law* 851

Queensland Crime Commission and Queensland Police Service, 2000, 'Child Sexual Abuse in Queensland: The Nature and Extent: Volume 1. Project Axis' (Report, Queensland Crime Commission and Queensland Police Service, June 2000)

Reilly, Alex, 'How Sorry Are We? The Limits of the Apology to the Stolen Generation' (2009) 34 *Alternative Law Journal* 97

Stolen Generations' Testimonies, Stolen Generations' Testimonies Foundation http://stolengenerationstestimonies.com

Van Rijswijk, Honni and Thalia Anthony, 'Can the Common Law Adjudicate Historical Suffering?' (2012) 36 *Melbourne University Law Review* 618

Watson, Nicole, 'The Northern Territory Emergency Response – Has It Really Improved the Lives of Aboriginal Women and Children?' (2011) 35 *Australian Feminist Law Journal* 147

Chapter 5

Border crossings

The transnational career of the television crime drama

Sue Turnbull

It begins, as so many television crime series do, with a body. This time, it is that of a woman found in the middle of the bridge spanning the Øresund Strait connecting Denmark to Southern Sweden. As we watch in the pre-title sequence, a car drives onto the bridge, the bridge lights go out and an unidentifiable person carefully places the body on a yellow line drawn to demarcate the border between Denmark and Sweden. When the detectives from the Swedish and Danish police arrive, Saga Norén from Malmo in Sweden and Martin Rohde from Copenhagen in Denmark, they are presented with the problem of deciding to whom the case belongs. Because the woman is immediately recognised as a well-known Swedish politician, Norén claims the body and the case. However, when the forensic team attempt to move the corpse, they discover that it has been cut in half. Even more puzzling, as is discovered in the subsequent forensic examination, the two halves don't match. The lower torso is that of a Danish prostitute who disappeared some two years earlier. The investigators are thus confronted with two murders that will force them to cross back and forth not only over the bridge, but also between two different legal jurisdictions.

The resulting Danish/Swedish co-production, *Broen/Bron*, aka *The Bridge* in English translations (DR1, SVT1 2011-), has been viewed and critically acclaimed in many different TV markets across the globe, although not by the kinds of viewing figures garnered by the American series *CSI*, which since its first appearance in 2001 has been touted as 'the most watched television series in the world'.[1] Nevertheless, since its original screening on both Danish and Swedish TV, *The Bridge* has (at time of writing in 2014) reportedly been shown in more than 174 different territories, achieving global distribution through DVD sales and downloads.[2] While the ratings for *Broen/Bron* in Denmark and Sweden

1 Sarah Bibel, '"CSI: Crime Scene Investigation" is the Most-Watched Show in the World' (Press Release, 14 June 2012).

2 Clive James, 'Clive James: The End of The Bridge? I Might Die of Despair' *The Telegraph* (London), 1 February 2014.

during its first showing in September 2011 were relatively low (under a million), when the first season of the series screened in the UK the following year, it fared rather better on the multi-channel station BBC 4 and on the BBC's Higher definition (HD) channel, without attracting the same kind of cult following as the earlier imported series, *The Killing (Forbrydelsen* DR1 2007–2012*)*. The series was also shown in Germany on the public service station ZDF from 18 March, as well as Poland, Brazil and Israel. So impressed was the Norwegian network NRK by the show, that they declared a desire to be involved in the second series. However, as Jensen has argued,[3] the further the series has travelled from its point of origin, the smaller and more niche the audience has tended to become. For example, in Australia, *The Bridge*, both the first and second seasons, was shown on the Special Broadcasting Service (SBS) with its remit to reflect to Australia's multicultural population, a public service network which attracts only a small share of the total television audience as measured by the ratings.[4]

The success of *The Bridge* as a television show with a global audience points to the recent rise in popularity of 'Scandi-noir' or 'Nordic-noir' in both crime fiction and on television. This success has been much commented upon in the international press and has become the focus of academic study.[5] In tracing the origins of this 'new wave' of global crime fiction and screen entertainment, Barry Forshaw[6] has suggested that long before well known Swedish crime writers Stieg Larsson created the character of Lisbeth Salander in *The Girl with the Dragon Tattoo*, the first of the Millenium series published in 2005, and long before Henning Mankell introduced Inspector Wallander in *Faceless Killers* in 1991 (English translation 1997), there had been other Scandinavian crime writers who achieved international recognition – and a movie deal. Husband and wife team Maj Sjöwall and Per Wahlöö wrote ten police procedurals featuring Detective Martin Beck which embraced a left-wing critique of what Sjöwall and Wahlöö perceived as the 'venal, bureaucratic dead-end of Sweden's social democracy'.[7] Borrowing the 'realist elements of the nineteenth-century novel', Sjöwall and Wahlöö thus succeeded, according to Lee Siegel, in turning the crime novel into 'a form of social criticism'.[8] As evidence of their international recognition, the fourth book in their ten-book series, *The Laughing Policeman*

3 Pia Majbritt Jensen, 'Export Patterns and Global Impact of Danish Drama Series' *Producers and Audiences Conference*, Lund, Sweden, 20 March 2014.

4 Ien Ang, Gay Hawkins and Lamia Dabboussy, *The SBS Story: The Challenge of Cultural Diversity* (University of New South Wales Press, 2008) 3.

5 Reference to conference at Lund, February 2014.

6 Barry Forshaw, *Nordic Noir: The Pocket Essential Guide to Scandanavian Crime Fiction, Film & TV* (Oldcastle Books, 2013) 13.

7 Lee Siegel, 'Pure Evil: Jo Neshø and the Rise of Scandanavian Crime Fiction' *The New Yorker* (New York), 12 May 2014, 40.

8 Ibid, 39.

(Rosenberg, 1973), was adapted as a film for Twentieth Century Fox starring Walter Matthau and Bruce Dern. This adaptation relocated Beck to San Francisco and turned him into an American: a form of cultural appropriation which has been routinely repeated in American as well as other TV markets in the adaptation of successful television shows from 'somewhere else', especially when these are in a language other than English.

The television landscape, however, has changed dramatically since the 1970s when the free-to-air networks were the primary source of production and distribution. With the rise of pay television, satellite and digital distribution, and the associated emergence of niche channels and cable networks, it is now possible for a television crime drama in a language other than English to find an enthusiastic and receptive audience well beyond its original centre of production. As a crime drama series that has travelled far from 'home' (Denmark/Sweden), the original *Broen/Bron* has therefore been viewed with subtitles on numerous niche TV channels and on DVD. Even more significant is the fact that it has been sold as a format in order to be remade in different cultural locations. These include the border between El Paso, Texas and Juaréz in Mexico in the US adaptation of *The Bridge* (FX 2013–) and the Channel Tunnel linking England and France in the Anglo/French adaptation *The Tunnel* (Sky Atlantic/Canal+ 2013–). The transnational career of *The Bridge* thus helps to shed light on the emerging features of a rapidly evolving post-broadcast global TV environment, an environment in which people are as likely to watch a TV series on a large flat screen in their living rooms as they are to download and watch a show on their tablet or computer.

However, in the context of this collection which is devoted to 'cultural legal studies', perhaps what is most interesting about *The Bridge* as a transnational drama series are the crimes with which it deals, and the ways in which these may or may not change when the series is 'translated' as a format into another production context and cultural setting. In this sense, we can observe the way 'law' itself crosses borders. Such transnational circulation therefore begs a number of questions including: What kinds of changes are deemed necessary to the original to make this series relevant to viewers in different cultural contexts? What kinds of crime are assumed to be 'global' and cross borders such that they will be understood by international audiences? Which are assumed to be culturally specific and therefore in need of cultural adaptation and localisation? In other words: What can the transnational television crime drama series tell us about the circulation of crime (and television) in an increasingly globalised world?

The importance of 'genre'

With its origins in popular fiction, film, and radio, as well as crime in the real world, the television crime drama has an extensive and vigorous root system. This helps to explain the diversity of a genre that encompasses police procedurals, mysteries, comedy-crime, thrillers, and drama-documentary as well as its capacity for hybridity and reinvention.[9] For example, early series such as *Dragnet* in the US and *Fabian of the Yard* in the UK usually derived their storylines from 'real' cases, exhibiting both a documentary impulse in their attention to police procedure as well as the stylistic influence of film noir (a style associated with a genre of American films as identified by French critics of the 1950s). The result was a type of stylistic hybridity that might result in some jarring juxtapositions. In terms of structure, each (usually) half-hour episode would delineate the trajectory of a different case that would inevitably be 'solved' by the conclusion. As a point of closure, *Dragnet* often included both the judgment and the penalty awarded,[10] while the eponymous *Fabian of the Yard* as played by actor Bruce Seton would morph into the 'real' Inspector Fabian who would produce some memento or evidence of his own involvement in the original case as evidence of the documentary 'truth' of what we had just witnessed.[11]

For some critics of the crime drama, this neat closure was an expression of the conservative and pro-establishment ideology of the early television crime drama which American critic David Marc once described as a 'comedy of public safety': a kind of sitcom without a laugh track in which The Law is married to Chaos.[12] While Chaos might step out of line in every episode, The Law will always manage to whip her back into shape before the final commercial. This characterisation, however, can be challenged with reference to a significant number of television police procedurals and crime drama series, both before 1984 when Marc was writing and after, that have suggested that the business of policing and the maintenance of law and order are far from easy. While in Britain, early examples of this more 'realistic' take on crime can be found in early social-realist police procedurals such as *Z-Cars* (BBC 1962–1978), in the US the most commonly cited example of an early crime drama which is considered to have mirrored the messy reality of crime and policing is *Hill Street Blues* (NBC 1981–1987).

It is therefore interesting to note that in terms of how the television crime drama series has been evaluated as a genre, it would appear that those series that have taken a more critical view of law and order issues, adopting what is often described as a 'social-realist' or 'gritty' aesthetic, while avoiding any easy resolution to the problem of crime, have tended to be judged more favourably than those series which opt for narrative resolution and a more vivid visual style. Thus while a popular series such as *CSI* with its stylistic debt to *Miami Vice* (NBC

9 Sue Turnbull, *The Television Crime Drama* (Edinburgh University Press, 2014).

10 Jason Mittell, *Genre and Television: From Cop Shows to Cartoons in American Culture* (Routledge, 2004) 133.

11 Susan Sydney-Smith, *Beyond Dixon of Dock Green, Early British Police Series* (I.B. Tauris, 2002) 101.

12 David Marc, *Demographic Vistas: Televisions in American Culture* (University of Pennsylvania Press, 1984) 69.

1984–1989) might be watched by a much larger global audience, it is the niche network HBO (Home Box Office) series *The Wire* (2002–2008) in all its 'gritty realism' which is appreciated by the relatively small cultural élite whose critical judgement appears to count. While *CSI* is for the most part a series in which one or two crimes are 'solved' in the space of its 'one hour' format (around forty plus minutes allowing for ad breaks), *The Wire* embraced what has been identified as a 'long form narrative structure', dealing with a single issue or theme in each of its five seasons, each of which foregrounded a different major theme and varied in overall length from ten to thirteen episodes.[13] Arguably, the seasonal story arcs of *The Wire* thus allowed for the development of more complex characterisation and narrative structure than the more episodic series, *CSI*.

Like *The Wire*, the Danish/Swedish production of *Broen/Bron* adopted the structure of a long-form police procedural in both its first and second seasons, depicting a related series of crimes over ten episodes. In terms of style, like *The Wire*, *Broen/Bron* also embraced an aesthetic that might be described as both social-realist and 'gritty', although the opening sequence of the first episode as the killer's car drives onto the Øresund bridge uses darkness, sources of bright and neon light in ways which recall the stylistic self-consciousness of the early and original *CSI* which I have argued elsewhere has had a profound influence on the aesthetics of the TV crime drama.[14] A 'realist' and 'gritty' look, however, is also the consequence of a set of production choices requiring just as much artistry and skilful management to successfully execute as any other. Furthermore, while this is also the aesthetic adopted by the British/French adaptation, *The Tunnel*, the first season of the Mexican/American version of *The Bridge* looks very different, set as it is in the arid borderlands and darkened alleyways and interiors of Juaréz and El Paso. This version also differs in terms of form, extending to thirteen episodes that open up a new and different set of narrative possibilities in the last three episodes as will be discussed in more detail below.

Format adaptations

In his ground-breaking work on the history of TV format adaptations, Albert Moran demonstrates that the process of adaptation has been a feature of the TV landscape since the 1950s in the UK and the US, as well as in Australia, when the 'copying' of ideas was rife and unregulated.[15] However, what

13 Tiffany Potter and C W Marshall, '"I am the American Dream": Modern Urban Tragedy and the Borders of Fiction' in Tiffany Potter and C W Marshall (eds), *The Wire: Urban Decay and American Television* (Continuum International Publishing Group, 2009) 1.

14 Sue Turnbull, 'The Hook and the Look: *CSI* and the Aesthetics of the Television Crime Series' in Michael Allen (ed.), *Reading CSI: Crime Television Under the Microscope* (I.B. Tauris, 2007) 15.

15 Albert Moran, *Copy Cat TV: Globalisation, Program Formats and Cultural Identity* (University of Luton Press, 1998) x.

constitutes a format may not always be clear given that this may comprise a number of different elements.[16] In the case of a game show this might be the rules and set design, while in the case of a drama this might entail a synopsis of the narrative situation, projected storyline, and an outline of the characters.[17] In his discussion of the long and successful career of Australian television mogul, Reg Grundy, Moran identifies four different periods in the evolution of the TV format.[18] This begins with the Foundation Stage in the 1950s when formats were appropriated by competing networks and across national and international boundaries with unregulated abandon, followed by the Primitive Stage lasting until 1980 and then the Formalization Stage initiated by the American ratification of the Berne Convention on Copyright in 1988. The fourth period, the Global Stage, extends from 2000 to the present and is, according to Moran, characterised by the 'game changers' of the format trade, quiz shows such as *Who Wants to be a Millionaire?* and reality TV shows such as *Big Brother* and *Survivor.*[19]

In the case of the quiz and reality shows, as Moran has demonstrated, the value of the format is that it leaves room for the show to be customised, and indeed 'nationalised', in terms of its specific cultural setting.[20] Thus the French adapted the original Dutch *Big Brother* format into a series entitled *Loft Story* (MC 2001–2002), the point of the competition between housemates being the production of a romantic couple rather than an individual winner as was the case in the original. The French emphasis on romance and sexual attraction thus ensured that sexual activity between the contestants was both anticipated and encouraged. Meanwhile, the Australian version of the *Big Brother* format, in its first iteration on Channel 10 in 2001, proved rather more 'tame', leading to the elimination of all but the most uncontroversial (and most appealing) male character. The only evident sexual activity involved a couple cuddling under what was somewhat coyly described as the 'dancing doona'. Thus the various national versions of *Big Brother* which appeared around the world were revelatory, not just in terms of how the different production companies orchestrated the format, but also in terms of the cultural differences these adaptations revealed.[21].

Although some kinds of television shows may lend themselves easily to format adaptation, there are others which are much trickier to relocate. As I have argued elsewhere, this is particularly true of a comedy series, given that 'getting the joke' may depend on forms of cultural knowledge which are only available to

16 Ibid.
17 Ibid, 14.
18 Albert Moran, *TV Format Mogul: Reg Grundy's Transnational Career* (Intellect, 2013) 224–225.
19 Ibid, 225.
20 Moran, above n 15.
21 Ernest Mathjis and Janet Jones, *Big Brother International: Formats, Critics and Publics* (Wallflower Press, 2004).

those who know the social context well.[22] So while there have been a number of successful cultural transplants such as the British sitcom *Till Death Us Do Part* (BBC1 1965–1975) successfully reimagined as *All in the Family* (CBS 1971–1979) and more recently *The Office* (BBC2 2001–2003), the American version of which gained traction the further it diverged from the British original, as has been admirably illustrated by Jeffrey Griffin,[23] there have also been conspicuous failures such as the American adaptation of Australian-produced *Kath and Kim* (ABC 2002–2005, Seven Network 2007). In this latter instance, while the script of the first episode followed that of the original fairly closely, what was missing in the adaptation was the ironic gap between how the central characters perceived themselves (as glamorous and attractive) and how they actually appeared (as self-deluded and grotesque). In the American version, as a result of casting attractive actresses in the central roles, the ironic gap was missing and the point of much of the humour deriving from the characters' mis-recognition subsequently lost.[24]

While the transnational career of television comedy has received some attention, rather less has been devoted to that of the crime series, although cross-cultural traffic in the genre has been evident since Moran's early 'Foundation Stage'. For example, the creator of the British TV series *Z Cars* (BBC 1962–1978), Troy Kennedy Martin, acknowledged in a number of interviews the inspiration provided by the America series *Highway Patrol* (Ziv Television Productions 1955–1959) for a British series featuring policemen in patrol cars connected via radio. A telling example of a crime drama adapted during Moran's later Formalization period is the intermittent series *Cracker* (ITV 1993–1995; 1996; 2006) starring Robbie Coltrane as criminal psychologist Dr Edward 'Fitz' Fitzgerald. In 1996 an American re-versioning of the show for the ABC network transplanted the action from Manchester to Los Angeles and starred a slimmed down Robert Pastorelli.[25] This re-make, however, met with a disappointing critical and ratings reception. Interestingly, in the case of *Cracker*, much of the response to the American re-make drew on comparisons with the original version that had already been shown in the US on a cable network. Clearly in an era of post-network TV when audiences have more access to shows from elsewhere, the possibility that an audience may have seen the original version of a TV crime drama (and prefer it) is increasingly likely. In other words, while some transplants might take, others may be rejected although the reasons for this rejection may vary.

22 Sue Turnbull, 'Mapping the Vast Australian Suburban Tundra: Australian Comedy from Dame Edna to Kath and Kim' (2008) 11(1) *International Journal of Cultural Studies* 15.

23 Jeffrey Griffin, 'The Americanization of *The Office*: A Comparison of the Offbeat NBC Sitcom and Its British Predecessor' (2008) 35(4) *Journal of Popular Film and Television* 154.

24 Sue Turnbull '"It's Like They Threw a Panther in the Air and Caught It in Embroidery": Australian Television Comedy in Translation' (2008) 159 *Metro* 110.

25 Mark Duguid, *Cracker* (British Film Institute, 2009) 130.

The fact that the original series of *Cracker* and other highly regarded British series of the same era, including the intermittent *Prime Suspect* (ITV 1991–2006), could be watched and enjoyed in the US without cultural translation can be attributed to what Joseph Straubhaar characterises as the 'cultural proximity' which exists between audiences in the US and the UK.[26] Such cultural proximity involves a number of factors including: a shared understanding of genre; the cultural values that are inherent in the text (including moral codes); and a shared understanding of the themes explored, such as gender inequality or immigration. Straubhaar further suggests that the most obvious line of demarcation in cultural proximity is language, arguing that in Europe in particular, differences in both language and culture may create effective barriers to the television program trade between countries, an observation made some ten years earlier by Sinclair, Jacka and Cunningham.[27] The global reach of *Broen/Bron* in its original Danish/Swedish format thus appears to both confirm and unsettle Straubhaar's propositions. More recently, Stehling has suggested a fourth type of cultural proximity resulting from globalisation and the movement of cultural goods and people across borders.[28] This Stehling identifies as 'transcultural proximity' arguing that 'different national audiences . . . may have more in common than expected' although she is careful to restrict her comments to Western-industrialised countries.[29]

Stehling's notion of transcultural proximity has particular relevance to the Australian reception for *Broen/Bron*, given that Australia is in effect a Western industrialised nation with a relatively small population of indigenous inhabitants that has been 'settled' by migrants from all over the world since its 'discovery' by European explorers in the seventeenth century. While it would be 'nice' in the context of an essay on the transnational career of the Scandinavian crime drama to suggest that the Vikings arrived here first and Australia's cultural proximity to Scandinavia therefore goes way back, there is apparently little archaeological evidence to suggest this. Of more relevance to the issue of transcultural proximity is the fact that *Broen/Bron* was not the first Scandinavian crime series to have been shown on SBS in Australia. Other shows have included *Unit One* (*Rejseholder* DR1 2000–2004); *The Eagle* (*Ørenen* DR1 2004–2006). *The Killing* (*Forbrydelsen* DR1 2007–2012), and the political drama *Borgen* (DR1 2010–2013). This suggests that the SBS audience for *Broen/Bron* might share not only generic, thematic and moral proximities, but would already be familiar with the Danish (and indeed the Swedish) TV crime drama as it has developed

26 Joseph Straubhaar, *World Television: From Global to Local* (Sage Publications, 2007) 26.
27 John Sinclair, Elizabeth Jacka and Stuart Cunningham (eds), *New Patterns in Global Television: Peripheral Vision* (Oxford University Press, 1996).
28 Miriam Stehling, 'From Localisation to Translocation: Audience Readings of the Television Format Top Model' (2013) 8(2) *Critical Studies in Television* 36.
29 Ibid, 48.

over the last fourteen years. Not forgetting, of course, that the original Swedish versions of the Inspector Wallander series adapted from the crime fiction of Henning Mankell, and the three telemovies based on the crime fiction of Stieg Larsson, had also screened on SBS.

Something in common

When it comes to a question of format adaptation, it is therefore interesting to consider what gets changed and what stays the same in different cultural and national contexts. Setting aside the interesting question of casting, which has played a significant role in how the three versions of *The Bridge* have been critically received in each of the locations where they have been shown, and focusing instead on the crimes which are intrinsic to the narrative structure of the plot, it is important to note that both *The Tunnel* and the American version of *The Bridge* retain the initial premise of the series and the central serial-killer plot. In genre terms, this includes the familiar trope of a pair of mismatched detectives who are forced to work together despite their differences. In each case, this includes not only their different gender and national backgrounds, but also key aspects of their personalities. In each adaptation, this pairing involves an affable middle-aged thrice-married male detective who has just had a vasectomy and an 'unusual' (blonde) female detective who appears to suffer from some kind of a personality disorder.

While this disorder is never specified, the implication in each case is that the female detective (who is named differently in each) has problems managing interpersonal relationships and understanding human emotion: a set of traits associated with the condition known as Asperger's syndrome located somewhere on the autism spectrum. This condition (Asperger's syndrome) is a trope that has become increasingly common in both crime fiction and the TV crime drama in recent years. For example, Lisbeth Salander in *The Girl with the Dragon Tattoo*[30] in the original crime novel the Swedish telefilm adaptation (dir. Oplev 2010), and subsequent American adaptation (dir. Fincher 2011) demonstrates similar characteristics. Like Saga and her American and British equivalents, Lisbeth appears particularly gifted as an investigator at the same time as she has difficulties establishing personal relationships. It is, of course, entirely possible that Lisbeth's social problems are a function of her traumatic childhood rather than any neurological disorder. Other examples would include the BBC's most recent incarnation of that famous nineteenth-century consulting detective Sherlock Holmes, *Sherlock* (BBC One 2010–), starring Benedict Cumberbatch. This series also suggests that the brilliant but socially inept Holmes might be located somewhere on the autism spectrum, although once again this is never

30 Stieg Larsson (Norstedts, Sweden 2005).

directly stated. And then there is Sarah Lund, the female detective central to the earlier Danish series, *The Killing* (*Forbrydelsen* DR1 2007–12). Lund also appears to have problems managing her personal life, although this might well be a product of the choices she has made to prioritise her work rather than her family or family relationships. Indeed, the trope of the brilliant but solitary and socially dysfunctional detective (usually male) is one that would be immediately recognisable to those familiar with the genre.

In each of the adaptations, the major plot premise of the original series is retained. This includes the fact that some five years earlier the male detective had an affair with his colleague's wife. His colleague's wife and son are subsequently killed in a car crash as she attempts to leave the marriage, after which the colleague 'apparently' commits suicide. This is the 'original' crime in the past which is the impetus for the former colleague to become a serial killer. This is therefore the crime which the investigators in the present must discover before they can fully understand the motivation underlying the series of crimes in the present. In the original series and the British and American adaptations they fail to do so before the killer has carried out his revenge by destroying the detective's marriage and killing his oldest son. In its structure, this plot therefore constitutes what Russian formalist theorist, Tzvetan Todorov, has described as the dual structure of the classic detective story.[31] This duality encompasses the story of the crime in the past which must be discovered and the story of the investigation in the present as it unfolds, the specific twist here being that the male detective will gradually realise that he is personally implicated in both stories and is in fact the target of the serial killer's desire for revenge.

In the original version and the Anglo/French remake, the killer is nicknamed the 'Truth Terrorist' (or TT in the Anglo/French version) and his crimes appear ideologically motivated in that they are designed to highlight a series of social problems. These Five Truths, revealed over a series of episodes, are:

1 Social inequality before the law
2 The value of human life in that some people are more valued than others
3 The plight of the mentally ill and cuts to their services
4 The plight of immigrants and lack of social integration exacerbated by the police
5 The exploitation of child labour in the global economy

In the American version, rather than being identified as the Truth Terrorist, the killer is nicknamed the Bridge Butcher. Furthermore, while the killer's crimes follow a similar pattern, they also diverge in ways that may relate to the fact that the American screenwriters have no well established (although faltering)

31 Tzvetan Todorov, *The Poetics of Prose* (Cornell University Press, 1977).

social welfare or health care system to target, as in the Scandinavian and British contexts.

In the case of the first Truth, each of the three series begins with a female body on the bridge, one half of which belongs to a respected woman of high social status and the other to a woman of little status. In the original version, the bodies are those of a well-respected female politician, Kerstein Ekwall, chair of the Malmo council, and Monique Brammer, a Danish prostitute and drug addict. In the Anglo/French production, the French woman is again a politician and the prostitute, identified by the tattoos on her leg, is Welsh. In the American/Mexican version, the bodies are those of a well known American anti-immigration judge and a Mexican woman who was one of twenty-three dismembered bodies found in a 'death house' a year earlier whose deaths were largely ignored by the Juaréz police. While in each version, the killer wants to draw attention to inequality before the law (the death of the high status woman initiates an immediate and thorough police inquiry while that of a low status woman receives scant attention), in the American version this truth is expanded to include the fact that the murder rates between the two countries are outrageously disproportionate. As one of the co-writers and show-runner of the American adaptation, Elwood Reid, explained in an interview, the Mexican woman on the bridge is representative of the hundreds of women who have 'disappeared' in real life, caught up in the 'machinery of crime' along the border.[32]

In the case of the second 'truth', in the original Danish/Swedish series, in order to demonstrate that not all people are equally valued, the Truth Terrorist delivers poisoned wine to the homeless living on the streets while kidnapping a homeless man whom he films bleeding slowly to death. In the Anglo/French version, this is translated into the delivery of poisoned medication to the elderly in a nursing home who have been abandoned by their families. Their lack of social value is in contrast to that of a French war veteran whom he kidnaps and films freezing to death in a warehouse. In the American version, the focus is on the plight of illegal immigrants, one of whom the serial killer captures and stakes out in the desert. In each instance, the plight of the one person dying on camera is intended to highlight the fact that people only care about those they can 'see' while ignoring the larger problem.

For his third 'truth', in the Danish/Swedish and Anglo/French series, the Truth Terrorist draws attention to the plight of the mentally ill, manipulating a schizophrenic man into beheading his doctor with a samurai sword before committing suicide. The American adaptation, however, takes a different line, introducing a peripheral plot involving investigators from the Federal Bureau

32 Andy Greenwald, *The Andy Greenwald Podcast:* The Bridge *Co-showrunner Elwood Reid* (3 October 2013) ESPN http://espn.go.com/espnradio/play?id=9764101

of Investigations attempting to take over the case, but bungling it entirely. As a result, one of them is beheaded, his body dumped in a dumpster. This is the point at which the American series begins to diverge most obviously from the original and to become a very different kind of crime drama, a difference which is played out not only in terms of the narrative, but also in the production style, the 'look' of the series as a whole, This is therefore the moment to consider this particular adaptation in some further detail.

Re-locating *The Bridge*

While the production company, Shine, had proposed an American re-make set on the US/Canadian border, show-runner and writer Elwood Reid and his co-writer Meredith Stiehm were aware that such a production risked being too like the original: a criticism that had already been made of the American remake of *The Killing* set in Seattle.[33] Determined to make the show as different as possible in aesthetic and style to the original, Reid and Stiehm therefore opted for the Mexican/US border and the possibility of exploring the very complex cultural issues relevant to the El Paso, Texas and Juaréz, Mexico locations. To that end, Reid read up on local history, hung out in Juaréz, talked with a local journalist and immersed himself in the history of the drug cartels, immigration and border town politics of the region, all of which find their way into the American version of *The Bridge*.[34]

Writing on his blog about the first episode of the American adaptation of *The Bridge*, America TV critic Andy Greenwald vividly describes the city of Juaréz as 'an obscene cyclotron of unchecked capitalism and violence'. This he attributes to a number of factors, including globalisation, misogyny, drug trafficking, magic, 'or some unholy combination of the lot'.[35] While young women flock to the city to work in low-paid jobs in the duty-free American factories, young men in the thousands arrive to work in high-paying risky jobs with the Mexican drug cartels, 'both are killed with terrifying regularity'.[36] As evidence, Greenwald describes the hundreds of pink crosses which dot the deserts outside Juaréz that are intended to commemorate the victims and to shame 'the forces of local corruption and international apathy'.[37] It might be noted that a shot of these pink crosses features in the opening credit sequence of the American *Bridge*.

In terms of the production style and look, the director of the pilot episode, Gerardo Naranjo, had previously directed *Miss Bala* (2011), a highly regarded

33 Ibid.
34 Ibid.
35 Andy Greenwald, *The Bridge of Tears* (10 July 2013) Grantland http://grantland.com/hollywood-prospectus/the-bridge-season-1-epis t-eva/.
36 Ibid.
37 Ibid.

film which was selected as the Mexican entry for the Cannes film festival in that year. *Miss Bala* also dealt with the fate of women living on the Mexican border caught up in the drug trade. In contrast to the washed-out monochrome palette of the original Scandinavian and Anglo/French adaptation, Naranjo therefore establishes a very different look for the American series in the pilot. This encompasses daytime scenes in the desert under white-hot light and night time scenes of chiaroscuro gloom in the backstreets of Juaréz. Indeed, all of the night scenes are so underlit as to be almost undiscernible adding to the dark tone and mood. Sources of light are muted and faces barely distinguishable except for the light reflecting on sweating brows and cheek bones. The overall effect is one of discomfort, threat and danger.

Given his immersion in the politics of Juaréz and El Paso, the original serial killer narrative involving the Truth Terrorist was the least interesting aspect of the narrative for Reid.[38] In Reid's opinion, the serial killer as a genre trope had long lost its currency, a point incidentally underlined by the fact that the El Paso police lieutenant and Sonja's boss, Hank Wade, is played by actor Ted Levine who more than twenty years earlier had starred as the serial killer Jame Gumb in *Silence of the Lambs* (dir. Demme 1991), a moment when the device of the serial killer was at its zenith in crime fiction and television.[39] It might be noted that Levine's performance in that film was overshadowed by that of Anthony Hopkins who took out the Oscar for playing yet another serial killer with a more promising future career, Hannibal Lecter. Therefore, although Reid was obliged by the FX network to use the serial killer narrative as a device to motivate the action and to mobilise the relationship between the mismatched male and female detectives, he was very keen to steer the American version of *The Bridge* in a different direction. This is best illustrated by the ways in which Reid and Stiehm develop the storylines of the numerous peripheral characters.

For example, in each of the series, in the initial scene on the bridge or in the tunnel there is a wealthy couple in an ambulance who are trying to get through the police blockade in order to get help for the husband who has been taken ill and who subsequently dies. In each case, the major plot function of the wife is the fact that she later has sex with the male detective, thus establishing his moral weakness and philandering ways. In the American version, however, the bereaved wife, Charlotte Millwright (Annabeth Gish) becomes a central figure in the ongoing narrative when she chooses to be a major player in the on going cross border crime rackets. This is enabled by the secret tunnel on her land, formerly operated by her husband without her knowledge, through which drugs,

38 Andy Greenwald, *The Andy Greenwald Podcast:* The Bridge *Co-showrunner Elwood Reid* (3 October 2013) ESPN http://espn.go.com/espnradio/play?id=9764101.

39 Sue Turnbull, 'A Terrible Beauty: Thomas Harris, *Red Dragon* and the Serial Killer in Crime Fiction' in Alan McKee (ed.), *Beautiful Things in Popular Culture* (Blackwell, 2007) 49.

guns, people and even bodies are being smuggled between Juaréz and El Paso. By the end of the thirteenth episode, Charlotte has been established as a key on going figure in the projected second season.

Another example of how the American series differs in its treatment of a peripheral character is evident in the storyline involving the journalist to whom the killer communicates his crimes. In each version, this journalist is presented as a morally reprehensible and unlikeable character. However, while in the Danish/Swedish and Anglo/French versions, this character is killed off by the Truth Terrorist once he has fulfilled his function, in the American *Bridge*, this character survives. Despite being seriously injured and in a wheelchair, the alcoholic and drug-taking Daniel Frye (Matthew Lillard) appears to be in the process of redeeming himself with the aid of his lesbian Mexican fellow journalist, Adriana Mendez (Emily Rios). In the finale episode of the series, Adriana's own sister disappears, thus tying her and Daniel's peripheral narrative back into the story of the lost girls of Juaréz which is clearly being set up as the major narrative focus of season two.

And then there's the character of the social worker. In the original Danish/Swedish version, he is called Stefan Lindberg, an ambiguous figure presented as a possible suspect in the Truth Terrorist's crimes. Lindberg's subplot involves a long-lost sister living on the streets who is one of the Truth Terrorist's first victims, as well as his actions in rescuing a battered woman and her child from an abusive husband. In a subsequent scene he kills the violent husband with an iron when he is attacked in his flat, is arrested in episode seven, and does not feature again. In the British/French version, the character of Stephen Beaumont is again ambiguous. This time he appears to run some kind of hostel for illegal immigrants and is trying to save a woman and her child from the clutches of a pimp who wants to sell her into prostitution. Beaumont's sister is also implicated in that the pimp is her boyfriend and she too becomes a victim of the Truth Terrorist when she steals and takes the poisoned opiates intended for her patients in an old-people's home. Echoing the plot of the original, Beaumont batters the pimp to death with an iron but commits suicide by jumping overboard from the cross-channel ferry when cornered by the police.

In the American version of *The Bridge*, this incidental character, now called Stephen Linder, is even more ambiguous and threatening than in the earlier versions. This is largely due to the performance of Australian actor Thomas M Wright who portrays Linder as a buttoned-up misfit (literally, his shirts are awkwardly buttoned right up to the chin), who speaks as if his mouth were full of marbles. We first see Linder tailing a young woman, Eva Guerra (Stephanie Sigman), through the streets of Juaréz. He then kidnaps her, placing her in the boot of his car before taking her over the border to his trailer in the desert outside El Paso. As it emerges, this is Linder's 'safe place' where he takes all the women that he rescues from a future life of prostitution. Here he treats their injuries and feeds them before delivering them to a ranch which functions as safe house run by some kind of 'minister'. When Eva's pimp/boyfriend comes looking for her, Linder again kills him but this is far from the end of Linder's story. Indeed, Linder's love for Eva, his desire to marry her, and his search for her when she again disappears from the safe house is the central narrative thread left open at the end of the first season. In episode twelve, Linder joins a group of women pacing through the desert, scraping at the soil between the pink crosses, searching for the remains of their loved ones.

Thus while both the Danish/Swedish and British/French adaptations conclude with the death of the detective's son in episode ten, the American version of *The Bridge* extends by a further three episodes, setting up the narrative premise for a second season addressing the still unsolved crimes of the lost girls and the traffic in people and goods across the border which are specifically relevant to the American/Mexican setting.

Dénouement

The trope of a pair of mismatched detectives, and a serial killer determined to exact revenge on a former colleague who has cuckolded him apparently needs little cultural translation and remains the same in the two adaptations of the original series. The themes of infidelity, loyalty and trust appear to travel easily across cultural locations, as does the detail of male vasectomy. These genre and thematic factors remain a constant even as the locations change.

Also constant is the tension between the two cultures as represented by the police who are forced to co-operate in the investigation across their related jurisdictions. This tension, however, was not always easy to distinguish for those unfamiliar with the cultural contexts. I know from anecdotal reports that colleagues and friends in Australia often found it difficult to determine whether they were in Sweden or Denmark in the original series, given the two countries looked so similar and the language differences were so hard to distinguish for the untrained ear. This was true despite the fact that Danish policeman Martin Rhode clearly has difficulty making himself understood to his Swedish colleagues in episode one. This comedic moment was therefore largely lost on those who did not 'hear' the difference in accent and language or understand the kinds of cultural nuances described by a Danish guide to visitors on a Scandinavian crime tour:

> In Scandinavia we are not brothers and sisters [. . .] The Danish cop is flawed and the Swedish cop suffers from Asperger's. She has no empathy, which is a caricature of how we see the Swedish. They see us as drinking too much.[40]

40 Lee Tulloch, 'On the Crime Trail' *Sydney Morning Herald* (Sydney), 15 June 2013.

While such cultural tensions may have been hard to discern for non-Scandinavian viewers, the tensions between the English/French and American/Mexican police were much easier to identity given that these were highlighted through frequent critical asides made by the characters (in their own languages) about each other's cultural propensities and failings. The language differences thus clearly demarcated the characters as French or English; Spanish or Mexican and were also very useful in identifying the locations. Therefore, although each series addresses the cultural tensions between the two jurisdictions represented, in some instances these were much easier to discern than in others.

Where the series differ most, however, is in the degree to which the two format adaptations adhere to the original story-line in the representation of the serial killer's 'truths'. And it is here that the American series diverges most dramatically. By choosing to focus on the 'lost girls' of Juarèz and the traffic in drugs and people across the Mexican/US border, the American version of *The Bridge* effectively re-imagines and re-orients the focus of the original series. While the serial killer narrative is still present, and the focus on key themes of family and betrayal, through increased attention to the more peripheral characters, the American version of *The Bridge* becomes a much more encompassing critical commentary about a particular national and social context. Far from this being a disadvantage in terms of the series' success and appeal, I would argue that this renders the American series all the more effective as a result.

This conclusion suggests a final observation about how audiences may watch a television crime drama from 'somewhere else', and here I am going to draw on my own viewing experience as an illustration of the kinds of 'transcultural proximities' that may obtain. As a British citizen living in Australia who has travelled across the Øresund Bridge, I was immediately captivated by the opening shots of the original *Bridge* and by the location shooting in Malmo and Copenhagen, both of which I had visited. As the series unfolded, even as I became engaged in the narrative and the fate of the characters, I found myself frequently distracted by the production design, including at one critical home-furnishing decision moment, Martin Rhode's dining chairs. *The Bridge* thus afforded me pleasurable forms of virtual tourism and ideas about interior design at the same time as it offered a compelling thriller narrative and social commentary.

As someone who has both lived and studied in both France and England, I watched *The Tunnel* with a similar traveller's gaze. Once again, I enjoyed the locations, the opportunity to revisit familiar places and spaces without, sadly, being nearly so excited about the décor. Watching the American version of *The Bridge* about a part of the United States I did not know, I learned that my husband had been a frequent visitor to Juarèz in the 1970s, in search of authentic Mexican cuisine. It was, he reminisced, 'a lovely place'; an observation which clearly cast a different light on the portrayal of Juarèz as a 'cyclotron of unchecked capitalism and violence'.[41] What these observations reveal is that even for an

41 Greenwald, above n 36.

avid viewer of the television crime drama, the pleasures of the text are not always dependant on the crime narrative. Indeed, it is possible to watch a television crime drama from 'somewhere else', precisely because of its difference or its familiarity.

What each of these versions of *The Bridge* also offered was insight into the kinds of social and cultural issues that the writers wished to highlight through the medium of the television crime drama. In the process, each version drew attention to its specific national context by revealing the tensions that occur when the forces of the law attempt to cross borders and jurisdictions to deal with the crimes that observe no such boundaries. At its most ambitious (especially in the American adaptation), *The Bridge* reflects the transnational career of crime more generally, the traffic in people and goods in a global economy and the reverberations this illegal trade may have in local and national contexts. At the same time, in each of its versions, *The Bridge* is an all too familiar human comedy about love, betrayal and revenge. Therein lies the secret of the transnational career of *The Bridge* as a television crime drama: the careful arrangement of the strange and the new in terms of the cultural context with the easily recognisable and familiar in terms of the genre: And we're back where this story began, contemplating two halves of what appears to be a whole. Only this time the body that confronts us, artfully arranged, is a fascinating corpus of work.

Bibliography

Ang, Ien, Gay Hawkins and Lamia Dabboussy, *The SBS Story: The Challenge of Cultural Diversity* (University of New South Wales Press, 2008)

Bibel, Sarah, '"CSI: Crime Scene Investigation" is the Most-Watched Show in the World' (Press Release, 14 June 2012)

Duguid, Mark, *Cracker* (British Film Institute, 2009)

Esser, Andrea, 'TV Formats: History, Theory, Industry and Audiences' (2013) 8(2) *Critical Studies in Television: The International Journal of Television Studies*' 54

Forshaw, Barry, *Nordic Noir: The Pocket Essential Guide to Scandanavian Crime Fiction, Film & TV* (Oldcastle Books, 2013)

Greenwald, Andy, *The Bridge of Tears* (10 July 2013) Grantland http://grantland.com/hollywood-prospectus/the-bridge-season-1-epis t-eva/

Greenwald, Andy, *The Andy Greenwald Podcast:* The Bridge *Co-showrunner Elwood Reid* (3 October 2013) ESPN http://espn.go.com/espnradio/play?id=9764101

Griffin, Jeffrey, 'The Americanization of *The Office*: A Comparison of the Offbeat NBC Sitcom and Its British Predecessor' (2008) 35(4) *Journal of Popular Film and Television* 154

James, Clive, 'Clive James: The End of The Bridge? I Might Die of Despair' *The Telegraph* (London), 1 February 2014

Jensen, Pia Majbritt, 'Export Patterns and Global Impact of Danish Drama Series' *Producers and Audiences Conference*, Lund, Sweden, 20 March 2014

Marc, David, *Demographic Vistas: Televisions in American Culture* (University of Pennsylvania Press, 1984)

Mathjis, Ernest and Janet Jones, *Big Brother International: Formats, Critics and Publics* (Wallflower Press, 2004)
Mittell, Jason, *Genre and Television: From Cop Shows to Cartoons in American Culture* (Routledge, 2004)
Moran, Albert, *Copy Cat TV: Globalisation, Program Formats and Cultural Identity* (University of Luton Press, 1998)
Moran, Albert, *TV Format Mogul: Reg Grundy's Transnational Career* (Intellect, 2013)
Potter, Tiffany and C W Marshall, '"I am the American Dream": Modern Urban Tragedy and the Borders of Fiction' in Tiffany Potter and C W Marshall (eds), *The Wire: Urban Decay and American Television* (Continuum International Publishing Group, 2009) 1
Salleh, Anna, 'Pseudoarchaeology says Vikings Came to Australia', *ABC Science* (online), 29 August 2007 www.abc.net.au/science/articles/2007/08/29/2013186.htm
Siegel, Lee, 'Pure Evil: Jo Neshø and the Rise of Scandanavian Crime Fiction' *The New Yorker* (New York), 12 May 2014
Sinclair, John, Elizabeth Jacka and Stuart Cunningham (eds), *New Patterns in Global Television: Peripheral Vision* (Oxford University Press, 1996)
Stehling, Miriam, 'From Localisation to Translocation: Audience Readings of the Television Format Top Model' (2013) 8(2) *Critical Studies in Television* 36
Straubhaar, Joseph, *World Television: From Global to Local* (Sage Publications, 2007)
Sydney-Smith, Susan, *Beyond Dixon of Dock Green, Early British Police Series* (I.B. Tauris, 2002)
Todorov, Tzvetan, *The Poetics of Prose* (Cornell University Press, 1977)
Tulloch, Lee, 'On the Crime Trail' *Sydney Morning Herald* (Sydney), 15 June 2013
Turnbull, Sue, 'A Terrible Beauty: Thomas Harris, *Red Dragon* and the Serial Killer in Crime Fiction' in Alan McKee (ed.), *Beautiful Things in Popular Culture* (Blackwell, 2007) 49
Turnbull, Sue, 'The Hook and the Look: *CSI* and the Aesthetics of the Television Crime Series' in Michael Allen (ed.), *Reading CSI: Crime Television Under the Microscope* (I.B. Tauris, 2007) 15
Turnbull, Sue, '"It's Like They Threw a Panther in the Air and Caught It in Embroidery": Australian Television Comedy in Translation' (2008) 159 *Metro* 110
Turnbull, Sue, 'Mapping the Vast Australian Suburban Tundra: Australian Comedy from Dame Edna to Kath and Kim' (2008) 11(1) *International Journal of Cultural Studies* 15
Turnbull, Sue, *The Television Crime Drama* (Edinburgh University Press, 2014)

Chapter 6

Theatre and the law in the twenty-first century

Peter Robson

On the face of it, while people are able, as one might expect, to identify a major law and justice film – from *12 Angry Men* to *Jagged Edge* and *Law Abiding Citizen* – or a prominent TV legal series – from *Perry Mason* to *Rumpole of the Bailey* and *The Good Wife* – the task becomes trickier with dramas. There is, however, as indicated, a range of theatrical productions with which audiences watching over several decades will be familiar most probably from their screen versions – *The Winslow Boy*;[1] *Witness for the Prosecution*;[2] *Libel*;[3] *A Man for All Seasons*;[4] *The Crucible*.[5] As I hope to demonstrate the debt of the cinema of justice to the stage has always been extensive and remains so. Indirectly then, as indicated, if not as noticeably as film and television, theatre is one of the influences on popular legal consciousness.[6]

This chapter complements debates on the way in which law has parallels with the theatrical which was covered most recently in the 2010 Special Issue of the journal *Law Text Culture* on Law and Theatricality. It also links to the work of Douglas Hay[7] and Pat Carlen[8] in the 1970s on the symbolism of the courtroom. The current work is concerned with a more limited field of inquiry in relation to drama. It looks at the theatre as a source for film scripts. It is focused on the representation of law and justice in film. This chapter looks in detail at the theatrical roots of four major courtroom dramas – *Witness for the Prosecution, Inherit the Wind, Nuts* and *A Few Good Men*. It is hoped that this study will provide the

1 1948 with Cecil Hardwicke and 1998 with Nigel Hawthorne.
2 1957 with Marlene Dietrich, Tyrone Power and Charles Laughton.
3 1959 with Dirk Bogarde.
4 1968 with Paul Scofield; also filmed in 1988 with Charlton Heston in a TVM version.
5 1955 with Simone Signoret and 1996 with Winona Ryder.
6 Lawrence M Friedman, 'Law, Lawyers and Popular Culture' (1989) 98 *Yale Law Journal* 1579.
7 Douglas Hay, 'Property, Authority and the Criminal Law' in Douglas Hay *et al.* (eds), *Albion's Fatal Tree: Crime and Society in Eighteenth-Century England* (Pantheon, 1975) 17.
8 Pat Carlen, 'The Staging of Magistrates' Justice' (1976) 16(1) *British Journal of Criminology* 48; Pat Carlen, *Magistrates' Justice* (Martin Robertson, 1976).

basis for a subsequent more extensive consideration of specific aspects of the relationship between film and the older art form.

Context of current inquiries

Sara Ramshaw suggested in 2010 that '(m)uch has been written on the theatrical aspects of law or the relationship between law and theatre or law as performance'.[9] She cites four essays which do indeed look at the theatricality of law as a broad notion which are touched on below. The actual traditional works of theatrical drama themselves, have, however, been largely overlooked in the scholarship of law and popular culture. Those writers whom she cites are, indeed, concerned with the law/theatre interface. The focus, though, as she indicates, is on examining the performance aspects of law and theatre and the extent to which the theatricality of law assists in providing law's cloak of legitimacy.[10] As Milner Ball expressed it, 'the "theatrical quality" of trials allows actors, judge and jury . . . to play parts in a government of laws and not of people'.[11] There is also interesting work on how the more recent staging of actual real courtroom dramas and related public inquiries have been portrayed within the modern theatre.[12] The potential impact of this development links into the fictional works of drama which I examine. Of course, this was a theme which had been adverted to in some of the early work in socio-legal studies. Pat Carlen suggested that the location of the bench in traditional courts created a symbolic space of awe[13] and Douglas Hay pointed out that this geography helped reinforce law's power in eighteenth-century England with the visiting Assizes as a source of theatrical retribution ostensibly for all classes.[14] It is a theme that has resurfaced in the discussions of the relationship between space and justice in both work on architecture[15] and the focus on law and space in modern urban writing.[16]

9 Sara Ramshaw, 'Jamming the Law: Improvisational Theatre and the "Spontaneity" of Judgment' (2010) 14 *Law Text Culture* 133.

10 Jack Balkin and Sanford Levinson, 'Law as Performance' in Michael Freeman and Andrew Lewis (eds), *Law and Literature: Current Legal Issues* (1999) vol 2, 729; Julia Stone Peters, 'Legal Performances: Good and Bad' (2008) 4 *Law Culture and the Humanities* 179.

11 Milner S Ball, 'The Play's the Thing: An Unscientific Reflection on Courts Under the Rubric of Theater' (1975) 28 *Stanford Law Review* 100.

12 Nicole Rogers, 'The Play of Law: Comparing Performances in Law and Theatre' (2008) 8 *Queensland University of Technology Law & Justice Journal* 429.

13 Pat Carlen, 'The Staging of Magistrates' Justice' (1976) 16(1) *British Journal of Criminology* 48.

14 Douglas Hay *et al.* (eds), *Albion's Fatal Tree: Crime and Society in Eighteenth-Century England* (Pantheon, 1975).

15 Judith Resnick and Dennis Curtis, *Representing Justice: The Creation and Fragility of Courts in Democracies* (Yale University Press, 2010); Linda Mulcahy, *Legal Architecture: Justice, Due Process and the Place of Law* (Routledge-Cavendish, 2011); Peter Robson and Rodger J, A Spatial Approach to Justice: The Development of Scottish Court Architecture (forthcoming, 2015)[0].

16 Andreas Philippopoulos-Mihalopoulos (ed.), *Law and the City* (Routledge-Cavendish, 2007).

This chapter then, is concerned with a more limited field of inquiry in relation to drama. It looks at the theatre as a source for film scripts. It starts the process of gauging the impact of theatre on the cinema of justice – that body of films which are directly concerned with the portrayal of legal themes both within and outside the courtroom.[17] It traces the theatrical sources of a number of significant films on law and justice and is the start of a process which, in due course, will provide a taxonomy of theatre-based films as well as a guide to those works of 'legal theatre' which have not been adapted for the screen. This then aims, *inter alia,* to see what features make a stage drama work as film and what do not. It attempts to divine any pattern in the use of stage drama sources at different times. It locates this discussion within the scholarship which has emerged in related fields and assesses what this work contributes to a richer picture of the theatre of justice. It goes on to examine the theatre-film work within the framework of adaptation theory encountered principally in literature/film discussions. This chapter, then, as indicated, looks at the theatrical roots of four major courtroom dramas – *Witness for the Prosecution*, *Inherit the Wind*, *Nuts* and *A Few Good Men.*[18]

Theatricality

In addition to the discussions on the way in which law has parallels with the theatrical adverted to in the works cited by Ramshaw, there is another general approach to the law/theatre interface which has attracted attention. In the Special Issue of the journal *Law Text Culture* on Law and Theatricality the editors hoped that their call for papers in relation to 'the revitalised field of theatricality' would allow the foregrounding of 'ideas of frame, the body, appearance, rhetoric, and image as key intersections for understanding the work of the law in producing, shaping and staging justice'.[19] There are two principal strands where theatricality is explored in these essays. First, there is a focus on the theme of theatricality within formal legal settings. There is also the arena where the political is the focus. The essays range from theatrical politics[20] to theatricality

17 Steve Greenfield, Guy Osborn and Peter Robson, *Film and the Law: The Cinema of Justice* (Hart Publishing, 2nd edn, 2010) passim.

18 A perusal of the major 'trial movies' compiled by Bergman and Asimow reveals that some 10 per cent of the films selected for in-depth analysis appeared initially as stage plays (Bergman and Asimow, 2006).

19 Marett Leiboff and Sophie Nield, 'Introduction: Law's Theatrical Presence' (2010) 14 *Law Text Culture* 1[0].

20 Ibid; Theron Schmidt, '"We Say Sorry": Apology, the Law and Theatricality' (2010) 14 *Law Text Culture* 55; Mamari Stephens, '"Tame Kaka" Still? Maori Members, and the Use of Maori Language in the New Zealand House of Representatives' (2010) 14 *Law Text Culture* 220; Connal Parsley, 'The Mask and Agamben: The Transitional Juridical Technics of Legal Relation' (2010) 14(1) *Law Text Culture* 12.

within the legal process[21] and changed ways of representing justice issues within theatre.[22]

The essays open up a thriving world of theatre, looking at contemporary struggles and revealing theatre's potential to bring to life what might seem dull official enquiries and reportage. Most recently, Denis Brion has looked again at the theatricality of the criminal trial in the adversarial system. He focused specifically on the impact of images in the courtroom and verdicts in the context of the concept of theatre as a semiotic process developed by the Prague School in the 1930s and 1940s.[23] He concludes that the visual elements in trials combine to create prejudice against defendants and deny them, in effect, due process. Beyond these interventions, however, theatre remains relatively unexplored by scholars of law and popular culture.

Law and literature

Theatre makes a number of appearances in the vast scholarship concerning the field of law and literature. We find, for instance, discussion of the 1975 play on the Supreme Court and its internal dynamics, *First Monday in October*. This material was subsequently made into a film with Jill Clayburgh and Walter Matthau as the sparring conservative and liberal justices in 1981. What was a worthy and rather wordy debate in the theatre with undertones of romantic possibilities is transformed into a romantic-comedy (rom/com) thriller in the screen version. Ray discusses this in the context of a collection of those instances where Supreme Court Justices are portrayed in the novel, drama and on film[24] and the manner of this portrayal. Her conclusions, as far as *First Monday in October* is concerned, are interesting in themselves of course. What is of greater fascination in this context is that they seem to be unique in addressing the literary, theatrical and cinematic forms in a single piece. As has been noted elsewhere, scholars have tended to focus on literature or film and more recently television.[25]

21 Michael Bachmann, 'Theatre and the Drama of Law: A "Theatrical History" of the Eichmann Trial' (2010) 14 *Law Text Culture* 94; Karen Walton, 'Chamber Theatre' (2010) 14 *Law Text Culture* 309.

22 Olivera Simić, 'Breathing Sense into Women's Lives Shattered by War: Dah Theatre Belgrade' (2010) 14 *Law Text Culture* 11; Caroline Wake, 'Caveat Spectator: Judicial, Political and Ontological False Witnessing in CMI (A Certain Maritime Incident)' (2010) 14 *Law Text Culture* 160; David A Williams, 'Legal Language and Theatrical Presence: Transforming a Legal Inquiry into Theatre' (2010) 14 *Law Text Culture* 188; Karen Crawley, 'The Farce of Law: Performing and Policing "Norm" and "Ahmed" in 1969' (2010) 14 *Law Text Culture* 247.

23 Denis J Brion, 'The Criminal Trial as Theater: The Semiotic Power of the Image' in Anne Wagner and Richard K Sherwin (eds), *Law Culture and Visual Studies* (Springer, 2014) 329.

24 Laura Ray, 'Judicial Fictions: Images of Supreme Court Justices in the Novels, Drama and Film' (1997) 39 *Arizona Law Review* 151.

25 Peter Robson and Jessica Silbey (eds), *Law and Justice on the Small Screen* (Hart Publishing, 2012).

There is also, what is in reality, a separate area about aspects of law and justice in the plays of Shakespeare. The specific focus on lawyers is dealt with in Kornstein's *Kill All the Lawyers?*[26] Ian Ward's later work on Shakespeare is also principally concerned with what he terms the 'legal imagination'.[27] Notwithstanding the persistence of Shakespeare at the core of the traditional theatre in the United Kingdom as well as other playwrights of his era,[28] this chapter leaves these high cultural issues to one side, at least for the present, as a quite distinct zone, related to, but distinct from popular legal culture.

Approaches to adaptation

Adaptation studies, as a discrete area of cultural studies, has centred principally on the way books have been altered for the purposes of the screen.[29] In this context several approaches to adaptation have been identified over the years. One early classification suggested one could identify transposition, commentary and analogy.[30] Those filmmakers involved in transposition simply sought to render the book's content faithfully in a visual form. Wagner cites *Wuthering Heights* (1939), *Jane Eyre* (1944), *Madame Bovary* (1949) and *Lord Jim* (1965). In other adaptations, filmmakers used the text as a departure point for a slightly different and new creation. This might involve re-emphasis or re-structuring and *Catch 22* (1970) and *A Clockwork Orange* (1972) were the examples Wagner gave. Finally *Cabaret* (1972) and *Death in Venice* (1971) were put forward as using different techniques to make a very different work of art from the original for which Wagner used the term analogy. McFarlane has suggested that context plays a major role in determining what form the adaptation takes. He notes that the non-literary, non-novelistic influences at work on any film are often crucial. The conditions within which the film industry and the prevailing cultural

26 Daniel Kornstein, *Kill All the Lawyers?: Shakespeare's Legal Appeal* (Princeton University Press, 1994); see also Roger Stritmatter, 'Shakespeare's Legal Appeal: *Kill All the Lawyers?* Seen Through the Prism of Authorship' (1997) 33 *Shakespeare Oxford Newsletter* 3.

27 Ian Ward, *Shakespeare and the Legal Imagination* (Butterworths, 1999).

28 Pascale Aebischer, *Screening Early Modern Drama: Beyond Shakespeare* (Cambridge University Press, 2013).

29 Stuart Y McDougal, *Made into Movies: From Literature to Film* (Hole, Rinehart and Winston, 1985); Neil Sinyard, *Filming Literature: The Art of the Screen Adaptation* (Croom Helm, 1986); Brian McFarlane, *Novel to Film: An Introduction to the Theory of Adaptation* (Clarendon Press, 1996); James Griffith, *Adaptations as Imitations: Films from Novels* (University of Delaware Press, 1997); John M Desmond and Peter Joseph Hawkes, *Adaptation: Studying Film and Literature* (McGraw Hill, 2006); Dennis Cutchins, Laurence Raw and James M Welsh (eds), *Redefining Adaptation Studies* (Scarecrow Press, 2010); Pascale Aebischer, *Screening Early Modern Drama: Beyond Shakespeare* (Cambridge University Press, 2013); R Barton Palmer and William Robert Bray (eds), *Modern British Drama on Screen* (Cambridge University Press, 2013).

30 Geoffrey Wagner, *The Novel and the Cinema* (Farleigh Dickinson Press, 1975).

and social climate at the time of the film's making are major determinants in shaping any film. Such matters, he owns, are difficult to pin down in contrast to the question of literary 'faithfulness'.[31]

Somewhat different issues arise in adaptations from stage to screen. This is an area where, until very recently, there has been limited work and as yet, no focus on the law and justice within adaptations.[32] None of the plays and films in the thirteen essays in Palmer and Bray's 2013 collection discuss the issue, ranging as they do from Shaw's *Pygmalion* through *Look Back in Anger* to *The History Boys*. Although superficially a mystery, *Sleuth*, one of the plays on which an essay is written, is rather about masculinity and about subverting generic expectations.[33] While there is, of course, scope for new creations and wholly different works of art, the attraction of the stage play as the source for film has been the relative simplicity of having a pre-ordained dramatic form by virtue of the traditional Theatre Act format. Some plays have indeed been filmed without any attempt to create a cinematic experience. One example that I use in teaching to illustrate the difference between the theatrical and cinematic form, is the trial scene from *The Merchant of Venice*. The contrast between the Al Pacino film version and the Henry Goodman/Royal Shakespeare Company (RSC) version is stark. The text, of course, remains the same but the potential for the film version to expand the cast and the scope of the action is taken advantage of to provide a bustling court setting with a menacing baying crowd for Shylock's speech highlighting the anti-Semitic elements much more forcefully than the sparsely populated set of the RSC stage.

It is also worth noting in this context, the recent marketing development in the use of cinemas as venues for operas, concerts and plays themselves. These productions are beamed live to audiences in the same way as has happened with sporting events for most of the past century, and are seen by some as the possible saviour of cinema.[34] Their ability to screen live top-class theatre, opera and ballet implies a blurring of lines, for consumers at least, of the demarcation between live performance, a film version and a filmed live performance.

31 Brian McFarlane, *Novel to Film: An Introduction to the Theory of Adaptation* (Clarendon Press, 1996); but see George Bluestone, *Novels into Film* (University of California Press, 1957); James Griffith, *Adaptations as Imitations: Films from Novels* (University of Delaware Press, 1997).

32 R Barton Palmer and William Robert Bray (eds), *Modern British Drama on Screen* (Cambridge University Press, 2013).

33 Monika Pietrzak-Franger, '*Sleuth* On Screen: Adapting Masculinities' in R Barton Palmer and William Robert Bray (eds), *Modern British Drama on Screen* (Cambridge University Press, 2013) 169.

34 Jonathan Owen, 'Event Cinema: Live Screenings of Opera and Ballet are the British New Wave' *The Independent* (UK), 27 January 2013.

Realism and beyond

The simplest approach, then, which the filmmaker may adopt, is to film the play in an arresting way. Discussing his highly successful film version of the Frederick Knott play *Dial M for Murder* (1953), Alfred Hitchcock is reported as saying 'I didn't really need to go to the studio, I could have phoned that one in'.[35] There is just one setting in the stage play: the living-room of the family flat in Maida Vale in London. Hitchcock's film adds a second setting in a gentleman's club, a few views of the street outside and a courtroom montage. The extent of opening up the action has been relatively modest but significant in most of the plays which I have hitherto examined. The skill of the filmmaker in many cases has been to disguise the original source in such a way that the audience has little sense of simply watching a filmed play or as Hitchcock again put it 'photographs of people talking'. This will form the core of the closer examination of theatrical films undertaken in this chapter. The matter though is perhaps rather more complex than adding in a few external shots and conversation, and that film has advantages which the static theatre can never enjoy.

Sinyard notes, for instance that '(f)ilm has clearly more possibilities for variety of time, space, point of view than the theatre'[36] which become available when the play is adapted for the screen. There are further differences. These include the nature of the theatrical and cinematic performances. The contrast between 'acting' and 'reacting' as well as the different use of the eyes. The fixed point of view of the theatre also contrasts with the ability of the camera to alter the shot; to dissolve; to go into close-up; to move backwards and forwards in time. Levels of realism are different with stylised violence seen as symbolic on stage in a way which film would deal with realistically. Viewer expectation would suggest that with its wider audience a play would have to be simplified or diluted. The solutions for the filmmaker include 'ventilating' the play by providing an alternative to the static interior with which film audiences will be bored. As Sinyard points out, the jump from stage to screen has been managed most effectively in some instances on different occasions as in the different film versions of Hecht and MacArthurs' *The Front Page* (1928).[37]

The cinema of justice has generally limited itself to transposing in a simple way the principal narrative thrust of the original book to the screen. Some sub-plots may be sacrificed and some locations altered but the reader of the book will recognise the film instantly. The kind of change that does take place is one of storyline detail. In the film version of John Grisham's work about corporate

35 Neil Sinyard, *Filming Literature: The Art of the Screen Adaptation* (Croom Helm, 1986) 157.
36 Ibid, 158.
37 Ibid, 165–166.

responsibility, *The Runaway Jury* (1997), the film indicts the gun industry in place of the tobacco industry. There is a relative absence of examinations of the cinematic qualities of law films in the scholarship. This derives, I would suggest, from the limited use of interesting cinematic techniques when bringing to the screen real-life human dramas like *A Civil Action* or *Erin Brockovitch* and the books of writers like Barry Reed (*The Verdict* (1981)) and Scott Turow (*Burden of Proof* (1996)). Only in very rare instances, like *The Devil's Advocate* (1991) do we have anything outwith the shift of the story from the novel to screen in the simplest transpositional mode. The reasons for this lack of alternative approaches stems from both financial as well as artistic considerations. Insofar as film reaches much wider audiences than books and the theatre, the temptation to 'leave well alone' with adaptations of already proven products is obvious. Elaborate sub-plots and superfluous plot twists can be sacrificed where book adaptations are concerned. We see this in the films of the Grisham legal novels.[38] Somewhat different considerations apply where the source is the one- or two-set stage play. As Hitchcock implied, filming talking heads for hours requires a commitment from the audience which few directors are willing to risk. We find this, for instance in the adaptation of *First Monday in October* where a stolid if worthwhile debate on the nature of censorship, free speech and libertarianism is transformed into a rom-com thriller with a few elements of the theatrical debate occupying very limited screen time.

The unheralded source of the cinema of justice

Hollywood and the film industry generally has sought its inspiration from a variety of existing sources, most notably books and drama. As Palmer and Bray point out, this relationship stretches back to the very earliest days of silent cinema with cinema seeking the cultural respectability of the theatre as well as the technical experience of the older art form.[39] In the scholarship on the cinema of justice the focus of attention, hitherto, has been on the recurrent narrative themes and how these have altered. The heroic white male lawyer and his transformation over the years have occupied much space.[40] There has also been a wealth of analysis of individual films and their significance for those interested

38 Peter Robson, 'Law and Popular Culture' (2001) 28(1) *Journal of Law and Society* 147.

39 R Barton Palmer and William Robert Bray (eds), *Modern British Drama on Screen* (Cambridge University Press, 2013) 6.

40 Nicole Rafter, 'American Criminal Trial Films: An Overview of their Development 1930–2000' (2001) 28(1) *Journal of Law and Society* 9; Michael Asimow, 'Bad Lawyers in the Movies' (2000) 24 *Nova Law Review* 533; Steve Greenfield, 'Hero or Villain? The Cinematic Lawyer and the Delivery of Justice' (2001) 28(1) *Journal of Law and Society* 25; Steve Greenfield, Guy Osborn and Peter Robson, *Film and the Law: The Cinema of Justice* (Hart Publishing, 2nd edn, 2010).

in a range of themes.[41] While there have been a couple of explorations of the adaptation of the work of specific authors onto the screen,[42] the source of the screenplays has been largely ignored by the law and film movement.[43] This chapter is a modest attempt to redress this balance and to shed some light on the different cultural products.

Initially, at this stage I have chosen to look at four well known films with a dramatic theatre source to see if any patterns and questions emerge which can be explored in the wider field. The plays/films are principally set in the courtroom or lawyers' chambers. The films also involve extensive time in the courtroom and have been termed 'trial movies'.[44] The conventions of this sub-genre are encountered with missing evidence and the collapse of witnesses in the witness box.[45] The films range across different themes and do not focus solely on the traditional staple of the cinema of justice – the capital murder trial. They cover not only this theme but also freedom of speech and the abuse of power of individuals and the state. Their specific selection derives from watching the Barbra Streisand film *Nuts* and being struck by how unlike a film it was and how much like a film of a stage play it seemed to be. It is sufficiently significant to be included as one of the four films on the cover of the second edition of Bergman and Asimow's groundbreaking examination of law on film along with *To Kill a Mockingbird* (1962), *The People versus Larry Flynt* (1996) and *Legally Blonde* (2001).[46]

Looking at the backgrounds of a number of the classic cinema of justice films I covered in my teaching, I noticed that the original source of these were plays. For instance, the clips used to illustrate one of the conventions of the courtroom drama – the implosion of the witness in the witness box – came from *Witness for the Prosecution, Inherit the Wind* and *A Few Good Men*. All turned out to have been adapted from stage plays and all came from successful dramatists. Since these seemed to be award-winning and commercially successful films in their own right this original source had not really suggested itself to me. It seemed

41 Leslie Moran *et al.* (eds), *Law's Moving Image* (Routledge-Cavendish, 2004); Austin Sarat, Lawrence Douglas and Martha Merrill Umphrey (eds), *Law on the Screen* (Stanford University Press, 2005).

42 Phil Meyer, 'Why a Jury Trial is More Like a Movie than a Novel' (2001) 28(1) *Journal of Law and Society* 133; Peter Robson, 'Adapting the Modern Law Novel: Filming John Grisham' (2001) 28(1) *Journal of Law and Society* 147.

43 Stefan Machura, 'An Analysis Scheme for Law Films' (2007) 36 *University of Baltimore Law Review* 329.

44 Paul Bergman and Michael Asimow, *Reel Justice – The Courtroom Goes to the Movies* (Andrews McMeel Publishing, 2nd edn, 2006).

45 Steve Greenfield, Guy Osborn and Peter Robson, *Film and the Law: The Cinema of Justice* (Hart Publishing, 2nd edn, 2010) 53.

46 Paul Bergman and Michael Asimow, *Reel Justice – The Courtroom Goes to the Movies* (Andrews McMeel Publishing, 2nd edn, 2006).

worthwhile investigating what it was that had happened in these three films that they were so significantly different from the Streisand film.

Agatha Christie, although her reputation has fluctuated wildly over the years, did produce twenty-seven long running plays and is the playwright people are most likely to have encountered; *Witness for the Prosecution* was a play derived from a short story which appeared in *Flynn's Detective Weekly* in 1925. Twenty years later Agatha Christie was persuaded to dramatise it and took the opportunity to add a twist to the original tale of a callous murderer using the legal system to his own ends.[47] A critically and commercially successful Hollywood version, with a screenplay by Billy Wilder and Harry Kurnitz, was produced in 1957 with major international stars, Marlene Dietrich, Tyrone Power and Charles Laughton taking the leading roles of Christine Helm, Leonard Vole and Sir Wilfrid Robarts and returning $9 million on a $3 million budget. Part of the play's fascination comes from its fidelity to the original theatrical storyline. It retains the basic plot of a young man, Leonard Vole, being accused of the murder of a middle-aged widow he has befriended and who inherits her considerable wealth on her death. In the course of the trial the wife retracts her account of events on the night of the murder leaving Leonard with no alibi. To this bare plot, what Wilder and his co-screenplay adapter have added is a chronic health problem for the eminent barrister, Sir Wilfrid Robarts. This, in turn, leads to an ongoing framing relationship between Sir Wilfrid and the nurse looking after his health, Miss Plimsoll. This sub-plot between Charles Laughton and his actual wife, Elsa Lanchester, changes the mood and focus of the film and provides light and shade. The portrayal by Tyrone Power of Leonard Vole as a rather jolly and chipper defendant also alters what is a rather dour stage play into quite a light comedy, albeit on a deadly theme. It is also one which intrigues audiences, judging by the interval reactions and speculation about who did murder Emily French when I last saw this play on tour in 2010. The sub-plot and the actors involved in the film are so dominant that the fate of Leonard becomes almost incidental and, unlike the play, it ends on quite a positive note.

Visually the play has been opened out extensively. In addition to the two sets found in the play – the barrister's Chambers and the courtroom – we have a range of changes. The Chambers acquire an elaborate set of stairs and a stair-lift providing comedy and dramatic moments. The chance to use the vast and faithful recreation of the Old Bailey courtroom is a contrast with what is possible on even the most extensive proscenium arch stage. In addition, there are scenes outside the court in the corridors of the court, in the nightclub where Leonard meets Christina, and her flat, as well as in the London street outside the hat shop where Vole meets the widow. In addition, in place of the cramped stage recreation of the Old Bailey and a simple office, the film versions of these are

47 Agatha Christie, *Witness for the Prosecution and Selected Plays* (Harper Collins, 1995).

exotic and soaring spaces. What was a simple, rather plodding, whodunnit with a slightly overbearing barrister becomes a battle between the nurse and her patient in which the conflict happens to take place around a murder trial. It is a sub-plot, but one which alters the whole tone of the production. It is Wilder's creation and has none of the turgidity that is associated with the plays of Agatha Christie. She had no role in its production and her brief 'comic' interaction between Chambers' staff at the start of the play is excised. Wilder, then has taken this modest 'twist on the final page' whodunnit and transformed it into a much richer and more complex mixture of plot and vehicle for a new character to emerge. Watching the play and then encountering the film of *Witness for the Prosecution* involves a wholly new piece of art being constructed and a quite different cultural product emerging.

The authors of *Inherit the Wind*, Lawrence and Lee had other successes with *Mame* as well as *First Monday in October* and the musical version of James Hilton's book, The Lost Horizon, *Shangri La*. Like Agatha Christie they did not have any authorial input into the screen version of *Inherit the Wind*. The play was first produced at the Dallas Theatre in December 1955. This play recreates the 1925 Tennessee Monkey trial in which a young student, John Scopes, was put on trial for teaching about Darwin's theory of evolution contrary to the laws of the State of Tennessee.[48] He was defended by the renowned lawyer, Clarence Darrow and the prosecution was undertaken by Woodrow Wilson's former Secretary of State and himself three times a Presidential candidate, William Jennings Bryan.[49] Its authors explained that the play was about contemporary post-war attacks on free speech rather than competing versions of the source of the universe. *Inherit the Wind* has been filmed on three occasions with the names of the principal protagonists altered. The essential structure of the 1960 film was retained for the 1975 and 1997 versions. Although it initially made a loss of $1.7 million on a budget of $2 million, it garnered critical praise and awards at the Berlin Film Festival as well as Oscar nominations. It was also influential on a whole generation of neophyte lawyers.[50] It is the Stanley Kramer version of 1960 with Spencer Tracy and Fredric March (a Jennings Bryan look-alike),

48 John T Scopes and James Presley, *Center of the Storm: Memoirs of John T. Scopes* (Henry Holt, 1967).

49 Darrow (1857–1938) was by the time of the trial famous for his work on behalf of organised labour and more sensationally the teenage murderers Leopold and Loeb – this was his penultimate case in a long career as a leading advocate of the American Civil Liberties Union; Jennings Bryan (1860–1925) had been Woodrow Wilson's Secretary of State (1913–1915) and had stood as the Democratic Party's Presidential candidate in 1896, 1900 and 1908 as well as campaigning for prohibition and woman's suffrage before latterly taking up the cause against Darwinism.

50 Nell Minow, '"An Idea is a Greater Monument than a Cathedral": Deciding How We Know What We Know in Inherit the Wind' (1996) 30 *University of San Francisco Law Rev* 1225.

as civil libertarian defence lawyer Henry Drummond (Clarence Darrow) and Matthew Harrison Brady (William Jennings Bryan) as the washed up demagogue who is seeking to recreate his glory days through channelling the power of religious fundamentalism which lives on in DVD form. The play has a two-level set with the courtroom on the lower level and the town on the upper level. The acting edition of the play notes that 'It is important to the concept of the play that the town is visible always, looming there, as much on trial as the individual defendant'.

In terms of plot the play remains broadly unchanged except for the dramatic courtroom demise of the prosecutor, Brady which actually befell Jennings Bryan five days after the end of the trial. A young man is arrested for teaching in his biology class that man is descended from primates and in turn from the very simplest forms of life. He is prosecuted by a major political figure, William Jennings Bryan and defended by the leading defence lawyer in the United States, Clarence Darrow. Such teaching of Darwin's theory of evolution had been declared to be unlawful by a 1925 Tennessee statute.[51] The play, then, is based on the prosecution of John Scopes in Tennessee in 1925 for breach of this statute. It was one of the statutes affecting many States in this era proscribing such teaching. The actual Scopes case was a 'set up' being engineered and funded by the American Civil Liberties Union and was a challenge to the unjust nature of the laws rather than stemming from an actual crackdown on deviant teaching. The paradox for the Tennessee authorities in the actual Scopes case was that the text books produced for students in the State themselves contained references to the theory of evolution.

The film has a number of outdoor sequences including the arrival by carriage and bus of the principal protagonists. While authorial intention is only one factor in reading cultural products it is worth noting their claims about the play. The authors Jerome Lawrence and Robert E Lee make clear in their notes for those producing the play that their intention in writing the play was to focus on the 'dignity of the human mind'.[52] They also collaborated on the legally centred play *First Monday in October*. As they put it 'Humanity is on trial. Anyone who would limit thought is on trial'. They stress in their Production Notes that *Inherit the Wind* is 'not about the theory of evolution versus the literal interpretation of the Bible'. Rather it 'assault[s] those who would constrict any human being's

51 Tennessee Evolution Statute 1925 (Butler Act) which enacted in section 1 'That it shall be unlawful for any teacher in any of the Universities, Normals and all other public schools of the State which are supported in whole or in part by the public school funds of the State, to teach any theory that denies the story of the Divine Creation of man as taught in the Bible, and to teach instead that man has descended from a lower order of animals.' It was not repealed until 1967.

52 Jerome Lawrence and Robert Edwin Lee, *Inherit the Wind* (Dramatists Play Service, 2000) Notes.

right to think, to teach, to learn'. In their drama on the narrow-minded hounding of unconventional ideas by an intolerant anti-liberal majority, then, the authors were responding to the 1940s HUAC hearings and the blacklisting of writers like Carl Foreman and Lillian Hellmann. Interestingly, since the 1950s, with the resurgence of fundamentalism and emergence of creationism as a significant force in education in some areas, the play has disturbing fresh resonances in which the literal interpretation of the Bible has become a bizarre feature of modern life in the United States as well as having echoes in other religions reliant on 'sacred' texts.

Visually, in place of the split stage and the town overshadowing the courtroom we have a naturalistic portrayal of the small town of Hillsboro with large crowd scenes and the festive atmosphere of a County Fair as the accompaniment to the trial. The whole process is expanded so that the boarding house where Brady and Drummond both stay plays a major part as the location for their discussions on the nature of freedom of thought and expression and the suppression of heretical unconventional speech. These direct conversations replace the interaction between Drummond and his client, Bert Cates, in the courtroom annexe. They humanise Brady and show him up in a rather more sympathetic light than he appears in the play. We understand that he and Drummond are fighting on behalf of the dispossessed. In Brady's case he has become intoxicated by adulation and is guilty of hubris. Again with the opening out of the play and the changes in the interaction between Drummond and both Brady and his wife, a fresh sub-plot on their relationship emerges with Drummond as the political ally as well as a probable rejected suitor of Mrs Brady. By the same token, the struggle between, Bert Cates's sweetheart, Rachel Brown, and her dogmatic and unbending father Reverend Brown is highlighted in the film, while merely hinted at in the play.

Looking to the models suggested in adaptation theory, what appears to have happened in *Inherit the Wind* is that, without altering the structure or plot significantly, Kramer has managed to create a cinematic work which disguises its theatrical roots effectively, while retaining the dramatic tension of the courtroom battle of ideas. This process stems from the replacement of the split stage and the possibility of a full size overbearingly hot and stuffy courtroom. It is also altered through the subtle introduction of the more personal elements. It remains a cerebral and wordy piece but one whose theatrical roots are not glaringly obvious and which feels like a work of cinema.

The contrast with *Nuts* is marked with its small-scale intimate, almost claustrophobic courtroom setting. *Nuts* was first produced in New York in 1980 at the Biltmore Theater. Its author, Tom Topor, also wrote the screenplay for the powerful Jodie Foster gang rape film, *The Accused*,[53] as well as a courtroom

53 1988, UIP/Paramount.

related TVM on sexual abuse [*Judgment* (1990)] and a Vietnam massacre reputation rehabilitation TVM [*Word of Honor* (2003)].

The action of the play *Nuts* is set in a courtroom in the psychiatric hospital of Bellevue Hospital, New York. All three Acts of the play are located there. The play revolves around a high class call girl, Claudia, who kills a client and who is resisting being locked up as insane rather than being tried for her alleged crime with the assistance of a Public Defender lawyer. Her family and the State authorities seek to have her declared insane. She is able to satisfy the judge that, indeed, she is sane and fit to plead.

In the 1987 film version Barbra Streisand plays the part of Claudia, Richard Dreyfuss is her Public Defender lawyer and Karl Malden is her concerned father. The denouement and crux of the whole piece is the revelation that it is her father's abusive conduct which led his daughter to go off the rails in the first place. She ends up killing one of her sadistic clients. The play's single set is maintained in the film version. There are a few short illustrative flashbacks to Claudia's life as a high class call girl as she gives evidence in the style developed for television audiences in the 1950s by Perry Mason and revived in the 1970s by Anthony Petrocelli. That apart, this film is the closest we get to a straightforward filmed play. The claustrophobic atmosphere of the courtroom is maintained by the location of so much of the actual action in the one small space. Just as the play makes do with a single stage where all the action takes place, the film is restricted to three 'sets' – in addition to the court, the courtroom hallway and the court's holding cell. The filming of *Nuts* seems as close to a filming of a play as is possible to imagine. It was also adapted for the screen by the author, Tom Topor along with Darryl Ponicsan and Alvin Sargent. This presence of the original author along with a relatively modest budget may have inhibited the urge to create a fresh oeuvre and seems to have led to little more than a filming of the action. On a budget of $25 million it recouped some $30 million. It was neither a great critical nor a huge commercial success. Comments included 'exceptionally talky and becalmed' (*New York Times*), 'a futile exercise in courtroom cliches' (*Chicago Sun Times*), and 'a facile script' (*Washington Post*). This seems a perfect illustration of the transpositional approach to adaptation. It lives on in the box set of the Barbra Streisand Collection along with *Up the Sandbox* (1972), *What's Up Doc?* (1972) and *The Main Event* (1979).

A rather different arrangement is found in the play and film *A Few Good Men.* It was one of the first pieces of work from the prolific and successful screenwriter Aaron Sorkin, whose credits include *Sports Night, The West Wing, Studio 60 on the Sunset Strip*, and *The Newsroom* as well as screenplays for *Charlie Wilson's War* and *The Social Network.* Unlike the other material examined, the screenplay was solely in the hands of the play's author, Sorkin. It centres on the court martial of two marines whose involvement in an initiation rite has resulted in the death of a fellow recruit. They admit the actions resulting in the death. The defence of the two marines is assigned to Lieutenant Daniel Kaffee. He is a lawyer son of a famous navy lawyer of the rank of Admiral, counting down the days until he can enter a lucrative legal practice. We soon learn that he is proud to avoid the stress and hassle of pleading in court and has managed to plea bargain all his previous caseload. The play centres on his development into a truth-seeker rather than chasing convenience and how this exposes the alternative code of serving soldiers with a commitment to their units and regiments above all. We discover that this alternative set of rules means that the two accused soldiers subjected their colleague to an initiation process because they were under orders. Obedience to whatever their superior tells them is a crucial part of their code – Unit, Corps, Country. How the defence strategy develops is the centrepiece of the play and how it works in practice is the climax.

A Few Good Men also contains both structural and visual changes, including a stunning opening sequence of close order drill impossible to produce on stage in a standard theatre. The shifts to Cuba and the preoccupation of Kaffee with baseball on an actual baseball field rather than this merely being a conversational topic allow us to see Kaffee as physically disengaged from his lawyerly duties. In terms of plot and dramatic moments it perhaps comes as a surprise to discover that the most quoted sequence in the film, the explosion of Colonel Nathan Jessup, is taken directly from the play and is not deliberately engineered to suit Jack Nicholson's irascible persona and that Daniel Kaffee was written as a smiling charmer before Tom Cruise imprinted his own particular style upon the young naval officer. The line 'You can't handle the truth!' was voted the twenty-ninth greatest American film quote of all time by the American Film Institute in 2005 and the film was voted the fifth best Courtroom Drama by the same organisation in 2008. In the play we simply have separate zones to represent Cuba, the offices and the courtroom. The narrative, however, does not alter, other than to highlight the extensive and stressful nature of trial preparation which has become a motif for all films about trial lawyers.

This modest roster of adapted plays suggests that, as far as the cinema of justice is concerned, the original theatrical material has been mainly used to create quite distinct cinematic artefacts with few traces of their origin as stage plays. In this examination, three of the films examined involved major changes and opening out and one did not. The neat explanation of authorial involvement does not emerge as the sole explanation. The role of the playwright in the filming of the transpositional film – *Nuts* – would possibly suggest a crucial limiting element where there was such involvement. It does not, however, sit happily with one of the other films – *A Few Good Men* – where such a role did not hinder a very different piece of work appearing. A detailed examination of a wider range of films, however, might yield a clear and consistent link between authorial involvement and the nature of the kind of adaptation undertaken.

Although unfashionable and perhaps simplistic, the notion of the *auteur* may also be worthy of some consideration. Within these films, distinguished and influential directors in their heyday like Billy Wilder, Stanley Kramer and Rob Reiner, have created something quite novel and distinct as contrasted with a rather tired production from veteran Martin Ritt in his penultimate directorial role after a thirty-year career. This too might turn out to be the most powerful marker of change in plays adapted to films in the cinema of justice.

The suggestion of McFarlane, that there are likely to be other factors, may also prove telling. Non-literary, non-novelistic influences at work may be crucial, such as the conditions within the film industry and the prevailing cultural and social climate may be a more helpful indicator. As indicated, with a large group of films in the cinema of justice having a theatrical source, it seems worthwhile to explore these possibilities across the full range of this sub-genre.

Changing boundaries

As indicated, though, there have been two related developments within the past decade which suggest that there is more to the theatre of justice than merely providing a conduit to cinematic prestige. In the general context of a flourishing theatre scene, at least in the UK,[54] there has been something of a revival of theatrical performances of the original plays which were the source of film scripts in the past. A steady stream of film and television actors have been bringing back to life forensic stage plays. The commercial theatre has seen in recent times on both sides of the Atlantic versions of *A Few Good Men*, *Inherit the Wind*, *The Winslow Boy*, *Witness for the Prosecution* and *Twelve Angry Men*.[55]

There have also been intimations of a shift in the hitherto natural process of moving from theatre to film. In addition to the play versions of films,[56] we now have the shift from TV to stage with versions of television successes on the stage in which either members of the original cast or their sound-alikes provide a live version of their television selves from *'Allo 'Allo*, *Hi de Hi*, *Dinner*, *Corrie*, *Yes Minister* and *Yes Prime Minister*. The health of this form of theatre appears rude.

In this chapter there has been a very modest start to the process of gauging the significance of the theatre on the cinema of justice. The theatrical sources of a small number of significant films on law and justice have been explored and there has been the start to a process which, in due course, will provide a full taxonomy of theatre-based films as well as a guide to those works of 'popular legal theatre' which have not been adapted for the screen and possible reasons for their omission. This chapter has indicated those features which seem to make a stage drama work as film and what does not. The use of stage drama as a source throughout the history of the cinema of justice has been noted. The study

54 Live Analytics, *State of Play: Theatre UK Growing, Evolving, Diverse* (Ticketmaster International, 2013) 5.

55 Originally this play started out life as a 1 hour TV drama, with author Reginald Rose producing a play version after the success of the film.

56 Including most recently the bizarre experience reported of film readings on stage of such films as Quentin Tarantino's film *The Hateful Eight* – see John Patterson, 'Lights, No Camera, Action: The Joy of Live Film Readings' *The Guardian*, 25 April 2014.

has located the theatre-film work within the framework of adaptation theory encountered principally in literature/film discussions and pointed to the limited nature of this work in relation to theatre.

This initial exploration of the interaction between cinema and theatre has produced some potential connections. The contrast between the theatrical text/performance and the film version offers the opportunity for reflection on the nature of the phenomena of law, film and drama and their relationship. As we have seen, the four plays which have been covered have elements of the transpositional approach to adaptation. In three of them, however, it is fair to say that an almost unrecognisable version greets us when we see the filmed version. With the exception of *Nuts*, the films are markedly different in tone from what they would be if their creators had not had any ambition beyond producing filmed versions of the plays. In the other plays, the transformations have been both visual and narrative. In *Witness for the Prosecution* the drama's tone is altered with changes to the narrative via the introduction of sub-plots as well as the benefit of impressive creations of the courtroom setting and Chambers. The original form in *Inherit the Wind*, suggested a world outwith the confines of the stage in a stylised manner like the Ascot Racecourse scene in *My Fair Lady* (1959). The transforming elements involve the extensive use of external settings and scenes as well as shifts in the narrative and relationship of the principal characters. What remain are the core structures of the originals. The source models already contain the theatricality inherent in a drama based in the courtroom. What has been added are relationships and characters not found in the originals. The same has occurred with *A Few Good Men* but with the film having the simpler tasks of fleshing out the characters and locations for a cinematic rather than a theatrical experience. The next step is to explore beyond these films which have been selected and see whether or not these practices are borne out once one looks elsewhere in the cinema of justice. In addition, what has emerged is that the relationship between the staged and filmed artistic product is not a static one of source followed by screen adaptation. Not only have the original sources continued to have a life of their own but a process of films, as well as television, as a source for the theatre seems to have developed. Given that most of this work operates firmly within the context of the commercial market, two courses of further research beckon. One is to explore to what extent the addition of sub-plots and locations and changes of tone are encountered in the rest of the cinema of justice derived from theatre. The other, which parallels the course charted for film and television, is to explore in depth the economic elements driving the reverse film/theatre adaptation developments and seek to uncover whether this is a temporary phase or a permanent phenomenon.

Bibliography

Aebischer, Pascale, *Screening Early Modern Drama: Beyond Shakespeare* (Cambridge University Press, 2013)

Asimow, Michael, 'Bad Lawyers in the Movies' (2000) 24 *Nova Law Review* 533
Bachmann, Michael, 'Theatre and the Drama of Law: A "Theatrical History" of the Eichmann Trial' (2010) 14 *Law Text Culture* 94
Balkin, Jack M, 'Idolatry and Faith: The Jurisprudence of Sanford Levinson' (2003) 38 *Tulsa Law Review* 553
Balkin, Jack and Sanford Levinson, 'Law as Performance' in Michael Freeman and Andrew Lewis (eds), *Law and Literature: Current Legal Issues* (1999) vol 2, 729
Ball, Milner S, 'The Play's the Thing: An Unscientific Reflection on Courts Under the Rubric of Theater' (1975) 28 *Stanford Law Review* 100
Bergman, Paul and Michael Asimow, *Reel Justice – The Courtroom Goes to the Movies* (Andrews McMeel Publishing, 2nd edn, 2006)
Bluestone, George, *Novels into Film* (University of California Press, 1957)
Brion, Denis J, 'The Criminal Trial as Theater: The Semiotic Power of the Image' in Anne Wagner and Richard K Sherwin (eds), *Law Culture and Visual Studies* (Springer, 2014) 329
British Film Institute, *BFI Statistical Yearbook* (2013)
Carlen, Pat, 'The Staging of Magistrates' Justice' (1976) 16(1) *British Journal of Criminology* 48
Carlen, Pat, *Magistrates' Justice* (Martin Robertson, 1976)
Christie, Agatha, *Witness for the Prosecution and Selected Plays* (Harper Collins, 1995)
Crawley, Karen, 'The Farce of Law: Performing and Policing "Norm" and "Ahmed" in 1969' (2010) 14 *Law Text Culture* 247
Cutchins, Dennis, Laurence Raw and James M Welsh (eds), *Redefining Adaptation Studies* (Scarecrow Press, 2010)
Desmond, John M and Peter Joseph Hawkes, *Adaptation: Studying Film and Literature* (McGraw Hill, 2006)
Freeman, Michael and Andrew Lewis (eds), *Law and Literature* (Oxford University Press, 1999)
Friedman, Lawrence M, 'Law, Lawyers and Popular Culture' (1989) 98 *Yale Law Journal* 1579
Greenfield, Steve, 'Hero or Villain? The Cinematic Lawyer and the Delivery of Justice' (2001) 28(1) *Journal of Law and Society* 25
Greenfield, Steve, Guy Osborn and Peter Robson, *Film and the Law: The Cinema of Justice* (Hart Publishing, 2nd edn, 2010)
Griffith, James, *Adaptations as Imitations: Films from Novels* (University of Delaware Press, 1997)
Halliday, Simon (ed.), *An Introduction to the Study of Law* (W Green, 2012)
Hay, Douglas, 'Property, Authority and the Criminal Law' in Douglas Hay *et al.* (eds), *Albion's Fatal Tree: Crime and Society in Eighteenth-Century England* (Pantheon, 1975) 17
Hay, Douglas, Peter Linebaugh, John G. Rule, E. P. Thompson and Cal Winslow (eds), *Albion's Fatal Tree: Crime and Society in Eighteenth-Century England* (Pantheon, 1975)
Kornstein, Daniel, *Kill All the Lawyers?: Shakespeare's Legal Appeal* (Princeton University Press, 1994)
Lawrence, Jerome and Robert Edwin Lee, *Inherit the Wind* (Dramatists Play Service, 2000)
Leiboff, Marett and Sophie Nield, 'Introduction: Law's Theatrical Presence' (2010) 14 *Law Text Culture* 1
LiveAnalytics, *State of Play: Theatre UK Growing, Evolving, Diverse* (Ticketmaster International, 2013)

McDougal, Stuart Y, *Made into Movies: From Literature to Film* (Hole, Rinehart and Winston, 1985)
McFarlane, Brian, *Novel to Film: An Introduction to the Theory of Adaptation* (Clarendon Press, 1996)
Machura, Stefan, 'An Analysis Scheme for Law Films' (2007) 36 *University of Baltimore Law Review* 329
Machura, Stefan and Peter Robson (eds), *Law and Film* (Blackwell, 2011)
Mermiri, Tina, *State of Play: Theatre UK Growing, Evolving, Diverse* (Ticketmaster International, 2013)
Meyer, Phil, 'Why a Jury Trial is More Like a Movie than a Novel' (2001) 28(1) *Journal of Law and Society* 133
Minow, Nell, '"An Idea is a Greater Monument than a Cathedral": Deciding How We Know What We Know in Inherit the Wind' (1996) 30 *University of San Francisco Law Rev* 1225
Moran, Leslie, Emma Sandon, Elena Loizidou and Ian Christie (eds), *Law's Moving Image* (Routledge-Cavendish, 2004)
Mulcahy, Linda, *Legal Architecture: Justice, Due Process and the Place of Law* (Routledge-Cavendish, 2011)
Owen, Jonathan, 'Event Cinema: Live Screenings of Opera and Ballet are the British New Wave' *The Independent* (UK), 27 January 2013
Palmer, R Barton and William Robert Bray (eds), *Modern British Drama on Screen* (Cambridge University Press, 2013)
Parsley, Connal, 'The Mask and Agamben: The Transitional Juridical Technics of Legal Relation' (2010) 14(1) *Law Text Culture* 12
Patterson, John, 'Lights, No Camera, Action: The Joy of Live Film Readings' *The Guardian*, 25 April 2014
Peters, Julia Stone, 'Legal Performances: Good and Bad' (2008) 4 *Law Culture and the Humanities* 179
Philippopoulos-Mihalopoulos, Andreas (ed.), *Law and the City* (Roudledge-Cavendish, 2007)
Pietrzak-Franger, Monika, '*Sleuth* On Screen: Adapting Masculinities' in R Barton Palmer and William Robert Bray (eds), *Modern British Drama on Screen* (Cambridge University Press, 2013) 169
Rafter, Nicole, 'American Criminal Trial Films: An Overview of their Development 1930–2000' (2001) 28(1) *Journal of Law and Society* 9
Ramshaw, Sara, 'Jamming the Law: Improvisational Theatre and the "Spontaneity" of Judgment' (2010) 14 *Law Text Culture* 133
Ray, Laura, 'Judicial Fictions: Images of Supreme Court Justices in the Novels, Drama and Film' (1997) 39 *Arizona Law Review* 151
Resnick, Judith and Dennis Curtis, *Representing Justice: The Creation and Fragility of Courts in Democracies* (Yale University Press, 2010)
Robson, Peter, 'Adapting the Modern Law Novel: Filming John Grisham' (2001) 28(1) *Journal of Law and Society* 147
Robson, Peter, 'Law and Popular Culture' (2001) 28(1) *Journal of Law and Society* 147
Robson, Peter and Jessica Silbey (eds), *Law and Justice on the Small Screen* (Hart Publishing, 2012)
Robson, Peter and Rodger J (2016) A Spatial Approach to Justice: The Development of Scottish Court Architecture (forthcoming)

Rogers, Nicole, 'The Play of Law: Comparing Performances in Law and Theatre' (2008) 8 *Queensland University of Technology Law & Justice Journal* 429

Sarat, Austin, Lawrence Douglas and Martha Merrill Umphrey (eds), *Law on the Screen* (Stanford University Press, 2005)

Schmidt, Theron, '"We Say Sorry": Apology, the Law and Theatricality' (2010) 14 *Law Text Culture* 55

Scopes, John T and James Presley, *Center of the Storm: Memoirs of John T. Scopes* (Henry Holt, 1967)

Simić, Olivera, 'Breathing Sense into Women's Lives Shattered by War: Dah Theatre Belgrade' (2010) 14 *Law Text Culture* 117

Sinyard, Neil, *Filming Literature: The Art of the Screen Adaptation* (Croom Helm, 1986)

Sorkin, Aaron, *A Few Good Men* (Samuel French, 1998)

Stephens, Mamari, '"Tame Kaka" Still? Maori Members, and the Use of Maori Language in the New Zealand House of Representatives' (2010) 14 *Law Text Culture* 220

Stritmatter, Roger, 'Shakespeare's Legal Appeal: *Kill All the Lawyers?* Seen Through the Prism of Authorship' (1997) 33 *Shakespeare Oxford Newsletter* 3

Topor, Tom, *Nuts* (Samuel French, 1981)

Wagner, Anne and Richard K Sherwin (eds), *Law Culture and Visual Studies* (Springer, 2013)

Wagner, Geoffrey, *The Novel and the Cinema* (Farleigh Dickinson University Press, 1975)

Wake, Caroline, 'Caveat Spectator: Judicial, Political and Ontological False Witnessing in CMI (A Certain Maritime Incident)' (2010) 14 *Law Text Culture* 160

Walton, Karen, 'Chamber Theatre' (2010) 14 *Law Text Culture* 309

Ward, Ian, *Shakespeare and the Legal Imagination* (Butterworths, 1999)

Williams, David A, 'Legal Language and Theatrical Presence: Transforming a Legal Inquiry into Theatre' (2010) 14 *Law Text Culture* 188

Woods, Alan, *The Selected Plays of Jerome Lawrence and Robert E Lee* (Columbus, 1995)

Part III

Law's technologies and cultural legal studies

Chapter 7

Picturing justice in a fraught legal arena

Fetuses, phantoms and mandatory ultrasounds

Jessica Silbey

Introduction

Since the US Supreme Court legalised abortion in the United States with *Roe v Wade* in 1973,[1] individual states have legislated to restrict that right through the regulation of medical practice and speech. Recently, anti-abortion groups have been advocating for laws that compel a pregnant woman to view a fetal ultrasound prior to an abortion. At their core, these mandatory ultrasound laws aim to prevent abortions because they assume that after viewing the ultrasound a woman will change her mind and decide to continue her pregnancy rather than terminate it.

The logic behind these laws relies on a misguided understanding of the ultrasound image, the circumstances of its viewing, and its female audience. This chapter aims to correct this understanding. It argues that these laws should be repealed, or else amended to reflect a twenty-first-century understanding of how digital images create meaning. Without an updated understanding of how images work on their audiences, rooted in contemporary aesthetic and cultural theory, the mandatory ultrasound laws thwart the very interests they claim to maintain: autonomy, freedom of choice and conscience, and objective, non-coercive decision-making.

Part I of this chapter describes the legal framework in the United States by focusing on two recent, opposing court cases about the legality of mandatory ultrasound laws. Part II analyses the competing discourses that animate the legal and cultural debates over reproductive choice, consent and information disclosure. Part III looks at the 'ideology of the image' and engages in a critique of medical imaging generally and ultrasound imaging in particular as an authoritative discourse intended to silence and coerce audiences. In the context of women's equality and reproductive liberty, this last part asks how photographs circulate in culture in order to interrogate how ultrasound images are relevant (if at all) to the debate concerning the morality and legality of abortion. The

1 *Roe v Wade*, 410 US 113 (1973).

chapter concludes by offering a critique that seeks to repeal or amend the mandatory ultrasound laws. This critique is grounded in aesthetic and cultural theory of which the law should take account in order to promote the justice it promises.

A case of two states: Texas and Oklahoma

From regulating the space and licensing of health clinics, to sexual education curricula, to mandating the provision of specific medical or non-medical services during clinic evaluations and procedures, anti-abortion pressures have been persistent and far-reaching since *Roe v Wade* in 1973. Mandating a fetal ultrasound is one of the most recent trends in anti-abortion politics. Its express goal is for the pregnant woman to visualise the embryo or fetus so that she contemplates her pregnancy in its visual dimension in addition to all the other ways she is experiencing it.

As of this writing, twenty-four states across the US regulate the provision of ultrasound by abortion providers.[2] Ten states require the ultrasound be performed and shown to the pregnant woman seeking an abortion. In three states, the woman must look at the ultrasound and the doctor must describe it to her, identifying the approximate gestational age, fetal length, identifying organs if visible, and in some cases making the heartbeat audible. In seven states, the ultrasound and description are mandatory, but the woman can decline to look or listen. The other fourteen states require a woman be given the opportunity to view an ultrasound if requested or if it is performed as clinic routine. In most of these twenty-four states, laws mandate that during pre-procedure counselling, the pregnant woman be told that an ultrasound will occur prior to the abortion. This counselling and the ultrasound may happen several days or hours before the procedure, depending on the mandatory state waiting periods. Because as many as 87 per cent of abortions in the US terminate pregnancies that are less than twelve weeks old,[3] mandatory ultrasounds in order to visualise the fetus are likely performed with a vaginal probe (a wand an inch in diameter that is inserted and pressed on the woman's cervix to get close to the uterus). Fetuses between five and nine weeks old (the majority of aborted pregnancies) are so small that abdominal ultrasounds produce less distinct images and sounds than the vaginal probe.[4]

2 Guttmacher Institute, *Induced Abortion in the United States Fact Sheet (2014)* (July 2014) www.guttmacher.org/pubs/fb_induced_abortion.html.

3 Ibid.

4 At week five, the spinal cord, heart and brain start to form; the fetus is approximately the size of a pen tip. At seven weeks, the fetus is the approximate size of a pencil eraser and arm buds begin to grow. At nine weeks, the fetus develops bones and is approximately 20 millimetres long. For more detailed medical facts, see Mayo Clinic, *Fetal Development: The 1st Trimester* (10 July 2014) www.mayoclinic.com/health/prenatal-care/PR00112.

The legality of mandatory ultrasound laws is in flux. Several courts already held parts of them unconstitutional. These court decisions are awaiting appellate review. Two recent cases, from Oklahoma and Texas, are on opposite sides of the constitutional divide. The Oklahoma case, *Nova Health Systems v Pruitt*, from 2012, held that the mandatory ultrasound requiring a simultaneous description of the fetus inflicted an undue burden on the woman's constitutional right to terminate a pregnancy of a non-viable fetus.[5] It thus violated the rule of *Planned Parenthood of Pennsylvania v Casey*, the US Supreme Court decision from 1993.[6] The Texas case, *Texas Medical Providers Performing Abortion Services v Lakey*, also from 2012, held that a similar law did not create an unconstitutional burden and instead promoted informed consent for women seeking abortions.[7] These cases suggest that the Supreme Court may eventually grant certiorari to resolve the conflict in light of *Roe v Wade* and its progeny.

Roe v Wade is primarily about the protection of the decision-making autonomy of a woman as she consults with her physician over her medical treatment.[8] *Roe* held that the governmental interest in a non-viable fetus does not outweigh the woman's control over her reproductive freedom. The state could only justify its interference with a woman's pregnancy during the first and second trimester if regulation serves to preserve the woman's health. Under *Roe*, until the fetus is viable and can live outside the woman's body the state cannot constitutionally interfere with or prohibit abortions to protect unborn fetuses for their own sake.

Criticism of *Roe* is manifold and varied. Some say it forced a decision judicially that should have been resolved through the democratic process, fomenting a backlash against the pro-choice movement.[9] Others criticise *Roe* for its legislative reasoning,[10] saying that it resembles technical line-drawing rather than the fact-dependent or generalised rules that courts are equipped to defend under the principle of *stare decisis*.

Whatever the criticisms of *Roe*, however, no one doubts that at its centre is the protection and celebration of women's control over their bodies in private consultation with their doctor. The state's interests in a woman's pregnancy cannot be separated from the state's interests in protecting her physical well-being and her individual liberty. Until the fetus can live independently of the woman the state has no compelling interest in protecting its life or its health at

5 *Nova Health Systems v Pruitt*, 292 P 3d 28 (Okla, 2012).
6 *Planned Parenthood of Southeasterrn Pennsylvania v Casey*, 505 US 833 (1992).
7 *Texas Medical Providers Performing Abortion Services v Lakey*, 667 F 3d 570 (5th Cir, 2012).
8 *Roe v Wade*, 410 US 113 (1973).
9 Linda Greenhouse and Reva B Siegel, 'Before (and After) *Roe v Wade* New Questions About Backlash' (2011) 120 *Yale Law Journal* 2028; Robert Post and Reva Siegel, 'Roe Rage: Democratic Constitutionalism and Backlash' (2007) 42 *Harvard Civil Rights Civil Liberties Review* 373.
10 Paul Brest *et al.*, *Processes of Constitutional Decisionmaking* (Aspen Publishers, 5th edn, 2006) 1405.

the expense of the woman's physical liberty and decisional autonomy. The mother's physical safety, however, remains paramount throughout her pregnancy well past the fetuses' viability, which explains the 'life and health of the mother' exception in all laws that prohibit late-term abortions.[11]

In 1992, *Planned Parenthood of Pennsylvania v Casey* blurred the focus on the private doctor–patient relationship. But in doing so, it re-emphasised the decisional autonomy women have regarding their reproductive health before fetal viability. *Casey* concerned several provisions of a Pennsylvania law that (1) required spousal notification of the wife's intention to terminate her pregnancy; (2) parental notification of a minor child's intention to terminate her pregnancy; and (3) the provision of certain truthful information twenty-four hours before the abortion about the health risks of abortion and of childbirth, and the probable gestational age of the fetus. The Supreme Court struck down the spousal notification requirement stating that it amounted to a veto by the husband over the wife's decision, which impermissibly reflected outmoded and hierarchical relationships between marital partners.

> The husband's interest in the life of the child his wife is carrying does not permit the State to empower him with this troubling degree of authority over his wife. [. . .] A state may not give to a man the kind of dominion over his wife that parents exercise over their children. [12]

For the same reason, the parental notification provision was upheld with a judicial bypass to protect the child against potential abuse from violent parents. Parents are guardians of their minor children, who are presumed to have diminished capacity regarding their medical decisions.

The court also upheld the 'informed consent' provisions[13] emphasising that providing truthful, non-misleading information about the procedure ensures that a woman apprehends the full consequences of her decision. The court affirmed provision of information related to the abortion, childbirth and the 'probable gestational age' of the fetus.[14]

> A requirement that the physician make available information [about the fetus] . . . was described in [previous cases] as an outright attempt to wedge the Commonwealth's message discouraging abortion into the privacy of the informed consent dialogue . . . We conclude, however, that informed choice need not be defined in such narrow terms . . . [R]equiring that the woman

11 *Casey*, 505 US 833 (1992), 850–851.
12 Ibid, 883, 898.
13 Ibid.
14 Ibid, 883.

> be informed of . . . fetal development and the assistance available should she . . . carry the pregnancy to full term is a reasonable measure to ensure an informed choice . . .[15]

This support for the state's provision of certain truthful, non-misleading information about the fetus is the foundation on which mandatory ultrasound laws are based.

At its best, the *Casey* court considers the provision of information empowering women to make the right choice for themselves. Given the unconstitutionality of the spousal provision, this informed consent provision imagines and presumes that women understand the information their doctor provides about the risks of abortions and childbirth. Except in unusual circumstances, in which the doctor in the exercise of her medical judgment thinks providing the information will harm the patient, considering truthful information about the abortion procedure is, to this court, the hallmark of autonomy and strength.

Moreover, the court approves the delivery of truthful non-misleading information that also delivers a message that childbirth is preferable. The puzzle of informed consent laws is here: how can we assess the information as truthful and non-misleading (a constitutional mandate if the information is required) at the same time as countenance the provision of the state's own moral critique of abortion in the delivery of the information?

This requires us to consider which part of ultrasound technology and its information is 'truthful and non-misleading'. It further requires us to determine how the ultrasound image and its narration contain the state's message of moral disapproval of abortion. And finally, it requires us to consider whether either element goes beyond the line *Casey* draws unduly burdening a women's constitutional right to privacy. Otherwise put, do the mandatory ultrasound laws imagine and help constitute the empowered female citizen that *Casey* describes? Or do they intrude both physically and intellectually into the body and mind of the woman becoming unconstitutionally invasive and degrading her independent status? Do they impermissibly manipulate an otherwise competent woman to effectuate the state's choice over her own?

Some courts take the first route, approving the state's means and message under *Casey* presuming the woman competent and nonetheless in need of more counselling. Other courts held these laws unconstitutional, also presuming the woman competent but deeming the mandatory counselling as unduly burdensome. The United States Court of Appeals for the Fifth Circuit, took the first route, upholding the 2011 Texas Woman's Right to Know Act (WRKA).[16] That law requires the physician to perform and display an ultrasound of

15 Ibid.
16 *Lakey*, 667 F 3d 570, 579 (5th Cir, 2012).

the fetus, make audible the fetus' heartbeat, explain to the patient the results of each procedure, and thereafter to wait 24 hours before performing the abortion.[17]

The court sees no problem of 'undue burden' under *Casey* because it understands sonograms and detecting fetal heartbeats as routine measures in pregnancy medicine today and thus not 'medically unnecessary' for the care of pregnant women (even if she seeks to terminate the pregnancy rather than keep it).[18] The court admits that 'the [Texas] statute's method of delivering this information is direct and powerful, but the mode of delivery does not make a constitutionally significant difference from the "availability" provision in *Casey*.'[19] Part III of this chapter will have more to say about this mistaken assertion that the 'mode of delivery' does not make a difference. Of course it does, as we see in the debates surrounding cameras in the courtroom and electronic surveillance. The medium matters.[20]

The court contends that 'denying [a woman] up to date medical information is more of an abuse to her ability to decide than providing the information.'[21] And '[o]nly if one assumes the conclusion of Appellees' argument, that pregnancy is a condition to be terminated, can one assume that such information about the fetus is medically irrelevant.'[22] Both these assertions assume the conclusions the court eventually reaches, which is that all information about the fetus is relevant to the woman's decision whether or not she wants to be a mother imminently. The court implies that women seeking abortions should be made to face the facts of their actions and no amount of true information will dissuade a woman who is sure of her choice. This is a view of women, as in *Casey*, as tough and independent. The court supports Texas' view that if women bend or waiver in the face of truthful information, their resolve has successfully been tested and at worst they have submitted to guidance by the state's normative values preferring childbirth to abortion.

The Oklahoma law invalidated in *Nova Health Systems v Pruitt* comes out the other way. The law parallels the Texas law in all relevant respects except two: it mandates a vaginal probe to produce a clearer ultrasound image, and it has no exceptions to the mandatory viewing. The Supreme Court of Oklahoma

17 A woman may decline to view the images or hear the heartbeat, but she may only decline to receive the narration of the images upon certification by the physician viewing the ultrasound is contraindicative to her physical or mental health. The Texas law also requires that the physician maintain a copy of the signed form for seven years. A physician who violates the law's provisions could lose their licence. (Tex HS Code Ann § 171.012(a)(4)).

18 *Lakey*, 667 F 3d 570, 579 (5th Cir, 2012).

19 Ibid.

20 Marshall McLuhan, *Understanding Media: The Extensions of Man* (McGraw-Hill, 1964).

21 *Lakey*, 667 F 3d 570, 579 (5th Cir, 2012).

22 Ibid.

invalidated the state law applying *Casey*'s undue burden test, albeit in a highly conclusory fashion. In a four-paragraph opinion, the Oklahoma Court said the '[t]he challenged measure is facially unconstitutional pursuant to *Casey*. The mandate of *Casey* remains binding on this Court until and unless the United States Supreme Court holds to the contrary.'[23]

Factual and legal justification for the Oklahoma court's ruling can be found in the trial court briefing. The undisputed facts were that while gestational age is directly relevant to the abortion procedure and to the choice between

> having a surgical abortion or a medication abortion, ultrasound imaging as a visual aid to the patient is unnecessary to provide that information . . . just as it is not necessary to use laboratory equipment as a visual aid when providing information about blood or urine results.[24]

Further, the court considered the undisputed facts from experts and peer-reviewed medical literature that 'seeing . . . an ultrasound image or hearing one described has no impact on a woman's decision' to continue a pregnancy despite causing significant distress.[25] In the record was evidence of women, undressed from the waist down undergoing a vaginal ultrasound, plugging their ears and contorting their body to avoid seeing and hearing about the ultrasound display.[26] Also undisputed at trial was the existence of the physician's ethical duty, thwarted in Oklahoma under the law in question, to avoid performing interventions that provide no medical benefit to a patient.

The Oklahoma court concluded that the state law placed a substantial obstacle before women seeking abortions for two reasons. First, it requires women to submit to unwanted, unnecessary and irrelevant medical procedures before obtaining an abortion. The state's interest in persuading the woman to refrain from terminating her pregnancy does not override her constitutional interest in physical freedom and self-determination when seeking medical care. Second, the Oklahoma law subjects women to demeaning and humiliating treatment as a condition of obtaining an abortion. The Oklahoma statute creates this physically and emotionally distressing circumstance for pregnant women only, implying that the state believes that these women alone require coaxing and regulation of their decisions. Together, these circumstances violate *Casey*'s rule and reasoning.

23 *Nova Health Systems v Pruitt*, 292 P 3d 28, [3] (Okla, 2012)
24 Ibid [16].
25 Ibid [17].
26 'One physician testified that her patients were so disturbed by the procedure that they stuck their fingers in their ears in an attempt to avoid hearing more.' R. on Appeal: Tab 17, App. 21, at 102:11–14.

The portrayal of vulnerable pregnant women and a harassing medical process conflicts with *Casey*'s description of tough, resilient women and a medical protocol that enlightens women rather than manipulates them. It also conflicts with *Roe*'s focus on protecting the private doctor–patient relationship. Requiring the provision and display of physically invasive and medically unnecessary ultrasounds with the express purpose of convincing a woman to change her mind about her choice to terminate her pregnancy interferes with the physician's medical judgment and the patient's bodily and decisional autonomy in response to that judgment. As the appellee *Nova Health Systems* writes in opposition to certiorari to the United States Supreme Court,

> [t]he burdens that the [Oklahoma] Act imposes on a woman's right to seek an abortion are so severe that they have not just the effect, but indeed 'the purpose . . . of presenting a substantial obstacle to a woman seeking an abortion'

rendering them unconstitutional under *Casey*.[27]

Competing discourses of choice, consent and disclosure

The impetus behind mandatory ultrasounds is to force a reckoning between the pregnant woman and her fetus. Although couched as 'informed consent' laws, there is no new information the ultrasound provides to the pregnant woman. She knows she is pregnant.[28] She is visiting a reproductive health centre precisely for that reason. She knows she could become a mother to this child. She seeks to avoid that destiny.

Informed consent laws require the provision of information relevant to the medical procedure, which includes the reason for and the nature of the medical procedure, its likelihood of success, its material risks, any alternatives and the consequences of doing nothing.[29] Rarely is the display of laboratory results, X-rays or ultrasound images part of the required 'information' provided to patients under informed consent regulations.

As Justice Blackmun points out in his concurrence in *Casey*, showing patients the contents of their bodies (e.g. an inflamed appendix) or a video of their impending procedure (e.g., to replace a heart valve) would be unnecessary to

27 Nova Health Systems, *et al.*, 'Brief in Opposition to Petition for Certiorari to the United States Supreme Court', Submission in *Pruitt v Nova Health Systems* US 12–1170, 3 June 2013, 22.

28 Informed consent must be understood in light of the 'reasonable' patient and physician. See Nadia Sawicki, 'The Abortion Informed Consent Debate: More Light, Less Heat' (2011) 21 *Cornell Journal of Law and Public Policy* 1, 19. '[T]he standard physician disclosure obligation under the law may be that of a "reasonable physician" or "reasonable patient": . . . Physicians generally have no duty to disclose information that would be obvious to the average patient.'

29 Ibid.

procure informed consent for a patient choosing to undergo an appendectomy or open-heart surgery. Indeed, it might actually be an inadvisable deterrent that causes unhealthy anguish and anxiety. Blackmun goes on to say that:

> the State's information must be 'calculated to inform the woman's free choice, not hinder it,' the measures must be designed to ensure that a woman's choice is 'mature and informed,' not intimidated, imposed, or impelled. To this end, when the State requires the provision of certain information, the State may not alter the *manner* of presentation in order to inflict 'psychological abuse,' designed to shock or unnerve a woman seeking to exercise her liberty right. This, for example, would appear to preclude a State from requiring a woman to view graphic literature or films detailing the performance of an abortion operation.[30]

The rest of the *Casey* court does not endorse or refute Blackmun's assertion that 'graphic literature' or 'films detailing . . . an abortion' would be impermissible because they inflict 'psychological abuse', designed to unnerve a pregnant woman seeking an abortion. Had they, the legality of the mandatory viewing and narration of fetal ultrasounds might be easier to answer.

The state appears to believe both that the ultrasound image simply conveys information in an unbiased and objective manner and that the ultrasound image is qualitatively different than an oral recitation of facts. Both cannot be true. And this is the first paradox embedded in mandatory ultrasound laws that reveals their illogic and illegality. As Carol Sanger writes:

> The . . . motivating belief is that a woman who sees her baby's image on a screen will be less likely to abort . . . [Compulsory ultrasound laws force women to] interrogate her decision over and over again. . . . Think harder, think longer . . . Mandatory ultrasound raises the stakes by producing an imagined showdown between the woman and her accuser, the fetus.[31]

Most commentators agree that this is the law's motivation, because *Casey* demands that women be audacious and stalwart in the face of manipulative government speech and not feeble or otherwise susceptible to influence in the face of medical facts they already know to be true.[32] Despite 'graphic . . . films'

30 *Planned Parenthood of Southeastern Pennsylvania v. Casey*, 505 US 833, 936–37 (1992) (Blackmun concurring in part and dissenting in part).

31 Carol Sanger, 'Seeing and Believing: Mandatory Ultrasound and the Path to a Protected Choice' (2008) 56 *University of California Los Angeles Law Review* 351, 358, 401.

32 The exception in *Casey* is when women are victims of domestic violence, which *Casey* describes as degrading and demeaning women, often rendering women unable to exercise autonomous choice regarding their reproductive destiny. Ironically, the court condones a state's influence over a woman's choice whether to become a mother but rejects a spouse's influence. Paternalism by the state is permitted, even applauded, but a husband's is constitutionally infirm.

intending to inflict 'psychological [trauma], . . . to unnerve a woman seeking to exercise her liberty right,'[33] a woman must be strong enough to face the ultrasound image, the fetus' cloudy image on the screen, and the fact of her pregnancy one last time before choosing to end it.

This rhetoric of courage, autonomy and choice whiplashes women and traps them between two incompatible and unrealistic identities. By mandating an ultrasound, the state appears to say:

> In order to make a decision of this significant moral magnitude, you must demonstrate substantial resilience and certainty to look upon your fetus and agree to kill it. Being this strong, you are free to exercise your choice under these circumstances. But if you are not this strong, you must become a mother, with all the responsibilities and strength that requires.

Embedded in this hypothetical paean to a woman's strength and autonomy is a related paradox concerning female gender stereotypes that otherwise render so many laws unconstitutional under US equality jurisprudence: A woman is presumed capable of being a mother – with the strength, resilience, time and resources that requires – simply because she has the capacity to reproduce. However, a woman is not presumed capable to make the other choice – not to become a mother – without undergoing state challenges to her decision. And this is because the first path of motherhood is her biological destiny; refusing it by terminating her pregnancy undermines accepted norms of gendered behaviour.[34]

Similarly, a third paradox exists in the required ultrasound law. Accepting one's maternal future in the face of the hurdles to the abortion may be noble (she has chosen life after all!) but it is also a sign of weakness: she couldn't withstand the state's proffer and persuasion. By contrast, the choice to abort having faced the state's hurdles is immoral (she chose death after all!) but it is also a sign of determination and courage: she withstood the state's proffer and persuasion. In what world do we accept laws that paint women in this bind of character and fitness in the process of choosing essential features of their future? If a pregnant woman succeeds in the face of the state's challenge, she is allowed to exercise her choice but she is immoral. If she is scared or deterred by the prerequisites to the abortion procedure, she becomes a mother with all the responsibilities that entails. This latter path is somehow simultaneously the more moral choice as well as the path that (according to the state) weaker or indecisive

33 *Casey*, 505 US 833 (1992), 937 n 7.

34 'To the extent women requesting abortions are expressly rejecting their maternal identity, we should reject mandated disclosures that reinforce this identity against the patient's will.' Sawicki, above n 28, 35.

women will more likely take. It is also the path the state encourages women to follow. In other words, the state hopes women are too weak and uncertain in the face of pregnancy and the state's obstacles that instead of women fortifying their will, they yield to biological destiny and the state's preference for childbirth. Yet this too conflicts with the essential tenets of *Casey*.

In addition to presuming that women can and shall be capable mothers simply by virtue of being female, these laws presume women have a diminished capacity to comprehend medical information and its social consequences. State legislative records make clear that behind the compelled speech and display laws around abortion is the long-discredited and insulting stereotype of women's limited capacity for scientific comprehension and their irrational temperament.[35] Under the auspice of the 'politics of protection' as Reva Siegel has written, these laws presume women to be frail and in need of the state's firm and guiding hand.[36]

But women seeking abortions are not confused about the fact of their physical state or the effect an abortion has on that physical state. They may not understand how the abortion proceeds or what its risks to their health may be, just as they may not understand how pregnancy proceeds or what its risk to health may be. The state may endeavour to require a physician to accurately apprise women of those risks to inform one's choice whether to remain pregnant. But the forced display of an ultrasound image does not dispel confusion about one's *current* state, the abortion procedure or the pregnancy process. Instead, it projects the state's desire for the woman's *future* state as mother on to this fetus as her future child.

Compelled ultrasounds also interfere with the private and autonomous relationship between the pregnant woman and her physician. Requiring doctors to speak on behalf of the state, or to comingle their advice with that of the state, may reasonably be a source of confusion for women. Most physicians describe mandatory disclosures concerning pre-abortion ultrasounds as onerous because they interfere with the trust and authority between doctors and patients.[37] Patients trust doctors to tell them objective truths about their health and prognosis and to be neutral in the face of moral or religious beliefs. Non medical information

35 Reva Siegel, 'Dignity and the Politics of Protection: Abortion Restrictions Under Casey/Carhart' (2008) 117 *Yale Law Journal* 1694, 1705, 1726. These laws presume women are uniquely confused in the face of the abortion decision (and not other medical decisions) and therefore are susceptible to being coerced and misled regarding this particular procedure. See Sawicki, above n 28, 19 (citing Reva Siegel and her references to South Dakota's law). See also Maya Manian, 'The Irrational Woman: Informed Consent and Abortion Decision-Making' (2009) 16 *Duke Journal of Gender, Law and Policy* 223, 225–226; Zita Lazzarini, 'South Dakota's Abortion Script – Threatening the Physician-Patient Relationship' (2008) 359 *New England Journal of Medicine* 2189, 2190.

36 Siegel, above n 35, 1726.

37 Caroline Mala Corbin, 'Compelled Disclosures' (2014) *Alabama Law Review* (forthcoming) (draft on file with author).

provided by a physician but for the state distorts the doctor–patient relationship, shifting the power dynamic from one where the physician enables a patient's free choice to one in which the physician under threat of state sanction persuades the patient to exercise the state's choice. Cloaked in the guise of a white coat and selflessness ('I am only here to help you; I have your best health interests at stake'), the forced delivery of ultrasound images that resemble scientific information, but are really projections of a state's desire for women to become mothers, confuses and misleads patients as to their doctor's intention and interests. These laws do not allow doctors to say 'I am obliged by law to show and describe this ultrasound to you, but I disagree with this requirement,' a stipulation that would disentangle the doctor's counsel from the state's speech.

Reva Siegel writes that '[d]ignity-constraints on misleading counsel apply if the government is not open about the fact that it is engaged in advocacy or committed to inculcating a particular moral viewpoint.'[38] This argument supports those above, and brings us to the final point of this section: mandatory ultrasound laws commit privacy and dignity violations. If we start with the proposition that women are independent and capable decision-makers about their reproductive choices, a position equality jurisprudence requires, mandatory speech and display laws violate fundamental privacy and disrupt the autonomy the state claims to foster. It does so in several ways.

One: these laws mandate a physical intrusion via vaginal or trans-abdominal ultrasounds, forcing a woman to produce evidence for the state of her own pregnancy of which there is no doubt.[39] Two: they aim to deliver emotionally intense reports about the fetus by underplaying its current biological existence, which is as an underdeveloped human being, while simultaneously gesturing towards its potential future as a healthy, born child. This kind of account preys on fears or insecurities a patient might have about her circumstance: Is she a bad person? Could she be a good mother? Is this anyone else's business? Neither the state nor a physician should excite the emotions of patients in order to persuade them to make a particular decision. This is presumptively impermissible as a form of coercion and violates central tenets of informed consent doctrine.[40] Three: these laws mandating description and display of ultrasounds intrude intellectually into a patient's decision-making autonomy, a form of autonomy that is private and protected in US constitutional jurisprudence. Like the decision whether to engage in religious exercise, to be married, to engage in political speech, to treat one's own illness, deciding whether to be a parent free from coercion is central to the meaning of freedom and dignity in our constitutional democracy. Of course, as *Casey* says, 'what is at stake is the woman's right to

38 Siegel, above n 35, 1760.
39 Sanger, above n 31, 402.
40 Sawicki, above n 28, 17.

make the ultimate decision, not a right to be insulated from all others in doing so.'[41] But *Casey* also says that the state's regulations 'must be calculated to inform the woman's free choice, not hinder it.'[42] The state's deliberate, powerful intrusion into the privacy of a woman's judgment concerning this fundamental, intimate life choice has as its goal the encumbrance of women's freedom of conscience under these circumstances.[43]

Ultrasounds and the ideology of the image

Ideology of the image

The phrase 'ideology of the image' has a long pedigree.[44] A cultural history of the visual arts (and particularly of realism) would be incomplete without addressing the issue of how 'reality' is constructed in diverse visual media. One of the primary flaws of the mandatory ultrasound debate concerns its failure to address the ideology of the ultrasound image.

To be sure, medical imagery has revolutionised patient care. But physicians (and radiologists) are the first to admit that imaging is an interpretive practice; there are images (and opinions about images) that are better than others for the purposes they serve.[45] Central questions for medical professionals include: What is the image for? How does it help the patient outcome?

These are very different questions than those triggering the use of mandatory ultrasounds prior to abortions. Proponents of ultrasounds say that '[u]ltrasounds cut through all th[e] evasive rhetoric. They show the reality of the unborn baby.'[46] But images themselves must be understood as *rhetorical*. Indeed, the state relies on the rhetorical difference a photographic image makes in conveying a message about facts already known.

Physicians who conduct pre-abortion ultrasounds do so either because the law requires it or because locating the tiny embryo in the comparatively large womb facilitates the procedure. Sometimes physicians will conduct an ultrasound

41 *Casey*, 505 US 833 (1992), 877.

42 Ibid.

43 'In authorizing regulation that communicates the community's values with the aim of influencing a woman's abortion decision, Casey deviates from informed consent premises.' Siegel, above n 35, 1758.

44 See, eg, Bill Nichols, *Ideology and the Image: Social Representation in Cinema and Other Media* (Indiana Press, 1981); Walter Benjamin, *Illuminations* (Schocken, 1969); Roland Barthes, *Camera Lucida* (Hill and Wang, 1982); Susan Sontag, *On Photography* (Picador, 2001); André Bazin, *What is Cinema?* (University of California, 1968).

45 Neal Feigenson and Christina Spiesel, *Law on Display: The Digital Transformation of Legal Persuasion and Judgment* (New York University Press, 2009).

46 Jill Stanek, *With Her Typing Fingers on the ProLife Pulse* (6 February 2013) www.jillstanek.com/2013/02/real-reason-abortion-providers-oppose-ultrasounds-78-change-minds.

to confirm gestational age, but doing so via ultrasound is an inexact science with error ranges of four to eleven days.[47] And nowhere does the medical literature indicate that displaying an ultrasound image to the patient optimises her health outcomes for the abortion.

The display of the pre-abortion ultrasound may be analogised to the display of test results, biopsy tissue or other imaging technology. But physicians more often *describe* these results to the patient than display them, in large part because the visual results are inscrutable by the lay-patient. We see numbers and abbreviations next to blood tests, or pieces of tissue, or a bone scan, and most patients cannot understand with any accuracy or contextual significance what they see. Indeed, at the same time as mandatory ultrasound laws espouse the persuasive clarity of ultrasound images for the purposes of delivering information to the patient, these same laws rely on the inscrutability of the ultrasound image for its rhetorical force. They are hazy pictures, magnified hundreds of times. Without a physician or technician's narration, a patient would not understand what she sees on screen. Thus many mandatory ultrasound laws require the physician to narrate the image, pointing to organs and limbs. This narration evidences the ultrasound's acute *lack of clarity* for the patient. Because of the ultrasound's ambiguities, patients are not urged to view the ultrasound image literally, but instead to project onto it future, potential or imaginary facts in order to render the image meaningful as a present image of their future baby.

Despite this, the political rhetoric surrounding the mandatory ultrasound laws asserts (without substantiation) that once patients see the fetal image, they are less likely to terminate the pregnancy. And so we must examine the relationship between the rhetoric of 'truth' and 'objectivity' justifying mandatory ultrasounds and the physician's narrative and inherent ambiguity in all images, including medical images. Does the insertion of the visual image in between the patient and her doctor, in light of its inscrutability and its necessary narration, exacerbate the loss of dignity and autonomy the woman experiences in the treatment room?

Proof of life?

Those supporting mandatory ultrasound requirements appear to approve the cultural movement that glorifies the fetus and idolises its image.[48] From the moment *Life Magazine* published Lennart Nilsson's photograph of an in-utero fetus on its cover in 1965 with the caption 'Drama of Life Before Birth', the

47 SOGC Clinical Practice Guidelines (2014) 26(2) *Journal of Obstetrics and Gynecology of Canada* 171, 175.

48 Rosalind Pollack Petchesky, 'Foetal Images: The Power of Visual Culture in the Politics of Reproduction' (1987) 13 *Feminist Studies* 263.

fetus has enjoyed a celebrated, public presence. How did this image unintentionally galvanise a prolife movement?[49] We must investigate not what the image purports to be (what it documents) but instead what it may *do* (how it persuades). How does a photographic image cultivate authority to generate collective understanding?

One way is to create a shared vision beginning with the assertion that 'this is worth seeing' to become part of our memory and who we are. On this issue, media critics are effusive. Photographic journalists describe photographs as 'lift[ing] past events . . . out of obscurity',[50] serving as 'bridge[s] connecting'[51] the photographer or viewer to the subjects photographed. The mere taking and displaying of an image appears to 'warrant deep reflection'[52] and may 'transform [. . .] human apathy'.[53] In the mandatory ultrasound context, it demands consideration of the image as if more worthy than other aspects of the procedure. By creating a common viewing experience, the mandatory ultrasound aims to transform those who look upon it from mere women and doctors into mothers and witnesses to young life worth protecting. When Lennart Nilsson's photograph of the fetus was first taken, his editors at *Life Magazine* demanded proof that the images were of an actual fetus because the images were so novel.[54] Now, images of fetuses much hazier and ambiguous are accepted as proof of life. But why? What is the connection between proof of life (if this is what the photograph is) and reproductive choice?[55]

First, most ultrasounds like the Nilsson photograph lack context that provide meaning. The fetus floats in the picture – autonomous, unconnected, primary – and the woman is omitted or made irrelevant by subsequent discourse that frames the picture.[56] As surely as she must be there, she is unseen. The doctor rarely points to the uterine wall or her ovaries or cervix. Instead, the doctor's

49 Richard Hughes, 'Burning Birth Certificates and Atomic Tupperware Parties: Creating the Antiabortion Movement in the Shadow of the Vietnam War' (2006) 68(3) *The Historian* 541, n 24.

50 Douglas Brinkley, 'Foreword' in Nick Yapp, *One Hundred Days in Photographs: Pivotal Events That Changed the World* (National Geographic, 2007) 11.

51 Chris Johns, 'Introduction' in Nick Yapp, *One Hundred Days in Photographs: Pivotal Events That Changed the World* (National Geographic, 2007) 17.

52 Brinkley, above n 50, 11.

53 Gordon Parks, 'Introduction' in *Life: 100 Photographs That Changed the World* (Life Books, 2003) 7.

54 Nilsson remembers that the editors were initially dubious of the authenticity of the picture and 'wanted to have a witness to say that this was really the case' because 'it was a very sharp picture'. Eventually convinced, *Life* ran many more photos. NOVA, *Behind the Lens: An Interview with Lennart Nilsson* (2013) Public Broadcasting Service www.pbs.org/wgbh/nova/odyssey/nilsson.html.

55 Petchesky, above n 48, 268.

56 Ibid, 277.

description contains anatomical details of the fetus alone and often omits qualifying language such as 'developing' or 'underdeveloped'. Doctors say instead: 'here are the kidneys, the heart, head, legs,' not 'here are the developing organs' or 'here are the leg buds'. Fetal imagery, as one scholar writes, 'epitomizes the distortion inherent in all photographic images: their tendency to slice up reality into tiny bits wrenched out of real space and time.'[57] As such, this ultrasound image (as with most images) can be made to mean almost anything.[58] '[N]one of this viewing and measuring and recording of bits of anatomical data gives [us] the slightest clue as to what *value* should be placed on this or any other fetus, whether it has a moral claim to heroic therapy or life at all, and who should decide.'[59] The use of the picture as a mechanism for judgment is political, not evidential. And it is hardly objective because it is already a statement about the hierarchy of values and persons.[60]

Second, the autonomy of the fetus in the ultrasound image bolsters its status as hero and innocent victim. Without taking into account context and its underdeveloped biological existence, the fetus becomes a baby well before its birth. Like the famous 'man on the moon' photograph of Buzz Aldrin taken only a couple of years after Nilsson's photographs, both fetus and astronaut appear floating in space, unattached and autonomous. Each represents the 'Hobbesian view of . . . human beings as disconnected', isolated, and free.[61] Although Buzz Aldrin wears a space suit, we see in him, as we do in the fetus, images of ourselves: our beginnings and our potential achievements. The images provide evidence of something we will never see with our naked eyes. Some people also thought that the man on the moon photograph was fake.[62] But when eventually embraced, it became evidence of human possibility. Similarly, medical imagery and its potential for diagnosis and cure provides us a sense of our mortality and an empowering glimpse into our (hopeful) future. This kind of framing endears the photograph to us; we resist interpretations that critique its clarity or undermine its message because of the pleasurable fantasies these messages create.

Third, as with the authoritative and trusted commentary of US news anchorman Walter Cronkite announcing the moon landing, the photographic image is undeniable. Rendering images authoritative through narrative is called 'verbal overshadowing'. It shapes perceptions and memories of ambiguous images. Commonly analysed in the context of advertising images and criminal photographic identifications, verbal overshadowing can affect substantive

57 Ibid, 268.
58 This is the way fetish objects work. Ibid, 270.
59 Ibid, 274.
60 Ibid, 272.
61 Ibid, 270.
62 Peter Stepan, *Photos That Changed the World: The 20th Century* (Prestel, 2006) 124.

evaluation of images. 'One study shows that verbalizing perceptions of a face's attractiveness shifted subjects' ratings toward extremes: a better-than-average face became beautiful, and a below-average face became ugly.'[63] With fetal ultrasounds, where at best a woman may see a black and white cloud of ovals and rods, she now sees a living person, or she thinks she does. To some women, the redirecting of emotion and care from oneself to one's fetus is welcome. But to others, this experience is unwelcome and traumatic. Women who look upon the ultrasound of an unwanted pregnancy do not necessarily see a present or future baby until they are told that is what they should see.

The doctor's narration, combined with the ultrasound's ubiquity in popular culture as baby's 'first portrait',[64] intentionally inaugurates the woman's journey into motherhood, whether or not welcomed. To suggest otherwise denies how the ultrasound is used and what is omitted from its display (the woman) and from the narration (her choice and the fetus' immaturity). Like Justice Potter Stewart's infamous claim to judging obscenity – 'I know it when I see it' – mandatory ultrasound laws expect patients to accept the judgment of others and acquiesce in the cultural narrative of maternal obligation.

But image theory defies this necessary result. Its critical application to the mandatory ultrasound context would restore integrity to the legal situation. Were we to insist on truth and objectivity in providing information to women facing the choice to terminate their pregnancies (as *Casey* commands), we would require critical analysis of the image and its narration. The suppression of critical reflection in these instances injures the autonomy and dignity of women whose free choices the law protects. Insofar as mandatory ultrasound laws are premised on their capacity to sway a woman's choice in non-rational ways by virtue of the furtive power of images, they are ethically impermissible under long-standing informed consent laws.[65] Critical analysis and the opportunity for self-reflection are necessary to revive the informed consent that these laws purport (but fail) to provide.

Historicizing representational practices and applying critical theory to the ultrasound image

In *The Public Life of the Fetal Sonogram*, Janelle Taylor, through extensive historical and sociological research, describes the evolution of the ultrasound technology in response to the varying needs and desires of doctors, technicians and patients. (Today ultrasound machines produce different 'modes' of viewing, each of which

63 Rebecca Tushnet, 'Looking at the Lanham Act' (2011) 8 *Houston Law Review* 862, 879 (citing Bretton Talbot *et al.*, 'The Verbal Overshadowing Effect: Influence on Perception' (2008) 4 *Intuition* 12, 12–15).

64 Sanger, above n 31, 372.

65 Sawicki, above n 28, 33.

produce vastly different-looking images.[66]) This evolution was driven by patients' perceptions of the ultrasound machine and its images as irrelevant and intrusive.[67] Moreover, Taylor describes how not until the 1970s and 1980s did the ultrasound became more accepted in obstetric practice.[68] Even then (as now), it is primarily a diagnostic tool for specific circumstances, not a mechanism for bonding.[69]

The potential for the ultrasound image to mean what the state urges ('this is a human life worth saving') depends on viewers ignoring the history of ultrasound technology and the indeterminacy of images. Image theorists confirm our tendency to ignore semantic flexibility in photographs. Susan Sontag writes that 'photograph[y] furnish[es] evidence. Something we hear about, but doubt, seems proven when we're shown a photograph of it.'[70] Sontag's words 'evidence' and 'proven' situates photography as powerful rhetoric. André Bazin, speaking of film, says that moving pictures appear to 'bear [. . .] unimpeachable witness to "things as they are"',[71] perpetuating the myth of total cinema: representing the world transparently and without distortion.

These critics confirm that photography or film are particularly persuasive representational forms through which to account for a person or event. Roland Barthes famously wrote that 'the Photograph's essence is to ratify what it represents', to confirm to its audience the 'that-has-been'.[72] Photographs are documentary traces. But none of these critics suggest that the 'that-has-been' corresponds to an essential meaning, as the state insists with ultrasound images. The ontology of the image is just that: it does not go beyond signifying *being* to signifying *discrete knowledge or connotation.*[73] Even photojournalists, who are in the business of documenting past events, echo these critics. Errol Morris says that photographs appear to present merely 'ocular proof'.[74] Lennart Nilsson describes photography as 'reproducing what you are seeing.'[75] Morris has argued that the persuasion of photographs 'stop us from thinking, encourages *not* to

66 Ibid, 35.
67 Janelle Taylor, *The Public Life of the Fetal Sonogram: Technology, Consumption, and the Politics of Reproduction* (Rutgers University Press, 2008).
68 Ibid.
69 Ibid, 58–62.
70 Susan Sontag, *On Photography* (Picador, 2001) 5.
71 Robert Stam *et al.*, *New Vocabularies in Film Semiotics: Structuralism, Post-Structuralism and Beyond* (Routledge, 1992) 185–186 (discussing the writings of film theorist André Bazin).
72 Roland Barthes, *Camera Lucida* (Hill and Wang, 1981) 76–80, 85.
73 This is what Barthes meant when he said a photograph is a 'message without a code.' Roland Barthes, *The Responsibility of Forms* (University of California Press, 1991) 5.
74 Errol Morris and Michael Meyer, 'Recovering Reality: Errol Morris on Abu Ghraib' (2008) *Columbia Journalism Review* 2 (5 March 2008) www.cjr.org/behind_the_news/recovering_reality.php.
75 Lennart Nilsson, *Lennart Nilsson Biography* www.lennartnilsson.com/biography.html.

think.'[76] Indeed, both Morris and Nilsson contest photography's epistemological dominance, Morris as he mobilises film to tell counter-factual stories[77] and Nilsson as he emphasises disconnection between his famously clear photographs of early-stage fetuses and the ambiguity surrounding scientific, political, ethical and cultural understandings of life's beginning.[78]

Over the years, concerns arose from arenas as diverse as news organisations, police, courts and civic government over the authority of photographs. Appearing autonomous and bearing 'silent witness' to facts or events, audiences are asked to question photographic referentiality and truth demanding 'authentication' of the photographic image before it can be used as evidence.[79] We do so with reference to the photographer (a trusted source), a verified caption (confirming information), context (situational authority), more photographs and framing (alternative points of view), and independent verification (human authentication). And even while we may be assured of certain facts contained in the image[80] – this is a fetus, it has a developing head and organs – the meaning of the facts, their relevance and significance, remain disputed and mutable depending on the story they illustrate.

How do we alleviate the harm mandatory ultrasound laws cause? William Mitchell suggests that a new phase of image study 'encourage[s] prolonged contemplation, second and third looks, reversals of perceptual fields . . . [so] that pictures might themselves be sites of theoretical discourse.'[81] Mitchell's recent work asks that we attend to the nature of pictures to learn better that and how they captivate us. John Tagg, by contrast, questions whether seeing is believing and asks instead about the history of the photograph: 'The photograph is not a magical "emanation" but a material product of a material apparatus set to work in specific contexts, by specific forces, for more or less defined purposes. It requires therefore not an alchemy but a history.'[82]

76 Morris and Meyer, above n 74.

77 Errol Morris, 'Which Came First, the Chicken or the Egg? (Part One)' *The New York Times* (New York), 25 September 2007 (discussing Roger Fenton's photographs 'Valley in the Shadow of Death').

78 Ibid. See also Hasse Persson, *Q&A with Lennart Nilsson* www.lennartnilsson.com/q_a.html.

79 US Federal Rules of Evidence 1001 (authenticating documents).

80 Of course, there are plenty of cases in which the photograph 'lies' and the facts it contains are false. See Hany Farid, 'Digital Doctoring: How to Tell the Real From the Fake' (2006) 3(4) *Significance* 162–166; Hany Farid, 'Seeing Is Not Believing' (2009) 46(8) *IEEE Spectrum* 44–48.

81 Asbjørn Grønstad and Øyvind Vågnes, 'What do Pictures Want?: An Interview with W J T Mitchell' *Image & Narrative* (online), November 2006 www.visual-studies.com/interviews/mitchell.html.

82 John Tagg, *Burdens of Representation: Essays on Photographies and Histories* (University of Minnesota Press, 1993) 3.

Whereas Mitchell initially looks inward at the nature of images and how they act on us, Tagg focuses outward at the photograph's material production of meaning through its making and circulation. Both approaches are central to becoming more self-aware of our tendency to underestimate the burden and power of photographs. Both approaches expose the injustice of mandatory ultrasounds in terms of reproductive rights jurisprudence that requires we protect the autonomy and dignity of women in the face of unwanted pregnancies.

To do so, we first consider the author of the ultrasound image, the person who authorises the image in the first instance. The 'photographer' in the ultrasound context is the technician or the physician. Aside from the possibility of faulty machines or a hesitant doctor, the 'source' of the image and its situational context appears convincing and respected. Moreover, the image is made in a medical office, wrapped in its own situational objectivity, authority and domination.

Second, the image's physical framing shapes and directs its interpretation. What is in the frame and what is not in the frame matters. For example, the absence of the woman's body signals a hierarchy of importance: baby first, woman second. The fuzziness of images demand narration and audience supplementation of more information and detail to make sense of what we think we see. As with photos of the Loch Ness monster or the Zapruder film detailing the assassination of JFK, photos do not provide the whole (or even enough) of the story. As we piece it together bringing our own perspective and understanding to the viewing, we become invested in the story that makes sense to us. All of this is supplementation beyond the actual image, which itself is a digital enhancement and requires professional training to interpret. In other words, the facts in the picture and the story the frame conveys often come from outside it.

Third, point of view matters. Images taken from one perspective can distort or recharacterise the same image when taken from a different perspective. Consider the 'zoom' or 'close up'. A shot of a person from far away is less emotionally intense and striking than is a close-up of that same person's face, her expression and her facial features clear and readable. The close-up concentrates the audience's attention and builds interest. We 'experience' closeness to the person, and thus we 'feel' close to the person. We see anxiety, fear, love or devotion on the face in the frame and those emotions stir in us too. Close-ups work by fuelling empathy through visual alignment. The fetal sonogram is a close-up.[83] We may not see facial expressions on the fetus, but descriptions of 'kicking' 'thumb sucking' 'rolling' 'sleeping' 'strong' or 'quiet' movements imbues the magnified image with intentionality and autonomy. The zoom or magnified focus of the image makes us feel physically and emotionally

83 Sanger, above n 31, 372.

closer to the fetus as a baby. We do not experience it as a bean-sized organism over which we have possession because it resides in our body, but as an autonomous and wilful child whose privacy we are invading by peeking into the womb.

Fourth, social situations affect how the patient and the doctor interpret the ultrasound. Does the patient come to the exam room under conditions of a wanted pregnancy or an unwanted one? With a partner or without? Having had children previously or not? Is the patient a young adult or a mature woman? For example, those who have lost a family or friend to cancer may differently view images of patients fighting the disease than those who are lucky to be untouched by cancer. Or, someone who lost a wanted pregnancy might bring intense anxiety to the ultrasound experience, knowing that not all pregnancies end happily.[84] Images are not self-containing in their meaning or their message. Their significance depends on what comes before, what comes after, and what experiences we bring to them.

Absent a critical or historicising practice alongside the compelled disclosure, cognitive distortions are likely to occur precisely because of the interpretive control by the person or organisation that frames its viewing (here, the state). As Professor Caroline Corbin explains, certain framing 'techniques exploit a distorting heuristic embedded in people's decisionmaking' and thereby impermissibly intrude on an individual's decisional autonomy. As is the case with advertising, where sellers employ the technique of 'affective priming', the ultrasound is used by the state to convey a specific message that celebrates maternal care over independence and unborn babies over women. Affective priming works by

> mak[ing] [a] product attractive not by describing or illustrating its benefits, but by associating it with something the audience already views positively. The point is not to help the audience visualize, understand, or remember an informational claim, but to piggyback [the] product onto a pre-existing emotional connection the viewer already has to something completely unrelated.[85]

By harnessing the image's ambiguity and combining it with the ideological certainty of medical imaging and glorification of maternity and childbirth, mandatory ultrasound laws undermine women's independent choice by exploiting this well-known advertising technique.

In the cultural context in which these laws operate, mandatory ultrasounds rely upon and promote cognitive distortions degrading rather than enhancing

84 Ibid, 374.
85 Corbin, above n 37, 27.

the patient's autonomy. They are deceptive to the patient and coercive for the health care provider. As such, these laws should be rejected. Barring that, we might follow the critical process described above, cross-examining the text and questioning its situational veracity.

Conclusion

Despite the revolution in communication technology, visual images and instantaneous messaging do not enhance all spaces and interactions. For example, the debate continues in the US over cameras in the courtroom with the US Supreme Court for itself drawing a line between delayed textual transcripts and audio recordings of oral arguments, which are permitted, and the televised or filmed oral arguments, which are not. Justice Souter famously said, 'I think the case (against cameras) is so strong that I can tell you that the day you see a camera coming into our courtroom, it's going to roll over my dead body.'[86] Concerns range from how cameras bias juries, lawyers and witnesses, whether cameras compromise the dignity of the courtroom, if cameras distort the court proceedings and perceptions of the judicial system, and how might cameras threaten the autonomy and privacy of judicial decision-makers.[87] If cameras and visual imaging in the public courtroom remain troubling for their potential undue influence and distortion, why are they embraced without complication in the private and sensitive space of the doctor's exam room in the context of abortion?

Martin Scorcese has recently called for photographic and film literacy, writing that '[w]e need to educate [audiences] to understand the difference between moving images that engage their humanity and their intelligence and moving images that are just selling them something.'[88] Laws that assume or rely on knee-jerk reactions to images and the data they contain are laws worth repealing. We are accustomed to the critical evaluation of text and oratory as a long-standing habit in law, the sciences, and consumption of news. We have not yet developed a similar habit of scepticism and critique with regard to film and photographic images used demonstratively or substantively in these same settings. Leaving the ultrasound image to be narrated according to the state's script, or to be framed by the dominant cultural expectation that the image bonds the mother with her 'baby', encourages deceptive and misleading speech about an image that is ambiguous at best, and coerces women and their doctors

86 Tony Mauro, 'Roll the Cameras (or Soutersaurus Rex)' *Legal Times* (Washington DC), 8 April 1996, 9.

87 For an analysis of the arguments for cameras in the courtroom, see Nancy Marder, 'The Conundrum of Cameras in the Courtroom' (2012) 44 *Arizona State Law Journal* 1490.

88 Martin Scorcese, 'The Persisting Vision: Reading the Language of Cinema' *New York Review of Books* (New York), 15 August 2013.

to enact the state's moral judgment for the duration of the image's viewing. Short of abolishing compelled viewings of ultrasounds, we should encourage critical engagement with them, which includes qualifying the accompanying narrative with accurate medical terminology about fetal size, development and capacity. Doctors should be able to voice their disagreement with the viewing practice and be free to 'depart [. . .] the text'[89] as scripted by the state, especially when it distorts or selectively describes the 'facts' about the pregnancy. Image and aesthetic theory has much to say about the roles of images in law and policy. We should rely on both to foment more perfect freedoms and the equality the laws purport to protect.

Bibliography

Barthes, Roland, *Camera Lucida* (Hill and Wang, 1982)

Barthes, Roland, *The Responsibility of Forms* (University of California Press, 1991)

Bazin, André, *What is Cinema?* (University of California, 1968)

Benjamin, Walter, *Illuminations* (Schocken, 1969)

Breathed, Berkeley, *Goodnight Opus* (Little Brown Books for Young Readers, 1996)

Brest, Paul, Sanford Levinson, J. M. Balkin, Akhil Reed Amar and Reva B. Siegel, *Processes of Constitutional Decisionmaking* (Aspen Publishers, 5th edn, 2006) 1405

Brinkley, Douglas, 'Foreword' in Nick Yapp, *One Hundred Days in Photographs: Pivotal Events That Changed the World* (National Geographic, 2007) 11

Corbin, Caroline Mala, 'Compelled Disclosures' (2014) *Alabama Law Review* (forthcoming)

Farid, Hany, 'Digital Doctoring: How to Tell the Real From the Fake' (2006) 3(4) *Significance* 162–166

Farid, Hany, 'Seeing Is Not Believing' (2009) 46(8) *IEEE Spectrum* 44–48

Feigenson, Neil, and Christina Spiesel, *Law on Display: The Digital Transformation of Legal Persuasion and Judgment* (New York University Press, 2009)

Greenhouse, Linda and Reva Siegel, 'Before (and After) *Roe v Wade* New Questions About Backlash' (2011) 120 *Yale Law Journal* 2028

Grønstad, Asbjørn and Øyvind Vågnes, 'What do Pictures Want?: An Interview with W J T Mitchell', *Image & Narrative* (online), November 2006 www.visual-studies.com/interviews/mitchell.html

Guttmacher Institute, *Induced Abortion in the United States Fact Sheet (2014)* (July 2014) www.guttmacher.org/pubs/fb_induced_abortion.html

Hughes, Richard, 'Burning Birth Certificates and Atomic Tupperware Parties: Creating the Antiabortion Movement in the Shadow of the Vietnam War' (2006) 68(3) *The Historian* 541

Johns, Chris, 'Introduction' in Nick Yapp, *One Hundred Days in Photographs: Pivotal Events That Changed the World* (National Geographic, 2007) 17

Lazzarini, Zita, 'South Dakota's Abortion Script–Threatening the Physician-Patient Relationship' (2008) 359 *New England Journal of Medicine* 2189

89 Berkeley Breathed, *Goodnight Opus* (Little Brown Books for Young Readers, 1996).

McLuhan, Marshall, *Understanding Media: The Extensions of Man* (McGraw-Hill, 1964)
Manian, Maya, 'The Irrational Woman: Informed Consent and Abortion Decision-Making' (2009) 16 *Duke Journal of Gender, Law and Policy* 223
Marder, Nancy, 'The Conundrum of Cameras in the Courtroom' (2012) 44 *Arizona State Law Journal* 1490
Mauro, Tony, 'Roll the Cameras (or Soutersaurus Rex)' *Legal Times* (Washington DC), 8 April 1996, 9
Mayo Clinic, *Fetal Development: The 1st Trimester* (10 July 2014) www.mayoclinic.com/health/prenatal-care/PR00112
Morris, Errol, 'Which Came First, the Chicken or the Egg? (Part One)' *The New York Times* (New York), 25 September 2007
Morris, Errol and Michael Meyer, 'Recovering Reality: Errol Morris on Abu Ghraib' (2008) *Columbia Journalism Review* 2 (5 March 2008) www.cjr.org/behind_the_news/recovering_reality.php
Nichols, Bill, *Ideology and the Image: Social Representation in Cinema and Other Media* (Indiana Press, 1981)
Nilsson, Lennart, *Lennart Nilsson Biography* www.lennartnilsson.com/biography.html
NOVA, *Behind the Lens: An Interview with Lennart Nilsson* (2013) Public Broadcasting Service www.pbs.org/wgbh/nova/odyssey/nilsson.html
Parks, Gordon, 'Introduction' in *Life: 100 Photographs That Changed the World* (Life Books, 2003) 7
Persson, Hasse, *Q&A with Lennart Nilsson* www.lennartnilsson.com/q_a.html
Petchesky, Rosalind Pollack, 'Foetal Images: The Power of Visual Culture in the Politics of Reproduction' (1987) 13 *Feminist Studies* 263
Post, Robert and Reva Siegel, 'Roe Rage: Democratic Constitutionalism and Backlash' (2007) 42 *Harvard Civil Rights Civil Liberties Review* 373
Sanger, Carol, 'Seeing and Believing: Mandatory Ultrasound and the Path to a Protected Choice' (2008) 56 *University of California Los Angeles Law Review* 351
Sawicki, Nadia, 'The Abortion Informed Consent Debate: More Light, Less Heat' (2011) 21 *Cornell Journal of Law and Public Policy* 1
Scorcese, Martin, 'The Persisting Vision: Reading the Language of Cinema' *New York Review of Books* (New York), 15 August 2013
Siegel, Reva, 'Dignity and the Politics of Protection: Abortion Restrictions Under Casey/Carhart' (2008) 117 *Yale Law Journal* 1694
SOGC Clinical Practice Guidelines (2014) 26(2) *Journal of Obstetrics and Gynecology of Canada* 171, 175
Sontag, Susan, *On Photography* (Picador, 2001)
Stam, Robert, Robert Burgoyne and Sandy Flitterman-Lewis, *New Vocabularies in Film Semiotics: Structuralism, Post-Structuralism and Beyond* (Routledge, 1992) 185–186
Stanek, Jill, *With Her Typing Fingers on the ProLife Pulse* (6 February 2013) www.jillstanek.com/2013/02/real-reason-abortion-providers-oppose-ultrasounds-78-change-minds
Stepan, Peter, *Photos That Changed the World: The 20th Century* (Prestel, 2006) 124
Tagg, John, *Burdens of Representation: Essays on Photographies and Histories* (University of Minnesota Press, 1993) 3
Taylor, Janelle, *The Public Life of the Fetal Sonogram: Technology, Consumption, and the Politics of Reproduction* (Rutgers University Press, 2008)
Tushnet, Rebecca, 'Looking at the Lanham Act' (2011) 8 *Houston Law Review* 862, 879

Cases

Casey, 505 US 833 (1992), 850–851
Casey, 505 US 833 (1992), 877
Casey, 505 US 833 (1992), 937 n 7
Lakey, 667 F 3d 570, 579 (5th Cir, 2012)
Nova Health Systems v Pruitt, 292 P 3d 28 (Okla, 2012)
Nova Health Systems v Pruitt, 292 P 3d 28, [3] (Okla, 2012)
Nova Health Systems, *et al.*, 'Brief in Opposition to Petition for Certiorari to the United States Supreme Court' Submission in *Pruitt v Nova Health Systems* US 12–1170, 3 June 2013, 22
Planned Parenthood of Southeastern Pennsylvania v Casey, 505 US 833 (1992)
Roe v Wade, 410 US 113 (1973)
Texas Medical Providers Performing Abortion Services v Lakey, 667 F 3d 570 (5th Cir, 2012)
US Federal Rules of Evidence 1001 (authenticating documents)

Chapter 8

Peeping

Open justice and law's voyeurs

Katherine Biber[1]

'Open justice' is the belief that justice must be done in public, and it must be seen to be done.[2] One consequence of open justice is that 'law' becomes a popular cultural genre, performing for a civic audience. Legal proceedings publicly scrutinise conduct that might be personal, sensitive or secret. This chapter asks whether a discourse of voyeurism can be applied to the pleasure taken in peeping at law's secrets. It recognises that open justice sometimes has the effect of feeding voyeuristic impulses in law's subjects, disclosing the evident enjoyment we feel when we are given access to the intimate or humiliating secrets of litigants, witnesses, defendants and victims.[3]

I will argue that peeping might be a less intrusive form of looking, and thereby retain some of the dignity of law's participants.[4] This chapter examines voyeuristic photographs made in Japan – evidence of peeping – to explore the conflation of intimacy, disclosure and pleasure. Wherever intimate behaviour and feelings are witnessed, there is pleasure taken in intimacy's disclosure, and recognition that its intimacy is implicitly probative. Where intimacies are photographed, they provide the viewer with proof, but they also entrust the viewer with proof's residue: the secret. That secret demands some discretion or

1 Faculty of Law, University of Technology, Sydney, Australia. *Katherine.Biber@uts.edu.au* I am grateful to Kohei Yoshiyuki, and to his representatives at Yossi Milo Gallery, including Francesca Fanelli and Alissa Schoenfeld. Thanks also to Paula Kupfer at Aperture Magazine, Philip Gefter and Michael Lorenzini. I am fortunate to have so many colleagues and friends who have offered advice and guidance as this research developed: Isabella Alexander, Paul McCartan, Lesley Townsley, Honni van Rijswijk, Trish Luker, Rosanne Kennedy, Barbara Caine, Helen Groth, Glenda Sluga, Tess Lea and Julia Kindt. I thank Marett Leiboff sincerely for the support and encouragement she has given.

2 Joseph Jaconelli, *Open Justice: A Critique of the Public Trial* (Oxford University Press, 2002); Emma Cunliffe, 'Open Justice: Concepts and Judicial Approaches' (2012) 40 *Federal Law Review* 385; J J Spigelman, 'The Principle of Open Justice: A Comparative Perspective' (2006) 29(2) *UNSW Law Journal* 147; Colleen Davis, 'The Injustice of Open Justice' (2001) 8 *James Cook University Law Review* 92.

3 Katherine Biber, 'Inside Jill Meagher's Handbag: Looking at Open Justice' (2014) 39(2) *Alternative Law Journal* 73.

4 See also Rosemarie Garland-Thomson, *Staring: How We Look* (Oxford University Press, 2009).

judgment about *what we see* and *what we show*. Voyeurs find pleasure in seeing another's secrets, but they also deploy various strategies for guarding those secrets. This chapter argues that voyeurism is both an effect and a technique of open justice. While peeping sometimes exacerbates the harms done when law's secrets are revealed, through exploring voyeuristic cultural practices in Japan, we can see how peeping might also preserve qualities of discretion, safety, and maintaining a respectful distance.

In the digital era, open justice enables us to peruse the contents of a rape victim's handbag,[5] view images from a high profile suicide scene,[6] watch footage of a murder victim being smothered by her attacker,[7] and read the private diaries of victims and defendants.[8] Primarily exhibited in commercial media outlets, these materials are not released for the purpose of achieving transparency and accountability about court processes; they feed the voyeuristic impulses of a viewing public.[9] I have written elsewhere that open justice ought to be tempered with 'sensitivity', arguing that a 'jurisprudence of sensitivity' might achieve both openness and discretion. This chapter contributes to this project, arguing that voyeurism shows us how, where pleasure is taken in the intimacies or humiliations of others, some of the dignity of law's participants might be preserved by *looking discreetly*, or peeping. Part I introduces a series of voyeuristic photographs made in Tokyo in the 1970s, and describes the practices of peeping and exhibitionism which they represent. Part II explores Japanese geographies of sexuality, characterised by a distinctive interplay of revealing and concealing, indoors and outdoors, and in which peeping has an established history. Part III describes the Japanese concept of a 'public sanctuary', a space that is simultaneously public and hidden, and explains how this might be imagined as a technique for managing the intimate disclosures that are made in a regime of open justice.

5 See, for example, 'Galleries: Evidence in the Jill Meagher murder case' *Herald Sun* (online), 13 March 2013 www.heraldsun.com.au/news/law-order/gallery-fnat79vb-1226596531880?page=1

6 See, for example, 'More of Kurt Cobain's suicide scene pictures released by Seattle police' *The Sydney Morning Herald* (online), 31 March 2014 www.smh.com.au/entertainment/music/more-of-kurt-cobains-suicide-scene-pictures-released-by-seattle-police-20140331–35slu.html

7 See, for example, Emma Partridge, 'Video reveals the moments before Lisa Harnum died, and what Simon Gittany did next' *The Sydney Morning Herald* (online), 1 November 2013 www.smh.com.au/nsw/video-reveals-the-moments-before-lisa-harnum-died-and-what-simon-gittany-did-next-20131101–2wq4h.html

8 See, for example, Kate Kyriacou, 'Court releases journal entries by Allison Baden-Clay, one written days before she disappeared' *The Courier-Mail* (online), 15 December 2012 www.couriermail.com.au/news/queensland/brisbane-supreme-court-releases-journal-entries-by-allison-baden-clay-one-written-just-days-before-she-disappeared/story-e6freoof-1226537242449; see also 'Diary of a mum accused of killing her four babies' *The Sun-Herald* (online), 6 April 2003 www.smh.com.au/articles/2003/04/05/1049459859119.html

9 Katherine Biber, 'Evidence from the Archive: Implementing the Court Information Act in NSW' (2011) 33(3) *The Sydney Law Review* 575; Katherine Biber, 'In Crime's Archive: The Cultural Afterlife of Criminal Evidence' (2013) 53(6) *The British Journal of Criminology* 1033.

Part IV explains that Yoshiyuki's photographs, despite their exotic strangeness, speak to contemporary Western preoccupations with privacy, surveillance and voyeurism. It shows how transparency has the potential to tip over into exhibitionism, inviting pleasure to be taken in practices of disclosure. Part V draws connections between discourses of voyeurism and regimes of open justice. In seeking out a space between 'public' and 'private', where sensitive information is both known and guarded, cultural scholarship has proposed various concepts for thinking about this space. Lauren Berlant proposes 'intimacy', D.A. Miller suggests the 'open secret', Michael Taussig describes the 'public secret', and Berlant and Michael Warner investigate the 'counterpublic'. These concepts are helpful in articulating a 'jurisprudence of sensitivity', which urges the exercise of tact and restraint in a regime of open justice.

Peeping in the park

In the early 1970s in Tokyo, a photographer walked through Chuo Park in Shinjuku and saw a couple having sex. He noticed several men creeping towards the couple to watch. Afterwards, he began visiting Tokyo parks regularly, discovering that this activity was a common feature of the park landscape at night. Many couples frequented these parks for sexual pleasure, and many more people – always men – visited those parks to watch them. The photographer researched technologies that would enable him to photograph in the dark and within six months, claiming concord with the park's peepers, he began to take photographs.

Even in the digital era, where personal devices enable us to capture hidden moments, the photographs seem shocking for their candour and audacity. While all of the couples portrayed are captured in circumstances of intimacy, most of them are not engaged in sexual intercourse. Many are fully-dressed, and we might observe sweet details, such as the neatly-paired shoes beside them, or a coat laid out beneath them. The images suggest that these couples are unaware of the photographer's presence, and many have gone to the trouble to hide behind shrubs or trees; the couples also seem oblivious to the groups of men clustering nearby, watching them. It is this feature of the images – the voyeurs – that is most disquieting. Brazen clusters of peepers come surprisingly close to the intimate couples, and sometimes we see one of them reaching out and actually touching a woman. The fashions and styling clearly locate their participants in the 1970s, but the subject matter requires no captions, and every image is named *Untitled*.

The photographs were supposed to capture the peepers. They were representations of voyeurism – their subjects, their maker and the audience were all practising voyeurism. These were photographs about peeping, and from them we can learn something about how voyeuristic practices expose the pleasure taken when intimate secrets are seen by the public. This usage of the term 'peeping' is thought to have its origins in the eighteenth-century character of

Figure 8.1 Kohei Yoshiyuki. From the series *The Park. Untitled*, 1971. Gelatin Silver Print © Kohei Yoshiyuki, Courtesy Yossi Milo Gallery, New York

Peeping Tom who watched the naked Lady Godiva riding through Coventry; the term 'voyeur' was first recorded in French in 1900.[10] Whereas psychiatric and psychoanalytic literatures have recognised voyeurism as a deviant psychopathology, this chapter relies upon its more common usage as a cultural phenomenon.[11] While some voyeuristic practices are intrusive and unwelcome, this chapter also explores the possibility that peeping – looking discreetly – might inform some jurisprudence of open justice, enabling law to be done openly and in public, but ensuring that sensitivities or intimacies are revealed safely.

Some of these photographs were first published in 1972 in *Shukan Shinchō*, an independent magazine committed to taboo-free examination of social questions. The complete series *Kōen (Park)* was first exhibited at the Komai Gallery in Tokyo in 1979, which was dedicated to post-war Japanese art, and the photographer used the pseudonym 'Kohei Yoshiyuki'. The images were blown up to life size, the gallery was in complete darkness, and visitors were given a torch. Yoshiyuki said, 'I wanted people to look at the bodies an inch at a time . . . I really enjoyed watching people looking at the photographs'.[12] Despite the exhibition being an

10 Jonathan M Metzl, 'Voyeur Nation? Changing Definitions of Voyeurism, 1950–2004' (2004) 12(2) *Harvard Review of Psychiatry* 127, 129. See also *Oxford English Dictionary*, online edition (2001–).

11 See Clay Calvert, *Voyeur Nation: Media, Privacy, and Peering in Modern Culture* (Westview, 2000).

12 At the exhibition, Yoshiyuki also displayed stills he had made from sex videos filmed, and left behind, by patrons of a pay-by-the-hour 'love hotel'.

Figure 8.2 Kohei Yoshiyuki. From the series *The Park. Untitled*, 1973. Gelatin Silver Print © Kohei Yoshiyuki, Courtesy Yossi Milo Gallery, New York

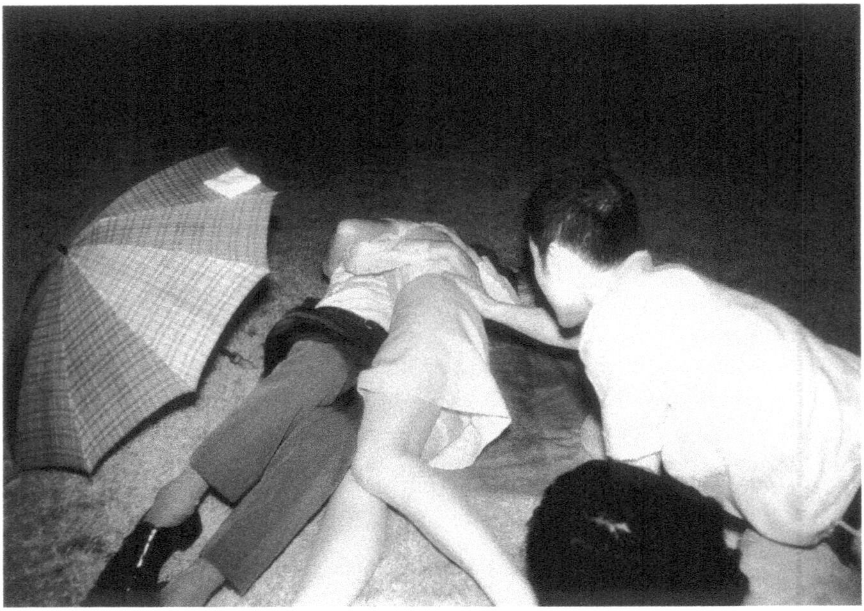

Figure 8.3 Kohei Yoshiyuki. From the series *The Park. Untitled*, 1971. Gelatin Silver Print © Kohei Yoshiyuki, Courtesy Yossi Milo Gallery, New York

underground success, afterwards the prints were destroyed, and a limited-edition book, *Dokyumento: Kōen (Document: Park)*, documenting the park images was published in 1980.[13]

Yoshiyuki's project, and its initial display in Japan, pre-dated the introduction of the 1985 Entertainment and Amusement Trades Control Law, which was responsible for the regulation, zoning and urban distribution of Japanese sexual practices. The law, which transformed Japan's vast and eclectic industry of 'love hotels', had the effect of creating new geographies of sex in Japanese cities.[14] Yoshiyuki's *Kōen* series captures a time before that law. With the publication in 2006 of Martin Parr's influential *The Photobook: A History – Volume II*, in which Yoshiyuki's park photographers were included,[15] new attention was drawn to his work. New York gallery, Yossi Milo, tracked down the artist, who agreed to reprint photographs.[16] During 2007, images from the series were acquired by the New York Museum of Modern Art, The Museum of Contemporary Art in Chicago, the Museum of Fine Arts in Houston and the San Francisco Museum of Modern Art. Later that year, the series was exhibited in New York at the Yossi Milo Gallery, with significant public curiosity and reportage. Yoshiyuki, whose real name has never been revealed, apparently continues to work as a commercial photographer in Japan.

Western critics and viewers felt that the photographs either confirmed[17] or contradicted[18] Western attitudes about Japan. Some saw them as part of a continuing Japanese art practice of portraying voyeurism is an erotic motif, from eighteenth- and nineteenth-century *Ukiyo-e* woodblock erotic prints to films like *In the Realm of Senses*.[19] Benjamin Genocchio wrote that photographs are 'by and large . . . not terribly well composed or printed . . . slightly out of focus . . . at times movement blurs the figures', but that all of these defects generate their 'allure', their 'grainy realism', and the 'naughty, clandestine' experience of looking at them.[20] Susan Kismaric referred to the 'predatory, animalistic' nature of the park's voyeurs;[21] Susan S. Phillips found them 'strangely unerotic';[22] for Vince Aletti, they recalled 'verité, vintage porn, frontline journalism and the

13 Philip Gefter, 'Sex in the Park, And Its Sneaky Spectators' *The New York Times*, 23 September 2007, Art 37. NYT, 23 Sept 2007, AR 37

14 See Mark D West, *Law in Everyday Japan: Sex, Sumo, Suicide, and Statutes* (University of Chicago Press, 2010); Sarah Chaplin, *Japanese Love Hotels: A Cultural History* (Routledge, 2007).

15 Martin Parr and Gerry Badger, *The Photobook: A History Volume II* (Phaidon, 2006), 296–267.

16 Rachel Wolff, 'A Lost Voyeur's Paradise: Images from Tokyo's furtive sex life, brought to light again' *New York* (online), 24 August 2007 http://nymag.com/nymag/guides/36605/

17 Parr, above n 15, 297; Yossi Milo, cited in Gefter, above n 13, 38.

18 Susan Kismaric, cited in Gefter, above n 13, 38.

19 Alexandra Munroe, cited in ibid.

20 Benjamin Genocchio, 'The Listings: Kohei Yoshiyuki: The Park' *The New York Times* (online), 7 September 2007 http://query.nytimes.com/gst/fullpage.html?res=9A0DE1D7153BF934A3575AC0A9619C8B63

21 In Gefter, above n 13, 38.

22 In ibid.

hectic spontaneity of paparazzi shots stripped of their glamour'.[23] For David Cohen, they represented a 'strangely wistful fusion of prurience and poignancy'.[24] Cohen questioned Yoshiyuki's motivations: 'Who is out there behind the camera each night: an anthropologist, an artist, a sexual deviant, a free love advocate, a blackmailer?'[25]

In an email interview with the *The New York Times*, Yoshiyuki explains the level of deception he practised in order to produce these 'candid' pictures:

> Before taking those pictures, I visited the parks for about six months without shooting them. I just went there to become a friend of the voyeurs. To photograph the voyeurs, I needed to be considered one of them. I behaved like I had the same interest as the voyeurs, but I was equipped with a small camera. My intention was to capture what happened in the parks, so I was not a real 'voyeur' like them.[26]

In these parks on these nights there were no police. While these acts were criminal, they were never criminalised. There were no charges laid, no police interviews, no witnesses, no trials, no judgments. There are just the photographs. When you take away the law's apparatus, all you're left with is the evidence. These photographs are the residue of crimes that never encountered the law, and in viewing them we perform the same voyeurism that might, in different circumstances, invoke the law. They are probative of illicit public sex, and the making and display of these images was also unlawful in Japan. Without law's structures, we see that our enjoyment of evidence is voyeuristic. In the presence of law, this enjoyment is diverted by rationality, procedure and doctrine, all of which seek to generate probative value from these illicit artefacts. By viewing these materials without legal justification, we recognise how much pleasure we can derive from evidentiary images.

In 1979, Yoshiyuki's interview with the photographic provocateur Nobuyoshi Araki was published in a Japanese porn magazine, *Weekend Super*:

YOSHIYUKI: You can't threaten people. You can photograph them, but the law . . .

ARAKI: So photographing them isn't illegal?

YOSHIYUKI: No, as long as you don't say anything. If you keep quiet, take your photographs and run, it's okay.

ARAKI: Really? It sounds almost criminal.[27]

23 In ibid.

24 David Cohen, 'Peeking In on the Social Set' *The New York Sun* (online), 6 September 2007 www.nysun.com/arts/peeking-in-on-the-social-set/62042/

25 Ibid.

26 Cited in Gefter, above n 13, 37–38.

27 Reprinted in English as 'Down in the Park: Yoshiyuki Kohei's Nocturnes: Interview by Araki Nobuyoshi' (2007) 188 *Aperture* 74.

What Yoshiyuki says here about the law is entirely untrue. It is illegal in Japan to engage in public indecency,[28] which includes public exposure of the genitals and also incidents which 'violate a sense of morality', which has been interpreted to include acts of exhibitionism and 'peeping' or voyeurism.[29] In Japan it is also illegal to produce, display or distribute sexually explicit material that is 'obscene',[30] with obscenity being defined by individual judicial officers charged with deciding whether it might evoke 'uncontrollable or disquiet reason'. It *was* illegal to have sex in the park, it was illegal to watch couples having sex in the park, it was illegal to photograph them, and it was also illegal to display or distribute those photographs. Jennifer Ray writes that Japanese obscenity laws 'made no exceptions for works of art'.[31] That these layers of voyeurism were not policed indicates one kind of discretion which, this chapter suggests, might protect intimacies in a regime of open justice.

In an interview with Cathy Lebowitz, the psychoanalyst Josefina Ayerza talked about the layers of voyeurism that are apparent in the Yoshiyuki photographs, but cautions against assuming that everyone who looks is equally a 'voyeur', or that the roles of voyeur and exhibitionist are stable. Ayerza says,

> The thrill with the voyeur who is the artist with his camera is that as soon as the photographs reach the gallery it is him who turns himself into an exhibitionist. And yes, in the same act we, the viewers, are transformed into voyeurs, but only in terms of structure – it does not make you perverse because you step foot in the structure.[32]

This reading of the photographs enables us to see that the structure is itself unstable, and that individuals might slip between the zones of public and private, exhibitionist and voyeur, revealing and concealing, or that they might occupy these categories concurrently.

Peeping in Japan

In order to understand how discretion might function to protect intimacies, it is necessary to know something here about the origins of a distinctly Japanese perversity, from which we can begin to imagine a 'jurisprudence of sensitivity', one which responds to practices and identities made manifest through both concealing *and* revealing.

28 Japanese Penal Code, Article 174, as explained in Milton Diamond and Ayako Uchiyama, 'Pornography, Rape and Sex Crimes in Japan' (1999) 22(1) *International Journal of Law and Psychiatry* 1.

29 Ibid.

30 Article 175 in ibid.

31 Jennifer Ray, *Repression and Rebellion: Cruising and its Depiction in Works by Minor White, Kohei Yoshiyuki, and Evergon* (MFA Thesis, Columbia College Chicago, 2012) 23.

32 Cathy Lebowitz, 'Kohei Yoshiyuki: The Park: Cathy Lebowitz interviews Josefina Ayerza' (2007) 30 *Lacanian Ink* 163, 166.

Fictional explorations of Japanese sexuality were transformed during the Meiji period (1868–1912), away from descriptive erotic writing towards a narrative that revealed interiority and identity.[33] McLelland described the new Japanese fiction as characterised by 'a hidden realm of desire in need of confession by the protagonist and elaboration by the author'.[34] He cites Yokota-Murakami who wrote, 'What is sexual thus emerges exactly as something that is private, that which has to be concealed, and therefore, to be revealed'.[35] The significance of this shift is that it represents a change in focus away from examining practices and towards recognising emerging identities; from what people *do* to who they really *are*.

Shortly after, the popularisation in Japan of Freudian psychoanalytic theories saw a discourse of public morality infused with discussions of 'perverse' or 'queer' desire (*hentai seiyoku*),[36] and a concurrent distinction drawn between normal (*seijō*) and perverse (*ijō*) sexualities. While McLelland observes that the period's aspiration for Japanese modernity had the effect of relegating 'perverse' practices to an imagined feudal past, remnants of feudal non-conformist practices maintained a tenacious grip on the contemporary imagination. For McLelland, the drawing of the normal/perverse distinction enables an opening of public discourse about perversity. In the popular therapeutic contexts in which perversity was confessed, diagnosed or treated, it was nevertheless disclosed or displayed and as a result, enjoyed. Of significance here, voyeurism was seen to be a perversion of, as well as a natural progression from, traditional forms of 'peeping'. Yokota-Murakami wrote:

> what distinguishes *debakame-shugi* (or, voyeurism) from the traditional forms of 'peeping' such as *kaimami* (a mere glimpse: occasional glimpses that princes and courtiers obtained of the courtly ladies who were enclosed by curtains and screens) is the ontological status the former gives to one who peeps.[37]

Yoshiyuki and Araki, in their conversation, and perhaps reflecting their transgressive aspirations, appear not to observe these distinctions, conflating the voyeur, the peeper, the photographer, the innovator and the pervert. Araki tells Yoshiyuki, 'The wonderful thing about this photograph is that it shows the peeper. It's a self-portrait. It shows your shadow. I really like that'.[38] In their discussion about the flash technology that enabled Yoshiyuki to photograph in the dark, they say:

33 Mark McLelland, *Queer Japan from the Pacific War to the Internet Age* (Rowman & Littlefield, 2005) 19–20.
34 Ibid, 19.
35 In ibid.
36 Ibid, 20.
37 In ibid, 20.
38 Araki, above n 27, 78.

ARAKI: It's fun when you have only seconds to get a shot, and the reaction is very clear.

YOSHIYUKI: Yes, it is fun.

ARAKI: Maybe everybody will be doing it by this summer, once word about the Sunpak flash unit spreads.

YOSHIYUKI: I heard the company had a lot of inquiries after my show.

ARAKI: Uh-oh!

YOSHIYUKI: Yeah, I won't be able to do my work anymore. *[Laughs]*

ARAKI: You mean nobody has ever come after you when you took photographs like this?

YOSHIYUKI: Never.

ARAKI: Wow! Maybe you're a ninja!

YOSHIYUKI: The guy who developed the Sunpak infrared strobe is a real lecher and a lot of fun.

ARAKI: Really? He must have done a lot of fieldwork.

YOSHIYUKI: I guess that's where the idea came from.

ARAKI: Lechers are the only hope for the twenty-first century. Only lechers come up with good ideas. Only lechers take good photographs. So are you one too?

YOSHIYUKI: I think I'm completely ordinary, but maybe there's a little lecher in everyone.[39]

Scholars differ in their views about Japanese attitudes to public sex. McLelland writes that public displays of affection were introduced to Japan by American soldiers after the Second World War,[40] and that American GIs sought out sex in public parks,[41] practices which were policed by US military patrols and ignored by Japanese police. He cites Yukio Mishima as authority for the claim that Japanese police 'would have been unable to arrest the Japanese partners anyway, "since there were no laws by which they might crack down"'.[42] McLelland writes, 'Public sexuality was suddenly visible and acceptable in a manner not seen prior to the war's end, and "petting" (*pettingu*) couples were conspicuous features of parks and shrine precincts'.[43] By contrast, Mark West cites Shōichi Inoue who, in his history of Japanese 'love space' wrote, 'At the beginning of the Twentieth Century, many couples made love outside. In fact, the general movement of male-female interaction from outdoors to indoors is said to be an extremely recent development'.[44] West quotes a 1916 news report stating that park benches were full of amateurs in the evenings: 'doctors and nurses, office workers and

39 Ibid, 78–79.
40 In McLelland, above n 33, 62.
41 In ibid, 68.
42 In ibid, 68.
43 In ibid, 62.
44 Cited in West, above n 14, 157.

female assistants, manual laborers, cooks and their girlfriends, reporters and their contacts, bank workers and female apprentices'.[45] He writes that, by the time of the US occupation, 'as the sun set, lovers gathered in places like the Imperial Palace grounds and Inokashira Park, and the next morning the grass was full of paper scraps and condoms'.[46] West also cites the novelist Aiko Gotō who, in 1973 said, 'Sex was originally something to be done while bathed in sunlight in the middle of a field. The need to seek stimulation behind closed doors shows how weak people have become'.[47] West advances the proposition that outdoor sex was practised by amateurs in plain view, and that sex professionals worked indoors until the 1930s, when *enshuku* first emerged, which were the precursors to the modern love hotel. Love hotels, a massive sector in the Japanese economy and a 'normal' feature of dating, marital, extramarital and professional sex, have been recognised as a highly-visible method by which sexual intimacy is hidden indoors.[48] Again, we see how Japanese sexuality holds in persistent tension the practices of revealing and concealing, with voyeurism – watching discreetly and for pleasure – now practised by the ethnographers who study love hotels.[49]

Public sanctuaries

At the same time that love hotels emerged as alternative zones of modern Japanese sexuality, there also emerged the categories of 'modern boys' (*mobo*) and 'modern girls' (*moga*) who 'socialized together away from the prying eyes of the family'.[50] These groups met in zones that an Anglophone readership would cast as 'public', although for *mobo* and *moga* cohorts these spaces were 'safe' for this reason, where propriety – so important among familiars – might be preserved among strangers.

There is a distinctly Japanese concept of the 'public sphere' that enables these notions of 'public' and 'safe' to cohere. In a European philosophical tradition, the 'public sphere' is the space where citizens engage in civil discourse; Cassegard writes that civic participation demands that Westerners 'temporarily bracket those dependencies, inequalities or everyday preoccupations that define our actual social status'.[51] However, in Japan, there are at least two distinct 'publics', of which only one is affiliated with the state. Cassegard explains that the character *ōyake/kō* has 'a distinct elitist connotation', as the character is

45 In ibid, 158.
46 In ibid.
47 In ibid, 157–158.
48 West, ibid; Chaplin, above n 14.
49 Ibid.
50 McLelland, above n 33, 24.
51 Carl Cassegard, 'Public Space in Recent Japanese Political Thought and Activism: From the Rivers and Lakes to Miyashita Park' (2011) 31(3) *Japanese Studies* 405, 407.

'etymologically linked to officialdom, government, or imperial authority rather than to popular political participation by citizens'.[52] The word '*kōen*' contains this character. However there is a second concept, *muen*, or 'non-relation', which is simultaneously 'outdoors' but separate from the state; in fact, *muen* offers sanctuary from the state and its agents. *Muen* has its medieval origins in religious temples, which were empowered to exclude secular, state authorities (*funyūken*),[53] and could offer asylum to those seeking sanctuary from the state and its agents. A wide range of places and groups were associated with *muen*, although not everyone was entitled to *muen's* protection – these were not universal rights, but locally distributed among certain places or groups.[54] In his writing on the origins of Japanese queer subcultures, McLelland identifies a similar class of spaces that are simultaneously public and separate. Collectively known as *hattenba*, or 'development spots', these can be found in parks, temples and public toilets, places where homosexual men could gather, usually after dark, without fear of exposure. The notion that a space can be both public and hidden is powerful in the context of a jurisprudence in which intimate secrets are disclosed as an act of justice.

In his writing on public parks in Japan, Cassegard says that the literal translation of *kōen* is 'public garden', and so it is significant that Kohei Yoshiyuki chose to name his series '*Kōen*', when the parks he photographed were in fact functioning as hidden sanctuaries for their users. Cassegard writes about Japanese parks occupied by homeless people, and the activists who defend their rights to do so by arguing that they are not *kōen*, but rather 'vacant lots'. These activists aim to reconceptualise the public sphere, away from *ōyake* or *kō* to *gōko*, *muen* or 'vacant lots',[55] attempting to 'reconnect the parks to their other and largely forgotten origin as places open to those in need'.[56] The vacant lot, in contrast to *kōen*, is a zone of hospitality and inclusion, sanctuary and security, and 'does not require a bracketing of things unworthy of public display, it allows for experiments in alternative forms of survival (squatting, scavenging, community gardening, black markets and barter) as well as various expressions of life that are subject to mainstream disapproval'.[57] In Cassegard's research with park activists, he noticed that their campaigns positioned *ōyake* or *kō* as Westernised concepts, alien to premodern Japanese ideas such as *gōko*, *muen* or *kugai* which, if recognised and reinvigorated, have the transformative potential to return to 'a once-vigorous idea of public life that has fallen into neglect or has been forgotten'.[58] It is an argument that has a seductive resonance for Yoshiyuki's photographs, and particularly their relation to – and reception by

52 Ibid, 410.
53 Ibid, 413.
54 Ibid, 414.
55 Ibid, 418.
56 Ibid, 416.
57 Ibid, 417.
58 Ibid, 417.

– Western audiences. That he named them '*Kōen*' implicitly suggests that he was provoking a Western notion of public space to operate in a zone that was, as his images plainly reveal, not understood in that way by its users. One interpretation of his chosen title, then, is that he is inviting his images to be seen as transgressions, its subjects issuing wilful challenges to public authority. However the scholarship of Cassegard, McLelland and others demonstrates that there is a legitimate alternative way of imagining these public intimacies, one that does not demand sanction for transgression, or more precisely, one that does not require transgression to be exhibited and judged *as* transgressive.

It is the public exhibition of these hidden secrets that achieves the shock, or power, of Yoshiyuki's photographs. The sense of the breached sanctuary, the shameful disclosure, the thrilling revelation, these are *also the effects of some acts of open justice*, revealing the pleasure in seeing a secret that has fallen out of place. It is important to distinguish these effects on a spectrum of pleasure; not all voyeurisms are equal. At one end we might find the insatiable hunter *(ryōki)*, trawling parks in the dark and physically touching couples engaged in public sex. The voyeur who hides behind a tree to watch might be engaged in a distinct category of behaviour, and the magazine reader, the photographer, or the gallery visitor enjoys a different kind of looking, and not all of them actively sought out the pleasure they received. Voyeurism demands an element of display, and voyeurs observe from a safe distance, although that distance varies. Decency and propriety might be preserved for the voyeur; they may experience the thrill of transgressing a boundary without necessarily crossing a line. In Yoshiyuki's photographs, it is when the voyeurs reach out and touch the couples in the park that some limit may be reached. Yoshiyuki's photographs manifest their perversity by never disclosing to us what sexual practices we are actually witnessing: are the couples exhibitionists, or have they been surprised by the voyeurs? Are the voyeurs content merely to watch, or are they active participants in these public sex acts? Are these public sex acts – which in Yoshiyuki's photographs appear relatively coy, with their participants mostly fully clothed – all that happened in these parks, or did he select not to exhibit more explicit sex acts? David Cohen, in his exhibition review, wrote, 'With photography, one perversion can segue into another. [. . .] Thus voyeurism begets a certain narcissism . . . The crucial ambiguity in Mr Yoshiyuki's work isn't his subjects' libidos but his own'.[59]

In an email interview with Philip Gefter of *The New York Times*, Yoshiyuki gave his own account of the practices he documented, one which suggestively refuses to resolve ambiguity:

> The couples were not aware of the voyeurs in most cases. The voyeurs try to look at the couple from a distance at the beginning, then slowly approach

59 Cohen, above n 24, 15, 19.

toward the couple behind the bushes, and from the blind spots of the couple they try to come as close as possible, and finally peep from a very close distance. But sometimes there are the voyeurs who try to touch the woman, and gradually escalating – then trouble would happen.[60]

His interview with Araki suggests that he witnessed explicit displays that were unambiguous,[61] and yet the images in the series *Kōen* seem adapted to some notion of propriety.

ARAKI: Are the people you photograph totally unaware of what's going on? [. . .]
YOSHIYUKI: The light flashes – a red light. I'd better not say anymore! [. . .]
ARAKI: They are amazing – because they are really screwing. Look at him giving it to her! You need a lot of nerve to take photographs like these. [. . .] These days it's the women who are aggressive. At Shinjuku Gyoen park, for instance, the women are always on top.
YOSHIYUKI: I saw that sometimes, too. But I can't photograph that. If the guy's on the bottom, he'll notice the camera.[62]

Here we see evidence of Yoshiyuki's own discretion, exercising careful judgment about what he sees and what he has chosen to show. For a jurisprudence of sensitivity, tact or restraint are crucial practices. In a regime of open justice, in the face of demands for disclosure, the law ought always to be attentive to the need, at times, for withholding. I have written elsewhere about another form of legal enjoyment, a '*jouissance* of restraint', in which there is evident pleasure taken in law's frugality.[63] However, here I propose the possibility that withholding might also be an act of justice.

Peeping at Japan

This chapter uses Yoshiyuki's photographs, and the Japanese context in which they were taken, to illustrate how Anglophone notions of open justice might be understood through a discourse of voyeurism. For this analogy to work, Yoshiyuki's images must be both exoticised *and* familiar. Some scholars advance coruscating criticism of the West's embrace of Japanese transgressive photo art, of which Nobuyoshi Araki is the most famous and prolific exponent. Christian Kravagna argues that Araki's work – best known for relatively hardcore scenes of naked women in scenes of bondage and penetration, but which also includes

60 Gefter, above n 13, 37–38.
61 Araki, above n 27.
62 Ibid, 74.
63 Katherine Biber, *Captive Images* (Routledge-Cavendish, 2007) 108.

images exceptionally similar to Yoshiyuki's park photographs[64] – is misogynistic and sexist, and yet it has been recuperated by Western proponents including Nan Goldin.[65] Jean-Christophe Ammann cautions that Araki's pictures 'may be shocking to our Western eyes', implicitly challenging Western audiences to overcome their 'shock', and suggesting that to Japanese eyes the images are banal.[66] Kravagna writes that Araki's sexism and exploitation of women and women's bodies is 'exonerated' through an 'exoticised reading' of his photographic practice; that various forms of 'legitimation' are deployed by Western audiences and critics 'repressing or rebutting the uneasiness' of his work.[67]

Responses to Yoshiyuki from Western critics have focused less upon the artist himself – likely because he has worked under a pseudonym and given very few interviews – and more upon the work itself. Whereas some viewers have recognised his work as emerging from a Japanese tradition, and some have seen his work as a commentary upon Japanese socio-sexual mores, most have sought to equate Yoshiyuki with Western practitioners of candid photography, and to identify his work as responding to contemporary Western preoccupations with privacy, surveillance and voyeurism. Yossi Milo, whose New York exhibition of Yoshiyuki's photographs was their first showing outside Japan, said 'The photographs are specifically of their time and place and reflect the social and economic spirit of the 1970s in Japan. Yet the work is also very contemporary', citing privacy discourse, voyeurism, surveillance, and 'a cultural climate obsessed with the personal lives of everyday people'.[68] Most of the Western responses to Yoshiyuki's work seek to connect it with Western themes and practitioners. Karen Irvine, curator of the Museum of Contemporary Photography in Chicago, sees Yoshiyuki as working in the same tradition as Weegee and Walker Evans, photographers who could 'capture public moments covertly'; Susan S. Phillips, photography curator at the San Francisco Museum of Modern Art, also compared Yoshiyuki with Weegee, 'one of the great photographers who was interested in looking at socially unacceptable subjects'.[69] Philip Gefter, in his writing on Yoshiyuki, cited other instances of photographers capturing transgressive behaviour and subjects, from Bressai's 1920s photographs of prostitutes in Paris, which were photographed with the consent of the subjects, to Merry Alpern's 1990s photographs of prostitutes in New York, captured covertly from an apartment window.[70] Kenneth Tam has compared Yoshiyuki with Alvin Baltrop, whose 'Pier Photographs' (1975–1986) chronicled the

64 For example, the untitled image reproduced in Akiko Miki, Yoshiko Isshiki and Tomoko Sato (eds), *Nobuyoshi Araki: Self. Life. Death* (Phaidon, 2005) 437.

65 Nan Goldin cited in Christian Kravagna, 'Bring on the Little Japanese Girls!' (1999) 13 *Third Text* 48, 69. See also Nan Goldin and Nobuyoshi Araki, *Tokyo Love* (Scalo, 1995).

66 Kravagna, ibid, 68.

67 Ibid, 65.

68 In Gefter, above n 13, 38.

69 In ibid, 38.

70 Ibid, 38.

transient visitors to a disused pier beside New York City's West Side Highway, and which attracted the homeless, drug users, gay cruisers, suicides, murders, and other illicit behaviours.[71] Baltrop, like Yoshiyuki, attempted to befriend his subjects first, acting as a participant as well as an observer, and going to considerable effort to capture his photographs. Jennifer Ray has compared Yoshiyuki with Minor White and Evergon, both of whom documented aspects of gay sexuality, and particularly gay cruising.[72]

The West's 'discovery' of Yoshiyuki's photographs is a narrative that slips clumsily off the page: chance encounters, walks in the park, hidden cameras, secret identities, a hidden world, the discovery of an unknown talent and, ultimately, a sell-out show. It is easy to be sceptical about claims that Western audiences stumbled accidentally upon Yoshiyuki's photographs, after they had spent over 30 years in the Japanese underground. More likely, given the contemporary Western fascination with surveillance, technology and identity, they were skilfully released at precisely the right moment to dilute a relatively toxic discourse – permeated by fears about state secrets, terrorists, total surveillance and the end of privacy – with a charming and surprising series of photographs from 1970s Tokyo parks after dark.[73]

Their off-the-rack 'fit' with existing Western concepts of voyeurism was demonstrated in 2008 by the American fashion photographer, Steven Meisel, who made a series of photographs for Italian *Vogue*. Styled by Andrew Richardson, the images undeniably referenced Yoshiyuki's *Kōen* photographs without actually citing them, portraying primarily Caucasian models in a park at night engaged in various acts of sexual exhibitionism and voyeurism, with some photographs closely matching scenes from Yoshiyuki's images. Despite commissioning the images as an editorial, Italian *Vogue* refused to publish them, and instead they appeared in *V* magazine under the title 'The State of Sex'.[74] Not acknowledging Yoshiyuki's images as their source, the *V* photographs were accompanied by the magazine's definition of 'dogging', identifying it as a distinctively British tradition:

> Dogging (verb): A British expression for participating in sexual acts in a semi-public place (usually a secluded car park or a forest preserve) or watching others doing so. Often, there are more than two participants . . . as watching is encouraged, voyeurism and exhibitionism are heavily

71 Kenneth Tam, *Disappearing in Plain Sight or How we used to have Casual Sex before Craigslist* (MFA thesis, University of Southern California, 2010). See also Douglas Crimp, 'Alvin Baltrop' (2008) 46(6) *Artforum* 269.

72 Ray, above n 31. White's erotic photographs were only published posthumously, in 1989, and were unknown during his lifetime.

73 Gefter, above n 13.

74 The images are reproduced as a slideshow in 'The State of Sex' *V Magazine* (online), V56, 2008 www.vmagazine.com/site/content/825/

associated with dogging. The people taking part often meet either randomly or arrange to meet up beforehand over the internet.[75]

That Yoshiyuki's photographs could be so seamlessly transformed into a generic visual register of high-end fashion, and that then-current British media reports about public sex could easily stand in for a distinctly Japanese perverse tradition, illuminates the universal recognition of voyeurism. We see how visual pleasure is taken in the exhibition of intimacies, and that intimacies are easily performed for a viewing public. As a metaphor for open justice, we see how unstable is the distinction between transparency and exhibitionism, a distinction that turns on whether it is pleasurable to look.

Open justice, visual pleasure

Open justice must be tempered with sensitivity; transparency without accountability and judgment becomes exhibitionism. Legal proceedings, and the evidence adduced in those proceedings, frequently disclose information that may be private, personal, sensitive, intimate or secret. While there are some existing legal principles or processes that protect some of this information from being disclosed, a 'jurisprudence of sensitivity' would see judgment exercised about whether and how to protect intimate or humiliating information disclosed in public proceedings. A jurisprudence of sensitivity could draw upon concepts used by cultural scholars to carve out a space between 'public' and 'private': Lauren Berlant invoked the term 'intimacy' for its capacity to unsettle the distinction between the public and the private.[76] D.A. Miller used the term 'open secret' to capture the tact or discretion required for managing personal secrets.[77] In Michael Taussig's work, the 'public secret' refers to 'that which is generally known, but cannot be articulated' because the secret, to retain its power, must be publicly shared *as a secret*.[78] David Bell, writing about public sex, recognised the 'ambivalence' of space that is simultaneously public and private, with corporeal practices transforming it from one to the other, and back again. Kevin Waldby argues that the notion of 'public sex' is misleading; instead preferring the term 'not private' sex, to highlight that 'the paradox of public sex is its hiding'.[79]

75 In ibid. See also David Bell, 'Bodies, Technologies, Spaces: On "Dogging"' (2006) 9 *Sexualities* 387. Martin Parr also linked Yoshiyuki's photographs with the then-contemporary phenomenon of 'dogging', above n 15, 297.

76 Lauren Berlant, 'Intimacy: A Special Issue' in Lauren Berlant (ed.), *Intimacy* (University of Chicago Press, 2000).

77 Cited in Eve Kosofsky Sedgwick, 'The Epistemology of the Closet' in H Abelove, M A Barale and D M Halperin (eds), *The Lesbian and Gay Studies Reader* (Routledge, 1993) 45–46.

78 Michael Taussig, *Defacement: Public Secrecy and the Labor of the Negative* (Stanford University Press, 1999), 5–6

79 Kevin Waldby, '"He asked me if I was looking for fags . . ." Ottawa's National Capital Commission Conservation Officers and the Policing of Public Park Sex' (2009) 6(4) *Surveillance and Society* 367, 369.

Berlant and Warner suggest the term 'counterpublic' to describe spaces which might be ephemeral or 'secret' sites.[80] They argue that the public/private distinction is produced by heteronormativity, which in turn reifies these categories and their relationship. They call for a queer refusal of the distinction and a concurrent refusal of heterosexual hegemony; public discourses of sex have the effect of creating a 'hegemonic national public around sex'; the notion that heterosexual 'privacy' is in any way 'private' relies on our failure to notice that the institutions of familial economy, health and reproduction, all of which are public and national, are not represented. While much of this chapter argues for some sensitivity about how we show what we know, Berlant and Warner's intervention demands that we are also attentive to what we have failed to notice. Broadly, they argue that where 'privacy' is protected, violations of privacy's norms are demonised (as perverted, obscene, exploitative, etc).[81] Further, the articulation of 'intimate life' as the '*elsewhere* of political public discourse' serves as a distraction from recognising the inequalities in our economic and political lives. They identify '[i]deologies and institutions of intimacy' as achieving *privatisation*, where the public sphere is purged of responsibility for its citizens.[82] Berlant and Warner argue that the privatisation of the sex act also renders private – or more precisely, unnoticed – the heterosexual hegemony implicit in a much wider range of acts that are not typically regarded as sex acts: 'paying taxes, being disgusted, philandering, bequeathing, celebrating a holiday, investing for the future, teaching', and so on.[83] They draw upon Foucault's *The History of Sexuality* to make the point that, in a civil society, confessional and expert discourses 'equate[s] true personhood with sex and surround[s] that sex with dramas of secrecy and disclosure'.[84]

Their account seems to narrate both Yoshiyuki's photographs and their critical reception in the West. Whereas some of the Japanese sources suggested that public intimacy, while visible, need not be disclosed, the *Kōen* images perform precisely the 'privatization' and the 'drama' that Berlant, Warner and Foucault cautioned against. Returning to the notion of open justice, perhaps we ought to keep perspective of the fact that, while some of law's disclosures may be shocking, humiliating or exploitative, most of the time law's business remains unseen, or unobserved, because nobody has come to watch. The principles of open justice are mostly sound, and also have the potential to respond to Berlant and Warner's urging of a radical visibility in response to the marginalisation of certain social cohorts. Consistently, they demand that society's 'outsiders' occupy spaces of visibility on the 'inside', and that in so doing they are seen. Berlant and Warner would likely welcome some of the visual pleasures that attend

80 Laurent Berlant and Michael Warner, 'Sex in Public' (1998) 24(2) *Critical Inquiry* 547.
81 Ibid, 550.
82 Ibid, 553.
83 Ibid, 555.
84 Ibid, 559.

a radical visibility, and they give their own account of a sex performance in a leather bar, where the crowd is 'transfixed by the scene of intimacy and display, control and abandon, ferocity and abjection', 'moaning softly with admiration', 'whistling, stomping, screaming encouragements'.[85] Yet it seems necessary to draw a distinction between intimacies that are performed to be seen, and those that were never intended to be seen. Taking pleasure in the former completes the performance; taking pleasure in the latter is voyeurism.

In my earlier writing on illicit public sex, with Derek Dalton, we used the term 'secret sex' to describe sex acts that occurred in public spaces but which were not meant to be seen, nor permanently recorded.[86] That writing was motivated by an artwork named *Tearoom* (1962–2007) by William E. Jones, a Los Angeles artist with a partially archive-based practice, much of whose work portrays gay sexuality. *Tearoom* is made from 55 minutes of film footage taken by police officers in 1962 in a men's public toilet in Mansfield, Ohio. The footage was captured secretly by a police officer hiding behind a two-way mirror, and caught men engaged in illicit homosexual sex acts; at least 31 men were convicted of sodomy as a result of the footage, serving mandatory minimum prison terms of 12 months. In our writing about Jones' work, the word 'secret' conveyed some of the inadequacy of the term 'private' for illicit conduct which occurs in public space. Bennett and Grant draw a distinction between 'privacy as an intrinsic or aesthetic value' and 'privacy as an instrumental or "strategic" value'.[87] This distinction offers a helpful way of conceptualising open justice, where decisions are routinely made to classify material as 'open' or 'closed' following instrumental or strategic guidelines, oblivious to the fact that 'open' and 'closed' also appear on an aesthetic register. Strategic disclosures imagine that information can be managed within a safe, lawful and bounded space; aesthetic disclosures linger on the illicit, risky and hidden aspects of personal intimacy. The aesthetic effect of seeing a secret exposed is powerful, and the impulse to watch is irresistible. Where the law orders disclosure, even in the name of accountability and transparency, it has the potential to transform us into voyeurs. Illicit images, or images of unlawful conduct, draw our attention to the fact that what is evidentiary might also be enjoyable. Law's generation of pleasure need not be implicitly problematic. We need to be attentive to law's capacity to do so, but more importantly, to law's unacknowledged *reliance* upon visual pleasure for its probative effects.

Yoshiyuki's photographs and their public reception play repeatedly upon the idea of the 'secret'. Yoshiyuki, in his elusive relationship with his public – his

85 Ibid, 564–565.

86 Katherine Biber and Derek Dalton, 'Making Art from Evidence: Secret Sex and Police Surveillance in the Tearoom' (2009) 5(3) *Crime Media Culture* 243.

87 C Bennett and R Grant (eds), *Visions of Privacy: Police Choices for the Digital Age* (University of Toronto Press, 1999) 4.

real identity is a secret – lets it be known that he discovered a secret world and that he was the first to document its existence. His first exhibition was held secretly:

ARAKI: I heard that you didn't issue many invitations. That was a bad idea. It's a shame you didn't make a really spectacular gesture.

YOSHIYUKI: I'm a coward.

ARAKI: Cowards don't go around spying on people and photographing them having sex. What was your motivation?[88]

Secrecy can function as an aesthetic strategy without any foundational necessity to conceal. Yoshiyuki's 'secrets', crucial to the success of *Kōen*, crumble when pressed. The world of public sex in Tokyo parks was evidently well-known; his photographs show that the parks were crowded with participants, and Mark McLelland's account of a *danshō* raid in which police and journalists documented a known yet hidden sexual subculture, demonstrates that photographers had visited Tokyo parks after dark 25 years earlier to capture their 'secret' world. Indeed, many of Yoshiyuki's viewers have already noted that his work follows an established Japanese artistic practice – from woodblocks to film – of documenting sexual voyeurs. And despite the claim that nobody knows who Yoshiyuki really is, he was easily found and contacted by New York art dealers and journalists. For a secret to retain its power, one needs to remain within the logic of the secret, and its necessary paradox. It is known *and* hidden, released *but* guarded. Perhaps this is crucial to law's management of intimate secrets. Within a regime of open justice, justice must be seen to be done, but the disclosure of the secret demands that somebody is there to see it. Law's gatekeepers generally function with cold efficiency, effectively excluding all those who cannot speak law's language, cannot access law's domain, or cannot decode law's secrets. While most of this chapter targets striking, and sometimes shocking, disclosures – where one of law's secrets has fallen out of place, resulting in harm or humiliation – we also need to concede that, most of the time, law's secrets are safe, because nobody has come to discover them.

In their conversation, Araki tells Yoshiyuki: 'They [the photographs] are powerful enough to thrill anyone who comes to see them';[89] Yoshiyuki says, 'at that time, nobody ever dreamed they'd be photographed'.[90] As a curator at the Museum of Contemporary Photography in Chicago, Karen Irvine, said, 'our appetite for observing people in extremely personal circumstances doesn't seem to wane'.[91] In Yoshiyuki's photographs we encounter subjects whose sexual

88 Araki, above n 27, 76.
89 Ibid.
90 Ibid, 78.
91 In Gefter, above n 13, 38.

secrets were never supposed to be captured, represented or made permanent; these were sexual liaisons that were supposed to disappear back into the darkness. Whereas voyeurs look without permission, are the beneficiaries of open justice really voyeurs? They – we – do not perpetrate any recognised legal or moral violations, and yet the experience of looking at law's secrets is often so powerful because we recognise some unspecified kind of trespass: we are looking at something that was never supposed to be represented, and never meant to be seen. The subjects of Yoshiyuki's images failed to anticipate the technological innovations that enabled their capture. Does that failure create an ethical obligation for those of us who might look at them? Does it limit our motivations for looking? Are we, for example, restricted to looking for the purpose of forming a judgment? We can adduce evidence of transgression and reach a proven finding? Can we look and learn? These images might enable us to study the history of public sex, or the history of surveillance, or voyeurism? Are we also entitled to look for pleasure? Can we look and be aroused? Disclosures will have multiple effects, not always predictable or governable. A regime of open justice achieves transparency through disclosure, in a technique that is designed to teach us about the processes of justice, and to give us confidence and trust in the regime. However, as this chapter has argued, open justice has the potential to function in ways that may be exhibitionistic, with the effect that it transforms us – its beneficiaries – into voyeurs. Disclosures, particularly sensational, intimate or humiliating disclosures, give us a taste for secrets, and feed an ongoing hunger for more disclosures, and for more shocking and strange disclosures. While we ought to remain vigilant about our processes of justice, and continue to scrutinise them, we need to remain attentive to what open justice might do to us.

Bibliography

Books and articles

Abelove, H, M A Barale and D M Halperin (eds), *The Lesbian and Gay Studies Reader* (Routledge, 1993)

Bell, David, 'Bodies, Technologies, Spaces: On "Dogging"' (2006) 9 *Sexualities* 387

Bennett C and R Grant (eds), *Visions of Privacy: Police Choices for the Digital Age* (University of Toronto Press, 1999)

Berlant, Laurent, 'Intimacy: A Special Issue' in Laurent Berlant (ed.), *Intimacy* (University of Chicago Press, 2000)

Berlant, Laurent (ed.), *Intimacy* (University of Chicago Press, 2000)

Berlant, Laurent and Michael Warner, 'Sex in Public' (1998) 24(2) *Critical Inquiry* 547

Biber, Katherine, *Captive Images* (Routledge-Cavendish, 2007)

Biber, Katherine, 'Evidence from the Archive: Implementing the Court Information Act in NSW' (2011) 33(3) *The Sydney Law Review* 575

Biber, Katherine, 'In Crime's Archive: The Cultural Afterlife of Criminal Evidence' (2013) 53(6) T*he British Journal of Criminology* 1033

Biber, Katherine, 'Inside Jill Meagher's Handbag: Looking at Open Justice' (2014) 39(2) *Alternative Law Journal* 73
Biber, Katherine and Derek Dalton, 'Making Art from Evidence: Secret Sex and Police Surveillance in the Tearoom' (2009) 5(3) *Crime Media Culture* 243
Calvert, Clay, *Voyeur Nation: Media, Privacy, and Peering in Modern Culture* (Westview, 2000)
Cassegard, Carl, 'Public Space in Recent Japanese Political Thought and Activism: From the Rivers and Lakes to Miyashita Park' (2011) 31(3) *Japanese Studies* 405
Chaplin, Sarah, *Japanese Love Hotels: A Cultural History* (Routledge, 2007)
Crimp, Douglas, 'Alvin Baltrop' (2008) 46(6) *Artforum* 269
Cunliffe, Emma, 'Open Justice: Concepts and Judicial Approaches' (2012) 40 *Federal Law Review* 385
Davis, Colleen, 'The Injustice of Open Justice' (2001) 8 *James Cook University Law Review* 92
Diamond, Milton and Ayako Uchiyama, 'Pornography, Rape and Sex Crimes in Japan' (1999) 22(1) *International Journal of Law and Psychiatry* 1
Garland-Thomson, Rosemarie, *Staring: How We Look* (Oxford University Press, 2009)
Goldin, Nan and Nobuyoshi Araki, *Tokyo Love* (Scalo, 1995)
Jaconelli, Joseph, *Open Justice: A Critique of the Public Trial* (Oxford University Press, 2002)
Kravagna, Christian, 'Bring on the Little Japanese Girls!' (1999) 13 *Third Text* 48
Lebowitz, Cathy, 'Kohei Yoshiyuki: The Park: Cathy Lebowitz interviews Josefina Ayerza' (2007) 30 *Lacanian Ink* 163
McLelland, Mark, *Queer Japan from the Pacific War to the Internet Age* (Rowman & Littlefield, 2005)
Metzl, Jonathan M, 'Voyeur Nation? Changing Definitions of Voyeurism, 1950–2004' (2004) 12(2) *Harvard Review of Psychiatry* 127
Miki, Akiko, Yoshiko Isshiki and Tomoko Sato (eds), *Nobuyoshi Araki: Self. Life. Death* (Phaidon, 2005)
Oxford English Dictionary, online edition (2001–)
Parr, Martin and Gerry Badger, *The Photobook: A History – Volume II* (Phaidon, 2006)
Ray, Jennifer, *Repression and Rebellion: Cruising and its Depiction in Works by Minor White, Kohei Yoshiyuki, and Evergon* (MFA Thesis, Columbia College Chicago, 2012)
Sedgwick, Eve Kosofsky, 'The Epistemology of the Closet' in H Abelove, M A Barale and D M Halperin (eds), *The Lesbian and Gay Studies Reader* (Routledge, 1993), 45–46
Spigelman, James Jacob, 'The Principle of Open Justice: A Comparative Perspective' (2006) 29(2) *UNSW Law Journal* 147
Tam, Kenneth, *Disappearing in Plain Sight or How we used to have Casual Sex before Craigslist* (MFA thesis, University of Southern California, 2010)
Taussig, Michael, *Defacement: Public Secrecy and the Labor of the Negative* (Stanford University Press, 1999)
Waldby, Kevin, '"He asked me if I was looking for fags . . ." Ottawa's National Capital Commission Conservation Officers and the Policing of Public Park Sex' (2009) 6(4) *Surveillance and Society* 367
West, Mark D., *Law in Everyday Japan: Sex, Sumo, Suicide, and Statutes* (University of Chicago Press, 2010)

Media

Cohen, David, 'Peeking In on the Social Set' *The New York Sun* (online), 6 September 2007 www.nysun.com/arts/peeking-in-on-the-social-set/62042/

Gefter, Philip, 'Sex in the Park, And Its Sneaky Spectators' *The New York Times*, 23 September 2007, Art 37. NYT, 23 Sept 2007, AR 37
Genocchio, Benjamin, 'The Listings: Kohei Yoshiyuki: The Park' *The New York Times* (online), 7 September 2007 http://query.nytimes.com/gst/fullpage.html?res=9A0DE1D7153BF934A3575AC0A9619C8B63
Kyriacou, Kate, 'Court releases journal entries by Allison Baden-Clay, one written days before she disappeared' *The Courier-Mail* (online), 15 December 2012 www.couriermail.com.au/news/queensland/brisbane-supreme-court-releases-journal-entries-by-allison-baden-clay-one-written-just-days-before-she-disappeared/story-e6freoof-1226537242449
Partridge, Emma, 'Video reveals the moments before Lisa Harnum died, and what Simon Gittany did next' *The Sydney Morning Herald* (online), 1 November 2013 www.smh.com.au/nsw/video-reveals-the-moments-before-lisa-harnum-died-and-what-simon-gittany-did-next-20131101–2wq4h.html
Wolff, Rachel, 'A Lost Voyeur's Paradise: Images from Tokyo's furtive sex life, brought to light again' *New York* (online), 24 August 2007 http://nymag.com/nymag/guides/36605/

Media – no named author

'Diary of a mum accused of killing her four babies' *The Sun-Herald* (online), 6 April 2003 www.smh.com.au/articles/2003/04/05/1049459859119.html
'Down in the Park: Yoshiyuki Kohei's Nocturnes: Interview by Araki Nobuyoshi' (2007) 188 *Aperture* 74
'Galleries: Evidence in the Jill Meagher murder case' *Herald Sun* (online), 13 March 2013 www.heraldsun.com.au/news/law-order/gallery-fnat79vb-1226596531880?page=1
'More of Kurt Cobain's suicide scene pictures released by Seattle police' *The Sydney Morning Herald* (online), 31 March 2014 www.smh.com.au/entertainment/music/more-of-kurt-cobains-suicide-scene-pictures-released-by-seattle-police-20140331–35slu.html
'The State of Sex' *V Magazine* (online), V56, 2008 www.vmagazine.com/site/content/825/

Chapter 9

The critical force of irony

Reframing photographs in cultural legal studies

Karen Crawley

Cultural legal studies forms part of the broader cultural turn in legal scholarship, which explores how law is formed and reformed through cultural practices, procedures, sites, interactions and agents. Within this broader turn, however, the methodology of cultural legal studies is distinctive: it takes representations seriously. Unlike what is often called 'the cultural study of law', which tends to reach 'beyond textual analysis' towards 'the networks of social practices'[1] through which culture and law shape each other, the diverse scholars pursuing cultural legal studies are united by their insistence on *reading* the text, or on focusing on the affective experience of *encountering* an image, in order to explore how the formal properties of literature, art, photographs, theatre, cinema and so on invite particular modes of engagement, engender certain perspectives, interpellate certain subjectivities, and encourage specific forms of relation. Against the facticity of the socio-legal tradition, cultural legal scholars frequently embrace and analyse the invention of fiction: imaginary and symbolic, yes, but no less powerful for that. Their intellectual toolkit therefore comes less from anthropology, sociology or cultural studies *per se* than from those interpretative methods sourced within the humanities tradition – philosophy, critical theory, literary studies, art history etc. – and developed by legal scholars through interdisciplinary inquiries into 'law and literature', 'law and the image', and 'law and film'.[2] Contemporary cultural legal scholars are turning to an increasingly broad range of popular representations – paintings, video games, advertising, reality television,

1 Sara L Knox and Cristyn Davies, 'The Force of Meaning: Cultural Studies of Law' (2013) 27(1) *Cultural Studies* 1, 1.

2 The literature is too voluminous to be cited here, but scholars whose work has been highly significant to the development of these fields over the last two decades include Maria Aristodemou, Peter Brooks, Ruth Buchanan, Wai Chee Dimock, Kieran Dolin, Costas Douzinas, Cathrine O Frank, Peter Goodrich, Rebecca Johnson, Orit Kamir, William MacNeil, Desmond Manderson, Lynda Nead, Penny Pether, Paul Raffield, Peter Rush, Austin Sarat, Richard Sherwin, Jessica Silbey, Gary Watt and Alison Young.

children's books, street art, hip hop music, comics and graphic novels[3] – to discover the contingencies and exigencies of jurisprudence, to imagine possibilities for justice beyond the law, and to understand the desires that enter into the experience of legal subjects.

Scholarship in law and the humanities has often remarked that modern law constitutes itself by denying its own status as representation. As Susan Sage Heinzelman writes, 'the law's dominant mode of representing itself has been as a discourse that is impervious to other discursive systems.'[4] Law and literature scholarship has long treated law as a distinct 'literary genre',[5] 'a kind of rhetorical and literary activity'[6] that denies its own literariness, rhetoricity or figurative nature. Scholars of legal performance have examined law as a mode of theatre that disavows its own theatricality.[7] Scholarship on law and the image has observed that:

> (l)aw pretends that it can close itself off from other discourses and practices, attain a condition of total self-presence and purity, and keep outside its domain the non-legal, the extraneous, the other – in particular the aesthetic, the beautiful and the image.[8]

For some socio-legal scholars, this feature of law is axiomatic and thus beyond scrutiny – in their introduction to a recent issue of *Cultural Studies* on 'Cultural Studies of Law', Sara L. Knox and Cristyn Davies state: 'We take it as given that the law must act to efface both its own rhetoricity and its interestedness in order to function as law, and in this way stands in awkward relation to culture, and to history.'[9] Cultural legal scholars, however, are generally not content to

3 See for instance Michael Freeman (ed.), *Law and Popular Culture* (Oxford University Press, 2005); Peter Robson and Jessica Silbey (eds), *Law and Justice on the Small Screen* (Hart Publishing, 2012); Luis Gomez Romero and Ian Dahlman, *Justice Framed: Law in Comics and Graphic Novels* (2012) 16 *Law Text Culture* Special Issue 1; Alison Young, *Street Art, Public City: Law, Crime and the Urban Imagination* (Routledge, 2013).

4 Susan Sage Heinzelman, 'Imagining the Law' in Austin Sarat, Matthew Anderson and Cathrine O Frank (eds), *Law and the Humanities: An Introduction* (Cambridge University Press, 2009) 213, 215.

5 Peter Goodrich, 'Law and Language: An Historical and Critical Introduction' (1984) 11 *Journal of Law and Society* 173, 174.

6 James Boyd White, *Heracles' Bow* (University of Wisconsin Press, 1985) 2.

7 Julie Stone Peters, 'Legal Performance Good and Bad' (2008) 4 *Journal of Law, Culture and the Humanities* 179; Karen Crawley, 'Farce of Law: Performing and Policing *Norm v Ahmed* in 1969' (2010) 14 *Law Text Culture* 247.

8 Costas Douzinas and Lynda Nead, 'Introduction: Law and Aesthetics' in Costas Douzinas and Lynda Nead (eds), *Law and Image: The Authority of Art and the Aesthetics of Law* (University of Chicago Press, 1999) 1, 4.

9 Sara L Knox and Cristyn Davies, 'The Force of Meaning: Cultural Studies of Law' (2013) 27(1) *Cultural Studies* 1, 1.

take this 'as given'. Since law draws its authority from pretending to stand outside of the culture it regulates, there is clearly something critical at stake in the task of 'eroding the pretence of law's purity and belief in its own separation from the aesthetic.'[10]

This chapter focuses on irony as a way of elucidating what is at stake in this project: as a way of characterising what is distinctive about cultural legal studies and the critical insights it generates into how law operates. Part I examines how work in cultural legal studies has focused on questions of form, style and affect in order to reveal the relationship between representation, subjectivity and law. Part II turns to the irony generated by an encounter between a censorious law and a controversial photograph in order to explore what this irony can reveal about the instability of the frames that structure our social ordering of desire and underwrite the law's coherence. Part III concludes by reflecting on irony's potential within cultural legal studies as a critical method for unravelling the strands that make up law's self-posturing, and for revealing how we, as legal subjects, identify with the imaginary and symbolic places from which law interpellates us.

Taking representations seriously in cultural legal studies

Legal scholars have long reached out to the humanities to explore the potential of representations to disrupt our established perspectives or ways of thinking, and the affective dimensions that give them transformative power. Cultural texts, images, and other forms of representation can be said to hold up a mirror to law. The relationship thereby engendered, however, is not one of simple mimetic reflection, in which a literary text or film provides an external 'commentary' upon law, but something much more complicated. Recent work in cultural legal studies has conceived of this relationship in increasingly sophisticated ways. Desmond Manderson seeks to overcome the 'mimetic fallacy' of previous law and literature scholarship – which flattens the text with its privileging of the signified over the signifier – by moving towards questions of form, style, and language itself. Drawing on Mikhail Bahktin's dialogic theory of the novel, Manderson's reading of D.H. Lawrence's *Kangaroo* shows how the form, style, language, syntax and multivocality of the modernist novel provides the reader with a 'a literary *experience* of justice'[11] that is both aesthetic and ethical: an experience of the dialogic between the formalism of rules and the impossibility

10 Rebecca Scott Bray, 'The Hart Island Project' in Peter Rush and Andrew Kenyon (eds), *Aesthetics of Law and Culture: Texts, Images and Screens* (JAI Press, 2004) 179, 200.

11 Desmond Manderson, *Kangaroo Courts and the Rule of Law: The Legacy of Modernism* (Routledge, 2012) 6.

but necessity of justice. Alison Young analyses cinema to ask how the spectator's desire – to judge and to be judged – is implicated in what is being shown on screen. For Young, 'the image' is a point of attachment and identification, one that interpellates certain kinds of legal subjectivities, and spectatorship is a 'haptic encounter' 'that allows an image to crawl under our skin, gripping us as subjects.'[12] In her account, law, image and spectatorship are thereby 'co-implicated' – 'the spectator and law, and the spectator and the image, are enfolded within each other, their contours and substances passing through and around each other.'[13] William MacNeil, turning a psychoanalytic gaze on the texts of popular culture, attends to how the text functions on the level of the Symbolic, which, he contends, does not merely repress the Real of politics and violence, but supports and symptomatises it.[14] His method of close reading maintains that the texts of popular culture do not simply convey legal themes like fairness, neutrality, and justice by analogy; rather, through the *action* of 'reading jurisprudentially'[15] these texts generate new intertexts that reveal legality as thoroughly informed by desire. This means that questions about the institution of law are questions about our subjective attachment to it, and law is best understood as a social subject driven to reproduce itself, over and over, through the texts that make up our lives. Each of these cultural legal scholars therefore insists on focusing their analysis on a register unique to representations, highlighting how questions of form relate to the conditions of our engagement with texts as readers, spectators, listeners, judges, legal subjects and critics – and how these questions have jurisprudential effect.

Behind these robust approaches to cultural representations – novels, images and films – lies a commitment to asking what art does (how we respond to it) rather than what it means (how we interpret it). This approach recognises that the force and political effectivity of art is not just a function of its transmission of a message, and that its significance cannot be exhausted by a historical, sociological, political, anthropological or institutional account of its production or reception. As Gilles Deleuze declared, '(t)he work of art is not communication',[16] but 'harbors within it an excess, a rapture, a potential of associations.'[17] Or as Susan Sontag wrote, '(a) work of art encountered as a work of art is an experience, not a statement or an answer to a question. Art is not only about

12 Alison Young, 'Arrested by the Image' (2013) 57 *New York Law School Law Review* 77, 83.

13 Ibid; see also Alison Young, *Judging the Image: Art, Value, Law* (Routledge, 2005) 10, 13.

14 William P MacNeil, *Lex Populi: The Jurisprudence of Popular Culture* (Stanford University Press, 2007) 10.

15 William P MacNeil, *Novel Judgments: Legal Theory as Fiction* (Routledge, 2012) 12.

16 Gilles Deleuze, 'What is the Creative Act?' in Sylvère Lotringer and Sande Cohen, *French Theory in America* (Routledge, 2001) 99, 106.

17 Jean-Francois Lyotard, 'Critical Reflections' W G J Niesluchawski trans (1991) 24(8) *Artforum* 92, 93.

something; it is something.'[18] Rather than attempting to read the art object for its (political) content, however socially determined, scholars working in this tradition concentrate on the affective and embodied *event* of viewing art, 'attending to the specificity of an art work and the specificity of the milieu in which the art object operates.'[19] On this account, art is distinctive for its capacity to facilitate 'a genuine encounter' that generates difference – that *does* something to us by short-circuiting our cognitive and conceptual capabilities.[20] The encounter between art and spectator is thereby both 'essentially performative'[21] and productive – as scholars writing about representations, we are always already implicated in the representation we encounter, and whatever we seek to bring to bear 'on' the object is already part of it, even as the encounter itself exceeds our analytical grasp and forms and transforms our subjectivity.

Cultural legal scholars study the effects and affect of representations in order to better understand the complexity of how law operates through and within its institutions and its subjects. To see law as an effect of processes of representation – as produced through the negotiation of knowledge, the telling of narrative, the exchange of symbols and the enactment of power relations – is to acknowledge its authority as contingent and conditional, constituted through a regime of images, texts and performances that must be repeated through time, articulated, displayed, and connected to bodies and places. It is not to deny its violent effects: law's authority is of course not *merely* symbolic, but grounded in the sanctioned violence it has the power to enact.[22] This violence, however, is not simply an outside force acting on a hapless pre-formed subject. Law is 'a practice of subject formation',[23] and as legal subjects, our attachment to the institution of law is about more than logic or fear of reprisal – it is the attachment

18 Susan Sontag, *Against Interpretation and Other Essays* (Picador, 2001) 17.

19 Simon O'Sullivan, 'The Aesthetics of Affect: Thinking Art Beyond Representation' (2001) 6(3) *Angelaki* 125, 130. It should be acknowledged that Deleuze disavowed the metaphysics entailed by the use of the term 'representation' – for Deleuze, the cinematic image is not a representation or a sign, rather, it is expressive and affective: 'not an image of a body, but the body as image.' Ed Mussawir, 'Cinematic Jurisprudence' (2005) 17(1) *Law and Literature* 131, 134–135.

20 Simon O'Sullivan, 'From Aesthetics to the Abstract Machine: Deleuze, Guattari and Contemporary Art Practice' in Simon O'Sullivan and Stephen Zepke (eds), *Deleuze and Contemporary Art* (Edinburgh University Press, 2010) 189, 194. Following Deleuze, Jill Bennett argues that an artwork is an 'encountered sign': a 'sign that is felt, rather than recognized or perceived through cognition.' Jill Bennett, *Empathic Vision: Affect, Trauma and Contemporary Art* (Stanford University Press, 2005) 7.

21 Peggy Phelan, *Unmarked: The Politics of Performance* (Routledge, 1993) 147.

22 Shoshana Felman, *The Juridical Unconscious: Trials and Traumas in the Twentieth Century* (Harvard University Press, 2002) 107. See Robert Cover, 'Violence and the Word' in Martha Minow, Michael Ryan and Austin Sarat (eds), *Narrative, Violence and the Law: The Essays of Robert Cover* (University of Michigan Press, 1995) 203.

23 Penny Pether, 'Language' in Austin Sarat, Matthew Anderson and Cathrine O Frank (eds), *Law and the Humanities: An Introduction* (Cambridge University Press, 2009) 315, 318.

of belief, the acting-out of purpose, the absorption of a narrative. As Austin Sarat and Thomas Kearns write, '(w)e have internalized law's meanings and its representations of us so much that our own purposes and understandings can no longer be extricated from them.'[24] In Robert Gordon's words, law's power

> consists less in the force that it can bring to bear against violators of its rules than in its capacity to persuade people that the world described in its images and categories is the only attainable world in which a sane person would want to live.[25]

The law must continually reform and resubstantiate its authority in the social psyche, and it achieves this by embedding itself within and colonising our cultural representations; as Peter Rush and Andrew Kenyon put it, these 'alter-egos of law . . . provid(e) the very material through which the legal institution becomes juridical.'[26] Cultural legal studies recognises that what is required is an account of what makes law, as a mode of representation, attach to and affect our bodies and life-worlds in this way: of how law 'inscribes itself on everyday life'.[27]

The critical project of cultural legal studies is usually framed as a corrective to an understanding of law as the application of rules, as well as an understanding of language that would reduce it to the communication of semantic content. H. L.A. Hart captured the easy plausibility of this understanding of law and language when he remarked that unless words were capable of standard meanings, 'nothing that we recognize as law could exist.'[28] This 'common-sense' starting point posits that the language employed by the institutions and agents of law is by and large unproblematic, and that when this language becomes fraught, compromised, paradoxical or ineffective, this is an episodic technical problem rather than a constitutive feature of language use. On this formulation, the authority of law is tied to its univocality, monism and consistency, its claim to an objective existence and its independence from the complexities of interpretation. The departure point for much critical legal scholarship has been to emphasise that this 'sovereign conceit'[29] is itself produced by representational efforts and effects that must be repeated throughout time. As Roland Barthes

24 Austin Sarat and Thomas R Kearns, 'Editorial Introduction' in Austin Sarat and Thomas R Kearns (eds), *The Rhetoric of Law* (University of Michigan Press, 1994) 12–13.
25 Robert W Gordon, 'Critical Legal Histories' (1984) 36 *Stanford Law Review* 57.
26 Peter Rush and Andrew Kenyon, 'Alter Egos: The Mise-En-Scène of Law and Aesthetics' in Peter Rush and Andrew Kenyon (eds), *Aesthetics of Law and Culture: Texts, Images and Screens* (JAI Press, 2004).
27 Peter Goodrich, 'Specula Laws: Image, Aesthetic and Common Law' (1991) 2 *Law and Critique* 233, 235.
28 H L A Hart, *The Concept of Law* (Oxford University Press, 1961) 124.
29 Judith Butler, *Excitable Speech: A Politics of the Performative* (Routledge, 1997) 16.

wrote, 'encratic language (the language produced and spread under the production of power) is statutorily a language of repetition; all official institutions of language are repeating machines.'[30] Similarly, Derrida argued that the founding violence of law must be repeated and consolidated, in that it repeats itself in every decision, every 'reinstating act of interpretation'.[31] Scholars have adopted literary and rhetorical modes of analysis in order to explore, in the words of Sarat *et al.*, 'how juridical language obscures its own agency, presenting itself as neutral and inevitable rather than forceful and world creating.'[32]

The critical move that analyses law as a form of representation has begun to put pressure on the conceptualisation of sovereignty in law. Following Philip Abrams, Rick Mohr characterises the state as a signifier: not 'the reality that stands behind the mask of political practice', but rather 'the mask itself', a 'collective (mis)representation' that emerges as 'a claim to domination'.[33] This claim, as legal pluralists have amply demonstrated, can only be maintained through the strategic, deliberate and continual neglect of the local and particular, of law's discursive and hybrid nature, and the productivity of human symbolic and embodied practices that negotiate multiple overlapping normative orders.[34] The need for the sovereignty of the Australian state, in particular, to be continually symbolically consolidated has been demonstrated through critical historiography emphasising the state's ongoing interaction with indigenous legal orders.[35] Since the law's performance of authority and the creation of the state is continuous, it is thus always liable to contingency and misfiring, to failure to constitute a successful claim to dominance. This misfiring is, as Derrida famously suggested, 'a stroke of luck for politics',[36] providing the entry point for critique.

30 Roland Barthes, *The Pleasure of the Text* (Richard Miller trans, Noonday Press, 1975) 40.

31 Jacques Derrida, 'Force of Law: The Mystical Foundation of Authority' Mary Quaintance trans (1990) 11 *Cardozo Law Review* 919, 961.

32 Austin Sarat, Matthew Anderson and Cathrine O Frank, 'Introduction: On the Origins and Prospects of the Humanistic Study of Law' in Austin Sarat, Matthew Anderson and Cathrine O Frank (eds), *Law and the Humanities: An Introduction* (Cambridge University Press, 2009) 1 at 37.

33 Philip Abrams, cited in Rick Mohr, 'Living Legal Fictions: Constituting the State or Submerging the Signifier' (2006) 19 *International Journal for the Semiotics of Law* 237, 238.

34 See in particular Martha-Marie Kleinhans and Roderick A Macdonald, 'What is a Critical Legal Pluralism?' (1997) 12 *Canadian Journal of Law and Society* 25.

35 See, among others, Rick Mohr, 'Shifting Ground: Context and Change in Two Australian Legal Systems' (2002) 15(1) *International Journal for the Semiotics of Law* 1; Stewart Motha, 'The Failure of "Postcolonial" Sovereignty in Australia' (2005) 22 *Australian Feminist Law Journal* 107; Honni Van Rijswijk, 'Stories of the Nation's Continuing Past: Responsibility for Historical Injuries in Australian Law and Alexis Wright's *Carpentaria*' (2012) 35(2) *UNSW Law Journal* 598.

36 Jacques Derrida, 'Force of Law: The Mystical Foundation of Authority' Mary Quaintance trans (1990) 11 *Cardozo Law Review* 919, 935.

The relationship between representation, subjectivity and law thus turns on the complex question of visibility, or exposure. Law is a public performance before an audience, and is thus perceived, performed and promulgated by and for its subjects. If Derridean accounts of performativity encourage us to think of law as a kind of subject formation in itself – one that authorises itself through the sovereign conceit but is in fact 'called into being in the act of calling others to account'[37] – then law's sovereign claims are vulnerable because of the ever-present possibility of an improper repetition or 'infelicitous performance'.[38] Psychoanalytic jurisprudence gives us another way of understanding the vulnerability of the public face of law, by offering 'a reading of the institution of law "as if" it were a subject and so driven to reproduce itself',[39] of law 'as a social subject ceaselessly laboring to create subjects'.[40] If performativity understands repetition as convention, psychoanalysis explores repetition as repression: the repression of an identification with a specific form of transgressing the law – in the parlance of psychoanalysis, enjoyment, and in its origin myths, patricide and incest – that guarantees the community's identity and the law's coherence.[41] For Slavoj Žižek, the vulnerability of the public legal order arises when this repressed transgressive enjoyment is staged or exposed: 'the obscene superego qua basis and support of the public law is operative only insofar as it remains unacknowledged, hidden to the public eye.'[42]

It is here, at the intersection of performative and psychoanalytic approaches to law, that we can position the law's encounter with a cultural representation as a misstep in law's own repetition, and an opening to a kind of critique that is not external but immanent to law's very subject-formation. The mirrored relationship between law and cultural representations is one of *refraction* – in which both are caught up together in an oscillating series of framings and reframings that are not resolved or fixed, but ongoing, and both are continually transformed in the process. Ironic moments are moments when this reframing is particularly noticeable, and the forces of power that stabilise the usual ways we look at things become uncertain or unbalanced, and law's self-instantiation and constitutive repression, normally kept backstage, are brought into focus. While not all encounters between law and cultural representations are ironic, some certainly are, and when they are, it's because of this drama of exposure,

37 Martha Merrill Umphrey, 'Law in Drag: Trials and Legal Performativity' (2011) 21 *Columbia Journal of Gender and Law* 114, 115.

38 J L Austin, *How to Do Things with Words* 2nd edn by J O Urmson and Marina Sbisà (Oxford University Press, 1975 [1955]) 14.

39 Peter Goodrich, 'The Unconscious is a Jurist: Psychoanalysis and Law in the Work of Pierre Legendre' (1996) 20(2) *Legal Studies Forum* 195, 199.

40 Ibid.

41 Slavoj Žižek, 'Superego by Default' in *The Metastases of Enjoyment* (Verso, 1994) 54, 55.

42 Ibid, 71.

when something becomes revealed that we couldn't see clearly before. This revelation is not the end of critical analysis, but its beginning.

Ironic encounters between law and art

Exactly what it means to consider law as a representational practice is perhaps nowhere more apparent than when legal institutions attempt – and 'fail' – to regulate controversial cultural texts: to limit or modify their affective trajectories, to decide what they will mean and where they will travel, who can read, view or listen to them and under what circumstances. As a strategy for containing representations, explicit censorship has a notorious tendency to backfire.[43] Historian Donna I. Dennis notes that the most widely expressed objection to obscenity regulation in the United States during the nineteenth century – far more than concerns about restrictions on freedom of speech or freedom of the press – stemmed from the realisation that such prosecutions often served to publicise the practices they were intended to eradicate.[44] Geoffrey Robertson calls 'the abiding irony of all censorship' 'the *Spycatcher* effect: attempt to ban by law any form of artistic expression, and the publicity you bestow upon it will only serve to promote massive sales.'[45] The perverse effects so often associated with regulatory censorship abundantly demonstrate that animating context or authorial intention does not determine the meaning or force of law's instantiation, suggesting the unstable connection between means and ends, forms and effects.

The irony of censorship is that it seems doomed to make present what it seeks to make absent. Judith Butler observes that in order for the law to regulate a phenomenon, it must transform it into legal discourse, and thus – inadvertently – 'establish it as a site of contestation, that is, as the scene of public utterance that it sought to preempt.'[46] She writes that 'the censor is compelled to repeat the speech that the censor would prohibit',[47] and 'language that is compelled to repeat what it seeks to constrain invariably reproduces and restages the very speech that it seeks to shut down.'[48] But, she warns, general appeals to this irony have limited explanatory power:

43 Sue Curry Jansen and Brian Martin, 'Exposing and Opposing Censorship: Backfire Dynamics in Freedom of Speech Struggles' (2004) 10(1) *Pacific Journalism Review* 29, 29–30; Derek Dalton and Catherine Schubert, 'When Classification Becomes Censorship: An Analysis of the Neutralisation and Resistance of Film Censorship in Contemporary Australia' (2011) 20(1) *Griffith Law Review* 31, 32–33.

44 Donna I Dennis, 'Obscenity Law and its Consequences in Mid-Nineteenth Century America' (2007) 16(1) *Columbia Journal of Gender and Law* 43, 92.

45 Geoffrey Robertson, *The Justice Game* (London, 1999) 47.

46 Judith Butler, *Excitable Speech: A Politics of the Performative* (Routledge, 1997) 130.

47 Ibid, 37.

48 Ibid, 129. See further Judith Butler, 'The Force of Fantasy: Feminism, Mapplethorpe, and Discursive Excess' (1990) 2(2) *Differences: A Journal of Feminist Cultural Studies* 105, 108.

> they cannot tell us when and why certain kinds of censorship are, in fact, more complete than others, why some operations of censorship seem to capture the offensive speech, and others seem quite helpless to effect any capture at all. What accounts for the efficacy and vulnerability to failure that characterizes different operations of censorship? Never fully separable from that which it seeks to censor, censorship is implicated in its own repudiated material in ways that produce paradoxical consequences.[49]

Butler's comment can be extended to the difference between cultural legal studies and the cultural study of law. Taking law's separability from culture as given, and thus merely pointing out the existence of law, represses inquiry into its own form, and ironically produces what it wants to prohibit – an analysis incapable of understanding how that attachment to an idea of law arises. This unquestioning attitude to law's form pervades traditional accounts of censorship that tend to posit a unilateral top-down exercise of power wielded by the censor on the censored, where each is understood as external to the power of censorship itself.[50] On this account, law is a pre-existing force externally imposed on artworks that become objects of criminalisation or governance, a force that artworks can then 'subvert'. But cultural legal studies, in its emphasis on law as constituted through representation, and its consequent attention to questions of form, affect and framing, gives us the analytical tools to pursue Butler's observation and to understand how law's own 'fantasy of sovereign action'[51] is called into question and transformed by its encounters and entanglements with its own repudiated texts.

The 2008 scandal over the work of Australian photographer Bill Henson provides an apt example of the ironies that surround controversial cultural texts, and what this can reveal about the complex relationship between representations, subjectivity and law. On 22 May, editorial writer Miranda Devine published a opinion piece in the *Sydney Morning Herald* decrying the sexualisation of children in the media, focusing on a particular photograph of a naked 13-year-old girl called 'N' that had appeared on the invitation to Henson's latest exhibition, due to open that night.[52] This editorial had a catalytic effect in a discursive scene already ripe for controversy. The issue of child sexualisation was on the political agenda in Europe, North America and Australia. An Australian Federal Parliament Senate Inquiry into the sexualisation of children in the media was

49 Butler, above n 46, 130.

50 Judith Butler, 'Ruled Out: Vocabularies of the Censor' in Robert C Post (ed.), *Censorship and Silencing: Practices of Cultural Regulation* (Getty Research Institute, 1998) 247, 247.

51 Butler, above n 46, 12.

52 Miranda Devine 'Moral backlash over sexing up of our children' *Sydney Morning Herald* (22 May 2008).

already underway.[53] The recent Federal government's intervention into the Northern Territory had been mobilised around the figure of 'the child in need of protection', which, in this era marked by what Barbara Baird called 'the fundamentalism of the child',[54] stood as an absolute truth outside bipartisan politics. Within a matter of hours, radio talk show hosts, politicians, journalists and television news crews had weighed in on Henson's exhibition, the gallery was besieged by phone calls, and complaints were being made to the NSW State Police. The exhibition was closed, and Henson, an acclaimed photographer made internationally famous in the 1970s for his dreamy photographs of nude adolescents, went to ground.

The following morning, in a now famous incident, the then-Prime Minister of Australia Kevin Rudd was shown several of Henson's photographs on Channel Nine's *The Today Show*. They were flashed on the screen in quick succession, covered with black bars, and captioned with the heading 'Outrage over child-porn art'. Rudd, who had not seen the images before, and so saw them for the first time with these bars, pronounced them 'absolutely revolting. Kids deserve to have the innocence of their childhood protected . . . for God's sake, let's just allow kids to be kids.'[55] Several hours later, police seized a large collection of Henson's photographs and announced their intention to proceed to prosecution for publishing a photograph of a child 'in a sexual context'.[56] The resulting furore – described by journalist David Marr as the 'biggest story in the country'[57] that year – had profound and highly public ripple effects throughout the legal, political and artistic communities over the following months, as police went on to seize further images which had long been held in several art galleries around the country, the art community re-evaluated its standards for the use of children in art, changes were suggested to remove the 'artistic defence' from the crime of indecent publishing in the *Crimes Act*, and prominent members of the international art community wrote an open letter calling on the Prime Minister and politicians to reconsider their comments.[58]

The Henson scandal unfolded in a similar way to controversies in the United States over photographs of children by Sally Mann, Robert Mapplethorpe, Jock Sturges and others: 'artistic' photographs brought to the public's attention by

53 Senate Report, Standing Committee on Environment, Communications and the Arts, *Sexualisation of Children in the Contemporary Media* (June 2008) www.aph.gov.au/binaries/senate/committee/eca_ctte/sexualisation_of_children/report/report.pdf.

54 Barbara Baird, 'Child Politics, Feminist Analyses' (2008) 23(57) *Australian Feminist Studies* 291, 295.

55 Kevin Rudd, on *The Today Show*, with host Karl Stefanovic, Channel 9 (23 May 2008).

56 *Crimes Act 1900* (NSW) s 91.

57 David Marr, *The Henson Case* (Text Publishing Company, 2008) 59.

58 Corrie Perkin and Lauren Wilson, 'Cate Blanchett calls on Kevin Rudd to soften Bill Henson art remarks' *The Australian* (28 May 2008).

the media provoked public outrage and an initially enthusiastic response from law enforcement, but did not in the end attract legal sanction.[59] A week after Devine's editorial was published, the Classification Board gave the unbarred image of 'N' a PG (parental guidance) classification, indicating that it was a 'mild' display of nudity.[60] As several members of the Classification Board noted, the addition of black bars when Henson's photographs were shown on television and in news media – and to Rudd – rendered 'a mild display of nudity' 'dirty and more confronting'.[61] Eventually, the police investigation into Henson was quietly dropped, after the NSW Director of Public Prosecutions advised the police that mere nudity in a photograph does not make it obscene or pornographic.[62]

The process by which the media's censorship invited, or incited, the law's subsequent censorship underlines the extent to which crime is produced through the discursive operations of what Young calls 'the crimino-legal complex', comprising 'legal judgments, the actions and pronouncements of police and administrative officials, the discourse of policymakers, and media representations of and popular discourses about crime.'[63] Ironically, in this case, it was not Henson who had produced pornography, but rather this crimino-legal complex that had done so *through the act of censoring the image*. The 'blacking out' did not only visually confirm but actually constructed the obscene nature of the photographs.[64] The censorial mechanisms by which sexuality was supposed to be warded off only amplified its effects. The bars immediately enlisted the fantasy

59 See for instance Robert Mapplethorpe's 'Jesse (McBride)' (1976) and 'Rosie' (1976), Sally Mann's photographs of her family in *At Twelve* (1988) and *Intimate Family* (1992), Jock Sturges, *The Last Days of Summer* (1991) and *Radiant Identities* (1994). See for instance Richard B Woodward, 'The Disturbing Photography of Sally Mann' *New York Times Magazine* (27 September 1992) 52.

60 Classification Board, report, 3 June 2008, T08/2235 cited in *Henson Case*, above n 57 at 118. The image with black bars appearing in the context of 'legitimate reportage' was an 'image of nudity that is very mild in viewing impact and justified by context,' and warranted a G classification. Classification Board, Attorney-General's Department, Canberra, reports T08/2273, T08/2275, T08/2274, T08/2278 and T082276, 29 May 2008. As David Marr notes, these decisions were not immediately reported in the media: Marr, above n 57, 117–118.

61 Classification Board, Attorney-General's Department, Canberra, reports T08/2273, T08/2275, T08/2274, T08/2278 and T082276, 29 May 2008.

62 Marr, above n 57,122–123.

63 Alison Young, *Imagining Crime: Textual Outlaws and Criminal Conversations* (Sage, 1996) 2.

64 For a similar analysis, see Sarah Edge and Gail Baylis, 'Photographing Children: the Works of Tierney Gearon and Sally Mann' (2004) 5(1) *Visual Culture in Britain* 75, 76. David Gurnham writes that some of Gearon's photographs were reproduced in UK newspapers with the genitals blacked out 'either to avoid causing offense or else to ensure that readers would interpret the photographs as sexual.' David Gurnham, *Memory, Imagination, Justice: Intersections of Law and Literature* (Ashgate, 2009) 113.

of the subject, just as any redaction of a text teases the fantasmatic.[65] The act of censoring the image thus elicited or generated the 'outrage' that such censorship was purporting to respond to. The irony apparent here draws our attention to the precarious nature of a legal regime that purports to stand apart from desire, but finds itself entangled in it.

As many commentators remarked, each side of the Henson debate – a political discourse concerned with harm to children, and an aesthetic discourse marshalled in Henson's defence – appeared to be 'speaking a different language'.[66] On one side was a political gaze, consumed with the spectres of child exploitation and paedophilic fantasy, and on the other side, a 'neutral', 'aesthetic' gaze, which, in emphasising the autonomy and pedigree of an 'art object' and the sacrosanct value of free artistic expression, evacuated the image of politics altogether. The (hysterical) over-politicisation of the image was answered by the (self-serving) under-politicisation of the image. But neither of these approaches can account for how particular images provoke a turn to law: how they seem to demand a response from the crimino-legal complex, or incite the desire for legal action. This is because both the purportedly neutral but ideologically-riven 'aesthetic gaze' and the overdetermined and externalised 'political gaze' tend to ignore, or else take as read, the complex affective experience of encountering the image itself. What is required is to re-aestheticise the image: to see what the image hails and brings to the surface, and what it judges and finds wanting in us.

The Henson photograph is politically troubling for precisely the reason it is artistically interesting: it directs our attention to the normally-invisible work of framing. To frame is to make something visible and at the same time to connect this visibility to that which cannot be seen (the outside of the frame) and what must not be seen (the frame itself). The characteristic of the frame is 'not that it stands out but that it disappears, buries itself, effaces itself, melts away at the moment it deploys its greatest energy.'[67] The frame is thus a visible invisibility – it's meant to be perceived, but not *noticed.* The Henson image confronts us directly with our semantic over-investment in the constructed and fragile frames that separate adult from child, art from pornography, sex from not-sex, real from representation. As a photograph, it is both real and not real, a representation, but also *not* a representation: this is the affect of indexicality.[68] The human body, and particularly the female body, is a particularly potent image, freighted with ideological and libidinal investments. As Devine's

65 Judith Butler, 'The Force of Fantasy: Feminism, Mapplethorpe, and Discursive Excess' (1990) 2(2) *Differences: A Journal of Feminist Cultural Studies* 105, 111.

66 Kate MacNeill, 'When Subject Becomes Object: Nakedness, Art and the Public Sphere' (2010) *Media International Australia* 82, 84.

67 Jacques Derrida, *The Truth in Painting* (Geoff Bennington and Ian McLeod trans, University of Chicago Press, 1987) 61.

68 Young, above n 13, 43–44.

description of the photograph on the invitation makes clear – 'the light shining on her hair, eyes downcast, dark shadows on her sombre, beautiful face, and the budding breasts of puberty on full display'[69] – the image of 'N' broke a particular taboo in showing developing breasts, a body in a liminal state between girlhood and womanhood. Mary Douglas explains that 'danger lies in transitional states, simply because transition is neither one state nor the next, it is undefinable.'[70] The limits of the body, the margins of genre, and the edges of categories, are the most critical in the construction of symbolic meaning, and are thus the sites at which policing is concentrated. 'Any structure of ideas is vulnerable at its margins.'[71] The liminality of and in the photograph begins to account for why the image hails the law: its borderline status is 'imagined as desiring a repressive response'.[72]

Politicians, policymakers and media commentators frequently employed the language of 'disgust' in relation to Henson's work. In addition to Rudd's initial statement, NSW Premier Morris Iemma, who was travelling in China at the time, quickly prepared a statement: 'As a father of four I find it offensive and disgusting.'[73] Rudd repeated this language when responding to a subsequent controversy over the *Art Monthly Australia* magazine cover – 'Frankly, I can't stand this stuff'[74] – and to the 'disgusting' news of how Henson recruited his models through school visits: 'I think parents would be revolted and horrified.'[75] Disgust is a reaction to matter out of place, generated by a failure of framing and a fear of contamination, of leaking boundaries.[76] The expression of disgust draws the line between who counts as human (those who feel disgust) and who is relegated as inhuman (those who inspire disgust – by feeling desire). These public performances of disgust – the identification and expulsion of deviant desire – form part of a legislative project by which deviant desires are identified and then located in one portion of the population who can be subjected to criminal sanction. This boundary-making activity, where the human and the pervert are distinguished from one another by idioms of disgust, involves 'a multivalent satisfaction'.[77] Politicians, police, journalists and media consumers became united

69 Miranda Devine, 'Moral backlash over sexing up of our children' *Sydney Morning Herald* (22 May 2008).
70 Mary Douglas, *Purity and Danger: An Analysis of the Concepts of Pollution and Taboo* (Routledge, 1966) 119.
71 Ibid, 122.
72 Young, above n 13, 44.
73 Cited in Clae Masters and Justin Valleyo, 'Who would call this art?' *The Daily Telegraph* (23 May 2008) 4.
74 'Australian PM in new nude art row' *BBC* (7 July 2008).
75 'Henson playground report disgusts PM' *ABC News* (4 October 2008).
76 Desmond Manderson, 'Possessed: Drug Policy, Witchcraft and Belief' (2005) *Cultural Studies* 35, 37.
77 Ummni Khan, 'Having Your Porn and Condemning It Too: A Case Study of a "Kiddie Porn" Expose' (2009) 5 *Law Culture and the Humanities* 391, 407.

in a shared moral and social community by the language of disgust, caught up in 'a cycle of desire and gratification'.[78]

To experience disgust at viewing a photograph of a child is to see someone else seeing the image in a certain way. It is thus an image of an image of another's desirous responses. To feel disgust at someone else's reading of an image is by necessity to perform that reading oneself – to have 'a filthy mind'. Disgust 'is inseparable from an intrinsic interest in the object' provoking the disgust.[79] As Nead notes, 'disgust is a strong response. The disgusted viewer is the affected viewer, highly motivated, in a state not unlike desire.'[80] These public performances of disgust, therefore, consist in identifying with desire, and then suspending that identification. The 'revolting' photograph revolts *in and through* the viewer, who then expels it. At the same time, the fear behind the disgust, the reason that such a performance is deemed necessary, the reason why it is felt *as* disgust, provides implicit support for the idea that such aberrant desires circulate throughout the social body and cannot be immediately disentangled from more 'legitimate' sexual desires. Motivating the display of disgust, then, is the fear and disturbance of seeing one's own socially constructed and encouraged desire – for the youth and beauty of the female form – reflected within a context that has been pre-condemned as abhorrent. The viewer's surprising identification with the paedophilic gaze leads them to disavow that gaze through the force of law.

Ironically, then, the crimino-legal complex's framework of outrage and condemnation not only hides the gratification of desire but forms the occasion of its possibility. Linda Williams coined the term 'on/scenity' to mark the unwitting paradox that the desire to prohibit a sexual representation is implicated in the desire to re-produce it – albeit within a framework of outrage.[81] Ummni Khan has demonstrated how media coverage of child exploitation stories is '*perverse.* They are sites where direct gratification is absent and yet displaced satisfaction and desire are engaged.'[82] 'Disgust licenses the reader to, if not completely violate, then at least relish the taboo of child pornography.'[83] Amy Adler has similarly argued that the primetime show *To Catch a Predator* 'continually stages the spectacle of the sexual child that it disavows.'[84] Like these

78 Lynda Nead, 'Bodies of Judgment: Art, Obscenity, and the Connoisseur' in Costas Douzinas and Lynda Nead (eds), *Law and Image: The Authority of Art and the Aesthetics of Law* (University of Chicago Press, 1999) 203, 206.
79 Aurel Kolnai, *On Disgust* (Open Court, 2004) 100.
80 Nead, above n 78, 213.
81 Linda Williams, 'Porn Studies: Proliferating Pornographies On/Scene: An Introduction' in Linda Williams (ed.), *Porn Studies* (Duke University Press, 2004) 1, 3–4.
82 Ummni Khan, above n 77, 394.
83 Ibid, 422.
84 Amy Adler, 'To Catch a Predator' (2011) 21(2) *Columbia Journal of Gender and Law* 138, 147.

other frameworks of opprobrium, the black bars on the Henson photograph make possible a double reading of the image. At the level of public appearance or public law, the text is censored, safe, cordoned off sexuality, and can be shown in mainstream media. But at the same time, the bars on the photograph bombard us with the injunction to enjoy, engage our fantasies, and let our imaginations go wild.

Crucially, this enjoyment or relish is not inconsistent with the public law's denunciation of a sexual interest in children. Rather, this enjoyment itself guarantees the coherence of the law's prohibition against paedophilic desire. As Žižek observes, what most deeply holds together a community is not so much identification with the law that regulates the community's 'normal' everyday circuit – here, the denunciation of paedophilia – but rather identification with a specific form of transgression of the law or a specific form of enjoyment.[85] The accessibility of this desire – its incitement or provocation as a fantasy which is socially constructed and therefore *available* to us – is necessary in order to maintain the coherence of the disgust – a disgust which would posit that deviant desires sit outside the law in individual bodies waiting to be eradicated. This desire is the unacknowledged obscene support *needed* for the maintenance of the 'disgusted' regulatory order – it cannot be extinguished, but must be sustained.

Acknowledging or exposing this co-implication between disgust and desire, transgression and condemnation, draws our attention to that which is frequently obscured by the polarising volatility of child sex panics. As Steven Angelides has argued in relation to the Henson scandal, the overt concern about children as the objects of sexualisation and exploitation hid a more palpable anxiety over 'the figure of the child as agentive sexual subject.'[86] This anxiety is even more acute in cases of sexting, in which the teenage girls who are the producers *and* subjects of the photographs are paradoxically figured both as victims needing the law's protection and as active agents who must be prevented from producing materials that are dangerous, both to themselves and to society, giving rise to the irony of a law that is supposed to protect young people being used against them.[87] The typical response, Angelides observes, to the 'social and discursive commingling of children and sexuality' is one of repression: children's sexual curiosities, desires, pleasures and agency are placed outside scrutiny or even acknowledgment. Neither side of the debate over Henson's photographs consulted children for their views, nor gave consideration to the interests that

85 Slavoj Žižek, 'Superego by Default' in *The Metastases of Enjoyment* (Verso, 1994) 54, 55.

86 Steven Angelides, 'What's Behind Child Sex Panics? The Bill Henson Scandal' (2011) 2 *Lambda Nordica* 101, 115.

87 See Jessica Whyte, 'Criminalising "Camera Fiends": Photograph Restrictions in the Age of Digital Reproduction'(2009) 31 *Australian Feminist Law Journal* 99, 116.

children might have in artistic expression.[88] Children in public discourse, Angelides argues, are typically 'objectified as homogenous Child, exalted in their innocence and demonized in their transgressions, endlessly spoken about and endlessly rendered mute.'[89] Perhaps, then, watching the law's authority falter and misfire in the Henson case has the potential to open up a conversation about the taboo of child sexuality in a way that is rarely available to public discourse.

For the taboo on child sexuality is subject to the same contradictory and ironic logic as censorship itself. The figure of the 'innocent' child that emerged as a historical product over the last few centuries has been primarily defined through absence or negation – lacking (sexual) guilt, knowledge or experience, the child is 'a set of *have nots*'.[90] The problem, as James Kincaid has pointed out, is that 'conceiving of something entirely as a negation brings irresistibly before us that which we're trying to banish.'[91] Saying 'don't think of an elephant' is guaranteed to make one think of an elephant. Once childhood is defined in terms of a *lack* of sexuality, it is thus defined sexually. This is because framing does not separate inside from outside, but irrevocably ties them together. Just like the black bars on the Henson photograph, negation engages the fantasmatic. Childhood is what is forbidden to sexuality, but what is forbidden is what sexuality strives for, what its fantasy constantly remakes – the prohibition is what generates the fantasy in the first place, the imaginative testing at the boundary. In short, once childhood gets defined as a-sexual, the sexualisation – and indeed fetishisation – of children begins. If sex is the limit of childhood, then the fantasy immediately suffuses images of children with sexual context, so to speak. We don't want it, and that is precisely why we have it.

Irony as critique: undermining the sovereign fantasy

The crimino-legal response to Henson's photograph provides an example of law being drawn into, and made vulnerable to, the representational dynamics it would seek to distance itself from and control. Shoshana Felman suggests that irony consists in 'dragging authority as such into a scene which it cannot master, of which it is *not aware* and which, for that very reason, is the scene of its own self-destruction.'[92] In the photograph made more sexual through censorship,

88 This was noted by both Andrew Kenyon and John Tobin in the public seminar 'Disturbing Australia: Art or Porn?' *Courting Controversy Lecture Series*, Melbourne University Law School (16 June 2008).
89 Angelides, above n 86, 115.
90 James Kincaid, *Erotic Innocence: The Culture of Child Molesting* (Duke University Press, 1998) 15.
91 Ibid, 55.
92 Shoshana Felman, 'To Open the Question' (1977) 55–56 *Yale French Studies* 5, 8.

the law that purports to judge the image is pulled inside the image's frame, dragged into the scene it cannot master, and drawn into the spectatorial relationship of affect, identification and desire that implodes its own claims to disinterested, objective judgment. Rebecca Clift suggests that irony depends upon 'the simultaneous presence of two dimensions of meaning: "inside" and "outside" meanings, the one framing the other.'[93] To perceive the irony of the Henson case is to simultaneously glimpse law's investment in remaining outside the image, as well as the fact that law is already inside the image by virtue of framing it. The law is '*not aware*' in these moments: irony exposes law's unconscious, 'the other dimension of law',[94] the repressions through which it constitutes itself. The fact that law is necessarily implicated in the libidinal investments it seeks to regulate does not automatically engender a crisis of legitimacy for public law, confirm the failure of legal regulation, or demonstrate that the law is irretrievably compromised in its efforts to deal with unwanted sexual desires. Rather, irony's exposure of this implication confronts us with the structures of our fantasies, the ordering principles of our symbolic universe, allowing our social and cultural understandings of sexual desire to be challenged and reworked, and law's own role in both producing and policing sexual desire to be better understood.

Irony arises between and by virtue of the layered and lived texts of our shared discourses, and marks the moments when our frames of reference collide and realign before us. It can be seen in the capacity of discourse to produce a reversal of effects, the tendency of utterances to escape the speaker's intent, and the susceptibility of forms to appropriation. It decentres – even destructs – authority by placing it within a scene larger than or outside itself, and thus undermining the authority of privileged meaning 'by staging a confrontation with the spectral presence of other possible meanings.'[95] As Claire Valier suggests, irony 'exists only in and through its demonstration. Irony, one might say, is the performative *par excellence*.'[96] This necessarily means that as critical and cultural legal scholars, we must look where and when irony strikes us, allowing the force of this irony to register as critique, as a glimpse into the institutional guise of law under pressure.[97] Whether in literature, art, or life, irony calls us to bear witness to a 'scene', addressing us as spectators and demanding that we interpret it.[98]

93 Rebecca Clift, 'Irony in Conversation' (1999) 28 *Language in Society* 523, 533.
94 Pierre Legendre, 'The Other Dimension of Law' in David Carlson and Peter Goodrich (eds), *Psychoanalysis and Jurisprudence: Essays in Law and the Postmodern Mind* (Michigan University Press, 1997) 175.
95 Claire Valier, 'The Spaces of Irony' in Ronnie Lippens (ed.), *Imaginary Boundaries of Justice: Social and Legal Justice Across Disciplines* (Hart Publishing, 2004) 97, 98.
96 Ibid, 97.
97 For irony as 'that on which the critic's eye falls,' see Joseph A Dane, *The Critical Mythology of Irony* (University of Georgia Press, 2011) 2.
98 Ruth L Smith, 'Morals and their Ironies' (1998) 26(2) *Journal of Religious Ethics* 367, 369. See further Linda Hutcheon, *Irony's Edge: The Theory and Politics of Irony* (Routledge, 1994) 18; Wayne Booth, *A Rhetoric of Irony* (University of Chicago Press, 1974) 245.

The irony that attends law's entanglements with cultural texts gives us the opportunity to see law 'in *the scene* of its own self-destruction' and thus to momentarily escape its thrall, to stand outside law's authority and realize its contingent and precarious hold on that authority. Through irony's 'double vision'[99] or 'multiple vision',[100] we witness law's authoritative self-instantiation and at the *same time* perceive it to be a fiction, constructed and vulnerable.

This chapter has explored irony as a means of appreciating the critical potential of understanding law as a representational practice, by focusing on the irony that can arise when the law is doubled in and through the representations it encounters. While the texts of culture are often said to hold a mirror up to law, a mirror does not create a copy so much as put into place a destabilising refraction, an uncanny doubling, or a radical non-relation (the impossibility of being here, and there too). Likewise, the ironic encounter between law and art does not consist of art's rendering of law or law's rendering of art, but in their complex and refracted relationship. Henson's photograph did not just reflect or subvert the crimino-legal prohibition brought to bear upon it, but enabled us to glimpse how law is constituted through the representational dynamics – of identification, framing, spectatorship, desire and affect – it tries to distance itself from and control. Irony thus becomes a departure point for analysing the precariousness of law's sovereign performances: as text (canonised and not pornographic, for instance), as theatre (a display of authority and not a farce), and as remaining outside the image (not implicated or desirous). This enables an immanent critique of law that remains sceptical about its formal self-presentation and claims to mastery over meaning, and remembers that the law that is created culturally is also un-created and re-created culturally, and could be different next time.

References

Adler, Amy, 'To Catch a Predator' (2011) 21(2) *Columbia Journal of Gender and Law* 138

Angelides, Steven, 'What's Behind Child Sex Panics? The Bill Henson Scandal' (2011) 2 *Lambda Nordica* 101

Austin, J L, *How to Do Things with Words* 2nd edn by J O Urmson and Marina Sbisà (Oxford University Press, 1975 [1955])

Baird, Barbara, 'Child Politics, Feminist Analyses' (2008) 23(57) *Australian Feminist Studies* 291

Barthes, Roland, *The Pleasure of the Text* (Richard Miller trans, Noonday Press, 1975)

Bennett, Jill, *Empathic Vision: Affect, Trauma and Contemporary Art* (Stanford University Press, 2005)

Booth, Wayne, *A Rhetoric of Irony* (University of Chicago Press, 1974)

99 Valier, above n 95, 98.

100 Smith, above n 98, 367.

Bray, Rebecca Scott, 'The Hart Island Project' in Peter Rush and Andrew Kenyon (eds), *Aesthetics of Law and Culture: Texts, Images and Screens* (JAI Press, 2004) 179
Butler, Judith, 'The Force of Fantasy: Feminism, Mapplethorpe, and Discursive Excess' (1990) 2(2) *Differences: A Journal of Feminist Cultural Studies* 105
Butler, Judith, *Excitable Speech: A Politics of the Performative* (Routledge, 1997)
Butler, Judith, 'Ruled Out: Vocabularies of the Censor' in Robert C Post (ed.), *Censorship and Silencing: Practices of Cultural Regulation* (Getty Research Institute, 1998) 247
Clift, Rebecca, 'Irony in Conversation' (1999) 28 *Language in Society* 523
Cover, Robert, 'Violence and the Word' in Martha Minow, Michael Ryan and Austin Sarat (eds), *Narrative, Violence and the Law: The Essays of Robert Cover* (University of Michigan Press, 1995) 203.
Crawley, Karen, 'Farce of Law: Performing and Policing *Norm v Ahmed* in 1969' (2010) 14 *Law Text Culture* 247
Dalton, Derek and Catherine Schubert, 'When Classification Becomes Censorship: An Analysis of the Neutralisation and Resistance of Film Censorship in Contemporary Australia' (2011) 20(1) *Griffith Law Review* 31
Dane, Joseph A, *The Critical Mythology of Irony* (University of Georgia Press, 2011)
Deleuze, Gilles, 'What is the Creative Act?' in Sylvère Lotringer and Sande Cohen, *French Theory in America* (Routledge, 2001) 99
de Man, Paul, 'The Concept of Irony' in Andrzej Warminski (ed.), *Aesthetic Ideology* (University of Minnesota Press, 1996) 163
Dennis, Donna I, 'Obscenity Law and its Consequences in Mid-Nineteenth Century America' (2007) 16(1) *Columbia Journal of Gender and Law* 43
Derrida, Jacques, *The Truth in Painting* (Geoff Bennington and Ian McLeod trans, University of Chicago Press, 1987)
Derrida, Jacques, 'Force of Law: The Mystical Foundation of Authority' Mary Quaintance trans (1990) 11 *Cardozo Law Review* 919.
Douglas, Mary, *Purity and Danger: An Analysis of the Concepts of Pollution and Taboo* (Routledge, 1966)
Douzinas, Costas and Lynda Nead, 'Introduction: Law and Aesthetics' in Costas Douzinas and Lynda Nead (eds), *Law and Image: The Authority of Art and the Aesthetics of Law* (University of Chicago Press, 1999) 1
Edge, Sarah and Gail Baylis, 'Photographing Children: the Works of Tierney Gearon and Sally Mann' (2004) 5(1) *Visual Culture in Britain* 75
Felman, Shoshana, 'To Open the Question' (1977) 55–56 *Yale French Studies* 5
Felman, Shoshana, *The Juridical Unconscious: Trials and Traumas in the Twentieth Century* (Harvard University Press, 2002)
Freeman, Michael (ed.), *Law and Popular Culture* (Oxford University Press, 2005)
Goodrich, Peter, 'Law and Language: An Historical and Critical Introduction' (1984) 11 *Journal of Law and Society* 173
Goodrich, Peter, 'Specula Laws: Image, Aesthetic and Common Law' (1991) 2 *Law and Critique* 233
Goodrich, Peter, 'The Unconscious is a Jurist: Psychoanalysis and Law in the Work of Pierre Legendre' (1996) 20(2) *Legal Studies Forum* 195
Goodrich, Peter, 'Screening Law' (2009) 21(1) *Cardozo Studies in Law and Literature* 1
Gordon, Robert W., 'Critical Legal Histories' (1984) 36 *Stanford Law Review* 57
Gurnham, David, *Memory, Imagination, Justice: Intersections of Law and Literature* (Ashgate, 2009)

Hart, H L A, *The Concept of Law* (Oxford University Press, 1961)
Heinzelman, Susan Sage, 'Imagining the Law' in Austin Sarat, Matthew Anderson and Cathrine O Frank (eds), *Law and the Humanities: An Introduction* (Cambridge University Press, 2009) 213
Hutcheon, Linda, *Irony's Edge: The Theory and Politics of Irony* (Routledge, 1994)
Jansen, Sue Curry and Brian Martin, 'Exposing and Opposing Censorship: Backfire Dynamics in Freedom of Speech Struggles' (2004) 10(1) *Pacific Journalism Review* 29
Khan, Ummni, 'Having Your Porn and Condemning It Too: A Case Study of a "Kiddie Porn" Expose' (2009) 5 *Law Culture and the Humanities* 391
Kincaid, James, *Erotic Innocence: The Culture of Child Molesting* (Duke University Press, 1998)
Kleinhans, Martha-Marie and Roderick A Macdonald, 'What is a Critical Legal Pluralism?' (1997) 12 *Canadian Journal of Law and Society* 25
Knox, Sara L. and Cristyn Davies, 'The Force of Meaning: Cultural Studies of Law' (2013) 27(1) *Cultural Studies* 1
Kolnai, Aurel, *On Disgust* (Open Court, 2004)
Legendre, Pierre 'The Other Dimension of Law' in David Carlson and Peter Goodrich (eds), *Psychoanalysis and Jurisprudence: Essays in Law and the Postmodern Mind* (Michigan University Press, 1997)
Lyotard, Jean-Francois, 'Critical Reflections' W G J Niesluchawski trans, (1991) 24(8) *Artforum* 92
MacNeil, William P, *Lex Populi: The Jurisprudence of Popular Culture* (Stanford University Press, 2007)
MacNeil, William P, *Novel Judgments: Legal Theory as Fiction* (Routledge, 2012)
MacNeill, Kate, 'When Subject Becomes Object: Nakedness, Art and the Public Sphere' (2010) *Media International Australia* 82
Manderson, Desmond, 'Possessed: Drug Policy, Witchcraft and Belief' (2005) *Cultural Studies* 35
Manderson, Desmond, 'Modernism and the Critique of Law and Literature' (2011) 35 *Australian Feminist Law* 105
Manderson, Desmond, *Kangaroo Courts and the Rule of Law: The Legacy of Modernism* (Routledge, 2012)
Marr, David, *The Henson Case* (Text Publishing Company, 2008)
Mohr, Rick, 'Shifting Ground: Context and Change in Two Australian Legal Systems' (2002) 15(1) *International Journal for the Semiotics of Law* 1
Mohr, Rick, 'Living Legal Fictions: Constituting the State or Submerging the Signifier' (2006) 19 *International Journal for the Semiotics of Law* 237
Moran, Leslie J. and Derek McGhee, 'Perverting London: The Cartographic Practices of Law' in Carl F Stychin and Didi Herman (eds), *Law and Sexuality: The Global Arena* (University of Minnesota Press, 2000) 100
Motha, Stewart, 'The Failure of "Postcolonial" Sovereignty in Australia' (2005) 22 *Australian Feminist Law Journal* 107
Mussawir, Ed, 'Cinematic Jurisprudence' (2005) 17(1) *Law and Literature* 131
Nead, Lynda, 'Bodies of Judgment: Art, Obscenity, and the Connoisseur' in Costas Douzinas and Lynda Nead (eds), *Law and Image: The Authority of Art and the Aesthetics of Law* (University of Chicago Press, 1999) 203
O'Sullivan, Simon, 'The Aesthetics of Affect: Thinking Art Beyond Representation' (2001) 6(3) *Angelaki* 125

O'Sullivan, Simon, 'From Aesthetics to the Abstract Machine: Deleuze, Guattari and Contemporary Art Practice' in Simon O'Sullivan and Stephen Zepke (eds), *Deleuze and Contemporary Art* (Edinburgh University Press, 2010) 189

Peters, Julie Stone, 'Legal Performance Good and Bad' (2008) 4 *Journal of Law, Culture and the Humanities* 179

Pether, Penny, 'Language' in Austin Sarat, Matthew Anderson and Cathrine O Frank (eds), *Law and the Humanities: An Introduction* (Cambridge University Press, 2009) 315

Phelan, Peggy, *Unmarked: The Politics of Performance* (Routledge, 1993)

Robertson, Geoffrey, *The Justice Game* (Vintage, 1999)

Robson, Peter and Jessica Silbey (eds), *Law and Justice on the Small Screen* (Hart Publishing, 2012)

Romero, Luis Gomez and Ian Dahlman, *Justice Framed: Law in Comics and Graphic Novels* (2012) 16 *Law Text Culture* Special Issue 1

Rush, Peter and Andrew Kenyon, 'Alter Egos: The Mise-En-Scène of Law and Aesthetics' in Peter Rush and Andrew Kenyon (eds), *Aesthetics of Law and Culture: Texts, Images and Screens* (JAI Press, 2004)

Sarat, Austin and Thomas R Kearns, 'Editorial Introduction' in Austin Sarat and Thomas R Kearns (eds), *The Rhetoric of Law* (University of Michigan Press, 1994)

Sarat, Austin, Matthew Anderson and Cathrine O Frank, 'Introduction: On the Origins and Prospects of the Humanistic Study of Law' in Austin Sarat, Matthew Anderson and Cathrine O Frank (eds), *Law and the Humanities: An Introduction* (Cambridge University Press, 2009) 1

Sarat, Austin, Matthew Anderson and Cathrine O Frank (eds), *Law and the Humanities* (Cambridge University Press, 2010)

Smith, Ruth L, 'Morals and their Ironies' (1998) 26(2) *Journal of Religious Ethics* 367

Sontag, Susan, *Against Interpretation and Other Essays* (Picador, 2001)

Umphrey, Martha Merrill, 'Law in Drag: Trials and Legal Performativity' (2011) 21 *Columbia Journal of Gender and Law* 114

Valier, Claire, 'The Spaces of Irony' in Ronnie Lippens (ed.), *Imaginary Boundaries of Justice: Social and Legal Justice Across Disciplines* (Hart Publishing, 2004) 97

Van Rijswijk, Honni, 'Stories of the Nation's Continuing Past: Responsibility for Historical Injuries in Australian Law and Alexis Wright's *Carpentaria*' (2012) 35(2) *UNSW Law Journal* 598

White, James Boyd, *Heracles' Bow* (University of Wisconsin Press, 1985)

Whyte, Jessica, 'Criminalising "Camera Fiends": Photograph Restrictions in the Age of Digital Reproduction' (2009) 31 *Australian Feminist Law Journal* 99

Williams, Linda, 'Porn Studies: Proliferating Pornographies On/Scene: An Introduction' in Linda Williams (ed.), *Porn Studies* (Duke University Press, 2004) 1

Young, Alison, *Imagining Crime: Textual Outlaws and Criminal Conversations* (Sage, 1996)

Young, Alison, *Judging the Image: Art, Value, Law* (Routledge, 2005)

Young, Alison, *The Scene of Violence: Cinema, Crime, Affect* (Routledge, 2010)

Young, Alison, 'Arrested by the Image' (2013) 57 *New York Law School Law Review* 77

Young, Alison, *Street Art, Public City: Law, Crime and the Urban Imagination* (Routledge, 2013)

Žižek, Slavoj, 'Superego by Default' in *The Metastases of Enjoyment* (Verso, 1994) 54

Legislation and government reports

Crimes Act 1900 (NSW) s 91
Classification Board, Attorney-General's Department, Canberra, reports T08/2273, T08/2275, T08/2274, T08/2278 and T082276, 29 May 2008
Senate Report, Standing Committee on Environment, Communications and the Arts, *Sexualisation of Children in the Contemporary Media* (June 2008) www.aph.gov.au/binaries/senate/committee/eca_ctte/sexualisation_of_children/report/report.pdf

Newspaper, radio and television sources

'Australian PM in new nude art row' *BBC* (7 July 2008)
Disturbing Australia: Art or Porn?' *Courting Controversy Lecture Series*, Melbourne University Law School (16 June 2008)
'Henson playground report disgusts PM' *ABC News* (4 October 2008)
Devine, Miranda, 'Moral backlash over sexing up of our children' *Sydney Morning Herald* (22 May 2008)
Masters, Clae and Justin Valleyo, 'Who would call this art?' *The Daily Telegraph* (23 May 2008)
Perkin, Corrie and Lauren Wilson, 'Cate Blanchett calls on Kevin Rudd to soften Bill Henson art remarks' *The Australian* (28 May 2008)
Rudd, Kevin, *The Today Show*, with host Karl Stefanovic, Channel 9 (23 May 2008)
Woodward, Richard, 'The Disturbing Photography of Sally Mann' *New York Times Magazine* (27 September 1992) 52

Chapter 10

Bodies, cinema, sovereignty

Using visual culture methodologies to think about other ways that law might work

Kirsty Duncanson

Prologue

> *1941*
> *. . . the German war machine is rolling up the map of Europe: country after country falling like dominoes. Nothing can stop it . . .*
> *Until one tiny, damp little island says, 'No. No; not here.'*
> *A mouse in front of a lion.*
> *You're amazing, the lot of you.*[1]

It is the ninth episode in the first season of the remodelled BBC classic children's television program *Doctor Who*. The new series is shiny, loud, bombastic. The new Doctor is angry, lonely, reflective and Northern. Each episode of the new series buzzes with special effects and edgy contemporary ideas about sexuality and morality, good and evil. But this moment is quiet. The Doctor slips into a soliloquy while the camera cuts between the listening girl-in-plaits and the character-filled 'handsome' face of the ninth generation Doctor. Set during the London Blitz, the soliloquy nostalgically eulogises the British war effort.

This is one of many stirring moments in the new *Doctor Who*, moving this particular Australian-based viewer-scholar to the edge of tears, even as her memories of a British childhood might really only be those of her parents. It is a moment of high patriotism, invoking a romanticised period of national unity and endeavour. But the stirring patriotism is not just conjured by the Doctor's words or a collective memory of the time. It is also generated by the cinematic play of light, sound, camera angle and shot sequencing within a narrative about time travel and aliens. By these means this scene calls on the bodies of its audience to engage with a set of ideas about the 'tiny, damp little island' that said 'no' to German invasion. Implicit within these are philosophical arguments about British sovereignty.

1 Russell T Davies (Dir), 'The Empty Child' (2005) *Doctor Who* [Television] UK: BBC.

In this chapter I investigate the relationship between the bodies of the Doctor's television audience and the jurisprudence of British sovereignty. While doing this, I explore the form of cultural legal studies I implement more generally in my research in order to think about ways that law might work through cultural texts and the bodies that encounter them. My argument is not simply that people 'feel' law in front of the telly, but that law is something experienced and produced on an affective level through the bodies of everyday life. For example, in my research with Henderson I explore the affective conditions of juries in rape trials contributing to jury decision-making.[2] However, in this chapter I retain my focus on the cinematic because the consumption of screen-based texts provides a particularly accessible model for exploring law and jurisprudence as they work through bodies.

In what follows below, I identify an argument concerning British sovereignty produced during the consumption of a particular two-episode storyline of *Doctor Who*: 'The Empty Child' and 'The Doctor Dances'.[3] A particular conceptualisation of sovereignty unfolds as a development of the Doctor's relationship with his companion Rose. I show that this relationship relies on a discourse of romance which has tacitly sustained the constitutional structure of Britain's body politic for the last few hundred years as a Crown in Parliament. The argument I trace in the science fiction storyline plays out as an international romance juxtaposing American polity against British, the latter of which is ultimately revealed as the superior sovereign order. While I locate this argument through narrative and dialogue I also examine how it is built through the affective combinations of genre, sound, image and the physiological context of consumption.

Cultural legal studies

The emergence of Cultural Legal Studies has meant the theoretical expansion of the concept of law, with methodologies drawn from the humanities used to recognise and examine law taking place and given meaning in the broader realms of social life. On the basis of its dominance as a culturally consumed product, cinema has been a popular site for this research, and cinema studies has provided much necessary theory and method. As cinema studies extends its analysis of movies into the bodies of audiences, so legal scholarship is equipped with tools for observing more deeply law's resonance in the flesh of its subjects. Using feminist legal critique, postcolonial, gender and queer theory together with visual culture methods, I investigate a jurisprudence of sovereignty occurring between screen-based texts and their audiences.

2 Kirsty Duncanson and Emma Henderson, 'Narrative, Theatre and the Potential Interruptive Value of Jury Directions for Rape Trials' (2014) 22 *Feminist Legal Studies* 155.
3 Russell T Davies (Dir), 'The Doctor Dances' (2005) *Doctor Who* [Television] UK: BBC.

Ideas about law pervade the cinematic; as central narratives, plot devices, points of reference, incidental allusions, or underlying logics that help hold together the aural and visual fragments constituting screen-based texts. Recent cultural legal scholarship has come to recognise law as *present* within these ideas. No longer are audio-visual texts treated as merely representations of law, or evidence of how law is (mis)imagined. Instead, such (mis)imaginings are understood to *be law*. Screen-based texts are thus a 'site of . . . theoretical enquiry rather than sociolegal representation'.[4] This is to treat 'cinema as jurisprudence', recognising cinema and television as screens 'onto which legal issues [are] projected and questioned.'[5] Thus, as McNamee observes, the 'analysis of films has moved beyond simply looking for legal themes or social themes with legal relevance, to looking for the (usually) hidden coherences in filmic texts which amount to . . . "alternative jurisprudences." '[6] The exchange of ideas between audience and text becomes a jurisprudential conversation, a collaborative consideration of legal concepts which is carried out of cinemas and living rooms by audiences and rendered material when implemented in the living of their everyday lives.

To see law in the encounter between audience and screen assumes an intertwined and productive relationship between law and culture, the 'political nature [of] all cultural production', and the presence of jurisprudential negotiation throughout popular culture.[7] The work of MacNeil, for example, reveals the broad reaching ways in which 'popular culture overtly and implicitly addresses jurisprudence.'[8] MacNeil finds philosophical consideration of abstract legal concepts in children's literature, cult television serials, fantasy fiction, mainstream science fiction and teen chick flicks. His work, he explains, is a 'recontextualisation of jurisprudence from the specialist to the generalist interpretive community.'[9] It is a 'democratisation' of legal philosophy that recognises productive negotiations of legal ideas happening outside the parameters of legal procedure and academia.

MacNeil's work follows the imperatives of feminist, post-structuralist legal theorist Grbich, who argues that if we were to 'conceive of legal reasoning without

4 William MacNeil, *Lex Populi: The Jurisprudence of Popular Culture* (Stanford University Press, 2007) 156.

5 Leslie J Moran, Emma Sandon, Elena Loizidou and Ian Christie 'Introduction' in Leslie J Moran, Emma Sandon, Elena Loizidou and Ian Christie (eds), *Law's Moving Image* (GlassHouse Press, 2004) xiv.

6 Eugene McNamee, 'Eye Witness – Memorialising Humanity in Steve McQueen's Hunger' (2009) 5 *International Journal of Law in Context* 281, 282.

7 Jessica Silbey, 'The Politics of Law and Film Study: An Introduction to the Symposium on Legal Outsiders in American Film' (2009) *Suffolk University Law Review* 755, 756.

8 MacNeil, above n 4, 157.

9 Ibid, 2.

its "law-ness," that is, not as a privileged representation but just as presentation, we all become its officials.'[10] To use Grbich's argument is to recognise the way in which law is produced, given meaning and made material by all of those who are subject to it. Each person is a site of legal authority. Correspondingly, MacNeil's work demonstrates legal philosophy spread across the social world, with 'untrained' legal subjects (including children and teenaged girls!) engaged in processes of comprehending and theorising law's existence, practice and authority. He calls this '*lex populi*': the law of the people, or popular jurisprudence.

Jurisprudence at the cinema may occur at a cognitive, if covert, level. But it is also experienced through bodies, often 'before conscious, reflective thought'.[11] This is because both cinema and law work their meanings, and their meanings are worked through the bodies of their subjects.

Embodied memories of sovereign knowledge

The entanglement of bodies and law became particularly apparent when feminist scholars dispelled the myth of an objective, disembodied legal mind and revealed that legal theory is an 'embodied imagination'.[12] Traditional law has been created, maintained and implemented predominantly by very particular bodies: male, white, middle-to-ruling class, abled and heterosexual. The particularity of these bodies has shaped law under the assumption that they are so normal they are objective, and all other bodies are anomalous. Consequently, anomalous bodies are pathologised, criminalised, punished, treated (or 'corrected') and dismissed as irrational (not objective). Being either a normal or anomalous body encountering law is to experience and know law in the body, to perform it and be shaped by it, even when the privilege of 'normality' allows a subject to be unaware that their experience concerns law or is limited to only a narrow group within society.

From its specifically embodied origins, law creates meaning in bodies by labelling and categorising them and their parts; demarcating movement; and taking action upon them. Law dictates the sex and race of bodies and when they are alive or dead. It decides when a body can be deprived of movement, life or death, and stipulates which experiences bodies can or cannot consent to. Law decides the ownership of bodies, their parts and tissues.[13] It specifies when, how and where bodies can be naked, intoxicated, touched, touching another or crossing a street.

10 Judith Grbich, 'The Body in Legal Theory' in Martha Albertson Fineman (ed.), *At the Boundaries of Law: Feminism and Legal Theory* (Routledge, 1995) 61 [69].
11 Vivian Sobchack, *Carnal Thoughts: Embodiment and Moving Image Culture* (University of California Press, 2004) 59.
12 Grbich, above n 10, 62.
13 Alan Hyde, *Bodies of Law* (Princeton University Press, 1997).

British sovereignty has consistently been imagined in corporeal form. From the medieval period, body parts and functions have been used to theorise the structure and operation of the body politic.[14] Even with growing disillusionment in the divine right to rule, Hobbes imagined sovereignty as the body of a giant male leviathan looming over the nation with a crown at its head. The limbs constituted the two houses of Parliament, and the torso was made up of subjects.[15] In Hobbes' lithograph, these tiny figures face into the greater body of the sovereign monster, indicating their integral part of and support for the structure of polity presented.[16]

But the physicality of sovereign jurisprudence extends beyond metaphor. Monarchy relies on a belief in a capacity and right to rule held by specific bodies, created through the sexual union of further specific bodies. This is a belief that a *corpus mysticum* of sovereign leadership transcends upon the death of the natural body of a monarch to their heir.[17] The same belief sustained the continuance of the British House of Lords as the site of inherited political office until the 1999 reform to an elected life peerage.[18] Until this time, seats in the Upper House descended through the bloodlines of a narrow group of families.

Hereditary power has been guarded by laws of marriage, property and inheritance, all of which depend on the categorisation of bodies into sexes and familial and sexual relationships. These laws work to restrict sexual practices to monogamous heterosexuality and reproduction. As such, they have had very real consequences for the acts that ruling class bodies participated in. The primacy of unambiguous legitimacy for inherited power and property generally excused adulterous husbands but had harsh penalties for women who had sex outside marriage. At different points in time, adulterous women have been executed, divorced, socially shunned and tolerated. Their lovers have been sued for trespass of property, and their murders sanctioned as a 'permissive remedy' by a state not otherwise able to execute the betrayed husband's vengeance itself.[19] On marriage women lost their legal subjecthood, and thus a husband could subject his wife to life-threatening violence, 'demand sex as a right, . . . starve her, banish her, . . . imprison . . . or incarcerate her in an asylum.'[20] Mohr argues

14 Jonathan Harris, *Foreign Bodies and the Body Politic* (Cambridge University Press, 1998).

15 Thomas Hobbes, *Leviathan* (Penguin, 1981).

16 Eve Darian-Smith, *Bridging Divides: The Channel Tunnel and English Legal Identity in the New Europe* (University of California Press, 1999) 26.

17 Ernst Kantorowicz, *The King's Two Bodies: A Study of Mediaeval Political Thought* (Princeton University Press, 1957).

18 *House of Lords Act* 1999.

19 Jeremy Weinstein, 'Adultery, Law and the State: A History' (1986–7) 38 *The Hastings Law Journal* 195, 196.

20 Aureen Waller, *The English Marriage: Tales of Love, Money and Adultery* (John Murray, 2009) no pagination.

that these past legal structures continue to haunt women as a petrifying (feeling of embodied *paralysing* fear) need to avoid disapproval because of their historical systemic vulnerability to those with legal power (predominantly men).[21]

In terms of same sex desire, Moran notes a contributing ideological factor to laws against sodomy has been the assumed threat of sex between men to the 'carnal order' in connection with property transfer.[22] Sex between men was understood as 'a violence to the system that circulates property between men', and as such required legal prohibition.[23] The myths about sex, desire, romance, gender and sexuality generated in conjunction with inheritance laws continue to circulate through the contemporary legal and popular imagination, shaping bodily knowledges and experiences.[24]

As authority to govern has become increasingly democratic, the ability to participate as a politician or voter has similarly relied on the assessment of bodies and placed physical demands on subject-citizens. The wrong genitals denied women suffrage and kept them out of the British House of Representatives until 1918, while the risk of universal suffrage leading to female franchise shaped requirements on lower class men in the British constitutional reforms of the 1800s. To participate in polity, men had to exercise bodily performances of 'civil' masculinity, such as having a family (ie: productive heterosexual sex) and engaging in military service.[25] Concurrently, suffragettes used their bodies to fight for the vote: marching, hunger-striking, and being trampled by horses.

In each of these encounters between bodies and law, bodies are discursively produced: they are compelled to perform and embody law. Simultaneously, the physiological reiterations of law's demands and proscriptions reinterpret law through small alterations of nuanced actions, and perform legal meaning anew. Anomalous bodies lay claim to previously restricted rights, and other bodies deliberately break the law. But even in resistance and subversion, bodies are engaged with law, experiencing it at a material level. In this manner, bodies 'know' law beyond cognitive awareness of the contents of legal documents or formal processes: bodies carry memories of the physical experience of law.

Cinematic bodies

Ott writes that bodies take memories of previous experiences into cinemas where the memories are triggered by the sensory stimuli of cinematic texts and used

21 Tara Mohr, 'Learning to Love Criticism' *The New York Times* (27 September 2014).

22 Leslie Moran, *The Homosexual(ity) of Law* (Routledge, 1996) 76.

23 Ibid.

24 See for example Ngaire Naffine, 'Possession: Erotic Love in the Law of Rape' (1994) 57 *Modern Law Review* 10.

25 Anna Clark, 'Gender, Class and Nation: Franchise Reform in England' in James Vernon (ed.), *Rereading the Constitution: New Narratives in the Political History of England's Long Nineteenth Century* (Cambridge University Press, 1996) 239

in the creation of textual meaning.[26] These are *bodies of experience*. Each body's repertoire of recollection includes memories created through cinematic and non-cinematic experience. Ott uses the example of repression experienced by many American bodies during the George W. Bush presidency, arguing that embodied memories of this repression are triggered by 'discursive and figural elements' of the film *V for Vendetta* to create an atmosphere of anxiety and build a convincing story about the necessity of political action against government.[27] Ott's theory echoes Sobchack's observation that cinematic meaning is produced by 'the entire bodily being' of the audience, which is 'informed by the full history and carnal knowledge of our acculturated sensorium.'[28] This is a system of sense receptors trained in the patterns of culturally specific significations of taste, smell, vibration, touch, pain, desire . . . and so on. In this chapter I seek to notice bodies of *legal* experience and knowledge responding to affective components of a television text, prompting them to engage in conversations about legal authority.

The sensorial nature of cinematic discourse is evident in the awareness shown by film and television producers of the physicality with which their products are consumed. For example, films are created for consumption in a darkened space with sound production exploiting the multiple speakers surrounding audiences. Camera angles, shot sequences and *mise-en-scène* are designed for oversized screens. Production decisions provoke sometimes planned, sometimes unpredicted reactions in the viewing body, causing it to jump in shock, recoil in disgust, snort with laughter, roar with delight and cry with empathic grief. Each of these responses happens before the intervention of cognitive processing, they are perceived and communicate meaning to audiences '*without a thought*'.[29]

Shepherd observes audiences physically engaged with cultural texts, shouting from their seats at live performers 'look out behind you!' or standing at football matches as the ball is kicked into goal.[30] He calls this 'muscular empathy' and 'physical contagion'.[31] MacDougall describes a similar reaction to film as imitation or mimicry that manifests, not in action, but in a frustrated desire to act.[32] This is a form of sometimes pleasurable, sometimes discomforting bodily tension. The much celebrated anecdote of children watching the original *Doctor*

26 Brian L Ott, 'The Visceral Politics of *V for Vendetta*: On the Political Affect in Cinema' (2010) 27 *Critical Studies in Media Communication* 39.
27 Ibid, 49.
28 Sobchack, above n 11, 63.
29 Ibid, 65.
30 Simon Shepherd, *Theatre, Body and Pleasure* (Routledge, 2006) 73–74.
31 Ibid.
32 David MacDougall, *The Corporeal Image: Film, Ethnography and the Senses* (Princeton University Press, 2006).

Who series from 'behind the sofa'[33] provides an example of physiological empathy with juvenile bodies exercising a carnal need to hide while imagining themselves with the Doctor and his companions confronting monsters from other times and places.

Although largely undocumented, this culturally pervasive *Doctor Who* anecdote also counters theorists' dismissals of television's capacity for affective audience engagement on the basis of its non-cinematic viewing context. Wheatley argues that the television is actually a significant site of affective consumption because of its domestic setting: it is a conduit for the uncertainties of the outside world reaching into the sanctum of the home and worrying the inhabitants.[34] The television provides 'the convergence of the domestic and familiar with the alien and repressed.'[35] It is a manifestation of, and medium for, the uncanny, a form of horror that provokes psychological thrills for audiences while stimulating bodily reactions of anxiety, unease and anticipation.

As one of the 'most disturbing' [36] stories of the new *Who* series 'The Empty Child' mobilises the televisually uncanny. A key example is the way in which a little boy's plaintive cries for his mummy are transmitted through a range of ordinary objects 'transforming their function and rendering them uncanny.'[37] The boy himself is disturbing because he appears neither truly alive nor dead, neither fully human nor alien in a zombie-like state, physically disfigured by a permanently fused gasmask. His liminal condition is simultaneously appealing and menacing because he seems at once vulnerable and dangerous: deeply familiar and disconcertingly strange. This discomforting dissonance penetrates moments of safety in the narrative by animating ordinary objects with his cries. Thus, just like the television's presence in the home as both familiar and disturbing, the boy's condition breaches spaces of ostensible shelter within the story by means of some superhuman capacity. Such layering of disrupted domesticity irritates the muscles of the young viewer to respond in a material manner, leading viewers to rise from their comfortable sofas and hide behind them. Thus, in its use of uncanny themes and conventions, the *Doctor Who* story I examine here is particularly illustrative of the affective condition of television watching.

33 Sam Leith, 'Worshipping Doctor Who from behind the sofa' *The Telegraph* (London) (4 July 2008); Kim Newman, *Doctor Who* (BFI Publishing, 2005) 6.

34 Helen Wheatley, *Gothic Television* (Manchester University Press, 2006) 6. See also Helen Wheatley, 'Uncanny Children, Haunted Houses, Hidden Rooms: Children's Gothic Television in the 1970s and '80s' (2012) 13 *Visual Culture in Britain* 383.

35 Quoting Alec Charles, Frank Collins, 'Monsters Under the Bed: Gothic and Fairy-tale Storytelling in Steven Moffat's Doctor Who' in Andrew O'Day (ed.), *Doctor Who: The Eleventh Hour – a Critical Celebration of the Matt Smith and Steven Moffat Era* (IB Tauris, 2014) 31.

36 James Chapman, *Inside the TARDIS: The Worlds of Doctor Who* (IB Tauris, 2006).

37 Collins, above n 35, 34.

Presumptions about the actual conditions of television viewing have been challenged by the proliferation of screens in a variety of sizes on which to watch programs wherever and whenever the viewer would like. However, the new *Who* series has been created to promote specific viewing conditions. The controlled release of heavily marketed fresh episodes based on carefully orchestrated secrecy and revelation place an urgency on watching each episode as soon as available, at scheduled broadcasting in traditional format. This strategy is most clearly evidenced by the fiftieth anniversary global simulcast episode 'The Day of the Doctor' (2013). Broadcasting companies in the United States, Canada, and Australia, across Europe, Asia, Latin America and Africa aired the episode at the same time as the originating broadcaster, the BBC in the UK. While the broadcast exemplifies a 'television event' of sorts in its break to the usual routine of television 'flows' and family routines,[38] it also emblematises the style of consumption encouraged throughout the revitalised *Who* series. For this reason, I am presuming certain conditions of viewing, including the excited expectation of an anticipated text, despite routine scheduling, and attentive viewers, rather than Ellis' distracted ones (who watch while doing other things).[39] Although *Doctor Who* is not created for a darkened theatre or surround sound, the quality of the new series is 'cinematic': it is made for larger, higher quality screens, with special effects and a symphonic score more common to film. These are the conditions and textual components I explore to find evidence of an embodied popular jurisprudential conversation about British sovereignty.

The story

Doctor Who had an almost thirty-year run from the 1960s before its ratings petered out. However, the cult of the Doctor remained in British popular consciousness, lending great energy and an established audience to the return of the series in 2005. The two-episode story examined in this chapter comes towards the end of the first season of the new series. The central, ongoing characters have been introduced and a relationship has been created with the original series that regulates inter-series signification.

'The Empty Child' begins with an action scene inside the Doctor's time and space travelling machine, the TARDIS. A danger alert has been picked up, and the Doctor sets coordinates to track it. The TARDIS lands in London in 1941 and as soon as they leave the craft, the Doctor and his companion are separated. Rose follows a boy in a gas mask plaintively calling for his mummy. She loses him as she takes hold of a rope, which pulls her into the middle of an air raid

38 Daniel Dayan and Elihu Katz, *Media Events: The Live Broadcasting of History* (Harvard University Press, 1992).

39 John Ellis, *Visible Fictions* (Routledge and Kegan Paul, 1982).

above the city. An American in Air Force uniform, going by the name of Captain Jack Harkness, saves her using his alien technology. They flirt.

Meanwhile, the Doctor discovers a band of homeless children led by Nancy, and frightened by the same gas-masked boy. Nancy warns the Doctor against touching the boy or answering the phone, through which the boy asks for his mummy. Later, Nancy confesses that he was her brother before a falling bomb crushed him. Resurrected to his zombie state, he wanders the streets transforming everybody he touches into a version of himself, creating a zombie army from which the Doctor, Rose and Captain Jack have to escape in various ways on a number of occasions.

Then Jack reveals that he is a human former time agent from the fifty-first century, turned conman who set up the danger alert and landed the device in the hope of working a con on his former employers. He had assumed the device, an abandoned alien ambulance, was harmless space junk. It is actually filled with 'nanogenes' compelled to repair any organic matter with which it makes contact. It was the ambulance that struck the boy, and the nanogenes that rendered him strange and dangerous in an attempt to 'fix' him.

When the Doctor makes the connections he realises that Nancy is actually the boy's mother. In the climax, as the zombie army converges once more on the Doctor and Rose, the Doctor prompts Nancy to tell the boy she is his mother. As she embraces the boy, telling him, 'I am your mummy; I always will be,' the nanogenes recognise the 'superior information of the parent DNA' and restore him correctly. Gathering the nanogenes with the new information, the Doctor directs them to the rest of the zombies, who are also immediately corrected.

Amidst the twinkling nanogenes and symphonically undulating music, Jack stops an activated bomb from falling on the scene. He proposes to redirect the bomb, thereby incidentally sacrificing his own life. However, just as he sips his last martini and contemplates his death, the TARDIS takes him on board. The episode ends with Rose asking Jack to dance, but the Doctor cuts in to foxtrot her around the consul to the upbeat swing of Glenn Miller's *In the Mood*. The credits roll.

International romance and the superiority of British sovereignty

A flirtatious edge was incorporated into the relationships between the Doctor and his companions in the regenerated *Doctor Who* series, animating the final dance sequence described above with the affective conventions of televised romance. The bodily stimuli generated through the romance genre stems from the deferred anticipation of erotic moments, which may never be realised.

In this section of the chapter I explore the way in which the inter-character flirtation mobilises a reworking of the politico-legally significant romance genre of international romance as a sexually playful love triangle rather than the usual heteronormative journey to committed monogamy. I argue that the conventions of the genre work in this television text to implicitly present the superiority of a certain kind of British sovereign order as the Crown in Parliament. Through my analysis, I identify cinematic and legal stimuli working the text's argument through the bodies of the television audience.

Within the first season's story arc of Rose and the Doctor's relationship, 'The Empty Child' presents a moment of disillusionment for Rose. Up until this episode, Rose has been aligned with the audience's awe, excitement and terror at the adventures the Doctor offers. As an ostensibly ordinary young, contemporary, English woman in a program made primarily for British audiences, Rose is the point of audience identification.[40] She facilitates and reflects the audience's emotional connection to the stories, events and characters while also executing an active involvement in the stories as an imaginary extension of the viewers' 'frustrated' sofa-based journeying with the Doctor. This audience connection includes an enthrallment with the Doctor.

However, as this story opens, she is presented as dissatisfied with the lack of precision of the Doctor's tools, which have failed to locate the alien object they are pursuing. She is also disappointed by his limited use of technology and his preference for old fashioned methods, such as *asking* people if they have noticed a strange object, rather than 'scanning for alien tech', as Rose suggests. In a reworking of a classic heterosexual argument in which female characters complain of their lover's lack of romance, Rose prompts the Doctor to 'give me some Spock for once – would it kill you?'

While Rose's disappointment provides an undulation in the affective journey of the Rose–Doctor romance, it pre-empts the introduction of Jack in eroticised opposition to the Doctor. When Jack enters the story Rose's flirtation with him is expressed in terms of his equipment, which she describes as 'flash' and 'very Spock'. She is delighted when he mentions 'scanning for alien tech'. Echoing her words of complaint against the Doctor aligns the two sets of technology into a relationship of comparison. Jack is thus presented as a competitor for the Doctor both in terms of technologically enhanced capabilities and for the affections of Rose.

Nationally specific accents mark a key point of difference between the two men, conferring national relevance to other points of difference between them, as well as their triangulated relationship with Rose. It is their nationalised signification that renders this subplot an 'international romance'.[41] International romance is a sub-genre of romantic comedy that eroticises and depoliticises power relationships between nations. Conventionally, the ultimate romantic union in these films is a heterosexual convergence of two nations gendered through

40 Lindy Orthia, '"Sociopathetic Abscess" or "Yawning Chasm"? The Absent Postcolonial Transition in *Doctor Who*' (2010) 45 *Journal of Commonwealth Literature* 207, 209.

41 Arthur Lindley, 'Translations of the Flesh: International Relations as Romantic Comedy in Recent Australian and British Film' (2003) 28 *Senses of Cinema* no pagination.

separated iconographic embodiments as one female and one male character, amorously drawn towards each other. Through the conventions of romance, the power and possible threat of the first nation is contained by its feminisation and its inevitable generic surrender to the masculine seduction of the second nation. But in this story, the international relations take place as a love triangle, in which sexual tension between the nations is partially (but importantly not entirely) rerouted through a shared love object, and both iconic manifestations of nation are male. Due to such a reconfiguration of the formula, instead of making harmless and desirable various contrasting iconographic aspects of national political character, this storyline sets the two nations in direct competition on the basis of their divergent jurisprudence of sovereign authority. The winner of the love object is implicitly configured as the superior of the two.

The love object herself is nationally emblematic. Although she does not bear the traces of sovereign signification that I will go on to demonstrate the men do, she *does* represent Britain. In part, her Britain-ness is due to her role as a point of identification for a British audience. It is enhanced by her name, which is celebrated as the title of the very first episode of this first season of the new *Doctor Who*. As the name for a white English female character, 'Rose' recalls the culturally imagined figure of an ideal British woman: the English Rose. The rose is also the national flower of England, and the Tudor Rose is that nation's heraldic emblem. Just as key London icons are used in the new *Who* to signify the location of stories as not just happening within London or England, but in Britain more generally, so the English are used to represent the British in the series (and the British represent the human race). In this particular story, Rose's Englishness is Britishness. Her symbolic function as 'Britain' is indicated by the Union Jack t-shirt she wears throughout both episodes, and most significantly as she dangles from a barrage balloon during a German air raid: the British flag emblazoned across her chest like a target for the German Luftwaffe.

While Jack is iconographically 'American', his Americanness is not simply symbolic of the nation but of the juridico-political order of the United States. In a similar manner, the English/Britishness of the Doctor is not symbolic of the nation but of the nation's sovereign. That is to say, the Doctor is not configured as Britain. This is because of the character's long running complex configuration as an alien who is also quintessentially British.

The ninth Doctor's Britishness is emphasised by his Northern English accent. Prior and subsequent characterisations of the Doctor (until the point of writing) have been played with Received Pronunciation (RP).[42] Although ostensibly class

42 This accent emerged through public school elocution lessons designed to disguise the regional origins of those seeking to rise through the British social classes. From the earliest years of the BBC, its Advisory Committee on Spoken English recommended RP for its announcers, although regional nuances were accepted. The privileging of this accent at the BBC has remained to the extent that it is also called 'BBC English'.

and region 'neutral' RP is very close to the South Eastern accents of the traditional ruling classes. Thus, the choice of allowing the actor playing the ninth Doctor to use his original accent is meaningful. This is highlighted in the 'Rose' episode by the Doctor's illogical response to Rose's question 'If you are an alien, how come you sound like you're from the North?' The Doctor's reply, 'Lots of planets have a North,' works paradoxically to remind the audience of the cultural specificity of England's North, and thus that a Northern English accent is indicative of a certain kind of Britishness rather than any kind of alienness.

At the same time, however, that the Doctor *is* alien endows him with skills beyond human capacity: he is more powerful, more intelligent and more able than humans. He has two hearts and can travel through time and space. In the new series, he has also been given the status of wielding a sentient-being made Law of the Universe as well as a natural universal moral order. For example, in the first episode he invokes 'Convention 15 of the Shadow Proclamation' to begin negotiations with the alien Nestene Consciousness, while in the later episode, 'Boom Town', he is presented as subverting the official laws of the universe by not delivering a criminal alien for prosecution (and execution), but instead using the TARDIS to reset the alien and thereby giving her 'a second chance'. Through his relationship with both levels of universal law, he is endowed with supra-human authority.

The doubled configuration of British and supra-humanity mimics the two bodies of the king Kantorwicz identified in the jurisprudence of European monarchy.[43] Monarchical sovereignty relies on a sustained, shared imagining within the ruled nation of a *corpus mysticum* as a second, dynamically charged body to the natural body of the ruler. The natural body is recognised as susceptible to the infirmities of any ordinary body, such as sickness, madness and death. The second body animates the first with extraordinary powers of sovereign authority. This body is neither subject to natural nor accidental infirmities, nor is it capable of doing or thinking 'wrong'.[44] Instead, it transcends the death of the monarch's natural body to rematerialise in the natural body of the heir. This 'undying royal body' has traditionally extended its mystical spirit to legitimise the inheritance of peerage in the House of Lords.[45]

The same fantasy provides a key premise for the Doctor as an alien whose abstract conceptual being transcends the death of each actor's contract to regenerate into the natural body of the next. This premise facilitated the 30 years of the original series, and has sustained a subsequent five more regenerations.[46] Thus, just as the British make the strange declaration 'the King

43 Kantorwicz, above n 17.

44 Ibid, 4.

45 Peter Goodrich, *Languages of Law: From Logics of Memory to Nomadic Masks* (Weidenfeld and Nicolson, 1990) 218.

46 Natasha Kulzac, 'Doctor Who Series Eight: First Full-length Trailer Shows Peter Capaldi's Time Lord Goes "Into the Dark Side"' *The Independent* (15 July 2014).

is dead; long live the King', so at 'the end of every Doctor, the beginning of a new Doctor emerges as another chapter in a never-ending story.'[47]

The Doctor can thus be recognised as an imaginative manifestation of the British sovereign: the cult of the Doctor relies on the same fantastical structure as that of the British Crown in Parliament. Implicit acceptance of the jurisprudential myth of monarchy by the viewing audience supports and naturalises acceptance of the same myth within the very popular science fiction television series.[48]

In direct contrast to the Doctor's embodiment of British sovereignty, Jack's personification of US sovereignty is constructed through a configuration of character traits emblematic of the United States' structure of democratic polity juxtaposed against the British. With a history of revolutionary independence from British monarchical rule, the United States appears new and progressive. Its constitutional philosophy distinguishes the nation's polity from European regimes entrenched in the past. In narratives of international romance, 'glamour will accrue to the American side' in conjunction with progress and 'present-ness' as signifiers of these jurisprudential differentiations from European sovereign order.[49]

In the character of Jack, American glamour, progress and present-ness are connected to the character's sexuality and technology. These connections are immediately established in the first scenes of his introduction. While Rose assesses his technology as 'flash' in comparison to the Doctor's, the combination of accent and uniform instantaneously invokes the British stereotyping of American World War II servicemen as 'oversexed, overpaid and over here'. The epithet articulates the threat perceived in these men who were not only in Britain while a significant number of young British men were not, but who also had access to otherwise largely unavailable goods such as nylon stockings and lipstick. The provision of luxury items to British women increased the cultural capital these men already had with their glamourously accented associations with US popular culture.

Hypersexuality is further accorded to Jack through his seduction of Rose. Jack has used his technology to save Rose. He flicks a switch and a bundle of twinkling lights appear, converging in Rose's tethered and cupped hands to repair her rope burns. He tells her they are nanogenes. Then, with a bottle of

47 Yue Yuan, 'The Regenerate: The Paradoxes of Nostalgia and Empire in the Doctor Who Series' (2014) 1 *Re:Search* 87, 89.

48 The recognition of the Doctor Who character as British sovereignty offers up an abundance of interesting explorations into contemporary popular jurisprudential negotiations of English, British and UK sovereignty within the context of European politics and the devolution (and possible independence) of Britain's distinct nations. These I hope to go on to explore in further work.

49 Lindley, above n 41, no pagination.

champagne in hand, he leads her to the roof where they are backlit by Big Ben's massive clock face, against which his invisible ship is tethered. Clicking a remote device, he switches on Big Ben's chimes. He clicks another and the swaying melody of Glenn Miller's *Moonlight Serenade* emits from nowhere. Jack grasps Rose by the waist as if for a close, slow dance or passionate kiss.

The music is important. Tension and anticipation, happiness and despair, relief and calm or swooning beguilement are generated through the tone, rhythm and melody of a musical score, reverberating through the ears, hearts and other organs of people in their living rooms. In this manner, music carnally cues an audience on 'how to feel about particular characters and events.'[50] It also conveys cultural ideology and meaning.[51] Giddens notes the way in which Miller created a sound that 'clings relentlessly to the collective memory.'[52] The meaning attached to the melody in 'The Empty Child' is not necessarily the meaning the music initially held, but it is one that has melded with particularly romanticised recollections of the period. *Moonlight Serenade's* slow swinging clarinet and saxophone is a moody reverie of 1940s seduction that, according to Giddens, clutches at the throat and softens the eye, while making everybody want to dance. The music triggers an embodied nostalgia, a collectively (re)configured memory of the charm and sexual activity during the war period. Because this information is born by music, and because a good musical score 'neither draws attention to itself, nor demands the listener's full attention', the audience is engaged in the music's meaning without cognitive processing. Thus, with Rose, the audience is beguiled by Jack, and relinquishes itself to him, the music, and the ideological 'memories' the music inspires.

The music also eroticises the triangle between Jack, Rose and the Doctor both as an affectively amatory piece of music, but also by announcing the thematic metaphor of dancing and sex that weaves through the two episodes, accentuated by the second episode's title, 'The Doctor Dances'. The musically enhanced dancing metaphor deepens the comparative opposition between the Doctor and Jack and situates it in the flesh of the audience.

From this scene, the extent of Jack's hypersexuality is progressively revealed, with hints of pan-sexuality and promiscuity in his flirtatious behaviour and euphemistic dialogue. However, when the Doctor mobilises the dance-sex metaphor to describe Jack's sexuality to Rose, his pansexuality is shown to reach beyond the human:

DOCTOR: He's a 51st century guy. He's a bit more flexible in his 'dancing'.
ROSE: How flexible?

50 Ott, above n 26, 47.
51 Kathryn Kalinack, *Film Music: A Very Short Introduction* (Oxford University Press, 2010) 27.
52 Gary Giddens, 'Stride and Swing: The enduring appeal of Fats Waller and Glenn Miller' *The New Yorker* (31 May 2004).

DOCTOR: Well, by his time, you lot were spread halfway across the galaxy.
ROSE: Meaning?
DOCTOR: So many species; so little time.
ROSE: What, that's what we do when we get there? . . . We seek new life and . . .
DOCTOR: Dance

Jack signifies cultural acceptance and progressive understandings of sexuality. As a future human, his pansexuality exists on a continuum in relation to the marginalised teenaged single mother from the British 1940s (Nancy) who has to pretend her child is her brother, through Rose's contemporary sexual agency tempered by monogamous heterosexuality, to his own overt promiscuity, libertarianism, bisexual and alien attractions. He represents a future human culture of open acceptance to difference. Such acceptance simultaneously signifies egalitarianism and a democracy that is inclusive of all, reminiscent of the fantasy of the United States as a democratic sovereignty of the people.

In contrast to Jack's dancing skills and smooth seductions, the Doctor appears awkward and uninterested by turns. The difference is brought into sharper relief by the repetition of the *Moonlight Serenade* scene. This time, when the music starts, Rose persuades the Doctor to dance. His clumsiness and her disappointment ('It didn't feel like dancing') imply the state of their romantic relationship. Framed in terms of international romance, Rose-as-Britain appears no longer compatible with traditional monarchical polity, and to have been seduced by an American philosophy of sovereign legitimacy.

The Doctor's poor dancing, with its metaphorical implications, follows the conventional characterisation of the British male nation in the international romance genre. Epitomised by Hugh Grant's characters in *Four Weddings and a Funeral* and *Notting Hill*, the masculine British nation-character lacks the flashy glamour and self-confident pick-up lines of their American female counterparts.[53] Self-deprecation and verbal and physical clumsiness are emphasised instead. Suggested by such sexual awkwardness and juxtaposed with American confidence, hypersexuality is monogamous heterosexuality. This is the ideological sexuality underpinning the structure of the British body politic. It is also the sexuality British law has sought to promote (in the regulation of possible breaches) in the guardianship of the nation's sovereign order based on primogeniture. In the more conventional international romances, the glamour of America is made less threatening, by its embodiment as female. The drive of generic romantic expectation enables the male nation to seduce her despite his comparative inadequacy.

53 Lindley, above n 41; Kirsty Duncanson, 'Embodiments of the English Constitution in the Romanticised Narratives of the Funeral of Diana, Princess of Wales and Four Weddings and a Funeral' (2008) 28 *The Australian Feminist Law Journal* 121, 138.

On a couple of levels, heteronormative dynamism works in the *Who* story to restore Britain's affections to its sovereign while also conquering the desires of the American. This reconfiguration of desire is ultimately presented in the final moments of the story, but the seeds are sown earlier. From the exchange concerning Jack's flexibility, Rose's loyalty and affection returns to the Doctor. In part this is presented through a mobilisation of cultural associations between bisexuality, promiscuity and unreliability. Jack's sexuality is entangled with the ambiguity of his other moral values: he is a conman, whose allegiance shifts overtly according to his interests. His moral laxity caused the corruption of the little boy and jeopardised the human race, and even though his proposed repentant sacrifice of his own life to relocate an activated bomb indicates reform, ambiguity is shown to remain by the Doctor's last line.

By comparison, the Doctor's awkwardness and clumsy dancing corresponds with his passionate devotion to the human race, and the British in particular. It is his devotion, his attempts to save humanity (as it is represented by the British in this storyline), which distracts him from sexual desire. His admiration of the British in wartime converges with the nation's collective memory of itself during that period, as affectively conjured by his soliloquy quoted at the top of this chapter. The righteousness of this admiration, and thus also his awkward fidelity, is confirmed by the enchanted twinkling lights of the nanogenes against a darkened set together with the undulating symphonic music and the impassioned deliverance of a solution that cures the zombie army and saves the human race.

Although Jack's ostensible self-sacrifice in bomb disposal is a potentially more glamourous and heroic gesture than the actions of the Doctor, it is presented as a climax of the character's conversion from conman to hero inspired and facilitated by the Doctor. Jack becomes the person he had been impersonating at the beginning of the story: an American in the British air force prior to US conscription, an American fighting a British cause. His conversion comes as a response to his realisation that he caused the zombie army in his cavalier pursuit of revenge against his former employers. It also happens through his flirtatious banter with the Doctor in which the Doctor mocks Jack's reliance on and pleasure in hyper-technology, and the Doctor's altruistic dedication to saving the British/humanity.

The final scene realises this reconfiguration moment through the dance metaphor. Although at first it appears that the Doctor is still unable to dance as he transforms a spin into an arm-breaking 'half Nelson' manoeuvre, on changing the music to the faster paced, brassier *In the Mood* he 'remembers'. But Rose has already invited Jack to 'cut in', and insists that 'Jack might like this dance.' When the Doctor replies, 'I'm sure he would, Rose. I'm absolutely certain. But who with?' Rose immediately returns to the Doctor and they execute a flawless foxtrot through the triumphantly climbing coda to the music's concluding percussive rim shot, at which the Doctor throws Rose into a low slung finishing embrace.

The exchange forms a light-hearted almost-forgettable post-climax moment to the 'most disturbing'[54] episode of the return series of *Doctor Who*, providing humorous relief at the end of the audience's journey through an uncanny adventure. Despite this, it contains significant conclusions to the playing out of eroticised international power relations. The synchronous exultant musical finale with the Doctor and Rose's embrace indicates the Doctor's (and British governance) 'winning' the love object. It appears that it is the Doctor's quip about who Jack wants to dance with that ultimately decides Rose's preference. Stripping the metaphors back to constitutional jurisprudence: Rose (as Great Britain) chooses the fidelity of awkward heterosexual monogamy that sustains constitutional monarchy over the promiscuous pansexuality of American democracy and its promises of difference-acceptance.

At the same time, the comment also implies that Jack is attracted to the Doctor (is it Rose with whom he'd like to dance . . . or is it really the Doctor?). This suggestion follows on from the more central narrative through which Jack's character has journeyed from cynical conman, to repentant hero. Although Rose played a role in this journey, it is the Doctor who has converted him to the extent that he almost sacrifices himself to save humanity. Thus the conventions of international romance are complete, with one nation succumbing to the attractions of the other. Jack joins the Doctor as yet another subordinate and adulating companion, (performed with necessarily limited agency). This configuration of erotic attraction between national signifiers places Britain's juridico-political structure as ultimately superior to the American, which is beguiled by the very characteristics its progressive democratic values had ideologically separated it from.

While I argue that the flirtation between the Doctor and Rose is a manifestation of British sovereign romance in this particular *Doctor Who* story, it also illustrates the affective conditions of watching television. For example, the banter between the Doctor and Rose creates a sexual tension that provides a greater 'emotional depth' to the new series than the original version allowed.[55] Such depth fosters speculation and the pleasurable anticipation of possible actual or frustrated union between them. This anticipation characterises the romance genre. It can be seen as a form of the frustrated embodied mimicry MacDougall describes in the consumption of cinematic texts.[56] In the instances of romance in long running television serials, frustration is intensified by the protraction of deferred union across one or several seasons. The bodies of the audience continually await an action that they know, even hope, will not unfold until the final moment of the last episode. This provides a strange embodied delight of

54 Chapman, above n 36, 200.
55 MacDougall, above n 32, 23.
56 Chapman, above n 36.

endless delay and near misses. Realisation of union is, in the end, only as powerful as the anticipation allows.

Conclusion: philosophical embodiments in the living room, and beyond

While signifiers held in image, dialogue and narrative render the Doctor a fantasy version of the British Crown in Parliament at a cognitively registered level, there is also a convergence of legal philosophy and bodily sensation at play in the conceptualisation of British sovereignty in these two episodes of *Doctor Who.* I have sought to identify some of this through my analysis so far. The convergence takes place in the encounter between the generic corporeal pleasures of un/conventional romance within an uncanny science fiction adventure and the embodied memories a British audience brings to their viewing concerning the jurisprudence of British sovereignty.

As I have argued above, British bodies still bear the traces of primogeniture laws that attempted to guarantee the transcendence of political power through limited family lines and sustain the mythical power of the King's (and the aristocracy's) second body or *corpus mysticum.* This is discernible in the continued customs of heterosexual courtship that apparently lead unproblematically to marriage contracts which are persistently performed by the contracting bodies with reverence to the heteronormative structures of monarchical power (brides 'given away' by their fathers; symbols of female virginity; vows echoing promises of obedience as well as fidelity; the legal subjecthood of family names replaced by that of the new propriety/male relative of the female body[57]). The ideological drive of primogeniture still shapes perceptions and thus also the embodied desires and experiences of sex and sexual violence, 'legitimate' and illicit hetero-, homo-, and further categorised sexual acts. At the same time, the demands of democratic participation also work through the flesh of citizen subjects, even in performed ambivalence to the civic 'duty' of voting. While suffrage has physical criteria and a history of bodily significance, it also provides a performative conceptual perception of bodies as bearing political agency[58] in conjunction with embodiments of monarchical subjecthood.

These are knowledges and memories of Britain's legal sovereign order that still shape, influence, and resonate through the bodies of people living in Britain, even as they are experienced as natural desires, pleasures, fears and compulsions. They form part of the *bodies of experience* Ott theorises in the cinema responding

57 R Shome, 'White Feminism and the Discourse of Nation: Re/membering Princess Diana' (2001) 1 *Feminist Media Studies* 323.

58 Diana Coole, 'Rethinking Agency: A Phenomenological Approach to Embodiment and Agentic Capacities' (2005) 53 *Political Studies* 122.

to the stimuli of cognitively and sensually perceived socio-legal and political semiotics.[59] As embodied memory, these legal experiences interact with implicit arguments concerning sovereignty that unfold at a sensually stimulating level through the television text. In this manner, components of politico-legal theory (the jurisprudence of sovereignty) is taking place at a carnal level, prior to what Sobchack calls 'conscious reflective thought'.[60] This is popular jurisprudence taking place through the bodies of 'untrained' legal subjects/experts. The product of such an encounter is a spectrum of embodied responses that reaffirm, rewrite or reconfigure the embodied legal knowledge of the consuming legal structures, to be carried into the next negotiation of law or legal philosophy.

'The Empty Child' and 'The Doctor Dances,' as a two-episode story of the *Doctor Who* series, provides one fleeting example of such embodied popular jurisprudential conversations. However, it is illustrative of a much more extensively practised engagement of law's subjects with law's meaning, authority and materiality in the very mundane performances of everyday life, as well as the grander, ostensibly more authoritative ceremonies of legal expertise.

For me, by participating in cultural legal studies to explore the interactions of law, bodies and culture enables deeper exploration of the ways law might be working not only in living rooms or at the cinema, but also in courtrooms. For example, drawing on the theoretical work of legal and cultural embodiments, has the potential for examining more deeply the components at work in the theatre of rape trial courtrooms influencing juror decision-making and the continued reluctance of juries to convict people accused of sexual violence.

Bibliography

Articles and books

Chapman, James, *Inside the TARDIS: The Worlds of Doctor Who* (IB Tauris, 2006)

Clark, Anna, 'Gender, Class and Nation: Franchise Reform in England' in James Vernon (ed.), *Rereading the Constitution: New Narratives in the Political History of England's Long Nineteenth Century* (Cambridge University Press, 1996) 239

Collins, Frank, 'Monsters Under the Bed: Gothic and Fairy-tale Storytelling in Steven Moffat's Doctor Who' in Andrew O'Day (ed.), *Doctor Who: The Eleventh Hour – a Critical Celebration of the Matt Smith and Steven Moffat Era* (IB Tauris, 2014) 31

Coole, Diana, 'Rethinking Agency: A Phenomenological Approach to Embodiment and Agentic Capacities' (2005) 53 *Political Studies* 122

Darian-Smith, Eve, *Bridging Divides: The Channel Tunnel and English Legal Identity in the New Europe* (University of California Press, 1999)

59 Ott, above n 26.

60 Sobchack, above n 11.

Dayan, Daniel and Elihu Katz, *Media Events: The Live Broadcasting of History* (Harvard University Press, 1992)
Duncanson, Kirsty, 'Embodiments of the English Constitution in the Romanticised Narratives of the Funeral of Diana, Princess of Wales and Four Weddings and a Funeral' (2008) 28 *The Australian Feminist Law Journal* 121
Duncanson, Kirsty and Emma Henderson, 'Narrative, Theatre and the Potential Interruptive Value of Jury Directions for Rape Trials' (2014) 22 *Feminist Legal Studies*
Ellis, John, *Visible Fictions* (Routledge and Kegan Paul, 1982)
Fineman, Martha Albertson (ed.), *At the Boundaries of Law: Feminism and Legal Theory* (Routledge, 1995)
Goodrich, Peter, *Languages of Law: From Logics of Memory to Nomadic Masks* (Weidenfeld and Nicolson, 1990)
Grbich, Judith, 'The Body in Legal Theory' in Martha Albertson Fineman (ed.), *At the Boundaries of Law: Feminism and Legal Theory* (Routledge, 1995) 61 [69]
Harris, Jonathan, *Foreign Bodies and the Body Politic* (Cambridge University Press, 1998)
Hobbes, Thomas, *Leviathan* (Penguin, 1981)
Hyde, Alan, *Bodies of Law* (Princeton University Press, 1997)
Kalinack, Kathryn, *Film Music: A Very Short Introduction* (Oxford University Press, 2010)
Kantorowicz, Ernst, *The King's Two Bodies: A Study of Mediaeval Political Thought* (Princeton University Press, 1957)
Lindley, Arthur, 'Translations of the Flesh: International Relations as Romantic Comedy in Recent Australian and British Film' (2003) 28 *Senses of Cinema* no pagination
MacDougall, David, *The Corporeal Image: Film, Ethnography and the Senses* (Princeton University Press, 2006)
McNamee, Eugene, 'Eye Witness – Memorialising Humanity in Steve McQueen's Hunger' (2009) 5 *International Journal of Law in Context* 281
MacNeil, William, *Lex Populi: The Jurisprudence of Popular Culture* (Stanford University Press, 2007)
Moran, Leslie, *The Homosexual(ity) of Law* (Routledge, 1996)
Moran, Leslie J, Emma Sandon, Elena Loizidou and Ian Christie, 'Introduction' in Leslie J Moran, Emma Sandon, Elena Loizidou and Ian Christie (eds), *Law's Moving Image* (GlassHouse Press, 2004) xiv
Moran, Leslie J, Emma Sandon, Elena Loizidou and Ian Christie (eds), *Law's Moving Image* (GlassHouse Press, 2004)
Naffine, Ngaire, 'Possession: Erotic Love in the Law of Rape' (1994) 57 *Modern Law Review* 10
Newman, Kim, *Doctor Who* (BFI Publishing, 2005)
O'Day, Andrew (ed.), *Doctor Who: The Eleventh Hour – a Critical Celebration of the Matt Smith and Steven Moffat Era* (IB Tauris, 2014)
Orthia, Lindy '"Sociopathetic Abscess" or "Yawning Chasm"? The Absent Postcolonial Transition in *Doctor Who*' (2010) 45 *Journal of Commonwealth Literature* 207
Ott, Brian L, 'The Visceral Politics of *V for Vendetta*: On the Political Affect in Cinema' (2010) 27 *Critical Studies in Media Communication* 39
Shepherd, Simon, *Theatre, Body and Pleasure* (Routledge, 2006)
Shome, R, 'White Feminism and the Discourse of Nation: Re/membering Princess Diana' (2001) 1 *Feminist Media Studies* 323
Silbey, Jessica, 'The Politics of Law and Film Study: An Introduction to the Symposium on Legal Outsiders in American Film' (2009) *Suffolk University Law Review* 755

Sobchack, Vivian, *Carnal Thoughts: Embodiment and Moving Image Culture* (University of California Press, 2004)
Vernon, James (ed.), *Rereading the Constitution: New Narratives in the Political History of England's Long Nineteenth Century* (Cambridge University Press, 1996)
Waller, Aureen, *The English Marriage: Tales of Love, Money and Adultery* (John Murray, 2009)
Weinstein, Jeremy, 'Adultery, Law and the State: A History' (1986–7) 38 *The Hastings Law Journal* 195, 196
Wheatley, Helen, *Gothic Television* (Manchester University Press, 2006)
Wheatley, Helen, 'Uncanny Children, Haunted Houses, Hidden Rooms: Children's Gothic Television in the 1970s and '80s' (2012) 13 *Visual Culture in Britain* 383
Yuan, Yue, 'The Regenerate: The Paradoxes of Nostalgia and Empire in the Doctor Who Series' (2014) 1 *Re:Search* 87, 89

Statutes

House of Lords Act UK 1999

Television series

Davies, Russell T (Dir), 'The Empty Child' (2005) *Doctor Who* [Television] UK: BBC
Davies, Russell T (Dir), 'The Doctor Dances' (2005) *Doctor Who* [Television] UK: BBC

Media

Giddens, Gary, 'Stride and Swing: The enduring appeal of Fats Waller and Glenn Miller' *The New Yorker* (31 May 2004)
Kulzac, Natasha, 'Doctor Who Series Eight: First Full-length Trailer Shows Peter Capaldi's Time Lord Goes "Into the Dark Side"' *The Independent* (15 July 2014)
Leith, Sam, 'Worshipping Doctor Who from behind the sofa' *The Telegraph* (London) (4 July 2008)
Mohr, Tara, 'Learning to Love Criticism' *The New York Times* (27 September 2014)

Part IV

Cultural legal studies as jurisprudence

Chapter 11

Popular culture's *lex vampirica*

The law of the undead in *True Blood*, the *Twilight* saga and *The Passage*

William P MacNeil[1]

Enjoy your vampire! 'Coming out of the coffin' and the right to desire differently in contemporary law and culture

From art house films (e.g., Jim Jarmusch's recent and brilliant *Only Lovers Left Alive*) to young adult fiction (e.g., Richelle Mead's entertaining 'Vampire Academy' series), from primetime *drek* (e.g, the truly execrable *Vampire Diaries*) to 'indie' cult movies (e.g., Swedish coming-of-age story, *Let the Right One In* – my personal favourite), the trope of the vampire looms large culturally, its present and (near) pervasive 'coming out of the coffin',[2] at once reflecting and refracting, as I shall argue here, our contemporary socio-legal debates, as much as our ongoing psychosexual concerns. A mirroring which – even if, famously and folklorically, vampires were *imago*-less, having no mirror refection – figures most prominently in two current vampire publishing phenomena, both having transitioned successfully from the printed page to the moving image, each being screen adaptations from their best-selling textual sources. I refer, first, to the big screen's *Twilight* saga, its strong box office showing a foregone conclusion given the unswerving loyalty of its literary fanbase – the original readership of

1 Griffith Law School Brisbane, Qld, Australia. This chapter was delivered, first, as a lecture to my upper year LLB elective, Legal Fictions: Representations of Law in Cinema, Philosophy and Literature at the Griffith Law School (Brisbane, Qld, Australia) and, second, as a paper given at 'A Symposium of Cultural Legal Studies Methodology – Wherefore Art Thou?', Legal Intersections Research Centre, School of Law, University of Wollongong (Wollongong, NSW). My thanks to the students of the former, as well as the attendees and organisers of the latter. Two people stand out as sources of inspiration for this chapter, to each of whom I owe a profound scholarly debt: first, to my American niece and god-daughter, Ms Catherine Elizabeth Harding (aka 'Catherine the Great'), for introducing me to the *Twilight* saga in the first place, many thanks (and always remember this piece of deathless prose, 'Edward chuckled darkly . . .'); and, second, to my longtime interinstitutional colleague, fellow law-and-litterateuse, and friend forever, Associate Professor Marett Leiboff for her many, many kindnesses over the years. To them, I dedicate this chapter with much love and affection.

2 Charlaine Harris, *A True Blood Omnibus* (Gollancz, 2007) 5.

the best-selling *oeuvre* of romancer *du jour*, Stephanie Meyer; and, second, to the small screen's *True Blood*, its seventh and final season now finished – in the end, an ailing franchise but, at least initially, a televisual *tour de force* by *Six Feet Under's* Alan Ball of Charlaine Harris's set of supernatural semi-*policiers*, the 'Southern Vampire Mysteries'. As vampire fictions – and, to my mind, as vampire *legal* fictions *non pareil* – both *True Blood* and *Twilight* take as their central and overarching theme, desire, as well as, more specifically, its 'right' to desire differently.

In each, however, this right plays out along very different narrative lines, following psychic scripts sharply at variance with each other – of which the next section of this chapter will detail at some length. But to foreshadow that argument, briefly: I contend that in *True Blood*, the right to desire differently is squarely hystericised, yielding for its cast of desiring subjects – at first, its principal leads, Bill and Sookie, then its supporting cast, Eric, Alcide, Sam, and so forth – an (il)logic that is iterative in the extreme, with one fantasmatic *objet petit a* replacing another, ultimately leaving, but for a brief wish-fulfilling epilogue, each character as unsatisfied, excluded or alone (or is that the autonomy of *bourgeois-liberal* legalism?) in the series' end as he or she was in its beginning. While, in *Twilight*, I wager, desire is properly obsessional, the static fixation of its right – Edward – consigning its principal desiring subject – Bella – to a state that is literally 'between two deaths': that of vampire bride and mother, whereby right accedes to duty – and its ethics of a higher good – in the astonishing 'shapeshift' of value (or is this the sublation of Hegelian dialectics?) with which the saga concludes. In so doing, both *Twilight* and *True Blood* – so I propound – mount a critique of law that is as *jurisprudential* as it is psychoanalytical, exposing behind the operations of *Recht*, whether it be defined as right (to be left alone, to freely choose) or duty (to connect with an identity, a family, a community), a *pathology*: a pathology which, whether symptomatised as hysterical (the rights of *True Blood*) or obsessive (the duties of *Twilight*), striates the socio-Symbolic, and its desiring 'Law'.

That is to say, legality comes (blood)stained in each of these vampiric 'tales from the crypt' with a Marx-like *jouissance* of possession, the all-consuming usufruct of which most definitely resides in, and redounds to the figure of the Master – or whichever one of the many aliases of the *Nom-du-Pere* he goes by: the 'anal father', the *jouisseur* – thereby enabling his alienation (*True Blood*) or subordination (*Twilight*), as reified objects, of the series' respective subjects of desire. That these 'objects, not subjects' – to invert Sandra Berns' pithy feminist phraseology[3] – turn out to be, in the main, *women* (i.e, Bella and Sookie) should come as no surprise to this chapter's genre-minded reader, given that 'the Gothic'

3 Sandra Berns, 'Women in English Legal History: Subject (Almost), Object (Irrevocably), Person (Not Quite)' (1994) 12 *University of Tasmania Law Review* 26.

– the canonical register in which each of these series is self-consciously inscribed – is always/already to sacrifice its 'Woman in White': that is, femininity *at risk*. The surrender of which may paradoxically call forth, as I will conclude in this chapter, a new species of law-bearer, one with a radically different rationale, as well as *modus operandi*. Specifically, a 'Slayer' who, like Amy in Pulitzer Prize-winning novelist Justin Cronin's dazzling 'undead' debut, *The Passage*,[4] out-'buffies' Buffy by, allegorically, impaling the hitherto dominant 'law of the undead' (i.e., rights, duties), installing in its place an alternative model of *nomos* indebted to another legal philosophy: namely, a 'law of nature', the love of which goes beyond, but also through *lex vampirica's* right to desire differently.

Psychoanalysing rights and duties: *True Blood* and *Twilight* as case studies in juris-*pathology*

True Blood*'s magic roundabout of rights: Sookie as* objet petit a

Rights saturate *True Blood* – much like the opening credits' vivid red wash when it smears, like a blood sample for 'Hep-V', its concluding frames. To push this sanguinary analogy further: rights circulate, blood-like, throughout the dense episodic capillaries of *True Blood*, seeping into its characters' dialogic addresses and asides;[5] oozing from those telling background details of its *mise-en-scene*, momentarily foregrounded by deep focus;[6] and, above all, coursing most strongly through those highly self-referential sequences which punctuate the series where we, the audience, not only watch, but watch the *watchers* watching . . . what else? Television! Here, the series' primetime players are recast as televisual spectators, their eyes, like ours, ever glued to the tube, only within the parallel world of *True Blood*, HBO or Showtime have been replaced by TBBN, aka 'Tru Blood Broadcasting Network' and its 24/7 on-air updates on, *inter alia*, vampiric rights: for example, the right to marry, broadcast in the televised news

4 See also, the sequel, Justin Cronin, *The Twleve* (Orion Books, 2012). A third instalment, concluding what will be a trilogy is due out late in 2014 and is to be entitled *The City of Mirrors*.

5 Rights are referenced – sometimes satirically, sometimes seriously – by, for example, characters as different as Russell Edgington, Pam, Governor Burrell and Marnie. In reference to 'equal rights', Edgington – the deposed vampire King of Louisiana – howls in high dudgeon, 'You are not our equals – we will eat you' (*TB*, 2011, Season 3, Episode 9). Meanwhile, Pam despairs, with her usual arch irony, of humans' 'constitutional rights to be idiots' (*TB*, 2012, Season 4, Episode 2). 'Human rights' are used by Burrell to justify his state of emergency, and looming pogrom against vampires (*TB*, 2014, Season 6, Episode 1). Finally, after an attack on her premises, Marnie squarely insists that Eric has 'no right' to interfere with her freedom of religion, i.e., Wiccanism (*TB*, 2012, Season 4, Episode 3).

6 Such as the tabloid headline announcing 'Angelina's' *rightful* adoption of a vampire baby, glimpsed in the clutter of Lettie Mae's ramshackle digs (*TB*, 2009, Season 1, Episode 3).

report shown, on the box, at 'Merlotte's' of New Hampshire's first legal vampire/human marriage (*TB*, 2010, Season 2, Episode 12). Structurally, these on-screen moments in the series appear to be, *prima facie*, the TV equivalent of the Shakespearean 'play-within-the-play', the reflexivity of which foregrounds, formally, its medium's aesthetic properties; but, here, by virtue of their recurrent nature – popping up over and over again throughout *True Blood* – these moments come to function more, in fact, like the chorus of Greek tragedy, often commenting upon or questioning, at other times ironically counterpointing the narrative's action, and, thereby, forging, in their substantive message's address, a social link between the text (the world of the story, its diegesis) and its context (the world of us, the audience).

Nowhere is this more the case than in those sharply crafted soundbites of Nan Flanagan as played by Jessica Tuck, the elegantly wan 'face' – or is that 'fang'? – of the Vampire Rights League (VRL), whose timely televisual interventions in 'undead' advocacy are a fixture of the series right up until her spectacular 'true death' in Series 4 (*TB*, 2012, Season 4, Episode 12). Prior to that, Nan had been a tireless campaigner – as well as savvy, even ruthless behind-the-scenes political operator – for vampire rights, battling against and sparring with, on a variety of 'TV programmes-within-the TV programme', any number of fictional antagonists[7] – most egregiously of all, Steve and Sarah Newlin (*TB*, 2010, Season 2, Episode 9)[8] – each of whom, like the current crop of paleo-conservatives dominating the American political landscape, would read rights restrictively, attempting to staunch its discursive flow to a trickle. Only, here, rights' flow is not, as the Tea Bag 'Republicunts'(*TB*, 2014a, Season 7, Episode 5)[9] fear, from straight to gay, but from vampire to human, the latter two being stand-ins for the former, and all the other 'culture wars' dualisms for which it is a correlate: native born/immigrant, *rentier*/working-class, white male/'Other', and so forth. Such a strong reality referent – of law's fractious politics, allegorised as vampire rights – is a series constant, present from the start of *True Blood*, its opening prologue, establishing the central historical premise of the show's alternate reality – that of the 'Great Revelation' of vampiric existence[10] – being coincident with Nan's first on-camera appearance: as the outspoken interviewee of, and more than a rhetorical match for real-life liberal satirist and social commentator Bill Maher who, playing himself, quizzes her relentlessly

7 Others include Rep. David Finch (*TB*, 2010, Season 2, Episode 9), and Rev. Theo Newlin (*TB*, 2009, Season 1, Episode 2).

8 See also Nan verbally jousting with a now solo Steve in 'Evil is Going On', (*TB*, 2011, Series 3, Episode 12).

9 A neologism delivered by – who else? – Pamela Swynford de Beaufort, played to high camp perfection by Kristin Bauer.

10 For more on this theme, see the graphic novel: Brian Cain, Gregg Hale and David Wohl, *True Blood: The Great Revelation* (Top Cow Publishing, 2008).

on the 'undead's' historical record prior to 'Revelation' and their demands, since, for recognition as citizen-subjects, as rights-bearers (*TB*, 2009, Season 1, Episode 1). 'We deserve basic civil rights', Nan avers, 'just like everyone else' (*TB*, 2009, Season 1, Episode 1).

It should come as no surprise then to the viewer when this historicising exchange over rights is, itself, instantly *historicised* as the first episode shifts from the prologue to the opening credits' dazzling montage of images (*TB*, 2009, Season 1, Episode 1), figuring a failing world of death and decay. Amidst its jump-cuts, pans, and close-ups of fetid waters, decomposing carcasses, gyrating bodies, unanswered prayers and crumbling, derelict structures – all to the darkly lascivious strains of Jace Everett's 'Bad Things'(2006), two images stand out as allusively resonant of rights' historicity: first, in the grainy black-and-white footage of '60s civil rights protestors, their street march well and truly overcome, indeed under violent assault from a brutally strong-arming riot police; second, in the short but memorable clip, taken from a moving car, of contemporary roadside signage, messaged 'God Hates Fangs', itself a waggish nod to the notorious Rev. Fred Phelps and his Westboro Baptist Church's virulently homophobic sloganeering, 'God Hates Fags' – fighting words, since their first appearance on placards at the Church's early '90s pickets, for gay rights activists everywhere.[11] In figuring so vividly these very real instances of oppression – racial and same-sex discrimination, respectively – both images summon up two originary and highly negative contexts rights were intended, in the first place, to address. But, as a positive presence, rights-*qua*-rights are missing from either camera shot here, conspicuous only by their absence, un-represented and, as discourse, perhaps un-representable. Until, that is, rights literally spring to life (rise from the grave?) in the first series' first episode taking on – or so I contend – characterological form in one of the unlikeliest of the *dramatis personae*, Bon Temps' last Confederate, still 'whistlin' Dixie' after all these (173!) years, Capt. William Compton, CSA, aka, 'Vampire Bill'.

I say 'unlikely' because Bill, as a former slave-owner, cuts – potentially – a very sorry figure indeed as a *prosopopoeia* of rights, an instantiation more suggestive of their *ab*use than use. But consider his character more carefully, not so much in terms of whom he is, but what he wants. Or, at least, what he says he wants. For when we first meet Bill at the series' opening, he claims that what he wants above all is what any jurisprude would recognise as the most fundamental of *bourgeois*-liberal rights, central to its rich tradition of autonomic 'negative liberties' – more integral than freedom of religion or speech, even more basic

11 The congregation receiving nationwide attention for their 1998 picketing of the funeral of gay hate crime victim, University of Wyoming student, Matthew Shepard. For more information on the activities of these 'Christians', so-called, see: Westboro Baptist Church Home Page, www.godhatesfags.com.

than the sanctity of property and contract: namely, *the right to be left alone*. Of course, as seasons 3 and 4 will disclose, Bill's motives in returning to Bon Temps were much more mixed, having been dispatched, by the Louisiana's Vampire Queen, Sophie-Anne, on a fact-finding mission (principally, to observe and study Sookie and her 'gift') that is driven by strategic advantage (to report back on how Sookie's unique abilities might best be deployed in the Queen's interest);[12] but, for the first two seasons, at least, the audience has no reason to doubt the sincerity of Bill's intentions to reclaim not only his old home – the now deserted Compton plantation, his direct descendants having died off – yet, even more significantly, his *humanity*. Which is precisely why Bill wishes, so desperately, to be alone: 'Vampires like me who live alone', he explains to Sookie, 'are a little better reminded of their former humanity'.[13]. By way of contrast, vampiric 'nesting' – as both the textual and televisual series 'avian-ise' undead domestic life – only intensifies their *in*humanity, especially their enjoyment in inflicting pain: 'When vampires live in nests', Bill continues, 'they become more cruel because they egg each other on. They see others like themselves constantly, and so they are reminded how far from being human they are'.[14]

All of which suggests that this most *unheimlich* notion of the 'homely' – or to give this term a more expansive spin, vampiric 'community' – is, for Bill, highly suspect, its problematic political, as well as moral and ethical basis of collective *connection* being repeatedly called into question here. Nowhere is this more the case than in the series' salacious, indeed highly 'pornified' depiction of this community's positive right to connect – in short, to desire an(O)ther – as a gruesomely Sadean sexual encounter, whereby 'the One' mercilessly and brutally 'enjoys' the body of 'the Other', penetrating, drinking, then draining it of life, as much as blood. Consider, from this dark vantage, the travelling *ménage a trois* of Malcolm, Diane and Liam, who, right up until their torched demise (*TB*, 2009, Season 1, Episode 7), cut quite a swath of 'enjoyment' through Bon Temps, terrorising and intimidating all and sundry, even exsanguinating mercilessly their human camp followers, a duo of all-too-willing 'fangbanging' sex slaves.[15] Certainly, these three – an *un*holy trinity if ever there was one –

12 Suggested first, when Bill's secret dossier on Sookie is revealed (*TB*, 2011, Season 3, Episode 2), and then gradually divulged throughout the Seasons 3 and 4, culminating in Sophie-Anne's assassination (*TB*, 2012, Season 4, Episode 2) carried in a palace coup by Bill, Eric and the Authority.

13 Charlaine Harris, above n 2, 67. For a similar sentiment, as well as wording, in the televisual series, see the episode entitled 'Mine' (*TB*, 2009, Season 1, Episode 3).

14 Charlaine Harris, above n 2, 67.

15 Namely, the treacherous Jerry, who hopes, as vengeful payback for the vampire-caused death of his lover, to infect this trio with the vamp STD, 'Hep V' (Season 1, Episode 3); and the much more biddable Janelle, last seen, horrifically, hanging from her heels – like an animal carcass in an *abattoir* – blood pouring from her punctured carotid artery (*TB*, Season 1, Episode 3).

could be dismissed as, and indeed, *are* 'rogues'; and, as such, are hopelessly out-of-step with the assimilationist policies of the vampiric powers-that-be, 'the Authority': 'Mainstreaming', snarls a defiant Liam, 'is for pussies' (*TB*, 2009, Season 1, Episode 7). But, as fully fledged, desiring citizen-subjects, vigorously exercising what Lacan would call their right-to-*jouissance* – think of an ecstatically growling Liam, caught on a sex tape, his head excitedly ricocheting from side to side, as he climaxes with, and into Maudette Pickens (*TB*, 2009, Season 1, Episode 1) – the trio are not so very far off the mating practices of much more integrated vampires, those whose principal – and, interestingly, highly policed – 'pleasure dome' is the deliciously dubbed 'Fangtasia'.

Despite, however, all its fabled security checks – the fearsome presence of Eric, presiding over proceedings as enthroned 'Sheriff'; of Pam, frostily vetting all entrants as 'door bitch' from hell; even of 'scream queen' Ginger, whose over-the-top shrieks function something like a built-in alarm system[16] – Fangtasia can still allow, on its club premises, consensual sexual congress between vamp and human to get seriously out of hand: as Jessica's extracurricular 'Ladies Room' hook-ups, when on the rebound from Hoyt, so amply attest (*TB*, 2012, Season 4, Episode 3). Not that Bon Temps' human contingent is any more restrained than Fangtasia's lewd vamps. If anything, the township's residents are far too apt to live up to the Mardi Gras motto that inspired their municipality's moniker – *laissez les bon temps roulez*, letting the 'good times' most definitely roll on, its waves of *jouissance* successively washing over and through Bon Temps' highways and byways, something like the floodtides of 'Hurricane Katrina', breaching New Orleans' fragile levees. The sluices of which are well and truly opened in the series' Season 2 by Maenad Maryann – a.k.a., Lilith, Isis, Gaia (*TB*, 2010, Season 2, Episode 7), whose Dionysian excess surges through Bon Temps, commanding its inhabitants, superegoically, to enjoy. 'Don't ever say No to yourself!' (*TB*, 2010, Season 2, Episode 4) is her anti-Oedipal injunction, its obscene 'pleasure(-in-pain) principle' engulfing the Bon Tempais(e), literally clouding their vision – their eyes, murkily opaque; and, thereby, rendering them insensibly sightless to their own self-mutilation,[17] *Fight Club*-style blows[18] and crazed, animalistic rutting, honouring the 'God Who (*Never*) Comes'.[19]

16 Who, as Season 7 reveals in a comical '80s flashback, came up with the original concept for Fangtasia, then pilfered by Pam (*TB*, 2014b, Season 7, Episode 4).

17 Like a madly giggling Jane Bodehouse, slicing off her finger as an offering for the 'Horned God' (*TB*, 2010, Season 2, Episode 11).

18 Such as Tara and Eggs, happily bashing each other as erotic foreplay, after consuming Daphne's heart, seared and served up by Maryann (*TB*, 2010, Season 2, Episode 8).

19 At a range of group encounters which include not only the couplings of the usual suspects – e.g., Arlene and Terry – but, comically, Coroner Mike Spencer, caught 'sodomising a pine tree' (*TB*, 2010, Season 2, Episode 8).

Even when not possessed by this orgiastic frenzy, Bon Temps' ever randy *hoi polloi* engage in all kinds of coital acts, which are anything but 'vanilla': rape fantasies, bondage scenes, sub/dom role play, up to and including old fashioned booty calls. The amorous career of that Southern fried Lothario, Jason Stackhouse is exemplary here, his Don Juanesque exploits – from V-addled Amy (Season 1) to viciously vengeful Violet (Season 5, 6), and all the others in between[20] – earning him the resolutely phallic sobriquet, 'sex on a stick'. A 'stick' which, as it turns out, can be just as much an instrument of punishment, as it can of reward – especially after the dubious 'enhancements' of that hyper-Viagra, 'V-juice', the addictive nature of which leaves Amy dead, Andy homicidal and, Jason, himself, with the worst case of priapism on primetime. Sex on a stick? With immodest residents such as these, Bon Temps is a town with sex on the *brain*. This is precisely Sookie's problem with her family, friends and neighbours because, even when the 'Law of the Father's Name' holds them firmly in check – its implacable 'No' tabooing enjoyment – their not-so-repressed *Wunschen* continually assail her consciousness. For Sookie is, *inter alia*, a telepath, gifted – or rather, as Charlaine Harris would have it,[21] 'cursed' with mindreading (dis)abilities, overhearing, among other things, cries for help, frustrated yearnings and angry rebukes[22] – but many of which are tinctured with carnal overtones, if not outright sexual fantasies. Recall the flashback of Sookie's disastrous dating history, a nonstarter precisely because her sixth sense susses all too well the closeted latency of one prospective *beau*[23] and the vulgar lasciviousness of the other.[24] No wonder that for Sookie, just like Bill, community is *the* enemy because its collective voice of *jouissance* – not just of lust, but of racism, homophobia, misanthropy, and so on – invades her, forever compromising her psychic privacy, undermining her inner self's integrity.

Silence, then, comes not just as a relief, but as deliverance from, potentially, psychosis – what, after all, is hearing voices? Voices, which on more than one

20 Including, fangbangers, Maudette and Dawn (Season 1); adulterous evangelist, Sarah (Season 2); hill-billy werepanther Crystal (Season 3); Hoyt's vamp girlfriend, Jessica (Season 4,5); and, in various same-sex fantasies and dreams – sometimes theirs, sometimes Jason's (!), Steve Newlin (Season 5, 6), Warlow (Season 6) and Eric (Season 7).

21 In an interview Harris stated that making Sookie telepathic is 'the worst thing I could think of to do to anybody'. She explained this further saying 'it would just be absolutely horrible to know what people really thought about you' (TheAuthorHour.com, 'Interview with Charlaine Harris' (On-Line Radio Interview, 19 November 2009).

22 Consider the first three Merlotte's customers Sookie waits on, and overhears in the premiere, with one praying to Jesus for the strength to resist another beer, another longing for brighter lights than Bon Temps, and yet another reprimanding a spouse for their imagined disapproval (*TB*, 2009, Season 1, Episode 1).

23 Longing to get over his 'hots' for Matt Damon, with Sookie as his bride – and beard (*TB*, 2009, Season 1, Episode 2).

24 One who wonders if she is a real blonde, her head hair the same as her pubic hair, ibid.

occasion – for example, the mourners at Adele Stackhouse's funeral (*TB*, 2009, Season 1, Episode 6), or those diners at Merlotte's after Tara's transformation (*TB*, 2012a, Season 5, Episode 4) – threaten, with their recriminations over the role Sookie played in each circumstance, to push her over the edge, provoking something like a *passage a l'acte*. These accusatory voices, however, are stilled with Bill – which is precisely why Sookie is drawn to him: because she cannot hear him, her eavesdropping aptitude, for once, failing her. This means that Bill is for Sookie – unlike anyone else in Bon Temps, from Lettie Mae Thornton to Maxine Fortenberry – an *enigma*, the riddle of which acts as an incredible lure, drawing her inexorably towards him, by directly speaking – ironically, in his very silence – to her hysteria. Hysteria? In what way, an astonished reader may very well query, is Sookie hysterical? Especially, since the usual somatic symptoms of the hysteric – a cough, a tic or a paralysis – are absent here. Yet, hysteria is more than a cache of symptoms; as Lacanian psychoanalysis teaches, it is a *structure*, discursively organised around a question – that of *identity*. 'What am I', asks the hysteric, repeatedly, 'a man or a woman?'.[25] At first blush, the series seems to answer this question in no uncertain terms, Alan Ball tricking Sookie out in what Joan Riviere would call parodic 'masquerades' of femininity (Riviere, 1986): the 'Hooters'-esque T-shirt and 'short shorts' of Merlotte's; the Lolita-like bikini worn while sunbathing at Gran's. But if there is one constant in *True Blood*, running throughout its seven seasons, then it is an interrogative that is posed to Sookie, over and over again – by Mary Ann (*TB*, 2010, Season 2, Episode 10), by Russell Edgington (*TB*, 2011, Season 3, Episode 6), by Eric (*TB*, Season 4, 2012, Episodes 2, 3), and, above all, by Bill (*TB*, 2009, Season 1, Episodes 1, 2) – that is, despite her 'girly' overcoding, a ventriloquised version of the hysteric's question: namely, 'What *are* you?'

The real thrust of this query here goes to the hysterical subject's *species*, rather than sexuation, because at stake for Sookie-as-hysteric is, not so much gender, as the engendering of identity itself – as human, faerie, or something in between. Not that questions concerning anatomical difference are entirely otiose either. For the source of Sookie's tremendous appeal is specified later in the series by reference to a highly gendered part-object: Sookie's 'precious faerie vagina', (*TB*, 2012, Season 4, Episode 12) as Pam so aptly metonymises here. This, in turn, metaphorises what Lacan might call, following Plato, her *agalma*;[26] that is, an unnameable 'X factor', an indefinable *je ne sais quoi* – wherein, as human/fae hybrid, lies her tantalising attraction. For make no mistake about it: in *True Blood*, Sookie is *the* not-so-'obscure object of desire', pursued by, fought over and, above all, *wanted* by the series' virile host: Bill, Eric, Alcide, Sam, Warlow

25 Jaques Lacan, *The Seminar of Jacques Lacan, Book III, The Psychoses, 1955–1956* (Jacques Miller (ed.), Russell Grigg trans with notes, W W Norton & Co, 1993) 171.

26 Dylan Evans, *An Introductory Dictionary of Lacanian Psychoanalysis* (Routledge, 1996) 125.

– enticing all, satisfying none. As such, Sookie functions not only as 'the Other' to the subjects of Law's desire here; rather, she comes to stand for the Law itself – or, at least, a critical remainder which its inauguration institutes: namely, that little piece of its Real, the Lacanian *object petit a*,[27] which will fill out the fantasy frame(s) of Law's subjects, enabling them to desire, properly, as *rights*-bearers. I italicise '*rights*-bearers', setting it off, because rights are, as legal philosophers as diverse as Costas Douzinas,[28] Renata Salecl,[29] and Ann Barron,[30] have observed or intimated, *the* discourse of desire, its internal logic holding out the promise of subjective recognition, even identic plenitude. Seen in this juridical light then, Sookie's circulation, throughout the series, between Law's desiring figures – Bill, *et al.* – is nothing less, in its mobility, than an allegory of rights discourse itself, especially as it moves from agent to agent, operating as a fungible *point de capiton*, or 'quilting point' that will confer an identity – as autonomic vampires, connected werewolves, longing shifters, 'queer' fae, and so on – at the very moment it 'hails' that subjectivity, interpellating it within the Symbolic of legal ideology.

This ongoing interpellative process recasts the role of Sookie's psychic powers. Instead of an assault or an invasion – essentially a crime against the person, her telepathy, when viewed from this vantage, becomes law-*full* (meaning full of law). 'Che vuoi?', asks Sookie, 'What do you want of me?' 'I want my rights!' – of *connaissance*, of recognition:[31] that is the impassioned reply she receives back from her many interlocutors – *True Blood's* vampires, werewolves, shifters and fae, all of whom are marked by castration's *beance*, the 'lack' of which rips their respective identities, rendering each hopelessly and dangerously ambiguous (Are they friend or enemy? Citizen or outlaw? Monster or mate?), thereby occasioning *meconnaissance* or 'misrecognition'. Sookie's response is classically hysterical, pointing and underscoring the hysteria which, as a discursive structure, informs rights. For rights, like Sookie, never give back by way of riposte what they seemed, at first blush, to afford. That is to say, both engage, then withdraw, failing to stitch up the tear in the Other that, as hysterical, each have vowed to close, unpicking it at the very moment of its repair. Why? Because to rethread this identic rent would, effectively, shut down desire, arresting its endless dialectic of subjective subversion that both rights and Sookie – as *objets petit a* – wish to sustain, their fantasmatic pledge tempting all, yet indefinitely postponing

27 Ibid.
28 Costas Douzinas, 'The Paradoxes of Human Rights' (2013) 20 (1) *Constellations* 51.
29 Renata Salecl, 'Woman as Symptom of Rights' (1993) 12 (2) *Topoi* 89.
30 Ann Barron, 'The Illusions of the I: Citizenship and the Politics of Identity' in Alan Norrie (ed.), *Closure and Critique: New Directions in Legal Theory* (Edinburgh University Press, 1993) 80.
31 William MacNeil, 'Law's *Corpus Delicti:* The Fantasmatic Body of Rights Discourse' (1998) 9 *Law and Critique* 37; William MacNeil, 'Taking Rights Symptomatically: *Jouissance, coupure, object petit a*' (1999) 8 (1) *Griffith Law Review* 134.

any determinate resolution to the 'Che vuoi' question. No wonder Sookie turns out to be half-fae, the most elusive and illusory of 'supernaturals' who, like rights as described by various traditions of 'critique' (e.g., Marxist, feminist, post-colonial), are never what they seem to be, constantly distorting appearances, continually concealing realities. Each – the fae, rights – wears a disguise, the cloak of which may slip now and then, but one that, on the whole, remains securely in place, captivating those in its thrall, enticing yet never satiating – much in the same way Sookie roams among and revolves around the series' succession of phallic signifiers, ever the object of, but at no time heeding their demand for rights.

Twilight's *'ethics of a higher good': Bella and the phallus*

In sharp contrast to the high turnover of Sookie's ever rotating 'magic roundabout' of desiring and desirable rights is the dutiful stasis of *Twilight*'s Bella. Fixity rather than flux define her condition and the saga is quite clear from its start wherein her attentions are focused: 'About three things I was absolutely positive. First Edward was a vampire. Second, there was part of him – and I didn't know how potent that part might be – that thirsted for my blood. And, third, I was unconditionally and irrevocably in love with him'.[32] That love, as Bella herself diagnosed, early on, is 'obsess[ional]'[33] – a point which Jacob picks up on, asking her 'Do you have obsessive-compulsive disorder'.[34] Not that the reader needs this, or any other kind of 'wild' analysis, the signs being easy enough to decipher, what with Bella staring at,[35] dreaming of,[36] even hallucinating about[37] her demon lover. 'Edward, Edward, Edward'[38] is her forlorn refrain, confirming in its compulsive iterability, the profoundly pathological nature of her all-consuming passion. Which raises, at this juncture, the properly diagnostic question: specifically, why is Bella so obsessed, to the point of psychosis – of which hallucinations are, indeed, classically symptomatic – with Edward Cullen? Of course, plenty of *reasons* abound accounting for his eminent suitability as a match, and the narrative goes out of its way to hymn his considerable physical attributes and comfortable material circumstances: his good looks, family's money, 'Old World' courtesy, street-smart savvy, courageous pluck, and flash car. No surprises then that *Pride and Prejudice's* similarly well-accoutred Mr Darcy provided Stephenie Meyer with her literary model here. But these *reasons* in no

32 Stephenie Meyer, *Twilight* (Atom, 2009) 171.
33 Ibid, 205.
34 Stephenie Meyer, *Eclipse* (Atom, 2009), 197.
35 Stephenie Meyer, above n 32, 35.
36 Ibid, 57.
37 Stephenie Meyer, *New Moon* (Atom, 2009) 99.
38 Ibid, 213.

way explain the *un*reason of Bella who, in her unhealthy fixation, resembles more a twenty-first century version of *Wuthering Heights'* Cathy ('I am Edward!') than one of Austen's more sensible heroines (who might very well have preferred, when all is said and done, boy-next-door Mike Newton).

Not that Edward's motives are anywhere near as inexplicable; far from it, as the saga's texts routinely remark upon just why he is attracted so powerfully here: simply, Edward likes the way Bella smells. So biology, nay chemistry at its purest – they *did* meet for the first time in a laboratory – is what drives Edward to distraction, Bella's 'mouth-watering' pheromones[39] sending out olfactory signals that are all too clearly 'derang[ing]'.[40] These aromatic ciphers, however, differ markedly in their legibility from, and are in bold contrast to the opacity of Bella's thoughts which, unlike everyone else's at the Forks, remain for Edward 'unreadable'.[41] But as to Bella: why *her* 'magnificent obsession' here? Surely, given the depths of Bella's feelings, there must be more to Edward than meets the eye, concealed beneath the radiance of his surface 'sparkle'.[42] I would hazard, by way of explanation, that here, in Edward, Bella senses *the* answer to the puzzle of her obsessional existence. For obsessives, according to Lacan, are just as much taken up with a question as hysterics – only, in the former's case, this interrogative is much more far-reaching, going well beyond that of identity to very core of ontological being. 'Am I dead or alive?'[43]: that is the question obsessives such as Bella ask – who are usually, by the way, *male*, just as hysterics are, more often than not, female. A gender coding that in the case of *Twilight* would seem to miss the mark – if, that is, gender was simply a question of primary and secondary sex traits. But as feminist theory, as much as Lacanian psychoanalysis has taught, gender is a 'construction', separate and distinct in its social nature from biological 'essentialism', its coordinates of 'masculine' and 'feminine' being constantly rearranged on a physiological grid that sometimes aligns with, sometimes departs from sexuated embodiment.

In terms of *Twilight* and its characterological system, the 'feminine' is corporealised most fully in the beautifully eye-catching Edward who, clearly, wants *to be* the phallus; that is, the visually pleasurable object, *a la* Laura Mulvey, of the desiring gaze. The passivity of which is all too evidenced in Edward's girlishly chaste refusal, not once, but twice – first, before his wedding; then, more surprisingly, on his honeymoon – of Bella's much more strident sexual overtures. While the 'masculine' is most clearly personified in the androgynous Bella who, despite her 'damsel-in-distress' antics (requiring rescue from skidding cars, drunken louts and stalker vampires) most definitely *has* the phallus. Endowed

39 Stephenie Meyer, above n 37, 267.
40 Stephenie Meyer, above n 32, 236.
41 Ibid, 43.
42 Ibid, 228.
43 Jacques Lacan, above n 25, 179–180.

with, but also thinking – as many men do – with this imagined appendage, Bella absolutely knows what she *wants*: a 'want' that includes, but also goes well beyond the carnal. What does Bella want? Essentially: to be made a vampire – a demand that she repeats to Edward, regularly, throughout the story's arc.[44] That is to say: Bella *in*sists, while Edward *ex*ists. With the answer to her insistent questioning about any future existence – alive or dead? – being *both*, Edward finally rendering her, as Lacan would put it, 'entre deux morts', neither living nor dead but one of 'the undead'. As such, Bella comes to occupy that most salubrious of nosological spaces – having her symptom, and enjoying it too, in a bestowal of vampiric immortality that, nevertheless, holds onto vitality's *jouissance*: 'I was amazing now – to them and myself. It was like I had been born to be a vampire . . . I had found my true place in the world, the place I fit, the place I shined'.[45] All accomplished, on her part, without ever having been bitten, Edward – typically – eschewing even vampiric penetration in favour of the far more clinical injection (a kind of prosthetic phallus?). But even so, in interweaving for Bella both life and death, Edward emerges in Meyer's fiction as a figure of what Jacques Alain Miller might dub strong 'suture'.[46]

Except for the fact that Edward – or, more precisely, the structural function that Edward performs in the narrative is always/already split, his role divided into a twosome of rival love interests that could have stepped out of the dramas of Shakespeare (some of which – *Romeo and Juliet*, *The Merchant of Venice* – are sources for *Twilight*) or, better, yet, the fictions of Scott with their two-by-two parade of fair and dark heroines. In light of this canonical literary context, one might say that the ethereal Edward is a vampiric version of *Ivanhoe's* Saxon (and flaxen) princess, Rowena; while the lusty Jacob Black – the sombre hue of his surname says it all – is a protean version of Rowena's Semitic counterpart, the raven-haired Rebecca of York? By cleverly recoding as supernatural this stock literary device, Meyer summons up in her vampire-werewolf dichotomy a whole host of binaries: anthropological (nature vs. culture), sociological (white hegemon vs. enraced 'Other'), historical (coloniser vs. Indigenous), physiological (organic vs. nonorganic), but, especially, psychoanalytical: unlike the triangulation that marks hysteria's relations with others, obsessives *double* their partners, a replication upon which Lacan[47] – as well as Salecl[48] and Miller[49] – have commented in

44 Stephenie Meyer, above n 32, 412–413; Stephenie Meyer, above n 37, 232; Stephenie Meyer, above n 34, 305; Stephenie Meyer, *Breaking Dawn* (Atom, 2009) 93.

45 Stephenie Meyer, above n 32, 485.

46 Jacques-Alain Miller, 'Suture: Elements of the Logic of the Signifier' (Jacqueline Rose trans) (2007) 8 (Winter) *The Symptom: On-line Journal for Lacan.com*.

47 Jacques Lacan, 'The Neurotic's Individual Myth' (1979) 48 *Psychoanalytic Quarterly* 405.

48 Renata Salecl, 'Love and Sexual Difference: Doubled Partners in Men and Women' in Renata Salecl (ed.), *Sexuation* (Duke University Press, 2000).

49 Jacques Alain-Miller, 'H2O: Suture in Obsessionality' (2003) 4 (Spring) *The Symptom: On-line Journal for Lacan.com*.

their respective readings of Freud's famous case study of obsessional neurosis, the 'Rat Man'.[50] What – or, more to the point, *who* will heal the rupture that this Edward/Jacob dualism indicates, bringing together and mending the *real* rift that threatens – more than Riley, more than Victoria, even more than the Volturi – the delicate equilibrium of Bella's new life-world, precariously balanced as it is between the living and the dead?

Surely, the solution to this dilemma – Bella loving both Edward and Jacob – lies in that most recent addition to the Cullen clan, that pint-sized character who turns out to be the real agent of suture in the saga, the 'sublime object' of all whether she be, for them, 'baby',[51] 'foetus',[52] 'thing'[53] or 'monster',[54] Renesmee. Though she may not be an 'immortal child'[55] of vampire lore, 'Nessie' is clearly miraculous, being the hitherto unheard of progeny of vampire-human coupling, one who will hybridise – just as the Amazonian crossbreed, Nahuel, does – not only the diet but affect, cognition and longevity of each. But even more than bridging the gap between vampire and human, Renesmee closes the breach between bat and wolf, Cullen and Quilete, being of course the receptor of Jacob's 'imprint'[56] – a shifter form of lifelong bonding.[57] Fission, thus, accedes to fusion here by hardwiring into the series' narrative schema what had hitherto been its principal floating signifier, the unplaceable Jacob (Is he a best friend? Brother *manqué*? Boyfriend?): first, as Nessie's protector and, later, potentially, as her lover and partner. The problem, however, with such overdetermined closure is that, in its rush towards resolution, tying up any and all of the plot's loose threads, it constructs a skein of law that is so tightly woven that it, effectively, strangles Bella's individuality. How? By transforming Bella's *choices* – here, to give birth; before that, to marry – predicated as each are on the free will of autonomic right, into a duty of the most onerous and taxing kind: a metamorphosis no less fraught than her excruciating transition from human to vampire. Indeed, the two processes are coincident. For in electing a vampire 'life', Bella turns her back on a whole range of alternative possibilities (college, career, and so on) in favour of what feminist critics of the saga[58] have rightly

50 Sigmund Freud, 'Notes upon a Case of Obsessional Neurosis' in Anna Freud (collab), *The Standard Edition of the Complete Psychological Works of Sigmund Freud, Vol 10* (James Strachey trans, Hogarth, 1955) vol 10, 151–318.
51 Stephenie Meyer, *Breaking Dawn* (Atom, 2009) 221.
52 Ibid, 254.
53 Ibid, 120.
54 Ibid, 164.
55 Ibid, 31.
56 Ibid, 330.
57 Stephenie Meyer, above n 37, 109–10, 156–157, 215.
58 Christine Jarvis, 'The *Twilight* of Feminism? Stephenie Meyer's Saga and the Contradictions of Contemporary Girlhood' (2014) 45 *Children's Literature in Education* 101; Lydia Kokkola, 'Virtuous Vampires and Voluptuous Vamps: Romance Conventions Reconsidered in Stephenie

decried as the most retrograde and limiting of options: that of wife and mother.

Of course, marriage and maternity are impossibly glamourised by Meyer here in that most deliciously decadent of Gothic figures: the vampire-bride. But, even more astonishing, the saga *ethicises* Bella's choice as the embrace of something approximating a 'Cause' (Occupy Edward?) and with it a 'higher good': that of the much touted 'veggie vampirism'[59] of the Cullens, the *ethos* of which is situated squarely within the context of the reconstituted contemporary family. For Bella does not simply marry Edward, the one merging with the other. On the contrary, and in a very real sense, she marries a familial *group* – albeit a highly unconventional one in which sons are older than their mothers (as with the case of Edward, the elder of Esme), siblings pair off (Rosalie with Emmett, Alice with Jasper) and fathers not only 'sire' but *birth*, as vampires, their offspring (like Carlisle does with his clan). As such, the Cullens, as a family unit, not only gesture towards the postmodern extended family (the 'yours, mine and ours' of spouses, de factos, ex-partners, children, step-children, half-siblings, and so on) but, at one and the same time, rehabilitate, in the Carlisle–Esme relationship, the high heteronormativity of the modern nuclear family. It may even raise from the dead something much more atavistic than that, a lost world of desire's *law* and its commanding correlative, duty. For Meyer's saga – and the films based upon them – are both consumed with an anxiety over what French social theorist and cultural critic Gilles Lipovetsky has called, presciently, the 'twilight of duty'.[60] A duty-waning dusk in which, as French Lacanian analyst Eric Laurent – following Lipovetsky – has summarised, 'the must has given way to the incantation of happiness, the categorical obligation to the simulation of the senses, the irrefragable prohibition to *a-la-carte* regulations'.[61] This aphanisis, or 'fading' of duty is registered in *Twilight's* very crepuscular title, the saga's successive titles – *New Moon*, *Eclipse* and *Breaking Dawn* – picking up and pushing forward this daily cycle, the diurnal following upon, and superseding the nocturnal, suggestive of a new day to come.

What is this new day if not the return of the patriarch and his law? A *Nom-du-Pere* that shall replace the impotent father of modernity (personified in the hapless Charlie, the Forks' near-Keystone chief of police), as well as the anal fathers of pre-modernity (incarnate in the malign royal triumvirate of the Volturi

Meyer's *Twilight* Series' (2011) 42 *Children's Literature in Education* 162; Anna Silver, '*Twilight* is Not Good for Maidens: Gender, Sexuality, and the Family in Stephenie Meyer's *Twilight* Series' (2010) 42 (1) *Studies in the Novel* 121; Anthea Taylor, 'The Urge Toward Love is an Urge Towards (Un)Death: Roamnce, Masochistic Desire and Postfeminism in the *Twilight* Novels' (2012) 15 (1) *International Journal of Cultural Studies* 31.

59 Stephenie Meyer, above n 32, 164.

60 Gilles Lipovetsky, *Le Crepuscule du Devoir* (Gallimard, 1992).

61 Eric Laurent, 'The Name of the Father: Psychoanalysis and Democracy' (2006) 1 (7) *Lacanian Compass: Psychoanalytic Newsletter of Lacanian Orientation.*

– Aro, Marcus and Caius), with a post-modernisation of paternity that lays down a law which says both 'No!' (specifically, to treating humanity as a natural food source) and 'Yes!' (namely, to a form of incest). Only, here, there is this hitch: that this reconfigured law, promulgated by the 'new, improved' patriarch, Carlisle, demands – as Alison Young would caution[62] – a sacrifice, one which, as ever, turns out to be 'Woman' herself, as legality's 'not-all', indeed as its very symptom. This is because no matter where you turn in *Twilight* – in its human, vampire or werewolf 'nomospheres', somewhere, and by someone, a woman is most definitely being beaten. She may not be bitten – but she's certainly bruised, like Bella on her honeymoon, 'decorated with patches of blue and black'.[63] A graphic detail which should recall and, in so doing, recast all the other 'accidents' that Bella has experienced since taking up with the Cullens, exposing them – whether they be perpetrated by Jasper, Laurent, James or Victoria – as highly coded variations on a theme of domestic violence. Not that Bella is alone here. Think of Emily on the reserve,[64] her beautiful face horribly scarred and disfigured by the animal (or male?) aggression unleashed by fiancé Sam's shapeshift; and who, as recompense, is allowed to stay on, playing Wendy to the Quiletes' wolf pack of 'lost boys', cheerily cooking for Paul, Embry, Jared and, of course, Jacob. The house-bound servitude of which, when read with the assaults on Bella itemised before, drives home *Twilight's* gendered context of not just pervasive inequity but very real misogyny. All of which bodes anything but well for the next generation of the saga's women – such as Renesmee. For with a protector as violently volatile as werewolf Jacob, and a father as battering as vampire Edward, what chance does little Nessie have? Especially, in light of Bella – *and* Emily – normalising, and thereby 'enabling' spousal abuse and its underlying *diktat* of duty: the subordination of women.

Come back Buffy, all is forgiven! Vampire slaying as a law of love

Not that the state Sookie is left in is any better than here – even after slaying the Oedipal father *manqué*, Bill. While her narrative world, with its rights fetishism, may hold out brighter prospects for gender equality than *Twilight's* duty-obsessed environment, it ends up producing eerily the same sort of female subservience as seen with Bella Cullen, *nee* Swann. For Sookie is last seen, five years hence, in the concluding postscript of *True Blood's* final episode, 'Thank You', (*TB*, 2014c, Season 7, Episode 10) as a Southern redneck version of the now *soignee* Mrs

62 Alison Young, '*Caveat Sponsa*: Violence and the Body in Law' in S Rice and J Brettle (eds), *Public Bodies, Private States* (Manchester University Press, 1994).

63 Stephenie Meyer, above n 51, 87.

64 Stephenie Meyer, above n 37, 291.

Cullen of the Forks, who is if not barefoot, then most certainly pregnant and, undoubtedly, largely in the kitchen, having spent easily the better part of the day preparing the lavish 'white trash' cookery of fried Thanksgiving comestibles for what appears to be the entirety of Bon Temps (Lafayette, James, Arlene, Hoyt, Jessica, Jason, Brigette, Holly, Andy, Adilyn, Wade and so on) and then some (non-resident outliers such as Sam, Nicole, and their children). With similar outcomes such as these, each reinventing gender oppression in the most sugar-coated and sentimentalised of ways, the rights of *True Blood* and the duties of *Twilight* turn out to be, in their mutual pathologies – hysteria and obsession – a *difference* without a difference. Instead of two stark options – whereby one is constrained to choose either one or the other, presumably because one might say, with a nod to Lacan, that *il n'y a pas rapport juridique*, here hysterical rights and obsessive duties turn out to be two sides of the same coin; that is, a Janus-faced duality, the impasse of which is constitutive of a Law that forever fails Woman as its subordinated, if not excluded Other. Given this, perhaps then the time has come for a jurisprudential 'reboot' of *lex vampirica*, with its circulating 'law stories' of the undead. All of which is to say: come back Buffy, all is forgiven – and bring your stake with you!

It is precisely this sort of Buffy-style circuit-breaker that is proffered by and carried out in Justin Cronin's stunning novel, *The Passage*, the first in his soon to be complete trilogy featuring a central antagonist who is a vampire slayer with a most definite twist. The twist being, of course, that Cronin's 'Drac'-duster, Amy is, herself, half-vampire – the hybrid result of a government experiment gone hideously wrong (is there any other kind?). After a lengthy, present-day prologue, detailing the disastrous fall-out from that experiment's bungling – thereby, unleashing, on an unsuspecting populace, a 'dirty dozen' (or is it an anti-apostolic cache?) of *uber*-vampires, *The Passage* fast-forwards ninety-two years into the future, now a bleak dystopian wasteland, North America having long been overrun – and depopulated – by 'the Twelve' and their multitudinous 'viral' progeny. Scattered throughout, however, are remnants of human civilisation, such as the Californian First Colony, whose survivors are hunkered down close to an abandoned power station, the lights of which – up to now, their salvation, warding off the vampiric 'jumps' – are, alas, failing. Still retaining traces of humanity, but with tremendously enhanced physical and psychic strength, the death-defying Amy wanders, one day, into this compound; and, from that point on, devotes herself to assisting the escape of these colonists, acting as their guide in the long and dangerous trek through the Southwest to Texas, with the intention of reuniting them there with other survivors who have formed a nascent sovereign state. On such a parlous exodus, Amy has no choice but to slay her own kind – but, unlike Buffy, whose dispatch of vampires had the finality of a Judge Dredd-like execution (not for nothing does she announce, Stallone-style, in Season 7, 'I am the Law')' (*BtVS*, 2004, Episode 5, Season 7) Amy's terminations are depicted as merciful rather than murderous, greeted by their victims as not only a blessed release but a welcomed restoration of identity.

For Amy, as the 'Girl with the Souls Inside Her'[65] can hear the collective cry of anguish of the vampiric multitude: 'Who am I who am I who am I?',[66] they call. To which, she responds 'You are . . . Smith. You are . . . Tate. You are . . . Duprey. You are Erie you are Ramos you are Ward you are Cho you are Singh';[67] and, so it goes, Amy luring the undead into the sunset, and their final – and joyful – oblivion through combustion.

Yet this 'true death' – to adopt the idiom of *True Blood* – allows these vampires to *live again* by reclaiming, at the very moment of their expiry, their long-lost humanity. By delivering this life-in-death, or death-in-life, Amy not only renews *lex vampirica*, she resacralises it, in fact '(re)christianises' it – though in terms that are anything but orthodox. What is this sacred law that Amy lays down? Surely, it is none other than a law of love which shows all the signs of a Christian theology in reverse: one that brings everlasting *death*, the repeated delivery of which turns Amy, as a *vampiric* vampire slayer, into a very christological Anti-Christ – *La Christa*? – who 'saves' all of us from the curse that a profane alliance of science, technology and policy are bringing about, not just in *The Passage*, but in the darkly 'interesting times' in which we, its readers, live. Specifically, the truly ghoulish prospect of the 'life everlasting' realised by, variously, genome projects, cloning initiatives and the new neurosciences, all here allegorised – at least, in its defeat of death – as vampirism. I make this claim because, despite the 'having it all' brouhaha of *True Blood*, *Twilight* and other like-minded popular fictions – with their undead depicted as forever young, sexually attractive, invincibly strong, and so on, vampires are, first and foremost, the exemplary figures illustrating the perils of too much life, damned for an eternity precisely because they are outside time, without end, infinite. If ever there was a case of *contra naturam*, then it is this species whose lack of mortality defies physical finitude, *the* universal 'law of nature'. As such, vampires – especially those redeemed in *The Passage* – should summon up a radically new and reconstituted natural law that would sublate but, nonetheless, go *through* rights and duties.

Unlike, however, the unlimited dominion promised humanity, historically, by theological natural law, or the boundless progress assured us, at present, by biological natural law, the law in question here would be very much a *dutiful* one of limits, of boundaries, of what we can and cannot do; yet, in so doing, it would solicit a new morality of *Recht*, of *right* – to surcease, to ends – capable of confronting, even managing the overriding legal, as well as philosophical, scientific, religious, political and cultural issues that vampirism knots together, emblematically: not just that of gender difference (male/female) or, even, ontic alternatives (alive/dead), but the core metaphysical problem of being and

65 Justin Cronin, *The Passage* (Orion Books, 2010) 721.
66 Ibid.
67 Ibid.

nothingness – and, with it, the possibility of a *jouissance* (a transcendent letting go) beyond *jouissance* (vitalist pleasure-in-pain). Not that *The Passage* or, for that matter, any other vampire fiction has any easy prescriptions here; however, I do conclude with, and urge upon my readers this proviso: that as to *lex vampirica's* potential reimagination of the law, socio-legality and jurisprudence, we adopt an attitude of openness that continues to invite the undead – and the abundant popular legal fictions about them – to come calling on us, regularly and routinely. But, equally, that we assume an air of discrimination towards this myriad of vampiric metaphors (Bill/Sookie, Edward/Bella, Wolgast/Amy), and the juridical models which they instantiate (rights, duties, love), that confront us on both page and screen. So that at the end of the day, as the sun sets, night falls and the hour of the vampire looms, we are quite sure that, after having rendered judgement, *we let the right one in.*

Bibliography

Textual

Barron, Ann, 'The Illusions of the I: Citizenship and the Politics of Identity' in Alan Norrie (ed.), *Closure and Critique: New Directions in Legal Theory* (Edinburgh University Press, 1993) 80

Berns, Sandra, 'Women in English Legal History: Subject (Almost), Object (Irrevocably), Person (Not Quite)' (1994) 12 *University of Tasmania Law Review* 26

Cain, Brian, Gregg Hale and David Wohl, *True Blood: The Great Revelation* (Top Cow Publishing, 2008)

Cronin, Justin, *The Passage* (Orion Books, 2010)

Cronin, Justin, *The Twelve* (Orion Books, 2010)

Douzinas, Costas, 'The Paradoxes of Human Rights' (2013) 20 (1) *Constellations* 51

Evans, Dylan, *An Introductory Dictionary of Lacanian Psychoanalysis* (Routledge, 1996)

Fink, Bruce, *Lacanian Psychoanalysis: Theory and Technique* (Harvard University Press, 1997)

Freud, Sigmund, 'Notes upon a Case of Obsessional Neurosis' in Anna Freud (collab), *The Standard Edition of the Complete Psychological Works of Sigmund Freud, Vol 10* (James Strachey trans) (Hogarth, 1955) vol 10, 151–318

Harris, Charlaine, *A True Blood Omnibus* (Gollancz, 2009a)

– *Dead as a Doornail* (Gollancz, 2009b)

– *Definitely Dead* (Gollancz, 2009c)

– *All Together Dead* (Gollancz, 2009d)

– *From Dead to Worse* (Gollancz, 2010a)

– *Dead and Gone* (Gollanncz, 2010b)

– *A Touch of Dead* (Gollancz, 2010c)

– *Dead in the Family* (Gollancz, 2011)

– *Dead Reckoning* Gollancz, 2012)

– *Deadlocked* (Gollancz, 2013)

– *Dead Ever After* (Gollancz, 2014)

Jarvis, Christine, 'The *Twilight* of Feminism? Stephenie Meyer's Saga and the Contradictions of Contemporary Girlhood' (2014) 45 *Children's Literature in Education* 101

Kokkola, Lydia, 'Virtuous Vampires and Voluptuous Vamps: Romance Conventions Reconsidered in Stephenie Meyer's *Twilight* Series' (2011) 42 *Children's Literature in Education* 162
Lacan, Jacques, 'The Neurotic's Individual Myth' (1979) 48 *Psychoanalytic Quarterly* 405
Lacan, Jacques, *The Seminar of Jacques Lacan, Book III, The Psychoses, 1955–1956* (Jacques Miller (ed.), Russell Grigg trans with notes, W W Norton & Co, 1993)
Lacan, Jacques, *The Seminar of Jacques Lacan, Book VII, The Ethics of Psychoanalysis, 1959–1960* (Jacques Miller (ed.), Dennis Porter trans with notes, W W Norton & Co, 1992)
Laurent, Eric, 'The Name of the Father: Psychoanalysis and Democracy' (2006) 1 (7) *Lacanian Compass: Psychoanalytic Newsletter of Lacanian Orientation* www.lacaniancompass.com/s/lacanian_compass_71.pdf
Lipovetsky, Gilles, *Le Crepuscule du Devoir* (Gallimard, 1992)
MacNeil, William, 'Enjoy Your Rights!: Three Cases from the Postcolonial Commonwealth' (1997) 9 *Public Culture* 377
MacNeil, William, 'Law's *Corpus Delicti:* The Fantasmatic Body of Rights Discourse' (1998) 9 *Law and Critique* 37
MacNeil, William, 'Taking Rights Symptomatically: *Jouissance, coupure, object petit a*' (1999) 8 (1) *Griffith Law Review* 134
Meyer, Stephenie, *Twilight* (Atom, 2009a)
– *New Moon* (Atom, 2009b)
– *Eclipse*, Atom (2009c)
– *Breaking Dawn* (Atom, 2009d)
Miller, Jacques-Alain, 'H2O: Suture in Obsessionality' (2003) 4 (Spring) *The Symptom: On-line Journal for Lacan.com*
Miller, Jacques-Alain, 'Suture: Elements of the Logic of the Signifier' (2007) 8 (Winter) *The Symptom: On-line Journal for Lacan.com* (Jacqueline Rose trans)
Riviere, Joan, 'Womanliness as Masquerade' in V Burgin, J Donald and C Caplan (eds), *Formations of Fantasy* (Routledge, 1986) 35
Salecl, Renata, 'Woman as Symptom of Rights' (1993) 12 (2) *Topoi* 89
Salecl, Renata, 'Love and Sexual Difference: Doubled Partners in Men and Women' in Renata Salecl (ed.), *Sexuation*, (Duke University Press, 2000)
Silver, Anna, '*Twilight* is Not Good for Maidens: Gender, Sexuality, and the Family in Stephenie Meyer's *Twilight* Series' (2010) 42 (1) *Studies in the Novel* 121
Taylor, Anthea, 'The Urge Toward Love is an Urge Towards (Un)Death: Romance, Masochistic Desire and Postfeminism in the *Twilight* Novels' (2012) 15 (1) *International Journal of Cultural Studies* 31
Wright, Elizabeth with Dianne Chisholm, J F MacCannell and Margaret Whitford (eds), *Feminism and Psychoanalysis: A Critical Dictionary* (Basil Blackwell, 1992)
Young, Alison, '*Caveat Sponsa*: Violence and the Body in Law' in S Rice and J Brettle (eds), *Public Bodies, Private States* (Manchester University Press, 1994)

Film, television, music and other media

'Bad Things', Song, 2006, on *Jace Everett*, Sony, CD, performed by Jace Everett
'Interview with Charlaine Harris' 2009, On-Line Radio Interview, 'The Author Hour – Your Guide to Fantastic Fiction', TheAuthorHour.com. [19 November 2009]
Buffy the Vampire Slayer – The Complete Seventh Season 2004, DVD, WB Television Network, USA

- 'Selfless', Episode 5, Season 7, wr Drew Goddard, dir David Soloman

True Blood: The Complete First Season 2009, DVD, prods, Alan Ball and Greg Feinberg, Warner Bros Entertainment Australia Pty Ltd

- Episode 2, 'The First Taste', wr Alan Ball, dir Scott Winant
- Episode 3, 'Mine', wr Alan Ball, dir John Dahl
- Episode 7, 'Burning House of Love', wr Chris Offutt, dir Marcos Siega

True Blood: The Complete Second Season 2010, DVD, prods, Alan Ball and Greg Feinberg, Warner Bros Entertainment Australia Pty Ltd Australia

- Episode 4, 'Shake and Fingerpop', wr Alan Ball, dir Michael Lehmann
- Episode 7, 'Release Me', wr Raelle Tucker, dir Michael Ruscio
- Episode 8, 'Timebomb', wr Alexander Woo, dir John Dahl
- Episode 9, 'I Will Rise Up', wr Nancy Oliver, dir Scott Winant
- Episode 10, 'New World in My View', wr Kate Barnow and Elisabeth Finch, dir by Adam Davidson
- Episode 11, 'Frenzy', wr Alan Ball, dir Daniel Minahan
- Episode 12, 'Beyond Here Lies Nothing', wr Alexander Woo, dir Michael Cuesta

True Blood: The Complete Third Season 2011, DVD, prods, Alan Ball and Greg Feinberg, Warner Bros Entertainment Australia Pty Ltd

- Episode 2, 'Beautifully Broken', wr Raelle Tucker, dir Scott Winant
- Episode 6, 'I Got the Right to Sing the Blues', wr Alan Ball, dir Michael Lehmann
- Episode 9, 'Everything is Broken', wr Alexander Woo, dir Scott Winant
- Episode 12, 'Evil is Going On', wr Alan Ball, dir Anthony Hemingway

True Blood: The Complete Fourth Season 2012, DVD, prods, Alan Ball and Greg Feinberg, Warner Bros Entertainment Australia Pty Ltd

- Episode 2, 'You Smell Like Dinner', wr Brian Buckner, dir Scott Winant
- Episode 3, 'If You Love Me, Why Am I Dyin'?', wr Alan Ball, dir David Petrarca
- Episode 12, 'And When I Die', wr Raelle Tucker, dir Scott Winant

True Blood: The Complete Fifth Season 2012a, DVD, prods, Alan Ball and Greg Feinberg, Warner Bros Entertainment Australia Pty Ltd

True Blood: The Complete Sixth Season 2014, DVD, prods, Alan Ball, Greg Feinberg, Alexander Woo and Brian Buckner, Warner Bros Entertainment Australia Pty Ltd

- Episode 1, 'Who Are You Really?', wr Raelle Tucker, dir Stephen Moyer

True Blood 2014a, TV programme, Series 7, Episode 5, 'Lost Cause', Craig Chester (wr), Howard Deutch (dir), HBO/Showtime, Australia [aired 20 July 2014]

True Blood 2014b, TV programme, Season 7, Episode 4, 'Death is Not the End', Gregg Feinberg (wr), Daniel Kenneth (dir), HBO/Showtime, Australia [aired 13 July 2014]

True Blood 2014c, TV programme, Season 7, Episode 10, 'Thank You', Brian Buckner (wr), Scott Winant (dir), HBO/Showtime, Australia [aired 24 August 2014]

Twilight 2009, DVD, dir Catherine Hardwick, Sony Pictures Home Entertainment Australia

The Twilight Saga: New Moon 2010, DVD, dir Chris Weitz, Summit Entertainment

The Twilight Saga: Eclipse 2010, DVD, dir David Slade, Summit Entertainment LLC

The Twilight Saga: Breaking Dawn – Part 1 2012, DVD, dir Bill Condon, Summit Entertainment LLC

The Twilight Saga: Breaking Dawn – Part 2 2013, DVD, dir Bill Condon, Summit Entertainment LLC

Westboro Baptist Church Home Page, www.godhatesfags.com.

Chapter 12

Reading the law made strange

Cultural legal studies, theology and speculative fiction

Timothy D Peters[1]

Introduction

In the 2013 re-boot of the Superman film franchise, *Man of Steel*, the Kryptonian General Zod threatens the destruction of Earth if humanity does not turn Kal-El (Clark Kent/Superman) over to him.[2] With a 24-hour time limit imposed, Kal-El weighs up whether or not he should acquiesce to Zod's request. Before making this momentous decision – not only whether to turn himself over to Zod, but also to reveal to the world that he is an alien who has been living among them for 33 years – Kal-El visits a church seeking guidance from the priest who is mopping the floors of the empty church building. The interaction between the priest and Kal-El makes little reference to God, Christianity and religion, except to suggest that, in Kal-El's hesitancy to trust the people of Earth with his secret, a 'leap of faith' is sometimes required first with trust coming later. The dichotomy of this scene, a 'man' of incredible power seeking the advice of a priest who appears somewhat unsure of himself, is amplified, however, by the background images and setting – in particular the stained-glass windows of this little country church. Behind Kal-El, when he is asking for advice, the viewer sees a window depicting Christ praying in the Garden of Gethsemane prior to the crucifixion. The resonances of this scene draw out in exceptional detail elements that have been within the superhero mythos since its origins: that of seeing Superman as a Christological or messianic figure with his coming to earth, sent by his 'heavenly' father (Jor-El), as embodying both *divinity* in terms of super-strength, X-Ray vision and the ability to fly with his very *human* appearances,

1 Many thanks to Dr Edwin Bikundo, Dr Karen Crawley, Dr Kieran Tranter and Professor William MacNeil for their insightful comments, feedback and suggestions on this chapter. Thanks also to Associate Professor Marett Leiboff and Dr Cassandra Sharp for both the opportunity to participate in the symposium 'Cultural Legal Studies Methodology Wherefore Art Thou?' and the invitation to contribute to this edited collection.

2 *Man of Steel* (Directed by Zack Snyder, Warner Brothers Pictures, 2013).

emotional struggles and desire to fit in.[3] *Man of Steel* heightens these references with this scene of contemplation and reflection representing Christ's fervent prayers before giving himself up to be crucified. When Kal-El presents himself to the US Army in the following scene he does so lifted up in the air with arms stretched wide, reflecting an image of Christ crucified. As such, *Man of Steel* situates itself within the Christian tradition and presents the archetypal superhero as a Christological-saviour come to save humanity.[4] In doing so, it raises a theological question about trust and faith – not so much about whether humanity should believe in, trust or have faith in God, but rather whether humanity can be trusted. What will humanity do with their saviour – receive and welcome or condemn and crucify?

This theological question is counterpoised in the climactic scene of the film where Zod, having lost all hope of gaining control of earth and building a new Krypton to replace the destroyed original, battles it out with Kal-El. Zod (who is now equally matched to Kal-El in every way), enraged by Kal-El's decision to protect humanity rather than see Krypton re-born, threatens to kill a number of innocent people caught in the battle as an attempt to spite Kal-El by making him watch them die. In a final moment of anguish Kal-El, in contradiction of over 80 years of comic book history, breaks Zod's neck and kills him. Superman, as the archetypal superhero – a figure of law, justice and the social order – traditionally refrains from taking a decision to kill his enemy, preferring to see him or her restrained (whether in jail or elsewhere). This scene, designed specifically to shock, goes in the end to a legal question, which sits alongside the theological question raised earlier: a question of judgment. Positioned as a supposed 'necessary act' of preventative violence – necessary because of Zod's threat to the innocent victims; supposed because, as with all 'necessary acts', there were other options (such as flying away with Zod in his arms, or taking the fight out of the city) – the film presents Kal-El's decision as an act of judgment and execution combined (Kal-El renders punishment for Zod's 'crimes against humanity'). What does it say that a film that has such strong references to Superman as a Christ-figure presents him engaging in the ultimate act of judgment by executing someone without trial or recourse to the law?

3 The Christological aspects of the filmic representations of Superman have been central since Richard Donner's *Superman: The Movie* (Directed by Richard Donner, Dovemead Films, 1978) and were developed, in particular, by Bryan Singer's *Superman Returns* (Directed by Bryan Singer, Warner Bros, 2006). See Ken Schenck, 'Superman: A Popular Culture Messiah' in BJ Oropeza (ed.), *The Gospel According to Superheroes: Religion and Popular Culture* (Peter Lang, 2005) 33; Adam Barkman, 'Superman: From Anti-Christ to Christ-Type' in Mark D White (ed.), *Superman and Philosophy: What Would the Man of Steel Do?* (John Wiley & Sons, 2013) 111.

4 Thus reflecting Grant Morrison's description of Superman as an 'American Christ': Grant Morrison, 143 *Wizard: The Comics Magazine* #143, 1 August 2003 180; Schenck, above n 3.

The foregoing visual and narratological analysis of *Man of Steel's* dramatic climax highlights the way in which texts of popular culture – and in particular speculative fiction (science fiction, fantasy, superheroes) – give rise to questions of what could be called legal theology or theological jurisprudence. This chapter seeks to identify a mode of analysing such instantiations of popular culture's theo-legality. This is not simply to identify an American form of Christianity that embraces the treatment of *Man of Steel* identified above, but rather to identify within the realms of popular culture itself resources for thinking through the theological aspects of law and our legal imaginary. Section 2 situates this approach in terms of the recent return to theology in critical theory, political science and jurisprudence as providing resources to understand and illuminate modern law and politics. This return calls into question the presumed secularity and neutrality of modern law, identifying that despite its attempts to relegate religion to either a historical antecedent long forgotten, or simply to an aspect of the private domain to be regulated and protected, that law itself remains caught in the theological. However, the theological aspects of modern law are often opaque and, as such, this chapter proposes that cultural legal studies' engagement with popular culture and speculative fiction provides a means for rendering visible the theological concepts of modern law. Section 3 draws on William MacNeil's intertextual jurisprudence and method of 'reading jurisprudentially' as an approach to cultural texts that, on the surface, have little to do with law or legality but which, on closer examination, unlock latent jurisprudential arguments. Section 4 examines the genres of speculative fiction as genres of estrangement that 'make strange' both the worlds they imagine and their representations of law, legality and justice. Section 5 explores, following Alison Milbank's analysis of G.K. Chesterton and J.R.R. Tolkien, the theological and world-envisaging nature of speculative fiction and the world-creating nature of law. Section 6 concludes by identifying the use of estrangement itself as a mode of cultural legal reading – one that renders visible the latent theologies of law and, at the same time, provides a space for imagining them differently.

Law and the theological (re)turn

We live in a world of law and legality, not just in the sense of the globalisation of the rule of law and the infiltration of legalistic thinking into all realms of life,[5] but in the sense of what Robert Cover called in 1983 a *nomos* – a normative universe where we 'constantly create and maintain a world of right and wrong, of lawful and unlawful, of valid and void.'[6] The formal institutions of law and

5 John L Comaroff, 'Reflections on the Rise of Legal Theology: Law and Religion in the Twenty-First Century' (2009) 53 *Social Analysis* 193, 193–196.

6 Robert M Cover, 'The Supreme Court, 1982 Term – Forward: Nomos and Narrative' (1983) 97 *Harvard Law Review* 4, 4.

justice form but a small part of this normative universe and it is only when they are situated within the 'narratives that locate [them] and give [them] meaning'[7] that we can understand their role. Yet the narratives that give rise to this *nomos* come from a range of sources and are not limited to the institutions represented by most forms of legal positivism in terms of the relationship between the individual and the state. This chapter argues that the stories told within popular culture – and in particular the forms of speculative fiction so favoured by Hollywood in recent times – both inform our concepts of law, legality and justice but also put those concepts into question, 'making strange' our traditional understanding so that we can see them anew.

If our understanding of law and the meaning that is constructed within it is caught up with the narratives we tell about it, then our modern concept of law is captured within what Mark Lilla describes as the fairy tales of modernity.[8] To describe modernity in relation to fairy tales seems to be somewhat paradoxical given modernity's significant distaste for myth, superstition and fantasy. Yet, the movements of modernity themselves – including those of modern law – are caught within a narrative mythos. As Peter Fitzpatrick has described it, modernity is mythic – it is the myth of being without myth.[9] In *The Stillborn God* Mark Lilla describes the stories that we tell ourselves about how our world came to be, including terms such as 'modernization, secularization, democratization [and] the "disenchantment of the world,"' as the 'fairy tales of our time'.[10] He argues that we should not see secularism and liberalism in our modern political situation as inevitable and irrevocable but rather as experimental and fragile – and having an urgent need to be nurtured and maintained. At the same time, Lilla's description of modernity is premised on a particular story that is seen as essential to modernity and modern law: the separation of theology from secular politics, religion from secular law, the church from the state. He describes his work not as a fairy tale but as about an 'intellectual rebellion against political theology in the West'[11] – an intellectual rebellion premised on the 'great separation' of theology and politics as the foundation of modernity and the modern state. The narratives of modern law are thus considered within this story of modernity identifying the 'immanence' of modern law (as opposed to its 'transcendence') with terms such as objectivity, secularity, rationality and neutrality. While acknowledging the role of religion and theology in its history, the dominant narratives of modern secular law operate alongside those of modernity and secularisation, relegating religion and theology to the private domain and minimising their role in the 'public sphere'. The 'secularisation

7 Ibid.
8 Mark Lilla, *The Stillborn God: Religion, Politics and the Modern West* (Knopf, 2007) 6.
9 Peter Fitzpatrick, *The Mythology of Modern Law* (Routledge, 1992) ix.
10 Lilla, above n 8.
11 Ibid.

thesis' presupposed the co-development of modernity and secularity, believing that modern development would undermine the need for, and authority of, religion and theology.[12] In recent years, however, the 'return of religion' (a term which seems to assume that religion has been away somewhere – exiled or on vacation) has seen the secularisation thesis come into disrepute and discussions of various forms of what has been described as the 'post-secular'. If the narratives of modern law include a presumption of its secularity, what might a post-secular law look like?

Max Weber's famous description of modernity as a 'disenchantment of the world' meant, for law, the move from primitive forms of law based on faith, magic and divination to modern bureaucratic and rationalistic forms based on universally applied rules and procedures.[13] As such:

> The separation of the state and of its various institutions, including law, from religion, and with this the religious neutrality of the state (and the political neutering of religion), has been conceived as not only central to the emergence of this new order, but also necessary for its preservation and for the achievement of the justice that it is supposed to guarantee.[14]

Scholars in recent years, however, have identified both the sustained influence of the theological, religious and sacred on modern 'secular' law. In his extensive history of the theological origins of Western law, Harold Berman argues that 'Western legal science is a secular theology, which often makes no sense because its theological presuppositions are no longer accepted.'[15] He goes on to note that:

> . . . the legal system of all Western countries, and of all non-Western countries that have come under the influence of Western law, are a secular residue of religious attitudes and assumptions which historically found expression first in the liturgy and rituals and doctrine of the church and thereafter in the institutions and concepts and values of the law. When these historical

12 See Jürgen Habermas, 'Secularism's Crisis of Faith: Notes on Post-Secular Society' (2008) 25 *New Perspectives Quarterly* 17, 17–18.

13 See Max Weber, *Economy and Society: An Outline of Interpretive Sociology* (University of California Press, 1978) 882; M D A Freeman, *Lloyd's Introduction to Jurisprudence* (Sweet & Maxwell, 8th edn, 2008) 839–842.

14 Winnifred Fallers Sullivan, Robert A Yelle and Mateo Taussig-Rubbo, 'Introduction' in Winnifred Fallers Sullivan, Robert A Yelle and Mateo Taussig-Rubbo (eds), *After Secular Law* (Stanford University Press, 2011) 1.

15 Harold J Berman, *Law and Revolution: The Formation of the Western Legal Tradition* (Harvard University Press, 1983) 165.

roots are not understood, many parts of the law appear to lack any underlying source of vitality.[16]

As such, our 'modern' conceptions of law, justice and judgment are drawn from theological underpinnings.[17] This complements Fitzpatrick's point, noted above, that modern law encompasses a form of mythology, sharing 'origins and a sustaining dynamic with the general mythology of modernity.'[18] That is, modern law's premise of being a separate, secular enterprise (in contrast to the religious or mythic 'other') in itself embodies the mythic and religious structures it seeks to reject.[19] Much of the work on law and religion follows this premise in identifying that 'law serves a social and cultural role analogous to that served by religion.'[20] Furthermore, the 'gesture of separation between religion and law', as Sullivan, Yelle and Taussig-Rubbo note, 'echoes, ironically, a fundamental concern of religion to distinguish between the "sacred and the profane", suggesting the closeness between sacred and secular modes of thought precisely at the point at which they are believed to be most distinct.'[21] Law itself encompasses modes of the religious. Despite the persistence of ritual in contemporary legal institutions, modern law is also seen as a product of an effort of de-ritualisation: the modern emphasis is on substantive law and legal realism over formalism and a disparaging of ancient modes of law as irrational or 'magical thinking'.[22] Yet, the supposed separation of law and religion is fraught with

16 Ibid, 166. See also Rick Mohr, 'The Christian Origins of Secularism and the Rule of Law' in Rick Mohr and Nadirsyah Hosen (eds), *Law and Religion in Public Life: The Contemporary Debate* (Routledge, 2011) 34.

17 Berman, above n 15, 171–185.

18 Fitzpatrick, above n 9, x.

19 Ibid; Sullivan, Yelle and Taussig-Rubbo, above n 14, 6. Fitzpatrick's more recent work furthers this connection between theology and law. See Peter Fitzpatrick, 'Legal Theology: Law, Modernity and the Sacred' (2009) 32 *Seattle University Law Review* 321.

20 Sullivan, Yelle and Taussig-Rubbo, above n 14, 3. See, e.g., Troy Harris-Abbot, 'On Law and Theology' (1990) 35 *The American Journal of Jurisprudence* 105; Martin E Marty, 'The Religious Foundations of Law' (2005) 54 *Emory Law Journal* 291; Cassandra Sharp, 'Religion and Justice: Atonement as an Element of Justice in Both Western Law and Christian Thought' in Rick Mohr and Nadirsyah Hosen (eds), *Law and Religion in Public Life: The Contemporary Debate* (Routledge, 2011) 151; Joshua Neoh, 'Text, Doctrine and Tradition in Law and Religion' (2013) 2 *Oxford Journal of Law and Religion* 175.

21 Sullivan, Yelle and Taussig-Rubbo, above n 14, 3, quoting David Kennedy, 'Images of Religion in International Legal Theory' in Mark W Janis and Carolyn Evans (eds), *Religion and International Law* (Martinus Nijhoff, 1999) 145.

22 Max Weber's tracing of secularisation to developments in Western Christianity during and after the Protestant Revolution famously identified society as becoming 'disenchanted' in the sense of being 'liberated from magic and personal charisma, as well as ritual formalism.' Sullivan, Yelle and Taussig-Rubbo, above n 14, 5. See Max Weber, *The Protestant Work Ethic and the Spirit of Capitalism* (Talcott Parsons trans, Charles Scribner's Sons, 1958).

problems and modern law itself remains caught within the sacred, religious and theological.[23] As such, the secularity of modern law is called into question.[24]

This insight gains greater significance when considered in light of the resurgence of interest in the concepts of political theology. At one level, such interest comes in terms of the theocratic claims to involvement in politics of what Jose Casanova calls 'public religions'.[25] This view of political theology retains the inherent modern sense of separation between fundamentalist theocracy on one side and secular democracy on the other. At a more fundamental level, however, are approaches to political theology that follow (in some form or another) Carl Schmitt's proclamation that 'all significant concepts of the modern theory of the state are secularised theological concepts.'[26] On this view, political theology is not so much a separate enterprise to modern secular politics and law, but rather the only way to understand modern politics itself.[27] That is, theology is the means for understanding the political. Giorgio Agamben's work in particular, drawing on Schmitt and Walter Benjamin (among others), uncovers the theological roots and concepts that underpin our modern political predicament.[28] Following Jacob Taubes' *The Political Theology of Paul*, other critical theorists have (re)turned to the writings of Saint Paul as fundamental texts of the Western tradition that need to be reclaimed, resituated and 'fought for', even in their process of being overcome.[29] In theology itself, the movement operating under the moniker 'Radical Orthodoxy', draws on traditional

23 For a discussion of an approach to 'law and theology' that is along these lines see Paul Babie, 'Breaking the Silence: Law, Theology and Religion in Australia' (2007) 31 *Melbourne University Law Review* 296.

24 See Mohr, above n 16.

25 Jose Casanova, *Public Religions in the Modern World* (The University of Chicago Press, 1994). For a variety of approaches to the interactions of law and religion in terms of political theology see: Hent de Vries and Lawrence E Sullivan (eds), *Political Theologies: Public Religions in a Post-Secular World* (Fordham University Press, 2006); Thomas G Kirsch and Bertram Turner, *Permutations of Order: Religion and Law as Contested Sovereignties* (Ashgate, 2009).

26 Carl Schmitt, *Political Theology: Four Chapters on the Concept of Sovereignty* (The University of Chicago Press, 2005) 35.

27 See, e.g., Paul Kahn, *Political Theology: Four New Chapters on the Concept of Sovereignty* (Columbia University Press, 2011); Clayton Crockett (ed.), *Religion and Violence in a Secular World: Toward a New Political Theology* (University of Virginia Press, 2006); de Vries and Sullivan, above n 25.

28 As Agamben notes: 'Modernity, removing God from the world, has not only failed to leave theology behind, but in some ways has done nothing other than to lead the project of the providential *oikonomia* to completion'. Giorgio Agamben, *The Kingdom and the Glory: For a Theological Genealogy of Economy and Government* (Stanford University Press, 2011), 287.

29 See Jacob Taubes, *The Political Theology of Paul* (Dana Hollander trans, Stanford University Press, 2004); Alain Badiou, *Saint Paul: The Foundations of Universalism* (Ray Brassier trans, Stanford University Press, 2003); Slavoj Žižek, *The Fragile Absolute – Or, Why is the Christian Legacy Worth Fighting For?* (Verso, 2000); Giorgio Agamben, *The Time That Remains: A Commentary on the Letter to the Romans* (Patricia Dailey trans, Stanford University Press, 2005).

theological sources to challenge the variety of modern and post-modern presuppositions of the division between theology and the secular.[30] John Milbank and Graham Ward, for example, both identify not only the theological origins and precursors of modernity but the way in which modernity itself is theological.[31] That is, the construction of modernity and secular social theory is always defined *against* or in terms of theology and can thus only be understood *as* a form of theology.[32]

In this sense, despite the presumed separation of theology and the secular, and, more specifically religion and law, theology has returned as a discourse *du jour*, at least so far as it can be used for an increased understanding of the immanent working of the state, politics and law. At the same time, the theological aspects of modern law are not always clear or visible. Agamben's work, for example, undertakes a laborious genealogical process to uncover the influence of such theological concepts. This chapter seeks to further the turn to the resources of theology as a way of understanding and re-thinking modern law. It identifies, however, that such resources find their illumination and engagement not simply within theoretical texts, political tracts or jurisprudential treatises. Rather, the turn to theology also provides a means of seeing the world as illuminated in a variety of ways, some of which include the many creative acts that go to co-create and constitute our world and which produce our social and legal imaginary and *nomos*. That is, theology is found in art as much as reason, and a theological account and critique of law needs to look to cultural texts as much as legal ones for its elaboration. Such creative works include (though are of course not limited to) the artefacts of popular culture that (albeit commercialised and reified by corporations and capitalism) contribute to the narratives via which we encounter the world. My argument is that the narratives of popular culture themselves provide the space for re-encountering and re-imagining law and its theology anew. As such, I argue for a turning away from the traditional canon of law and literature and the traditional genres of the 'law film' encompassing representations of lawyers, judges, trials and court scenes and rather engage in constructing a theological jurisprudence of *speculative* fiction – of superheroes, science fiction, mythic quests, fantastic stories and fairy tales.

30 John Milbank, Catherine Pickstock and Graham Ward (eds), *Radical Orthodoxy: A New Theology* (Routledge, 1999).

31 See John Milbank, *Theology and Social Theory: Beyond Secular Reason* (Blackwell, 1990) 3. See also Graham Ward, *Cities of God* (Routledge, 2000).

32 Even a cursory reading of Hobbes' *Leviathan*, which Mark Lilla takes to be a founding text of modernity and the inauguration of the 'great separation' between secular and religious in politics, identifies that Hobbes is engaging and responding to theology, as well as constructing his own. See Lilla, above n 8 (2007). See John Milbank, above n 31, ch 1.

Cultural legal studies as intertextual jurisprudence

The traditional focus of the disciplines of 'law and literature' and 'law and film' has been on what could be termed the socio-legal analysis of the representations of law, legal institutions and legal actors in cultural texts. In contrast to such methodologies, Professor William MacNeil has been progressing an approach that engages popular culture texts as a source for re-reading the traditional canon of jurisprudence. Articulating a method of analysis he entitles 'reading jurisprudentially', MacNeil explores popular culture (in the forms of literature, film and television – at times, all at once), bringing cultural texts into dialogue with theoretical texts of jurisprudence.[33] The focus of this analysis is not so much on the empirical identifying of how popular culture represents law, but that popular culture has something to say about law and legal theory itself. To do this he explores texts that do not appear to be about the law at all: *Buffy the Vampire Slayer*, *Harry Potter*, *The Lord of the Rings* (both Tolkien's and Jackson's), *Fight Club* and *Minority Report*.[34] Through a series of close readings he then identifies that these fictional and cultural narratives not only inform popular concepts of justice, rights and rules, but rather re-present, re-think and re-signify jurisprudence itself. As he outlines in *Lex Populi: The Jurisprudence of Popular Culture*, the process of 'reading jurisprudentially' develops and constructs a new intertext – a text between texts – out of both cultural texts and jurisprudence.[35] This method of 'intertextual jurisprudence' privileges the process of reading as much as the texts under consideration and it is this close reading of the texts that enables one to see them anew. He identifies that the strength of this mediation of law through fiction is that 'it produces not just mutually illuminating readings, but an alternative intertext' one which 'synthesizes, sublates . . . and enables us, in turn, to look at "the legal" and "the literary" *otherwise* – as a site of discursive difference rather than binary stasis, of theoretical inquiry rather than socio-legal representation.'[36]

In his most recent book, *Novel Judgements*, where he provides a more programmatic outline of the process of 'reading jurisprudentially', MacNeil turns to literature, in particular the novels of the nineteenth century as the 'privileged *and popular* medium of its era.'[37] The focus on a particular time period is not a

33 See William P MacNeil, *Lex Populi: The Jurisprudence of Popular Culture* (Stanford University Press, 2007) 1–2, 155–156; William P MacNeil, *Novel Judgements: Legal Theory as Fiction* (Routledge, 2012) 12–20.

34 See MacNeil, *Lex Populi*, above n 33, chs 1, 2, 3, 4, 5.

35 Ibid, 2.

36 William P MacNeil, 'One Recht to Rule Them All! Law's Empire in the Age of Empire' (2004) 34 *Studies in Law, Politics and Society* 279, 280. See also MacNeil, *Lex Populi*, above n 33, 155–156.

37 MacNeil, *Novel Judgements*, above n 33, 9.

move towards so much the historicity of the texts, but rather an analysis of what MacNeil describes as their deep structure:

> For what these deep structural depths reveal, once plumbed, is a different scene of explication, an alternative site of understanding; namely, a subtext of jurisprudence and legal philosophical import that releases rather than fixes meaning.[38]

MacNeil's process of 'reading jurisprudentially' is able to take what seems to be certain tropes of the cultural text and via an unpacking in relation to jurisprudence, develop a new way of seeing not only the cultural text, but jurisprudence itself. That is, instead of simply seeing pop culture as a representation of law or an allegory of justice, he identifies the way in which pop culture *re-reads* law and legal theory.

MacNeil's approach to reading cultural texts is thus unique in two respects. First, it identifies that texts that do not specifically engage in representations of law, the legal system or even traditional representations of crime or justice as their central focus, are still potentially sources of jurisprudential analysis. Texts from speculative genres such as fantasy, science fiction and the Gothic have as much, if not more, to say about law and legal theory that is of worth than many of the texts traditionally explored by law and popular culture scholarship. In this sense, a number of scholars have taken up MacNeil's project engaging in forms of jurisprudential analyses of science fiction, comic books and superheroes, and even role-playing games.[39] The second unique aspect is the approach to the text itself. MacNeil treats the text not simply as providing an insight into what people think about law but, through the text's modes of storytelling, its tropes, stylistic turns and plot devices, provides the possibility for re-thinking and 'doing' jurisprudence. This construction of an intertextual jurisprudence elevates the status of the cultural text to theoretical work that can re-sign, re-signify and re-imagine traditional understandings of law and jurisprudence

38 Ibid, 11.

39 See, eg, Kieran Tranter, '"Frakking Toasters" and Jurisprudences of Technology: The Exception, the Subject and Techne in *Battlestar Galactica*' (2007) 19 *Law and Literature* 45; Peter J Hutchings, 'From Offworld Colonies to Migration Zones: *Blade Runner* and the Fractured Subject of Jurisprudence' (2007) 3 *Law, Culture and the Humanities* 381; Timothy D Peters, '"The Force" as Law: Mythology, Ideology and Order in George Lucas's *Star Wars*' (2012) 36 *Australian Feminist Law Journal* 125; Jason Bainbridge, '"This is the Authority. This Planet is Under Our Protection" – An Exegesis of Superheroes' Interrogations of Law' (2007) 3 *Law, Culture and the Humanities* 455; Timothy D Peters, 'Comic Book Mythology: Shyamalan's *Unbreakable* and the Grounding of Good in Evil' (2012) 16 *Law Text Culture* 243; Scott Beattie, 'Voicing the Shadow – Rule-playing and Roleplaying in *Wraith: The Oblivion*' (2007) 3 *Law, Culture and the Humanities* 477.

in ways not possible via pop culture or jurisprudence themselves. As such, MacNeil breaks down certain disciplinary boundaries, as well as 'modern' divisions in respect to what can be considered the canonical or 'authoritative texts' of jurisprudence.

Here I propose to take up MacNeil's 'reading jurisprudentially' and extend upon it in both of the unique aspects identified above. First, by focusing specifically on texts of speculative fiction as sites of estrangement or 'making strange' that provide not only representations but sites of law for analysis. My argument is that within these fictional realms – these worlds imagined differently – we can find new spaces to imagine or re-imagine our concepts of law, legality and justice. Second, by extending the jurisprudential consideration into the realms of theology or theo-legality. The combination of these two aspects (which are addressed in the next two sections) will culminate in an articulation of the methodology of cultural legal reading as a form of 'making strange' itself – one that reveals and rethinks a theological account of law.

The law 'made strange': taking speculative fiction seriously

Speculative fiction as a category of literature, film and television (not to mention comic books, video games and other forms of narrative-based popular culture) is traditionally seen as a commercial, rather than literary, classification. Encompassing at least works of science fiction and fantasy, but also extending to 'utopian and dystopian fiction, magic realism, fantastic voyages, ghost stories, and the Gothic with supernatural elements'[40] speculative fiction's definitional limits and boundaries are somewhat nebulous to say the least.[41] R.B. Gill, having noted the limited consideration of speculative fiction as a literary genre, puts forward a working definition of speculative fiction as 'works presenting modes of being that contrast with their audiences' understanding of ordinary reality.'[42] That is, '[s]peculative fiction envisions a systematically different world in which not only events are different, but causes operate by logics other than normal ones.'[43] This envisioning of different worlds resonates with Carl Malmgren's analysis of both science fiction and fantasy in relation to their intersections in what he terms 'science fantasy'.[44] Having described fictional universes as

40 R B Gill, 'The Uses of Genre and the Classification of Speculative Fiction' (2013) 46 *Mosaic* 71, 72 referring to the listing of categories of stories included on the Internet Speculative Fiction Database.

41 Ibid, 71–72.

42 Ibid, 72–73.

43 Ibid, 73.

44 Carl D Malmgren, 'Towards a Definition of Science Fantasy' (1988) 15 *Science-Fiction Studies* 259.

consisting of the two major components of world and story, Malmgren identifies that for the genre of science fiction (and the same can be said of fantasy), what is unique is the question of the *world*, rather than the story.[45] What is distinctive about these genres is the way that they situate themselves in worlds '*other* than the basic narrative world', that is the empirical world of the author.[46] In contrast to 'realistic' or 'naturalistic' fiction which, while positing fictional narratives and characters, generally does so within a world that conforms to that of the author and reader, the genres of speculative fiction imagine a world that is fundamentally different to what the author or reader understands as ordinary reality.[47] The differences of such an imagined world may be naturalised via a scientific explanation as logically possible (as in science fiction) or relegated to the imaginable but impossible or unreal (as in fantasy) or explained with references to various modes of the supernatural (as in much Gothic literature).

One of the ways to discuss the differences of the world imagined by these genres is via the concept of estrangement or 'making strange'. Darko Suvin famously defined science fiction as a form of 'cognitive estrangement', situating it as one of a number of 'estranged genres' (including fairy tale, fantasy and myth), which he opposed to naturalistic ones.[48] In utilising the term or concept of estrangement, Suvin makes reference in particular to the work of Victor Shklovsky and Bertolt Brecht. Shklovsky, one of the Russian Formalists, in his essay 'Art as Technique' outlines the concept of *ostranenie* (translated as estrangement, defamiliarisation or simply 'making strange') in relation to a theory of art. For Shklovsky, the purpose of art is to 'impart the sensation of things as they are perceived and not as they are known.'[49] Rather than focusing on presenting the complex in the form of the simple – the unknown in terms of the known – the purpose of art is to 'de-autonomise' us from the world. In everyday life we become habitualised to the world around us and instead of seeing things clearly or noting things in detail, we become de-sensitised to them and treat them out of habit. Even when we look at the object specifically, we do not really see it for our habitualised understanding and perception gets in

45 Ibid, 259. Malmgrem specifies the world as 'including the total repertoire of possible fictional entities – i.e., the characters, settings and objects . . . that occupy the fictional domain.' The story, then, 'connects and combines the various entities that make up the world; at an abstract level it consists of a systematic set of rules governing the arrangement and interaction of those entities' at 259.

46 Ibid, 260. Darko Suvin describes this as the 'zero-world' of the author: Darko Suvin, *Metamorphoses of Science Fiction: On the Poetics and History of a Literary Genre* (Yale University Press, 1979) 11.

47 Malmgren, above n 44, n 2. See also Suvin, above n 46, viii.

48 Suvin, above n 46, 3–4, 7–10. See also Simon Spiegel, 'Things Made Strange: On the Concept of "Estrangement" in Science Fiction Theory' (2008) 35 *Science Fiction Studies* 369, 371.

49 Victor Shklovsky, 'Art as Technique' in Lee T Lemon and Marion J Reis (eds), *Russian Formalist Criticism: Four Essays* (University of Nebraska Press, 1965) 3, 12.

the way. We see what we think we are going to see, not what is actually there. Art, for Shklovsky, 'exists that one may recover the sensation of life; it exists to make one feel things, to make the stone *stony*.'[50] Rather than presenting a complex thing via a simple image, art should make objects 'unfamiliar' and '[i]ncrease the difficulty and length of perception because the process of perception is an aesthetic end in itself and must be prolonged. *Art is a way of experiencing the artfulness of an object; the object is not important*.'[51]

As such, for Shklovksy 'Art removes objects from the automatism of perception.'[52] In literature, such techniques can include: the avoidance of direct naming so that an event or familiar object is described as new or unfamiliar; the presenting of things from an unusual point of view; and the almost childlike description of something familiar as if it were seen for the first time.[53] Yet, while focusing on particular instances and particular authors, Shklovsky notes that 'defamiliarization is found almost everywhere form is found.'[54] For example, the purpose of an image is not so much to 'make us perceive meaning, but to create a special perception of the object – *it creates a "vision" of the object instead of serving as a means of knowing it*.'[55] Instead of providing a clear perception of the image, the aim is to impede or slow perception so that the focus is not on the directness of the image as representation, but on the presentation of the representation itself.

Bertolt Brecht made use of a similar understanding of estrangement in relation to theatre, particularly in the form of the *V-Effekt* or estrangement effect. Brecht defined *Verfremdung* (translated as alienation or estrangement) as follows: '[a] representation which estranges is one which allows us to recognise its subject, but at the same time makes it seem unfamiliar.'[56] While similar to Shklovsky's definition (and there is speculation as to whether Brecht was influenced directly by Shklovsky or not[57]) the focus for Brecht is political and didactic. The practice of the *V-Effekt* in theatre is aimed at blocking empathy and interrupting the audience's perception.[58] Instead of engaging or 'delving' into the play, in Brecht's

50 Ibid, 11–12.
51 Ibid, 12.
52 Ibid, 13.
53 Ibid, 13–18; see the discussion by Alison Milbank, *Chesterton and Tolkien as Theologians: The Fantasy of the Real* (T&T Clark, 2007) 36.
54 Shklovsky, above n 49, 18.
55 Ibid, 18.
56 Bertolt Brecht, 'A Short Organum for the Theatre' in J Willett (ed.), *Brecht on Theatre: The Development of an Aesthetic* (Farrar, Strauss, Giroux, 1964) 179, 192, quoted in Suvin, above n 46, 6 where he changes the translation of 'alienation' to 'estrangement'.
57 See the discussion in Galin Tihanov, 'The Politics of Estrangement: The Case of the Early Shklovsky' (2005) 26 *Poetics Today* 665, 687–688, n 42, referred to by Spiegel, above n 48, n 4.
58 Spiegel, above n 48, n 4; Brecht, above n 56, 190–192.

Epic Theatre, the spectator 'is obstructed from regarding it as "natural"'[59] and the activity occurring on the stage should be rendered visible in itself (not simply in terms of the world it represents). As such, the artifice of the performance (and thus, at the same time politics and the social order) and its constructedness should become clear. In seeking to develop a 'theater of the scientific age', Brecht sought to replicate the naïve, objective gaze of the scientists that would see things as estranged in terms of looking at them as if for the first time.[60] As Spiegel notes, the result of the estrangement techniques for Brecht should be 'the realization that things do not have to be the way they are, that any current state of things is not a natural given but a product of historical processes, which can change and will be changed.'[61]

Suvin's use of the term estrangement thus draws on both Shklovsky and Brecht's concepts, but he then takes them in a different direction by applying them to genre as opposed to technique. For Suvin, 'the approach to the imaginary locality, or localized daydream, practiced by the genre of S[cience] F[iction] is a supposedly factual one.'[62] In that sense, science fiction's focus on a 'factual reporting of fictions' implies the attitude of *estrangement* and particularly connects to Brecht's comparison between the look of estrangement in theatre and the detached gaze of the scientist. Suvin considers 'the look of estrangement' to be 'both cognitive and creative'.[63] He notes that in science fiction, moving away from the concept of estrangement in the 'realistic' or 'naturalistic' contexts of Brecht and Shklovsky, the 'attitude of estrangement . . . has grown into the *formal framework* of the genre.'[64] Suvin's use of the term estrangement at the level of genre has been criticised as misinterpreting Shklovsky's and Brecht's focus on technique.[65] However, given Shklovsky's approach to art as a means of making the familiar seem unfamiliar so that it can be seen anew, Suvin's discussion of the genre of science fiction (and other genres of estrangement) does sit within this framework (even though, within the stories themselves, that which appears estranged to the reader is naturalised at the level of the story).[66] Furthermore, Suvin's focus on the 'cognitiveness' of science fiction identifies that the genre is not only

59 Spiegel, above n 48, 370.
60 Ibid.
61 Ibid; Brecht, above n 56.
62 Suvin, above n 46, 5–6.
63 Ibid, 6.
64 Ibid, 7.
65 See Spiegel, above n 48, 375. For a more favourable rendering of Suvin's analysis of estrangement in science fiction, see Philippe Mather, 'Figures of Estrangement in Science Fiction Film' (2002) 29 *Science Fiction Studies* 186, 187.
66 See discussion of this by Spiegel, above n 48, 372–374; cf Mather, above n 65, 188–189.

> a reflecting *of* but also *on* reality. It implies a creative approach tending toward a dynamic transformation rather than toward a static mirroring of the author's environment. Such typical methodology of S[cience] F[iction] . . . is a *critical* one, often satirical, combining a belief in the potentialities of reason with methodological doubt in the most significant cases.[67]

That is, science fiction is aimed at being a reflection *on* reality, despite its engagement and creation of different worlds, novums and characters. The sense of estrangement created by the imagination of a world of advanced technology, space travel, alien life or simply a different engagement with the world, is all aimed at a reflection of and on the present world of the author (and reader). While this can also be articulated about most fiction, the genres of estrangement themselves provide a different entry onto the present world via their imagining of a starkly different one.

Speculative fiction's legal theology

While Suvin's focus is on science fiction as a form of cognitive and critical estrangement, the other genres that he describes as estranged (fairy tales, tragic myth and fantasy) can also be seen to be reflective on the world via levels of estranging thematics. Alison Milbank, in her analysis of the works of G.K. Chesterton and J.R.R. Tolkien, identifies the manner in which they both draw on concepts and techniques of defamiliarisation and 'making strange' in their speculative fiction. Milbank's argument is that Chesterton and Tolkien shared a view of art as 'revealing the createdness of the world' and the creative vocation of the artists in remaking it. As such, she situates Chesterton and Tolkien in the context of their Catholic theology, seeing art itself as mediatory – a 'theological tool for opening human eyes to see the reality of God and the reality, albeit contingent, of the world beyond itself.'[68] From this:

> the theology of the art of invention of stories, fantastic or otherwise, is derived. To tell a story, whether one's own or a traditional tale, is to mediate the world in its intentionality and narrative character . . . to tell a story is to affirm that there is meaning to life, and that experience is shaped and has an entelechy.[69]

The focus on the telling of stories, and, in particular marvellous or creative stories is not simply for entertainment – encompassing flights of pure imagination

67 Suvin, above n 46, 10.
68 Milbank, above n 53, xiv.
69 Ibid, 11.

and the construction of utopian or dystopian alternate worlds – but to affirm the independence of the world from our perception and appropriation of it. In this sense Chesterton and Tolkien see fairy tales as a way of looking at the world as storied and gifted. They enable us to see that 'the world of objects is not the product of our own mental perceptions but has its own reality.'[70] Referencing Tolkien's essay on fairy stories, Milbank notes that 'Faerie' for Tolkien 'is the site where we encounter other beings and the world itself not just as "enchanted" but as "other".'[71] This form of enchantment identifies not so much the complete separateness of things from each other but their inter-relatedness and relationality.[72]

Following Tolkien himself, Milbank identifies two forms of fantasy in Chesterton and Tolkien's speculative fiction. The first is a form of 'making strange' or 'defamiliarisation' associated with Chesterton's work, which is similar in form, though not necessarily in purpose, to Shklovsky's concept of *ostranenie*. For, whereas Shklovsky's defamiliarisation 'privileges the viewer or reader over the object described or pictured', Chesterton's focus is on empowering the object itself and its givenness as part of the world. [73] As Milbank argues, Chesterton's use of techniques of 'making strange' was to

> sunder our lazy ownership of perception, so that we lose our apprehension of the phenomenal world in order to find it again: as itself, as something coming to us which is a mystery in its quiddity, its individuality and its difference from ourselves. [74]

Chesterton made use of this type of defamiliarisation frequently in his Father Brown mystery stories where the technique was not so much to show a supernatural answer to the mystery, but rather to re-enchant the world in the uncovering of the logical explanation (which was far more mundane or diurnal than it originally appeared). That is, it is in the seeing of the world anew that we can apprehend its enchantment, not in the form of mystic supernatural occurrence but in terms of the sense of wonder of the world in its ordinariness.

The second category of fantasy, which Tolkien saw himself as engaging in (though he did also use techniques of defamiliarisation as well), was that of 'escape' – not in the sense of escapism but in the sense of how, in fairy stories, normal daily objects and materials such as stone, wood and iron 'are made all

70 Ibid, 12.
71 Ibid, referring to J R R Tolkien, 'On Fairy-Stories' in J R R Tolkien, *Tree and Leaf: The Homecoming of Beorhtnoth* (HarperCollins Publishers, 2001).
72 Ibid, 12.
73 Ibid, 36–37.
74 Ibid, 37.

the more luminious by their setting'.[75] While this focus on escape was similar to Chesterton's 'making strange' it was for a different purpose. Whereas Chesterton never takes the reader completely out of his own world, Tolkien does:

> [f]or the aim of escape combined with a recovery of vision is to undergird Tolkien's imaginary or sub-created fictional universe, and allows him to employ defamiliarization effects throughout his stories and novels for a slightly different function.[76]

Tolkien saw the artistic conception of an alternative world as a process of sub-creation that both reflects elements of the world of the artist but also sets those elements free. Whereas Chesterton's aim is to show the marvellous or transcendent *realism* of objects – making us actually *see* them – Tolkien's aim is to show their independence. Tolkien's belief was that fantasy aims towards the liberation of things to be themselves: 'By being freed into new life, however, they also become *more* than themselves.'[77]

Whereas Suvin identifies science fiction as a mode of cognitive estrangement, which is both a reflection of and on the world, Milbank and Tolkien identify the possibility of estranged genres to show the independence of the world itself. What this identification of the way that the genres of speculative fiction engage in modes of estrangement shows, is that they are not simply flights of fancy, realms of pure imagination with no relation or reference to reality. Rather, they produce a meditation *on* and a mediation *of* the world itself. That is, speculative fiction provides the ability for us to see the world anew via its various modes of estrangement. It is in this sense that the genres of speculative fiction can be explored as a mode of the cultural legal. Rather than focusing on the direct representations of law, the legal institution and legal actors within popular culture, the engagement of speculative fiction provides a way to understand and re-think the stories of and about law themselves. As such, in the analysis of motifs of law and legality, of justice, authority and legitimacy that are 'made strange' by their situation in worlds imagined differently, we find the potential to think and see them otherwise, not in the sense of simply a utopian (or dystopian) looking forward through the potential of the imagination, but an understanding that the imagination's setting free of these concepts enables a different reflection and understanding of them.

At the same time, law itself encompasses a form of envisioning of the world, a sense of what Robert Cover calls law's 'world creation' noting that the practices

75 Tolkien, above n 71, 59 quoted in Milbank, above n 53, 40.
76 Milbank, above n 53, 40.
77 Ibid, 51.

of law engage in 'the projection of an imagined future upon reality.'[78] In this sense law engages in a speculative activity, it is a 'bridge' in 'normative space', which connects our understanding of the world as it is with our projections of other worlds that might be.[79] While law's implementation or actualisation of such an imagined future encompasses a violence that brings it into force,[80] the frameworks within which law operates and is able to do this are mythic and narrative driven. That is, the narratives that we tell about law itself form the underlying myths (whether such a myth is factual or not), which encompass its legitimacy. The reading of the law 'made strange' through the modern myths told in popular culture thus provides a way to unpack and explore both the mythological and theological structures of law that we cannot always approach directly because we are, as Shklovsky would say, habitualised or autonomised to them. In considering the structures of law as they are 'made strange' by speculative fiction, we can not only see them anew (and thus also conceive them otherwise) but we can bring to light and make available for critique, the latent theologies of modern law. The normative aspects of legal analysis and legal interpretation are always about the enforcing of a particular vision of the world on the factual situation in which it engages. Thus, the legal imaginary that informs such a process of enforcement, must be seen as the process of world-building or world-creating and, in a sense, have similarities to the artist's process of creation or sub-creation in the production of art. The mythologies and stories of law themselves are engaged in a mode of speculative re-creating of the world. Yet, the risk of viewing the law in this way is that we see the world as being able to be simply constructed and created through law (a particular modern vision of the task of law itself). The possibility of speculative fiction, however, is that we can see the world as gifted and not simply constructed, created as well as contingent. That is to say, speculative fiction uncovers the *theological* aspects of law in the process of estranging our ordinary conceptions of it. In revealing the world as created and contingent, speculative fiction also reveals the possibility for different theological accounts of the world and of law.

Conclusion: towards a cultural legal theology

The method of cultural legal studies that I have been articulating here engages the concept of 'making strange' at three levels. In the first instance, the texts of speculative fiction present alternative worlds as the location of their stories and

78 Robert M Cover, 'Violence and the Word' (1986) 95 *Yale Law Journal* 1601, 1604. On law as 'world-creation' see Cover, above n 6, 12–19.

79 Cover, above n 6, 9–10.

80 Note Robert Cover's famous statement that 'Legal interpretation takes place in a field of pain and death.' As such, the interpretation of law is distinguished from the interpretation of literature: Cover, above n 78, 1601, 1607.

encompass elements of the fantastic, the uncanny or the marvellous. As such the *generic* contexts of speculative fiction are estranged through the imagining of different worlds. At a second level, when these texts represent or engage the concepts of law, legality or justice – the superhero's exceptional relationship to the law, the natural law of Tolkien's high elves or the questions of robotic rights and legality in science fiction – they present them as estranged from our normal perception of them. Simply exploring these different modes of legality provides a new way of conceiving law. But it is not simply a *different* conception of law, for speculative fictions' creative estranging of the law opens up its contingent nature and, I argue, reveals its theological underpinnings. This is not so much a focus on looking for theological content *in* the texts under consideration but that the texts, in themselves, reveal and engage in a process of theological creativity and speculation. The visions of such a legal theology may be distorted in terms of its commercial context (as we saw in the opening analysis of *Man of Steel*) but that distortion itself reveals an understanding of the world (no longer claimed as an autonomous secular space devoid of religion) and of law in theological terms. The third level of 'making strange' is the process of reading these texts as sites of the cultural legal – and thus constructing a cultural legal intertext. Taking speculative fiction seriously means that instead of seeing these texts as simply commercial mass-produced artefacts that are circulating in the never-ending run of capitalist exchange (now available for digital download and streaming on demand), we must sit, contemplate, 'read' and re-read these cultural texts as sites of law, of legal theology and of legal *and* cultural world-creation. It is this form of close reading of the text that 'makes strange' the works of speculative fiction and uncovers, unpacks and sets free the law and legal theory to be re-thought and otherwise re-imagined and for its theology – good, bad or otherwise – to be revealed and laid bare.

This process of 'making strange' – which draws on the way the concepts of law, legality and justice are not only represented but estranged in speculative fiction – both renders visible and obfuscates the fundamental distinctions of legal modernity: between theology and politics, religion and law, church and state. Following the turn to theology in critical theory, political science and jurisprudence, it makes it possible to uncover, identify and critique the latent theologies of modern law. Going further, however, this method of cultural legal reading attempts to open up and explore the way in which law is itself informed and undergirded by particular theological positions. Such positions are often hidden and opaque because, in the same way that John Milbank notes in relation to modern liberalism, 'this theological founding is a contingent fact, the result of people thinking in terms which are indebted to a certain religious heritage, linked to certain events, writings and claimed revelations.'[81] As such, the

81 John Milbank, 'Against Human Rights: Liberty in the Western Tradition' (2012) 1 *Oxford Journal of Law and Religion* 203, 217.

privileging of the stories of speculative fiction is because they are able to explore and unpack certain theological aspects of modern law by 'making strange' our ordinary, habitualised and autonomised perception of them. Considering the law 'made strange' and rendered otherwise by speculative fiction identifies that stories which have little to do with direct representations of law itself can be in fact imbued with a certain legality and also render visible a theological jurisprudence. In this sense it is, as MacNeil has said, through the plumbing of 'the depths of deep structure' of popular culture texts that we can construct an intertext of popular culture, jurisprudence and theology. That is, a cultural legal *theology* is uncovered through the process of 'making strange' itself.

Bibliography

Articles/books/book chapters

Agamben, Giorgio, *The Time That Remains: A Commentary on the Letter to the Romans* (Patricia Dailey trans, Stanford University Press, 2005)

Agamben, Giorgio, *The Kingdom and the Glory: For a Theological Genealogy of Economy and Government* (Stanford University Press, 2011)

Babie, Paul, 'Breaking the Silence: Law, Theology and Religion in Australia' (2007) 31 *Melbourne University Law Review* 296

Badiou, Alain, *Saint Paul: The Foundation of Universalism* (Stanford University Press, 2003)

Bainbridge, Jason, '"This is the Authority. This Planet is Under Our Protection" – An Exegesis of Superheroes' Interrogations of Law' (2007) 3 *Law, Culture and the Humanities* 455

Barkman, Adam, 'Superman: From Anti-Christ to Christ-Type' in Mark D White (ed.), *Superman and Philosophy: What Would the Man of Steel Do?* (John Wiley & Sons, 2013)

Beattie, Scott, 'Voicing the Shadow – Rule-playing and Roleplaying in *Wraith: The Oblivion*' (2007) 3 *Law, Culture and the Humanities* 477

Berman, Harold J, *Law and Revolution: The Formation of the Western Legal Tradition* (Harvard University Press, 1983)

Brecht, Bertolt, 'A Short Organum for the Theatre' in J Willett (ed.), *Brecht on Theatre: The Development of an Aesthetic* (Farrar, Strauss, Giroux, 1964) 179

Casanova, Jose, *Public Religions in the Modern World* (The University of Chicago Press, 1994)

Comaroff, John L, 'Reflections on the Rise of Legal Theology: Law and Religion in the Twenty-First Century' (2009) 53 *Social Analysis* 193

Cover, Robert M, 'The Supreme Court, 1982 Term – Forward: Nomos and Narrative' (1983) 97 *Harvard Law Review* 4

Cover, Robert M, 'Violence and the Word' (1986) 95 *Yale Law Journal* 1601

Crockett, Clayton (ed.), *Religion and Violence in a Secular World: Toward a New Political Theology* (University of Virginia Press, 2006)

de Vries, Hent and Lawrence E Sullivan (eds), *Political Theologies: Public Religions in a Post-Secular World* (Fordham University Press, 2006)

Fitzpatrick, Peter, *The Mythology of Modern Law* (Routledge, 1992)

Fitzpatrick, Peter, 'Legal Theology: Law, Modernity and the Sacred' (2009) 32 *Seattle University Law Review* 321

Freeman, M D A, *Lloyd's Introduction to Jurisprudence* (Sweet & Maxwell, 8th edn, 2008)
Gill, R B, 'The Uses of Genre and the Classification of Speculative Fiction' (2013) 46 *Mosaic* 71
Habermas, Jürgen, 'Secularism's Crisis of Faith: Notes on Post-Secular Society' (2008) 25 *New Perspectives Quarterly* 17
Harris-Abbot, Troy, 'On Law and Theology' (1990) 35 *The American Journal of Jurisprudence* 105
Hutchings, Peter J, 'From Offworld Colonies to Migration Zones: *Blade Runner* and the Fractured Subject of Jurisprudence' (2007) 3 *Law, Culture and the Humanities* 381
Kahn, Paul, *Political Theology: Four New Chapters on the Concept of Sovereignty* (Columbia University Press, 2011)
Kennedy, David, 'Images of Religion in International Legal Theory' in M Janis and C Evans (eds), *Religion and International Law* (Martinus Nijhoff, 1999) 145
Kirsch, Thomas G and Bertram Turner, *Permutations of Order: Religion and Law as Contested Sovereignties* (Ashgate, 2009)
Lilla, Mark, *The Stillborn God: Religion, Politics and the Modern West* (Knopf, 2007)
MacNeil, William P, 'One Recht to Rule Them All! Law's Empire in the Age of Empire' (2004) 34 *Studies in Law, Politics and Society* 279
MacNeil, William P, *Lex Populi: The Jurisprudence of Popular Culture* (Stanford University Press, 2007)
MacNeil, William P, *Novel Judgements: Legal Theory as Fiction* (Routledge, 2012)
Malmgren, Carl D, 'Towards a Definition of Science Fantasy' (1988) 15 *Science-Fiction Studies* 259
Marty, Martin E, 'The Religious Foundations of Law' (2005) 54 *Emory Law Journal* 291
Mather, Philippe, 'Figures of Estrangement in Science Fiction Film' (2002) 29 *Science Fiction Studies* 186
Milbank, Alison, *Chesterton and Tolkien as Theologians: The Fantasy of the Real* (T & T Clark, 2007)
Milbank, John, *Theology and Social Theory: Beyond Secular Reason* (Blackwell, 1990)
Milbank, John, 'Against Human Rights: Liberty in the Western Tradition' (2012) 1 *Oxford Journal of Law and Religion* 203
Milbank, John, Catherine Pickstock and Graham Ward (eds), *Radical Orthodoxy: A New Theology* (Routledge, 1999)
Mohr, Richard, 'The Christian Origins of Secularism and the Rule of Law' in R Mohr and N Hosen (eds), *Law and Religion in Public Life: The Contemporary Debate* (Routledge, 2011) 34
Morrison, Grant, 143 *Wizard: The Comics Magazine* #143, 1 August 2003 180
Neoh, Joshua, 'Text, Doctrine and Tradition in Law and Religion' (2013) 2 *Oxford Journal of Law and Religion* 175
Peters, Timothy D, 'Comic Book Mythology: Shyamalan's *Unbreakable* and the Grounding of Good in Evil' (2012) 16 *Law Text Culture* 243
Peters, Timothy D, '"The Force" as Law: Mythology, Ideology and Order in George Lucas's *Star Wars*' (2012) 36 *Australian Feminist Law Journal* 125
Schenck, Ken, 'Superman: A Popular Culture Messiah' in B J Oropeza (ed.), *The Gospel According to Superheroes: Religion and Popular Culture* (Peter Lang, 2005) 33
Schmitt, Carl, *Political Theology: Four Chapters on the Concept of Sovereignty* (The University of Chicago Press, 2005)

Sharp, Cassandra, 'Religion and Justice: Atonement as an Element of Justice in Both Western Law and Christian Thought' in R Mohr and N Hosen (eds), *Law and Religion in Public Life: The Contemporary Debate* (Routledge, 2011) 151

Shklovsky, Victor, 'Art as Technique' in Lee T Lemon and Marion J Reis (eds), *Russian Formalist Criticism: Four Essays* (University of Nebraska Press, 1965) 3

Spiegel, Simon, 'Things Made Strange: On the Concept of "Estrangement" in Science Fiction Theory' (2008) 35 *Science Fiction Studies* 369

Sullivan, Winnifred Fallers, Robert A Yelle and Mateo Taussig-Rubbo, 'Introduction' in W F Sullivan, R A Yelle and M Taussig-Rubbo (eds), *After Secular Law* (Stanford University Press, 2011) 1

Suvin, Darko, *Metamorphoses of Science Fiction: On the Poetics and History of a Literary Genre* (Yale University Press, 1979)

Taubes, Jacob, *The Political Theology of Paul* (Dana Hollander trans, Stanford University Press, 2004)

Tihanov, Galin, 'The Politics of Estrangement: The Case of the Early Shklovsky' (2005) 26 *Poetics Today* 665

Tolkien, J R R, 'On Fairy-Stories' in J R R Tolkien, *Tree and Leaf: The Homecoming of Beorhtnoth Beorhthelm's Son* (Harper Collins Publishers, 2001)

Tranter, Kieran, '"Frakking Toasters" and Jurisprudences of Technology: The Exception, the Subject and Techne in *Battlestar Galactica*' (2007) 19 *Law and Literature* 45

Ward, Graham, *Cities of God* (Routledge, 2000)

Weber, Max, *The Protestant Work Ethic and the Spirit of Capitalism* (Talcott Parsons trans, Charles Scribner's Sons, 1958)

Weber, Max, *Economy and Society: An Outline of Interpretive Sociology* (University of California Press, 1978)

Žižek, Slavoj, *The Fragile Absolute – Or, Why is the Christian Legacy Worth Fighting For?* (Verso, 2000)

Films

Man of Steel (Directed by Zack Snyder, Warner Brothers Pictures, 2013)

Superman: The Movie (Directed by Richard Donner, Dovemead Films, 1978)

Superman Returns (Directed by Bryan Singer, Warner Bros, 2006)

Chapter 13

Republicanism meets (dystopian) faërie

Harry Potter and the institutional disaster

Luis Gómez Romero

Introduction: once upon a time there was a best-selling novel

The popular series of novels that comprise the adventurous *coming-of-age* of a wizard named Harry Potter –the Potter novels[1]– published by Joanne 'Kathleen' Rowling[2] over a period of ten years between 1997 and 2007 *function as* a source of law. This is the main thesis that underlies this essay and I wish to clearly establish it from the very beginning, but I realise I must begin by clarifying two matters to justify the value and necessity of this claim. First, I need to establish the terms of my claim in the context of the *Law and Literature* movement. Second, I will justify why the Potter novels provide an exemplary site for this jurisprudential analysis.

In one sense, the idea of locating the Potter novels within a Law and Literature reading is not new. The *Law and Literature* movement has a long history in Anglo-American legal scholarship. Its origins can be traced to the early 1970s –when James Boyd White's groundbreaking work on the field was published.[3] Nonetheless, its epistemological aptness to understand the nature and functions

1 I will indistinctly refer to the Potter series both as stories and novels. The term *novel* is therefore used in its broadest possible sense, i.e., as a group of tales or stories that make up a larger literary work. Harry Potter's *corpus* comprises seven novels (*Harry Potter and the Philosopher's Stone*, *Harry Potter and the Chamber of Secrets*, *Harry Potter and the Prisoner of Azkaban*, *Harry Potter and the Goblet of Fire*, *Harry Potter and the Order of the Phoenix*, *Harry Potter and the Half-Blood Prince* and *Harry Potter and the Deathly Hallows*) and three ancillary books which purportedly have been authored by wizards and published in the wizardly world (*Fantastic Beasts and Where to Find Them*, *Quidditch Through the Ages* and *The Tales of Beedle the Bard*).

2 Joanne Rowling's pen name is 'J K Rowling' as a result of a merchandising strategy implemented by her agent, Christopher Little. He anticipated that, whereas girls would read books by male authors, boys would never read a book if the author was a woman. He advised Joanne to use androgynised initials, so she added her grandmother's name – Kathleen – to her own. See Sean Smith, *J. K. Rowling: A Biography* (Arrow Books, 2001) 175.

3 James Boyd White, *The Legal Imagination: Studies in the Nature of Legal Thought and Expression* (Little, Brown & Co., 1973).

of legal discourses has been constantly plagued by two fallacies that, following Desmond Manderson, I will respectively call *mimetic* and *romantic*.[4] The mimetic fallacy binds literature and law by ascribing to art the function of imitating nature or reality in such a way that literary texts are reduced to statements that convey information on facts that are relevant in terms of legal interpretation, critique, or review of legal institutions or standards.[5] The romantic fallacy states that the value of art consists in *healing the wounds of the world* or, in other words, that literature embodies the *absent justice* of law.[6]

The aesthetic value of literature, however – as Manderson rightly points out – does not lie in how coherently it depicts the so-called *real-world* or in the moral values it supports, but rather in the *form* and *style* of language that set up a significant aesthetic experience.[7] This aesthetic peculiarity of literature has been vehemently depicted by Roland Barthes, who defined literary creation as 'the splendour of a permanent revolution of language' [*la splendeur d'une révolution permanente du langage*] that enables both the artist and the reader enjoy it *outside and beyond any expression of power*.[8] In the case of fiction, thus, a text is provided with the qualities of *literature* not by its content, but by the way it is composed and the language strategies that are applied in the process of fictionalisation. In other words, the *aesthetic value* of fiction – novels, stories, and related literary genres – lies in the pre-eminence given to the voice of the artist over the events represented in his/her work.[9] I analyse the legal relevance of literary creations under this light: as a multiplicity of voices that – along with other many cultural elements – subverts, breaks, contradicts and challenges the cultural structure of law. In other words, I contend that the singular, unique and subjective aesthetic experience that is triggered by the style and form of literary texts converges in shaping the moral autonomy of the individual,[10] fragmenting hegemonic

4 Desmond Manderson, *Kangaroo Courts and the Rule of Law: The Legacy of Modernism* (Routledge, 2012) 9 ff.

5 See, for instance, Robin West, 'Authority, Autonomy, and Choice: The Role of Consent in the Moral and Political Visions of Franz Kafka and Richard Posner' (1985) 99 *Harvard Law Review* 384; from the same author, 'Submission, Choice and Ethics: A Rejoinder to Judge Posner' (1986) 99 *Harvard Law Review* 1449; Richard Posner, 'The Ethical Significance of Free Choice' (1986) 99 *Harvard Law Review* 1431; Martha Nussbaum, *Poetic Justice: The Literary Imagination and the Public Life* (Beacon Press, 1995); and Nicola Lacey, *Women, Crime, and Character: From Moll Flanders to Tess of the D'Urbervilles* (Oxford University Press, 2008).

6 For example, Nussbaum above n 5; Ian Ward, *Justice, Humanity and the New World Order* (Ashgate, 2003); and Melanie Williams, *Secrets and Laws: Collected Essays in Law, Lives, and Literature* (UCL Press, 2005).

7 Manderson, above n 4, 116–117.

8 Roland Barthes, 'Leçon' in Roland Barthes, *Œuvres Complètes* (Éditions de Seuil, 2002) vol 5, 427, 433. All translations are mine unless otherwise stated.

9 Manderson, above n 4, 16.

10 Milan Kundera, 'Discours de Jérusalem: le Roman et l'Europe' in Milan Kundera, *L'Art du Roman* (Gallimard, 1986) 191, 191 ff; Octavio Paz, *El Ogro Filantrópico* (Joaquín Mortiz, 1980) 7–8.

conceptions of justice[11] and stimulating semantic innovation to name new forms of justice.[12]

It is in this sense that the Potter novels represent a unique opportunity to shed light on ethical and cultural discourses that broadly analyse and criticise the intrinsic tensions of contemporary legal systems. *Pottermania* – the vast network of all things Potter as exemplified by the books, the movies and merchandising on a vast scale – is a cultural phenomenon framed by the unmistakable traits of contemporary capitalist globalisation,[13] with an astonishing sales record (325 million copies of the books sold by 2009).[14] The Potter novels have been translated into sixty languages –including extinct ones, as Latin or classical Greek – and have reached geographical locations (such as China) and cultural traditions (the Zulu in Southern Africa) that a few decades ago might have seemed too distant from the post-Thatcherite England that frames Harry Potter's adventures.[15]

Harry Potter's popularity is not enough to justify its aesthetic value or legal relevance. The nexus between popularity and aesthetic value on the Potter novels (or on any other literary work) is merely contingent. The question about the possibility of millions of readers being wrong when considering the Potter stories

11 Wai Chee Dimock, *Residues of Justice: Literature, Law, Philosophy* (University of California Press, 1996) 23 ff.

12 I have extensively analysed elsewhere the role literary texts play in the semantic innovation of legal discourses. See Luis Gómez Romero, *El Tiempo de los Débiles: Garantismo y Literatura* (Porrúa, 2008) 265 ff.

13 Globalisation is not an exclusively contemporary economic, legal, social and political phenomenon. From a legal perspective, the dissemination of Roman law after the recovery of the *Corpus Juris Civilis* in Northern Italy; the deep influence of Islam over legal institutions in the Iberian Peninsula (for example, through institutions as the *alcalde* in local governance, or the *albacea* in testate succession); or the reception of Napoleon's *Code Civil* around the world can be highlighted as highly significant past globalising processes.

14 *Harry Potter and the Order of the Phoenix* amounted to 40 per cent of book sales around the world the weekend after its launch. See Julia Eccleshare, '"Most Popular Ever": The Launching of Harry Potter' in Julia Briggs, Dennis Butts and Matthew Grenby (eds), *Popular Children's Literature in Britain* (Ashgate, 2008) 287, 287. Around 7 million copies of *Harry Potter and the Half-Blood Prince* were sold in the United States the first twenty-four hours after it was released. See Edward Wyatt, 'Potter Book Sets Record in First Day' *New York Times* (New York) 18 July 2005, E3. *Harry Potter and the Deathly Hallows* would beat that figure two years later: more than 8 million books were sold in the United States the day it was released (ninety copies per second!). See Motoko Rich, 'Harry Potter's Popularity Holds Up in Early Sales' *New York Times* (New York) 23 July 2007, A12.

15 Nancy K Jentsch has carried out a succinct analysis of the German, Spanish, French and English versions: 'Harry Potter and the Tower of Babel: Translating the Magic' in Lana Whited (ed.), *The Ivory Tower and Harry Potter: Perspectives on a Literary Phenomenon* (University of Missouri Press, 2002) 285. Gillian Lathey has examined the role the translations have played in the series merchandising. See: 'The Travels of Harry: International Marketing and the Translation of J. K. Rowling's Harry Potter Books' (2005) 29 *The Lion and the Unicorn* 141.

as a splendid aesthetic experience could possibly be answered with the laconic persuasiveness of Harold Bloom: 'yes'.[16] Nonetheless, we do not need to affirm high aesthetic value in the Potter novels to acknowledge that the aesthetic experiences that are maintained by the cultural industry are never entirely transparent or innocent. There are many interests at stake, including preserving the *status quo* of the current hegemonic classes and their socio-economic system, i.e., capitalism.[17] Popular cultural artefacts possess a high *representational value* since, on the one hand, they *depict* and *expose* the cultural conditions in which they are rooted and, on the other hand, they either *sustain* or *challenge* the ways in which we provide meaning to our individual and collective life experiences. The Potter novels have special interest for jurisprudential analysis because of such representational value and its substantive impact on the legal discourses it makes reference to, as I will show later on.

The demarcation of genre is fundamental to the success of any attempt at a jurisprudential reading of a literary text. Genres, as Fredric Jameson claims, are 'essentially literary *institutions*, or social contracts between a writer and a specific public, whose function is to specify the proper use of a particular cultural artefact.'[18] The definition of the Potter novels' genre has been a deeply contested issue in the field of literary studies. Either praised as the instrument for a renaissance in reading for children all over the world or dismissed as a conventional cultural commodity, the critics agree in explaining their tremendous popularity as a product of a generic mosaic (or hotchpotch) that combines the classical fairy tale with mystery novels, school stories and adventure fictions.[19] Nonetheless,

16 Harold Bloom, 'Can 35 Million Book Buyers be Wrong? Yes' *Wall Street Journal* (New York) 11 July 2000, A26.

17 Theodor Adorno and Max Horkheimer, *Dialektik der Aufklärung: Philosophische Fragmente* (Suhrkamp, 1990). For a specific critical analysis of the Potter novels on this basis, see Jack Zipes, *Sticks and Stones: The Troublesome Success of Children's Literature from Slovenly Peter to Harry Potter* (Routledge, 2001) 170 ff. Rowling lived in poverty before *Harry Potter and the Philosopher's Stone* was published. The manuscript was submitted to several publishing houses, all of which rejected it. Finally, in 1996, Barry Cunningham – an editor at Bloomsbury, a small publishing house in London – decided to publish the book, which was quietly released to bookstores. Three days after its publication, however, Arthur A Levine – editorial director of Scholastic Books, an American publishing house – bid $100,000 (£ 66,666) to buy the book rights for the American market. Rowling's story as a struggling mother who got a six-figure sum after writing a children's book in precarious conditions was quickly reproduced and exaggerated by media all over the world. Sean Smith compellingly summarises the consequences of this event in the following terms: 'Joanne's deal was undoubtedly big for a previously unpublished children's author and big enough for the hype to begin.' See above n 2, 179–184 and Lindsey Fraser, *Conversations with J. K. Rowling* (Scholastic, 2000) 44–47.

18 Fredric Jameson, *The Political Unconscious: Narrative as a Socially Symbolic Act* (Cornell University Press, 1981) 106.

19 See Anne Hiebert Alton, 'Generic Fusion and the Mosaic of Harry Potter' in Elizabeth E Heilman (ed.), *Harry Potter's World: Multidisciplinary Critical Perspectives* (Routledge, 2003) 141.

dystopia has rarely been discussed yet as one of the generic drifts in Harry Potter's literary medley.

Such an omission needs to be amended, as a prevailing theme in J K Rowling's narrative is not only the archetypal battle between good and evil so cherished by romance,[20] but also *legality*: the institutional framework through which justice is achieved. From criminal law to contracts or labour norms to civic statutes, Rowling depicts the legal system of Harry Potter's wizardly world with considerable detail.[21] The Potter series actually posits contemporary problems of political justice within unfair legal institutions. I propose thus to read the Potter novels as a dystopian narrative, that is, as a work of speculative fiction focused on the possible outcomes of the oppressive and unjust – though unexamined – historical tendencies entrenched in our daily life.[22] Dystopias are deeply political narratives that warn readers of the most dreadful sociopolitical tendencies rooted in the present that, if continued, could turn their lives into a nightmare. In order to achieve this, dystopian fictions represent dark potential scenarios that generate the opportunity for a cognitive encounter, first, with the worst social, legal and political features of our own times and, second, with what might be done to prevent the dreadful advent of the dystopian society.

For this reason, then, I will consider the representational value of the Harry Potter novels in relation to functionality of the *rule of law*. I will now divide my arguments into three parts. First, I will undertake a discussion of legalism from a pluralist standpoint to justify the inclusion of these novels (or, indeed, any other literary work) in the catalogue of sources of law. Second, I will situate the Potter novels within the dystopian tradition. Finally, I will examine the (dystopian) fictionalisation of the rule of law in the novels through a republican conception of political justice. This position has not been arbitrarily chosen. To consider the Potter stories as a source of law acknowledges the role of readers as *independent legal agents* that are culturally endowed with the power to create rules. This idea is radically republican as it liberates the citizens from suffering (*patior*) the legal system and, at the same time, makes them responsible for the symbolic endeavour (*ago*) of governing human actions under fair terms. I will

20 Northrop Frye, *Anatomy of Criticism: Four Essays* (Princeton University Press, 1957) 186 ff.

21 See Susan Hall, 'Harry Potter and the Rule of Law: The Central Weakness of Legal Concepts in the Wizard World' in Giselle Liza Anatol (ed.), *Reading Harry Potter: Critical Essays* (Praeger, 2003) 147.

22 I have thoroughly justified this reading of the Potter novels elsewhere. See Luis Gómez Romero, *Fantasía, Distopía y Justicia: La Saga de Harry Potter como Instrumento para la Enseñanza de los Derechos Humanos* (Ministerio de Sanidad, Política Social e Igualdad/Instituto de la Juventud, 2011). I assume marvellous literature as a general genre that comprises both fairy tales and science fiction. This way, I avoid circumscribing utopian and dystopian literature to science fiction – as some critics (e. g., Darko Suvin) do. See Tzvetan Todorov, *Introduction à la Littérature Fantastique*, (Seuil, first published 1970, 2005) 61–62.

conclude by considering the responsibility of each individual citizen in preserving the delicate balance between security and freedom within the boundaries of the *res publica* – 'public affairs' – or re-public, that concern the whole community.

Legalism v pluralism: the Potter novels as a source of law

Judith Shklar defines legalism as 'the ethical attitude that holds moral conduct to be a matter of rule following, and moral relationship to consist of duties and rights determined by rules.'[23] As with any other ethical attitude that has been strongly interiorised and is widely shared, legalism is not only expressed in the moral behaviour of individuals, but also in terms of how its influence is extended to hegemonic philosophical systems, political ideologies and social institutions. Courts and trials by law represent the most refined social paradigms of legalist morality.[24]

Legalism, however, is far more nuanced than any overt operation of law, for law plays an important symbolic function in modern complex societies as a cultural device that enables the stability and reproduction of pre-established social expectations. Legalism is a *conservative ideology* that reinforces this dimension of legal discourses.[25] Shklar defines legalism as an ideology since it fails to acknowledge both the (cultural) context and the (political and ethical) values that inevitably underlie law. In other words, legalism strips legislation, administration and adjudication of their complexity as *human* decisions by condensing law into an ideal purity detached from culture, politics or history. To put it in a nutshell, legalism endows the sources of law with the attributes of logical necessity.[26] Nevertheless, as Peter Goodrich suggests, whoever thinks of law under such terms is obliged to pay the double price of ignoring 'the irrationality and chance embedded in social life' as well as 'the instability and change intrinsic to human purpose and human personality'.[27]

A rigorous critical scrutiny of legalism requires a thorough revision of the doctrine of the sources of law.[28] Legal pluralism seems an obvious methodological course to achieve this goal. It is important to prevent, however, the temptation of yielding to a narrow and self-marginalising anthropology (a strategy that is

23 Judith Shklar, *Legalism* (Harvard University Press, 1964) 1.
24 Ibid, 2–3.
25 Ibid, 10.
26 Ibid, 11.
27 Peter Goodrich, 'Law and Modernity' (1986) 49(5) *Modern Law Review* 545, 545.
28 Peter Goodrich suggests a different methodological course based on the historical and comparative study of *minor jurisprudences*, that is, of 'discarded or failed laws, of jurisdictions denied, repressed or absorbed' by the hegemonic and all-powerful 'legal tradition'. See *Law in the Courts of Love: Literature and Other Minor Jurisprudences* (Routledge, 1996) 3.

frequently used by social and political actors that vindicate the acknowledgement of their differentiated cultural identity), and the false radicalism of anti-State romanticism (a common trend among social and political movements that focus on deepening and extending democratic participation). Boaventura de Sousa Santos correctly points out that these two forms of *naïve* pluralism tacitly accept the conceptions of law that legalism endorses and promotes.[29]

A pluralist critique of legalism, on the contrary, requires a comprehensive reconsideration of the sources of law beyond the structures of Western legal systems and the positivist thesis that represents the State as a *nomopoly* –a monopoly in the creation of law.[30] Boaventura de Sousa Santos analyses this matter from the perspective of what he calls *interlegality*, which consists in 'the conception of different legal spaces superimposed, interpenetrated and mixed in our minds, as much as in our actions, either on occasions of qualitative leaps or sweeping crises in our life trajectories, or in the dull routine of eventless everyday life.'[31] Sousa Santos reckons that these overlapping legal spaces are characterised by three structural normative components that transcend the State: rhetoric, bureaucracy (roughly understood as a regulation of social processes) and violence.[32] Drawing on the pluralist theses of Sousa Santos, the Potter stories (as well as other literary works) could therefore be read as rhetorical elements of the legal order that constitute both a (normative) mode of communication and a decision-making strategy based on persuasion.

The problem with this methodological approach is that it ultimately entails an implicit regression to legalism. By constructing literature as an instrument in the production of legal arguments, this pluralist perspective accordingly downgrades the Potter novels to cultural products that influence legal sources without forming part of them. Emmanuel Melissaris proposes an interesting solution to this dilemma by displacing legal theory from institutional *structures* – which are currently its privileged subject matter – to '*discourses* that are reduced to the binary schema of legal/illegal or permitted/forbidden.'[33] This binary code would make possible a distinction between legal discourses and other discourses – for example, ethics or etiquette – that use different codes to program their regulatory operations.

Melissaris admits that this coding criterion might obfuscate the semantic characterisation of legal discourses *vis-à-vis* other types of norms. It is therefore

29 Boaventura de Sousa Santos, *Toward a New Commonsense: Law, Science and Politics in the Paradigmatic Transition* (Routledge, 1995) 89 ff.
30 See Roderick Macdonald and David Sandomierski, 'Against Nomopolies' (2006) 57(4) *Northern Ireland Legal Quarterly* 610, 633.
31 Sousa Santos, above n 29, 437.
32 Ibid, 86–89.
33 Emmanuel Melissaris, 'The More the Merrier? A New Take on Legal Pluralism' (2004) 13(1) *Social & Legal Studies* 57, 74.

necessary to introduce in it further qualifying factors that are granted by the *institutionalisation* of law. It must be noted, however, that Melissaris conceives institutions as a *consequence* of legal discourses, rather than determining legal discourses through institutions – as legalism does. According to Melissaris, legal discourses are defined by the way in which they 'create generalized expectations that are confirmed by a third party by being either enforced or confirmed and re-established in cases of their having been disappointed.'[34] As a result, law is expanded beyond the discursive borders within which law has traditionally been framed by legalism. For instance, the security guard of a night club might be considered a third party that validates a legal regulation just as a court validates the legislation created by the State.

In sum, Melissaris characterises legal discourses by their ability to *authorise* and *evaluate* human actions. This means that facts and rules are not mutually excluding categories in the legal arena but, on the contrary, they are included in each other's constituency. Melissaris argues that, on the one hand, 'legal norms are always hinged on facts' and, on the other hand, 'the law does not develop separately from the way people normatively experience the world, but is rather constituted by those experiences.'[35] Law is therefore created from *shared normative experiences* that provide those who participate in them a common ability to shape the world through accepted normative commitments.[36] This way, the theory of legal pluralism advanced by Melissaris is empirical and normative at once because it assumes that 'participants [in a legal community] understand themselves as individuals, as well as in their collectivity in the world.'[37] The political effect of this take on legal pluralism is twofold: on the one hand, it carries away from the State and its legal professionals the production of law;[38] on the other hand, it merges the sources of law with the cultural context in which they usually work.[39]

It is true that formal coercive institutions – whose profile, constitution and function represent the core contents of curricula in law faculties all over the world – are important elements of current legal discourses. Nonetheless, even in our highly formalised contemporary legal systems institutionalisation within specific State-driven institutions is not an intrinsic feature of law. Legal contents and techniques are imbricated in our daily experiences; representations of

34 Ibid, 75.

35 Emmanuel Melissaris, *Ubiquitous Law: Legal Theory and the Space for Legal Pluralism* (Ashgate, 2009) 105–106.

36 Ibid, 109. On the cultural and narrative basis of such regulatory commitments, see Robert Cover, 'Foreword: *Nomos* and Narrative' (1983) 97(1) *Harvard Law Review* 4, 46.

37 Melissaris, above n 35, 115.

38 Ibid, 61–71.

39 Ibid, 79 ff.

institutionalised legal orders are couched in images and concepts drawn from everyday life.[40] Law is embedded in the symbolic order – broadly understood as the linguistic structure that facilitates coherent communication between human beings and therefore organises and regulates human subjectivity[41] – since its production is integrally connected to the spheres of our lives that inspire and form our identity: for example, the books we read, the music we listen to, the clothing we wear, and the art we grow up with.

It is in this sense that I claim that the Potter series of novels constitute a source of legal discourses. Popular culture is, as Marett Leiboff has compellingly suggested, the *tacit knowledge* of law.[42] Harry Potter is hence a popular cultural artefact that negotiates and transmits legal discourses throughout society. Dustin Kidd summarises this idea as he writes that '[o]wing to their massive audience and broad appeal the Potter novels are an extremely important source of social norms.'[43] The (dystopian) Potter stories are a constitutive element of *shared normative experiences* in our current globalised historical context.[44] In the following segments I will therefore prove that the works of J K Rowling are extremely suitable for a jurisprudential analysis precisely because they speak of the shortcomings of the legal discourses that broadly define and characterise the rule of law or *Rechtsstaat*.[45]

40 Roderick Macdonald, *Lessons of Everyday Law* (McGill-Queen's University Press, 2002); Daniel Jutras, 'The Legal Dimensions of Everyday Life' (2001) 16(1) *Canadian Journal of Law & Society* 45.

41 Jacques Lacan, 'Le Symbolique, l'Imaginaire et le Réel' (1982) *Bulletin de l'Association Freudienne* 1, 4.

42 Marett Leiboff, 'Talkin 'bout Law's Generations: Pop Culture, Intellectual Property and the Interpretation of Case' (2013) 29(1) *Law in Context* 95, 96.

43 Dustin Kidd, 'Harry Potter and the Functions of Popular Culture' (2007) 40(1) *Journal of Popular Culture* 69, 82. Desmond Manderson similarly claims that Harry Potter *has become law* 'in the lives of young readers.' See 'From Hunger to Love: Myths of the Source, Interpretation and Constitution of Law in Children's Literature' (2003) 15(1) *Law & Literature* 87, 96. The same idea is advanced by Aaron Schwabach, 'Harry Potter and the Unforgivable Curses: Non-Formation, Inconsistency and the Rule of Law in the Wizarding World' (2006) 11(3) *Roger Williams University Law Review* 309, 310–311.

44 This approach does not preclude cultural particularism, but simply acknowledges that Harry Potter has become a potent cultural symbol wherever the mechanical reproduction and distribution of cultural artefacts is technologically affordable and widely practised. For an account of the reception of the Potter novels in specific cultural contexts see, for example, Hollie Anderson, 'Reading *Harry Potter* with Navajo Eyes' in Heilman, above n 19, 97 and Ann Towns and Bahar Rumelili, 'Foreign Yet Familiar: International Politics and the Reception of Potter in Turkey and Sweden' in Daniel Nexon and Iver B Neumann (eds), *Harry Potter and International Relations* (Rowman & Littlefield, 2006) 61.

45 See below n 79.

Defence against dark realities: the Potter novels as dystopian texts

Dystopia is a contemporary genre born in the first quarter of the twentieth century. Dystopian narratives – for example, Eugene Zamiatin's *Мы* (1924),[46] Aldous Huxley's *Brave New World* (1932)[47] or George Orwell's *Nineteen Eighty-Four* (1949)[48] – function as cultural indices of the anxieties of the twentieth century (destructive use of science and technology, conditioned obedience, limited freedom, crumpled individuality, or unrestrained state surveillance, among others[49]) and clever discursive means for calling attention to and identifying what needed to be changed in hegemonic institutions under specific historical contexts.[50]

Utopia and dystopia share the general vocation of utopianism that Lyman Tower Sargent embodies under the general label of 'social dreaming'.[51] The specific formal strategies of literary utopias and dystopias are distinct. The traditional utopian text conveys an alternative world by means of a travelogue consisting of the perambulation of a voyager throughout the utopian society vividly interspersed with his or her questionings and comments to a local guide.[52] The typical dystopian text, on the other hand, does not appeal to a *dis*locating narrative device to provoke estrangement: it simply opens right in the midst of a nightmarish world that appears to be far worse than anything experienced by a reader.[53]

The dystopian protagonist is already immersed in a polity deeply pierced by social and political wickedness. Harry Potter's *bildungsroman* is punctuated with narratives of slavery,[54] racial discrimination,[55] or the rise of a fascist regime.[56] As Raffaella Baccolini and Tom Moylan note, however, the dystopian story line then develops a counter-narrative 'as the dystopian citizen moves from apparent

46 Eugene Zamiatin, *We* (Gregory Zilboorg trans, Dutton, first published 1924, 1952 edn).
47 Aldous Huxley, *Brave New World* (Vintage, first published 1932, 2004 edn)
48 George Orwell, *Nineteen Eighty-Four*, in Irving Howe (ed.), *Orwell's Nineteen Eighty-Four: Text, Sources, Criticism* (Harcourt Brace Jovanovich, first published 1949, 1982 edn) 3.
49 Mark Hillegas, *The Future as Nightmare: H. G. Wells and the Anti-Utopians* (Oxford University Press, 1967) 3.
50 Tom Moylan, *Scraps of the Untainted Sky: Science Fiction, Utopia, Dystopia* (Westview Press, 2000) xi–xvii.
51 Lyman Tower Sargent, 'Three Faces of Utopianism Revisited' (1994) 5(1) *Utopian Studies* 1, 3.
52 Tom Moylan, *Demand the Impossible: Science Fiction and the Utopian Imagination* (Methuen, 1986) 36–37.
53 Sargent, above n 51, 9.
54 J K Rowling, *Harry Potter and the Chamber of Secrets* (Bloomsbury, first published 1998, 2000 edn) 133–134.
55 Ibid, 86–87.
56 J K Rowling, *Harry Potter and the Deathly Hollows* (Bloomsbury, 2007) 184 ff.

contentment to an experience of alienation and resistance.'[57] A general trait of fictional literature is precisely the pre-eminence of the diversity of voices (*heteroglossia*) over the unity of a normative shared language (*monoglossia*) as a ground of narrative style.[58] Dystopia particularises this general trait by staging a conflict between a narrative of hegemonic order and a counter-narrative of resistance personified in a singular misfit or a discontented social class and their eventual allies. J K Rowling situated her own storytelling within this conflicted literary tradition in her address accepting the 'Príncipe de Asturias' award in Spain in 2003:

> [. . .] I've always believed that Harry Potter books are highly moral. I wanted to portray the ambiguity of a society where intolerance, cruelty, hypocrisy and corruption are frequent, so I could better show how heroic it can be, no matter what your age is, fighting in a battle that will never be won. I also wanted to reflect the fact that life between 11 and 17 years old can be hard and confusing, even if one has a magic wand.[59]

Even though *l'auter est mort* [the author is dead],[60] Rowling's reflections on her own work still represent a valid hermeneutical standard to interpret its possible meanings.[61] The mundane structure of human or *muggle* – non-magical – politics permeates the stories. Rowling refers to a battle that must be fought even if it cannot be won. Dystopia is an open literary form: the resistant dissenters can either prevail or be crushed by the established power structures. In both cases, the dystopian discourse is made possible by a chilling view of our probable future which distances us from the present and transforms it, regardless of whether the alienated protagonist is finally victorious or defeated, in a moment of possibility that, paraphrasing Darko Suvin, reconciles the principle of reality with the principle of hope because social, legal and political evils are always historically contingent and thus historically reversible.[62]

Generally speaking, hope regards the world as a *laboratorium possibilis salutis*, that is, as an ongoing process in which our final salvation or perdition has not

57 Raffaella Baccolini and Tom Moylan, 'Introduction: Dystopia and Histories' in Raffaella Baccolini and Tom Moylan (eds), *Dark Horizons: Science Fiction and the Dystopian Imagination* (Routledge, 2003) 1, 5.

58 Mikhail Bakhtin, 'The Discourse in the Novel' in Michael Holquist (ed.), *The Dialogic Imagination: Four Essays by M. M. Bakhtin* (Caryl Emerson and Michael Holquist trans, University of Texas Press, 1981) 259, 308.

59 J K Rowling, *Príncipe de Asturias Prize Acceptance Speech* (25 October 2003) www.fpa.es/multimedia-es/videos/jk-rowling-premio-principe-de-asturias-de-la-concordia-200325.html

60 See Roland Barthes, 'La Mort de l'Auteur' in Roland Barthes, *Œuvres Complètes* (Éditions de Seuil, 2002) vol 4, 40, 45.

61 See Harold Bloom, *The Western Canon: The Books and School of the Ages* (Harcourt Brace & Company, 1993) 37.

62 Darko Suvin, *Positions and Presuppositions in Science Fiction* (Kent State University Press, 1988) 80–83.

yet been decided.[63] Dystopia needs hope both as a cognitive basis that rouses awareness of the fact that the current social, legal and political system is contingent and as an ethical principle that makes us, as readers, responsible for seizing the opportunity to resist an oppressive and unjust future. From a dystopian perspective, therefore, Harry Potter's world and our own historical realities are not hermetically sealed from one another. Harry Potter has raised his voice to prevent us from following the path that leads to the enthronement of a totalitarian Dark Lord resembling his nemesis, Voldemort, whose untrammelled power would take away our precious liberties.

The fickleness of (wizardly) law

Utopias and dystopias can be properly classified as *estranged narratives*. By means of estranged representation, we are able to recognise an object or a situation but, at the same time, we lose our familiarity with it.[64] Dystopia achieves estrangement by positing a flaw in the political and social fabric of a secondary world that strains our sense of the probable while not violating our attachment to the plausible.[65] This way, the marvellous context of Harry Potter's wizardly world displaces our everyday experience, situating it in an imaginary frame outside the known reality. Yet it is still recognisable, in a very real and present fashion. The basic dystopian flaws that pervade this secondary world can be summarised as follows:

(a) The constitutional structure of the wizardly government is entirely based on a Ministry of Magic that operates through an incompetent and corrupt bureaucracy that is free from any form of legal or popular control;[66]
(b) The criminal justice system is structured around an arbitrary and dreadfully violent penitentiary institution (Azkaban);[67]

63 Ernst Bloch, 'Kann Hoffnung Enttäuscht Werden?' in *Gesamtausgabe: Literarische Aufsätze* (Suhrkamp, 1985) 385, 392.
64 See Darko Suvin, 'On the Poetics of the Science Fiction Genre' (1972) 34(3) *College English*, 372, 374–375.
65 Irving Howe, 'The Fiction of Anti-Utopia' in Howe above n 48, 303, 308–309.
66 For an account of the organisation and functions of the Ministry see, for example, J K Rowling, *Fantastic Beasts & Where to Find Them* (Bloomsbury, 2001) xviii; *Harry Potter and the Philosopher's Stone* (Bloomsbury, 1997) 51, and *Harry Potter and the Order of the Phoenix* (Bloomsbury, 2003) 119–120. See also Gómez Romero, above n 22, 323 ff, and Benjamin Barton, 'Harry Potter and the Half-Crazed Bureaucracy' (2006) 104(6) *Michigan Law Review* 1523, 1523 ff.
67 See J K Rowling, *Harry Potter and the Prisoner of Azkaban* (Bloomsbury, 1999) 139–141, and *Harry Potter and the Half-Blood Prince* (Bloomsbury, 2005) 13. See also Gómez Romero, above n 22, 326 and 331 ff; Joel Fishman, 'Punishment in the Harry Potter Novels' (2005) 12(1) *Texas Wesleyan Law Review* 452, 452 ff, and Paul Joseph and Lynn Wolf, 'The Law in Harry Potter: A System Not Even a Muggle Could Love' (2003) 34(2) *University of Toledo Law Review* 193, 197 ff.

(c) Wizards arbitrarily dominate other species of magical creatures (giants, centaurs, or merpeople);[68]
(d) While the production of social wealth is achieved through the slavery of house-elves,[69] its distribution among wizards is highly unequal;[70] and
(e) The wizardly society is structured over rigid racial hierarchies that regard 'purity of blood' as a virtue and accordingly discriminate *mudbloods*, that is, wizards who descend from *muggles* (non-magical people).[71]

Legalism fails in adequately addressing these problems in the so-called *real world* as it isolates law from its political and social context. The Potter novels, in contrast, effectively convey through estranged narrative strategies an acute critique of what I will call, after Immanuel Kant, *wild powers*. In his treatise on the conditions of perpetual peace, Kant avows to regard 'with profound contempt' as 'a brutal degradation of humanity' the 'attachment of savages to their lawless freedom' [*gesetzlose Freiheit*] that ultimately rejects 'the magnificent liberty of rational beings'.[72] This reflection summarises a key tenet of republican freedom regardless of the Eurocentric prejudices behind it: to institutionalise lawless freedom amounts to affirming limitless power. Republicanism rejects the Hobbesian thesis that recommends those individuals who 'seek to make lesse' a 'Soveraign Power too great', to subject themselves 'to the Power, that can limit it; that is to say, to a greater.'[73] On the contrary, freedom is conceived from a republican standpoint as *non-domination*. 'One agent dominates another', writes Philip Pettit, 'if and only if they have a certain power over that other, in particular a power of interference on an arbitrary basis.'[74] What is required for a non-arbitrary – non-dominating exercise of power is that it fosters 'not the power-holder's personal welfare or world-view, but rather the welfare and world-view of the public.'[75]

This is precisely Niccolò Machiavelli's point when he defines republican liberties as a *plebeian* [*ignobili*] expression of freedom that consists in the sole desire

68 The history of the development of the constitutional notion of citizenship in the wizardly world is painstakingly explained in Rowling, *Fantastic Beasts*, above n 66, x–xiii. See also Gómez Romero, above n 22, 288 ff.
69 See above n 54 and J K Rowling, *Harry Potter and the Goblet of Fire* (Bloomsbury, 2000) 197–199 and 317–335. See also Gómez Romero, above n 22, 383 ff, and William MacNeil, *Lex Populi: The Jurisprudence of Popular Culture* (Stanford University Press, 2007) 17–23.
70 See Rowling, above n 69, 474. See also Gómez Romero, above n 22, 378 ff.
71 See above n 54. See also Gómez Romero, above n 22, 397 ff.
72 Immanuel Kant, *Zum ewigen Frieden* (Fischer, first published 1795, 2008 edn) 164–165.
73 Thomas Hobbes, *Leviathan or The Matter, Form and Power of a Commonwealth Ecclesiastical and Civil* (Penguin, first published 1651, 1985 edn) 260.
74 Philip Pettit, *Republicanism: A Theory of Freedom and Government* (Oxford University Press, first published 1997, 2010 edn) 52. See also Antoni Domènech, *El Eclipse de la Fraternidad: Una Revisión Republicana de la Tradición Socialista* (Crítica, 2004) 59.
75 Ibid, 56.

of living without being dominated [*solo desiderio di non essere dominati*] or dominating anyone else [*desiderio grande di dominare*].[76] It is Jean-Jacques Rousseau's point when he claims that 'force does not create right' [*force ne fait pas droit*], and that 'we are obliged to obey only legitimate powers' [*on n'est obligé d'obéir qu'aux puissance légitimes*].[77] It is no less Thomas Paine's point when he contends that '[r]epublican government is no other than government established and conducted for the interest of the public, as well individually as collectively.'[78]

Kant's (lawless) *wild powers* hence contrast with Rousseau's (and Machiavelli's and Paine's) *legitimate powers*. Republicans not only seek to combat the general effects of *dominium* in society, but particularly the unjust domination that can be associated with the *imperium* of government. In order to prevent the government's functions to be subject to manipulation on an arbitrary basis, the first constitutional condition that must be fulfilled is the empire-of-law or *nomocracy* (νομοκρατία), according to which government should operate by law.[79] In James Harrington's words:

> [. . .] if the liberty of a man consists in the empire of his reason, the absence whereof would betray him to the bondage of his passions, then the liberty of a Commonwealth consists in the empire of her laws, the absence whereof would betray her to the lust of tyrants. And these I conceive to be the principles upon which Aristotle and Livy [. . .] have grounded their assertion, 'that a Commonwealth is an empire of laws and not of men.'[80]

76 Niccolò Machiavelli, *Discorsi sopra la Prima Deca di Tito Livio* (Rizzoli, first published 1531, 2013 edn) 73.

77 Jean-Jacques Rousseau, *Du contrat social; ou, Principes du Droit Politique* in Jean-Jacques Rousseau, *Du Contrat Social* (Gallimard, first published 1792, 2010 edn) 177. It must be noted that David Held situates Machiavelli within the tradition of *protective republicanism* that stresses primarily the instrumental value of political participation for the protection of citizen's objectives and interests, while locating Rousseau within the tradition of *developmental republicanism* that emphasises the intrinsic value of political participation for the enhancement of decision-making and the development of the citizenry. See *Models of Democracy* (Polity, 3rd edn, 2012) 36 ff. Both traditions, however, converge in conceiving freedom as non-domination. See Roberto Gargarella, *Las Teorías de la Justicia después de Rawls: Un Breve Manual de Filosofía Política* (Paidós, 1999) 162–163.

78 Thomas Paine, *Rights of Man, Being an Answer to Mr. Burke's Attack on the French Revolution* in Thomas Paine, *Common Sense, Rights of Man and Other Essential Writings of Thomas Paine* (Signet, first published 1791, 2003 edn) 129, 286.

79 I follow here Philip Pettit's terminology because the phrase *empire-of-law* comprises both the broad Anglo-American *rule of law* concept and the more restricted concept of *Rechtsstaatlichkeit* (which is just one of the formal requirements of the *Rechtsstaat*, the legal State or State of law) that has been developed in Continental Europe. See Pettit, above n 74, 171 ff.

80 James Harrington, *The Commonwealth of Oceana*, in G A Pocock (ed.), *The Political Works of James Harrington* (Cambridge University Press, 1977) 155, 170.

Aristotle actually suggests that law is a better ruler than 'the best man' because law is passionless, whereas passion is innate to 'the heart of man'.[81] The empire-of-law condition thus requires laws to satisfy specific established constraints in order to prevent them from being arbitrarily manipulated. Laws, for example, should be general and apply to everyone, including the legislators themselves (*lex generalis*); they should be promulgated (*lex promulgata*) and made known in advance to those to whom they apply (*lex previa*); they should be intelligible and consistent (*lex manifesta*), and they should not be subject to constant change (*lex perpetua*).[82] The satisfaction of these constraints does not imply, of course – as legalism would suggest –, that legal actions are always bound to be for the good. The empire-of-law condition simply implies that, if laws satisfy these constraints, it is difficult for decision-makers to conduct their actions on an arbitrary basis.

'The wizard world depicted by Rowling,' wrote Susan Hall in 2003, '[. . .] does not recognize the rule of law [. . .] This absence of an understanding of the rule of law represents a fault line in the terrain of the wizard world on which the forces of chaos can apply maximum pressure.'[83] This early evaluation of the wizardly legal system proved to be quite accurate: the flaws in the empire-of-law condition within the wizardly constitutional structure ultimately prepare the rise of the fascist regime led by Lord Voldemort.[84]

A criminal process that is launched against Harry Potter shows the reader the extent to which the Ministry of Magic arbitrarily manipulates law for the sake of *wizardry security*.[85] Rowling lets her readers know that paragraph C of the *Decree for the Reasonable Restriction of Underage Sorcery* – enacted in 1875 – bans, under the penalty of being expelled from Hogwarts School of Witchcraft and Wizardry, the use of magic outside Hogwarts' premises by wizards under the age of seventeen.[86] Likewise, in terms of Section 13 of the *International Statute of Wizarding Secrecy*, any magical activity which could be noticed by *muggles* is considered to be a serious offence.[87] The rationale that supports such provisions goes back to the times of witch-hunting, as wizards supposedly seek to prevent violent incidents with *muggles* by hiding magic. Both the *Decree* and the *Statute*

81 Aristotle, *Politics* (H Rackam trans, Harvard University Press, 1977) 1286 a.

82 Pettit above n 74, 174. See also Antonio-Enrique Pérez Luño, *La Seguridad Jurídica* (Ariel, 1991) 20 ff.

83 Hall, above n 21, 147.

84 See Marett Leiboff and Mark Thomas, *Legal Theories: Contexts and Practices* (Thomson Reuters, 2nd edn, 2014) 188.

85 I propose this expression – which Rowling does not use – to highlight the parallels between the provisions that regulate security in the wizardly world and the regulations and policies that we, as *muggles*, usually categorise under the label of *national security*. For a compelling account of the trials in Harry Potter's world as curial performances of sheer governmental force see MacNeil, above n 69, 12–17.

86 Rowling, above n 54, 21.

87 Ibid.

become relevant in the Potter stories when, during a summer break, Harry Potter casts a spell in the presence of *muggles* to save his cousin Dudley from the mortal attack of *dementors* – cruel creatures whose role is to guard the inmates of Azkaban prison. Thus, Harry undergoes a trial for having breached both regulations.

Rowling cleverly makes her readers realise that Clause Seven of the *Decree* exempts Harry from liability as it establishes that 'magic may be used before *Muggles* in exceptional circumstances, and those exceptional circumstances include situations which threaten the life of a wizard or witch him- or herself, or any witches, wizards or *Muggles*.'[88] Nevertheless, she also points to the fact that the Ministry of Magic has a special interest in having those grounds for acquittal dismissed from Harry's defence. The Ministry's officials have a secret agenda: they claim that Voldermort is dead, while Harry and Albus Dumbledore – Hogwarts' principal – are planning to reveal the truth of his comeback to the general public. The officials prosecuting Harry thus intend to silence him by any means possible as they regard the information on Voldemort highly dangerous for the community at large.[89] It would help the Ministry's agenda to have Harry Potter declared guilty and expelled from Hogwarts, as this punishment would result in exiling him from the wizardly world through the destruction of his magic wand.[90]

During the process, Harry is aided by Dumbledore, who sustains a bitter argument with the prosecutor Cornelius Fudge – the Minister of Magic himself. There are three key aspects of Dumbledore's defence that I deem convenient to highlight.[91] First, he claims that the Ministry exceeded its powers twice (trying to have Harry expelled from Hogwarts and confiscating his wand before the judges had been notified of an accusation against him and heard his defence). Second, he argues the Ministry 'overlooked' some laws. Third, he observes that the law had been reformed *ex post facto*, in order to bring Harry (an underage wizard) to trial in a criminal court. The Ministry violated the empire-of-law constitutional condition by trampling the principles of *lex generalis* (the Ministry's officials do not consider themselves bound to the law they are supposed to enforce), *lex previa* and *lex perpetua*.

While legalism would be satisfied by simply verifying that rules have been complied with or violated, the dystopian and republican analysis of the Potter novels pushes the reader to evaluate the social and political consequences of the degradation of law into 'a playground for the arbitrary will of the authorities'.[92]

88 Rowling, *Order of the Phoenix*, above n 66, 135.
89 The Minister of Magic reckons that releasing the information about Voldemort would 'start a panic' that would 'destabilize' everything the magical community had worked for during 'the last thirteen years.' See Rowling above n 69, 613–614.
90 Rowling, *Order of the Phoenix*, above n 66, 29–30 and 35.
91 Ibid, 136–137.
92 Pettit, above n 74, 174.

The empire-of-law constitutional condition is closely related to the principle of legal certainty, according to which the law must provide those subject to it with the ability to regulate their own conduct. Legal certainty is a *sine qua non* requirement of republican freedom. In other words, freedom as non-domination should provide every individual with certainty about how to conduct his/her social and political life by calculating the legal consequences of his/her actions and, specifically, of the exercise of his/her rights. Machiavelli eloquently praises this virtue of the republican constitution when he states that the 'common usefulness which free life brings with it' [*comune utilità che del vivere libero si trae*] lies in being able to enjoy our 'possessions freely without any suspicion' [*potere godere liberamente le cose sue sanza alcuno sospetto*], and living without fearing for ourselves [*non temere di sé*] or 'being apprehensive' [*dubitare*] about the fate of our families or loved ones.[93] Approximately two centuries after Machiavelli, Montesquieu expressed a similar view as he declared that '[t]he political liberty of the citizen is a tranquillity of mind arising from the opinion each person has of his own safety' [*La liberté politique, dans un citoyen, est cette tranquillité d'esprit qui provient de l'opinion que chacun a de sa sûreté*].[94]

Rowling's dystopian storytelling is a powerful advocate of republican freedom. Few arguments possess such a persuasive strength regarding the importance of legal certainty as the devastating effects that the fickleness of wizardly law has over Harry Potter. Even though he is finally acquitted, 'the prospect of the disciplinary hearing filled every tiny particle of his brain', and he thought that he would be 'unable to bear it'.[95] The day of the hearing '[h]is insides were squirming' and, when he tried to eat, he felt he was 'chewing carpet'.[96] As soon as he entered the court, he 'gasped; he could not help himself' because it was a 'large dungeon' with walls 'made of dark stone, dimly lit by torches' where the accused was supposed to sit in a chair whose arms 'were covered in chains' that made him dizzy.[97]

Harry Potter's preposterous trial is not jurisprudentially relevant because of the information it conveys – in the *real world* there is no magical community of wizards and witches, or a prison called Azkaban or a magical court called Wizengamot – or the values it endorses, but because of the way in which it narratively subverts and challenges the legalist neglect of the political horizons embedded in the very notion of the empire-of-law. The anxiety that suffocates Harry is a (dystopian) warning about the perils of renouncing the empire-of-law – and, therefore, legal certainty – in the name of security. Though it is true

93 Machiavelli, above n 76, 104.
94 Montesquieu, *De l'Esprit des Lois* (Flammarion, first published 1748, 1979 edn) vol 1, 294.
95 Rowling, *Order of the Phoenix*, above n 66, 112.
96 Ibid, 113.
97 Ibid, 126.

that the empire-of-law on its own does not guarantee the survival of liberties or the disappearance of inequality, it is necessary to acknowledge that, without it, liberty and equality are frequently an illusion. It is legal certainty what allows people to be aware of the fact that liberties are not a temporal concession of wild powers, so that everyone can be sure that such liberties will not be taken away tomorrow, that they will stand strong in spite of any political or social upheaval because they are protected under the authority of law. In this way, the certainty provided by the empire-of-law projects into the future the republican ideal of freedom as non-domination.

Conclusion

Today the idea of forfeiting the law when it gets in the way of helping the government to be efficient in keeping social harmony has become widely accepted in face of the supposed threats that, all over the world, currently hang over several states (for example, terrorism, drug trafficking, organised crime, or other *calamities* that have been profusely documented). I believe this essay needs to conclude with an answer to such seemingly practical concerns.

The legal uncertainty that prevails in the wizardly world not only entails all sorts of dangers against civil liberties but, paradoxically, it also undermines the authorities that promote it. Let us remember that, in the Potter novels, the unreliability of the wizardly legal system creates a vacuum which Voldemort – who offers a perverted, violent version of social order – exploits. The importance of the dark dystopian prophesy implied in the story of the rise of Voldemort becomes hence evident as we consider that the instability of the wizardly world is not different from the one we currently experience in *our* world of indiscriminate state espionage, sinister anti-terrorism policies and Azkaban-like prisons as Abu Ghraib or Guantanamo. Both in Harry Potter's fictional world and in our historical reality, freedom has been sacrificed in exchange for the fake promise of keeping us safe. The price we have paid, however, has not being reflected in any substantial improvement of our security: lost liberties have not won the so-called *War on Terror*.

This paradox brings us back to the republican ideals of the empire-of-law and legal certainty. Jean-Jacques Rousseau once advised us against searching for tranquility in dungeons, where the misery is a condition of security.[98] Immanuel Kant similarly mocked the absurdity of envisaging the dream of perpetual peace in graveyards.[99] Harry Potter is now part of this illustrious republican tradition: his story will always remind us that security is worthless if it is not aimed at ensuring the enjoyment of freedom.

98 Rousseau, above n 77, 177.
99 Kant, above n 72, 152.

Bibliography

Adorno, Theodor and Max Horkheimer, *Dialektik der Aufklärung: Philosophische Fragmente* (Suhrkamp, 1990)

Alton, Anne Hiebert, 'Generic Fusion and the Mosaic of Harry Potter' in Elizabeth E Heilman (ed.), *Harry Potter's World: Multidisciplinary Critical Perspectives* (Routledge, 2003) 141

Anderson, Hollie, 'Reading *Harry Potter* with Navajo Eyes' in Elizabeth E Heilman (ed.), *Harry Potter's World: Multidisciplinary Critical Perspectives* (Routledge, 2003) 97

Aristotle, *Politics* (H Rackam trans, Harvard University Press, 1977)

Baccolini, Raffaella and Tom Moylan, 'Introduction: Dystopia and Histories' in Raffaella Baccolini and Tom Moylan (eds), *Dark Horizons: Science Fiction and the Dystopian Imagination* (Routledge, 2003) 1

Bakhtin, Mikhail, 'The Discourse in the Novel' in Michael Holquist (ed.), *The Dialogic Imagination: Four Essays by M M Bakhtin* (Caryl Emerson and Michael Holquist trans, University of Texas Press, 1981) 259

Barthes, Roland, 'Leçon' in Roland Barthes, *Œuvres Complètes* (Éditions de Seuil, 2002) vol 5, 427

Barthes, Roland, 'La Mort de l'Auteur' in Roland Barthes, *Œuvres Complètes* (Éditions de Seuil, 2002) vol 4, 40

Barton, Benjamin, 'Harry Potter and the Half-Crazed Bureaucracy' (2006) 104(6) *Michigan Law Review* 1523

Bloch, Ernst, 'Kann Hoffnung Enttäuscht Werden?' in Ernst Bloch, *Gesamtausgabe: Literarische Aufsätze* (Suhrkamp, 1985) vol 9, 385

Bloom, Harold, *The Western Canon: The Books and School of the Ages* (Harcourt Brace & Company, 1993)

Bloom, Harold, 'Can 35 Million Book Buyers be Wrong? Yes' *Wall Street Journal* (11 July 2000) A26

Cover, Robert, 'Foreword: *Nomos* and Narrative' (1983) 97(1) *Harvard Law Review* 4

Dimock, Wai Chee, *Residues of Justice: Literature, Law, Philosophy* (University of California Press, 1996)

Domènech, Antoni, *El Eclipse de la Fraternidad: Una Revisión Republicana de la Tradición Socialista* (Crítica, 2004)

Eccleshare, Julia, '"Most Popular Ever": The Launching of Harry Potter' in Julia Briggs, Dennis Butts and Matthew Grenby (eds), *Popular Children's Literature in Britain* (Ashgate, 2008) 287

Fishman, Joel, 'Punishment in the Harry Potter Novels' (2005) 12(1) *Texas Wesleyan Law Review* 452

Fraser, Lindsey, *Conversations with J K Rowling* (Scholastic, 2000)

Frye, Northrop, *Anatomy of Criticism: Four Essays* (Princeton University Press, 1957)

Gargarella, Roberto, *Las Teorías de la Justicia después de Rawls: Un Breve Manual de Filosofía Política* (Paidós, 1999)

Gómez Romero, Luis, *El Tiempo de los Débiles: Garantismo y Literatura* (Porrúa, 2008)

Gómez Romero, Luis, *Fantasía, Distopía y Justicia: La Saga de Harry Potter como Instrumento para la Enseñanza de los Derechos Humanos* (Ministerio de Sanidad, Política Social e Igualdad/Instituto de la Juventud, 2011)

Goodrich, Peter, 'Law and Modernity' (1986) 49(5) *Modern Law Review* 545

Goodrich, Peter, *Law in the Courts of Love: Literature and Other Minor Jurisprudences* (Routledge, 1996)

Hall, Susan, 'Harry Potter and the Rule of Law: The Central Weakness of Legal Concepts in the Wizard World' in Giselle Liza Anatol (ed.), *Reading Harry Potter: Critical Essays* (Praeger, 2003) 147

Harrington, James, *The Commonwealth of Oceana* in G A Pollock (ed.), *The Political Works of James Harrington* (Cambridge University Press, 1977) 155

Held, David, *Models of Democracy* (Polity, 3rd edn, 2012)

Hillegas, Mark, *The Future as Nightmare: H G Wells and the Anti-Utopians* (Oxford University Press, 1967)

Hobbes, Thomas, *Leviathan or The Matter, Form and Power of a Commonwealth Ecclesiastical and Civil* (Penguin, first published 1651, 1985 edn)

Howe, Irving, 'The Fiction of Anti-Utopia' in Irving Howe (ed.), *Orwell's Nineteen Eighty-Four: Text, Sources, Criticism* (Harcourt Brace Jovanovich, first published 1949, 1982 edn) 303

Huxley, Aldous, *Brave New World* (Vintage, first published 1932, 2004 edn)

Jameson, Fredric, *The Political Unconscious: Narrative as a Socially Symbolic Act* (Cornell University Press, 1981)

Jentsch, Nancy K, 'Harry Potter and the Tower of Babel: Translating the Magic' in Lana Whited (ed.), *The Ivory Tower and Harry Potter: Perspectives on a Literary Phenomenon* (University of Missouri Press, 2002) 285

Joseph, Paul and Lynn Wolf, 'The Law in Harry Potter: A System Not Even a Muggle Could Love' (2003) 34(2) *University of Toledo Law Review* 193

Jutras, Daniel, 'The Legal Dimensions of Everyday Life' (2001) 16(1) *Canadian Journal of Law & Society* 45

Kant, Immanuel, *Zum ewigen Frieden* (Fischer, first published 1795, 2008 edn)

Kidd, Dustin, 'Harry Potter and the Functions of Popular Culture' (2007) 40(1) *Journal of Popular Culture* 69

Kundera, Milan, 'Discours de Jérusalem: le Roman et l'Europe' in Milan Kundera, *L'Art du Roman* (Gallimard, 1986) 191

Lacan, Jacques, 'Le Symbolique, l'Imaginaire et le Réel', (1982) 1 *Bulletin de l'Association Freudienne* 4

Lacey, Nicola, *Women, Crime, and Character: From Moll Flanders to Tess of the D'Urbervilles* (Oxford University Press, 2008)

Lathey, Gillian, 'The Travels of Harry: International Marketing and the Translation of J K Rowling's Harry Potter Books' (2005) 29 *The Lion and the Unicorn* 141

Leiboff, Marett, 'Talkin 'bout Law's Generations: Pop Culture, Intellectual Property and the Interpretation of Case' (2013) 29(1) *Law in Context* 95

Leiboff, Marett and Mark Thomas, *Legal Theories: Contexts and Practices* (Thomson Reuters, 2nd edn, 2014)

Macdonald, Roderick, *Lessons of Everyday Law* (McGill-Queen's University Press, 2002)

Macdonald, Roderick and David Sandomierski, 'Against Nomopolies' (2006) 57(4) *Northern Ireland Legal Quarterly* 610

Machiavelli, Niccolò, *Discorsi sopra la Prima Deca di Tito Livio* (Rizzoli, first published 1531, 2013 edn)

MacNeil, William, *Lex Populi: The Jurisprudence of Popular Culture* (Stanford University Press, 2007)

Manderson, Desmond, 'From Hunger to Love: Myths of the Source, Interpretation and Constitution of Law in Children's Literature' (2003) 15(1) *Law & Literature* 87
Manderson, Desmond, *Kangaroo Courts and the Rule of Law: The Legacy of Modernism* (Routledge, 2012)
Melissaris, Emmanuel, 'The More the Merrier? A New Take on Legal Pluralism' (2004) 13(1) *Social & Legal Studies* 57
Melissaris, Emmanuel, *Ubiquitous Law: Legal Theory and the Space for Legal Pluralism* (Ashgate, 2009)
Montesquieu, *De l'Esprit des Lois* (Flammarion, first published 1748, 1979 edn)
Moylan, Tom, *Demand the Impossible: Science Fiction and the Utopian Imagination* (Methuen, 1986) 36–37
Moylan, Tom, *Scraps of the Untainted Sky: Science Fiction, Utopia, Dystopia* (Westview Press, 2000)
Nussbaum, Martha, *Poetic Justice: The Literary Imagination and the Public Life* (Beacon Press, 1995)
Orwell, George, *Nineteen Eighty-Four* in Irving Howe (ed.), *Orwell's Nineteen Eighty-Four: Text, Sources, Criticism* (Harcourt Brace Jovanovich, first published 1949, 1982 edn) 3
Paine, Thomas, *Rights of Man, Being an Answer to Mr. Burke's Attack on the French Revolution*, in Thomas Paine, *Common Sense, Rights of Man and Other Essential Writings of Thomas Paine*, (Signet, first published 1791, 2003 edn) 129
Paz, Octavio, *El Ogro Filantrópico* (Joaquín Mortiz, 1980)
Pérez Luño, Antonio-Enrique, *La Seguridad Jurídica* (Ariel, 1991)
Pettit, Philip, *Republicanism: A Theory of Freedom and Government* (Oxford University Press, first published 1997, 2010 edn)
Posner, Richard, 'The Ethical Significance of Free Choice' (1986) 99 *Harvard Law Review* 1431
Rich, Motoko, 'Harry Potter's Popularity Holds Up in Early Sales' *New York Times* (23 July 2007) A12
Rousseau, Jean-Jacques, *Du contrat social; ou, Principes du Droit Politique* in Jean-Jacques Rousseau, *Du Contrat Social* (Gallimard, first published 1792, 2010 edn)
Rowling, J K, *Harry Potter and the Philosopher's Stone* (Bloomsbury 1997)
Rowling, J K, *Harry Potter and the Chamber of Secrets* (Bloomsbury, 1998)
Rowling, J K, *Harry Potter and the Prisoner of Azkaban* (Bloomsbury, 1999)
Rowling, J K, *Harry Potter and the Goblet of Fire* (Bloomsbury, 2000)
Rowling, J K, *Fantastic Beasts & Where to Find Them* (Bloomsbury, 2001)
Rowling, J K, *Harry Potter and the Order of the Phoenix* (Bloomsbury, 2003)
Rowling, J K, *Príncipe de Asturias Prize Acceptance Speech* (25 October 2003) www.fpa.es/multimedia-es/videos/jk-rowling-premio-principe-de-asturias-de-la-concordia-200325.html
Rowling, J K, *Harry Potter and the Half-Blood Prince* (Bloomsbury, 2005)
Rowling, J K, *Harry Potter and the Deathly Hollows* (Bloomsbury, 2007)
Sargent, Lyman Tower, 'Three Faces of Utopianism Revisited' (1994) 5(1) *Utopian Studies* 1
Schwabach, Aaron, 'Harry Potter and the Unforgivable Curses: Non-Formation, Inconsistency and the Rule of Law in the Wizarding World' (2006) 11(3) *Roger Williams University Law Review* 309
Shklar, Judith, *Legalism* (Harvard University Press, 1964)
Smith, Sean, *JK Rowling: A Biography* (Arrow Books, 2001)

Sousa Santos, Boaventura de, *Toward a New Commonsense: Law, Science and Politics in the Paradigmatic Transition* (Routledge, 1995)
Suvin, Darko, 'On the Poetics of the Science Fiction Genre' (1972) 34(3) *College English* 372
Suvin, Darko, *Positions and Presuppositions in Science Fiction* (Kent State University Press, 1988)
Todorov, Tzvetan, *Introduction à la Littérature Fantastique*, (Seuil, first published 1970, 2005)
Towns, Ann and Bahar Rumelili, 'Foreign Yet Familiar: International Politics and the Reception of Potter in Turkey and Sweden' in Daniel Nexon and Iver B Neumann (eds), *Harry Potter and International Relations* (Rowman & Littlefield Publishers, 2006) 61
Ward, Ian, *Justice, Humanity and the New World Order* (Ashgate, 2003)
West, Robin, 'Authority, Autonomy, and Choice: The Role of Consent in the Moral and Political Visions of Franz Kafka and Richard Posner' (1985) 99 *Harvard Law Review* 384
West, Robin, 'Submission, Choice and Ethics: A Rejoinder to Judge Posner' (1986) 99 *Harvard Law Review* 1449
White, James Boyd, *The Legal Imagination: Studies in the Nature of Legal Thought and Expression* (Boston, Little, Brown & Co., 1973)
Williams, Melanie, *Secrets and Laws: Collected Essays in Law, Lives, and Literature* (UCL Press, 2005)
Wyatt, Edward, 'Potter Book Sets Record in First Day' *New York Times* (18 July 2005) E3
Zamiatin, Eugene, *We* (Gregory Zilboorg trans, Dutton, first published 1924, 1952 edn)
Zipes, Jack, *Sticks and Stones: The Troublesome Success of Children's Literature from Slovenly Peter to Harry Potter* (Routledge, 2001)

Index

For Product Safety Concerns and Information please contact our EU
representative GPSR@taylorandfrancis.com
Taylor & Francis Verlag GmbH, Kaufingerstraße 24, 80331 München, Germany

www.ingramcontent.com/pod-product-compliance
Ingram Content Group UK Ltd.
Pitfield, Milton Keynes, MK11 3LW, UK
UKHW020018200926
475702UK00014B/1949
* 9 7 8 0 8 1 5 3 8 2 2 0 1 *